The Changing Politics of Foreign

Also by Christopher Hill

NATIONAL FOREIGN POLICIES AND EUROPEAN POLITICAL COOPERATION (*edited*)

TERRORISM AND INTERNATIONAL ORDER (*with Lawrence Freedman, Adam Roberts, R. J. Vincent, Paul Wilkinson and Philip Windsor*)

CABINET DECISIONS ON FOREIGN POLICY: The British Experience October 1938–June 1941

TWO WORLDS OF INTERNATIONAL RELATIONS: Academics, Practitioners and the Trade in Ideas (*edited, with Pamela Beshoff*)

THE ACTORS IN EUROPE'S FOREIGN POLICY (*edited*)

DOMESTIC SOURCES OF FOREIGN POLICY: West European Reactions to the Falklands Conflict (*edited, with Stelios Stavridis*)

MARCHING TO CAPTIVITY: the War Diaries of a French Peasant 1939–1945 – Gustave Folcher (*translated and edited English version; first published in French, edited by Rémy Cazals*)

DOCUMENTS ON EUROPEAN FOREIGN POLICY (*edited, with Karen Smith*)

The Changing Politics of Foreign Policy

Christopher Hill

First published 2003 by
PALGRAVE MACMILLAN
Houndmills, Basingstoke, Hampshire RG21 6XS and
175 Fifth Avenue, New York, N.Y. 10010
Companies and representatives throughout the world.

PALGRAVE MACMILLAN is the new global academic imprint of the Palgrave Macmillan division of St Martin's Press, LLC and of Palgrave Macmillan Ltd. Macmillan® is a registered trademark in the United States, United Kingdom and other countries. Palgrave is a registered trademark in the European Union and other countries.

ISBN-13: 978-0-333-75421-4 hardback
ISBN-10: 0-333-75421-2 hardback
ISBN-13: 978-0-333-75423-8 paperback
ISBN-10: 0-333-75423-9 paperback

This book is printed on paper suitable for recycling and made from fully managed and sustained forest sources.

A catalogue record for this book is available from the British Library.

Library of Congress Cataloging-in-Publication Data
Hill, Christopher 1948–
      The changing politics of foreign policy / Christopher Hill.
         p. cm.
      Includes bibliographical references and index.
      ISBN 0-333-75421-2 (cloth) – ISBN 0-333-75423-9 (paper)
      1. International relations – Political aspects. 2. International relations –
Psychological aspects.   I. Title.
JZ1253 .H55 2002
      327.1 – dc21   2002075289

10   9   8   7   6
10   09   08   07   06

Printed and bound in China

For

Maria, Alice and Dominic

'Politics is a strong and slow boring of hard boards. It takes both passion and perspective.'

—**Max Weber**

Contents

List of Tables

List of Figures

List of Abbreviations

ACP	African, Caribbean and Pacific Countries
AIDS	Auto Immune Deficiency Syndrome
AIPAC	American Israel Public Affairs Committee
ANC	African National Congress
ANZUS	Australia, New Zealand, United States pact on security (1951)
ASEAN	Association of South East Asian Nations
BJP	Bharatiya Janata Party
CFC	Chlorofluorocarbons
CDU	Christian Democratic Union
CIA	Central Intelligence Agency
CHOG	Commonwealth Heads of Government
CSU	Christian Social Union
DGSE	Direction générale de la sécurité extérieure
EC	European Community
ECOFIN	(Council of) Economic and Finance Ministers
EMU	Economic and Monetary Union
ENA	École nationale d'administration
END	European Nuclear Disarmament
EU	European Union
FAC	Foreign Affairs Committee
FCO	Foreign and Commonwealth Office
FDP	Free Democrat Party
FPA	Foreign Policy Analysis
FRG	Federal Republic of Germany
GATT	General Agreement on Tariffs and Trade
IGO	Intergovernmental Organization
IMF	International Monetary Fund
INGO	International Non-governmental Organization
IPE	International Political Economy
IR	International Relations
IRA	Irish Republican Army

KGB	Komitet Gosudarstennoi Bezopasnosti (Soviet Security Service)
LDC	Less Developed Country
LDP	Liberal Democratic Party (of Japan)
MERCOSUR	Mercado Commun del Sur (Common Market of the Southern Core)
MITI	Ministry of International Trade and Industry (Japan)
NAFTA	North American Free Trade Agreement
NATO	North Atlantic Treaty Organization
NCG	Non Central Government
NIC	Newly Industrializing Country
NPC	National People's Congress (China)
NSC	National Security Council
OECD	Organization for Economic Cooperation and Development
OPEC	Organization of Petrol Exporting Countries
OSCE	Organization for Security and Cooperation in Europe
PF	Patriotic Front (of Zimbabwe African National Union)
PKK	Workers Party of Kurdistan
PLO	Palestine Liberation Organization
SEA	Single European Act
SOP	Standard Operating Procedure
TNA	Transnational Actor
TNE	Transnational Enterprise
UEFA	Union of European Football Associations
UNCTAD	United Nations Conference on Trade and Development
USAF	United States Air Force
WEU	Western European Union
WTO	World Trade Organization
ZANU–PF	Zimbabwe African National Union – Patriotic Front

Acknowledgements

There are a number of people and institutions I wish to thank for their help over the four years this book has been in the making, There are many more whose assistance I have drawn on over the much longer period in which my ideas about foreign policy have been gestating.

Throughout my time in the Department of International Relations at the London School of Economics and Political Science I have benefited from the intellectual stimulus and friendly support of gifted colleagues. It has been a tremendous environment in which to work, at once eclectic and rigorous. This is partly because we are kept up to the mark by an extremely able student body. Every week over twenty-five years I have learned something or been sharpened in my thinking in a seminar or tutorial, not least in the fortnightly 'foreign policy issues workshop' which I have run for interested research students, many of whom now are well-known scholars. The individuals whose theses I have had the privilege of supervising have been particularly helpful. It is well-known that the PhD student–supervisor relationship is a close and important one. What is less often acknowledged is that the benefits are two-way. All of my research students are in this book in one way or another.

I am most grateful to the Economic and Social Research Council of the United Kingdom. Their award (number R000222572) made it possible for me to take the leave during which this project got going during 1998. Professor Yves Mény and the Robert Schuman Centre at the European University Institute in Fiesole kindly provided me with research facilities at that time, and for shorter periods since. Professor Jan Zielonka, also at the EUI, has been a constant source of encouragement and ideas. The help of the library staff of the LSE, the EUI and the Royal Institute of International Affairs has been indispensable. My publisher at Palgrave Macmillan, Steven Kennedy, has displayed both the professional qualities of his trade and a committed interest in the content of this book. The Department of International Relations Staff Research Fund enabled me to employ two research assistants, at different points: Maria Ekenbratt did sterling work in checking footnotes, while Alan Chong both dug out sources and helped me clarify the argument. Jennifer Chapa, my administrative assistant at LSE, has gone well beyond her formal duties in helping out and her work has been immaculate. Alison Carter has always been willing to lend a hand. Keith Povey has been a most efficient and friendly editorial consultant, while my sister, Jane Hill, has willingly given her time and invaluable expertise to help me get the book to press. I very much appreciate everything they have all done.

I have also benefited greatly from being able to test the book's argument in the constructively critical atmosphere provided by university seminars. Michael Mastanduno at the John Sloan Dickey Center for International Understanding of Dartmouth College, Hans Maull and colleagues at the University of Trier, James Mayall at Cambridge, Martin Smith and Tony Payne at Sheffield, Alfred Tovias at the Hebrew University in Jerusalem, and Donatella Viola at the University of Plymouth, together with seminars at LSE and the EUI, have all provided hospitality and given me pause for thought.

The following individuals have generously provided the information, comments and criticisms, despite being pressed for time themselves, without which a wide-ranging comparative book of this kind could not have been completed. It is a pleasure to acknowledge their help: Chris Alden, David Allen, Filippo Andreatta, Philip Bell, Geoff Berridge, Pamela Beshoff, Christopher Brewin, Chris Brown, Elisabetta Brighi, Fraser Cameron, Nicola Catellani, Raymond Cohen, Christopher Coker, Michael Cox, Patricia Daehnhardt, Michael Donelan, Spyros Economides, Michel Girard, Ayla Göl, Gregor Hackmack, Mutsumi Hirano, Heidi Hobbs, Brian Hocking, Albert Jönsson, Daphné Josselin, Miles Kahler, Vinzenz Kastner, Patrick Keatley, David Keen, John Kent, Alan Knight, Henrik Larsen, Michael Lee, Michael Leifer, Roger Levermore, Richard Little, Andrew Linklater, Chris Lord, Peter Lyon, Roger Morgan, MacGregor Knox, Inderjeet Parmar, Chad Peterson, Leticia Pinheiro, Frank Rusciano, Helene Sjursen, Karen Smith, Michael Smith, Stelios Stavridis, James Tang, Paul Taylor, Kevin Theakston, José Valdes-Ugalde, Jana Valencic, Brunello Vigezzi, Andrew Walter and Stephen Wright. I also gratefully acknowledge the permission granted to me by the University of Birmingham Library to quote from the Chamberlain papers, and that of David Baldwin and the Princeton University Press to use the table adapted on page 150. Finally, the advice of Palgrave's anonymous readers helped me to improve the shape and scope of the book at a critical point.

Four colleagues have been particularly valuable in the writing of this book. It is a fortunate institution indeed which disposes of the wisdom on foreign policy of Fred Halliday, Margot Light, William Wallace and Michael Yahuda, and I have been privileged to be able to draw on their knowledge and advice. Margot and I have shared the pleasures and travails of teaching Foreign Policy Analysis at LSE, and I could have had no better comrade in arms.

Personal circumstances affect the writing of any book, for good and ill. I have been fortunate in being able to write much of this one in the pleasant rural environment of San Donato in Collina, ten miles beyond Florence towards Arezzo. This would not have proved possible without the generous hospitality and encouragement of friends in the locality. I am deeply grateful to the following, and to all their families: Cristina and Ugo Andreotti Lorenzetti, Rita and Lorenzo Butini, Jean and Luca Fanelli, Colette Kleemann, Sergio Lavacchini, Grazia Nocentini and Stefano Papola, Anneliese and Mario Poli, Floriano and Elisabetta Poli, and Giovanni Tinti.

My family and friends have been the foundation on which everything has been built. In particular I wish to pay tribute to the woman whom I always knew as Carole Knight, whose friendship and sensibility so many people have missed since her tragic death in 1998. As ever, I have relied most on the keen judgements and tender feelings of my wife Maria McKay, while our children, Alice and Dominic, are the two people who make everything worth while.

CHRISTOPHER HILL

Preface

In the mind of the reading public, foreign policy is a subject written about by journalists, retired diplomats, and ministers looking for a place in history. There is certainly a lot to learn from the accounts of these experienced riders on the carousel of international meetings, conflicts and conspiracies. There is, however, another literature altogether dealing with foreign policy, in the academic world. This has grown up over the last fifty years under the name of 'foreign policy analysis' (FPA), and is nested in the general subject area of International Relations, itself a close relative of political science. Some of the concepts of foreign policy analysis have leaked into our general political vocabulary, such as 'crisis-management', 'misperception' and even 'groupthink', but for the most part it has remained an in-house activity. Ironically, in the last decade or so FPA has paid the price for its introspection as many in the new generation of scholars have come to see foreign policy as integral to the played-out Westphalia states-system, and of only residual intellectual interest.

This book argues that such neglect is understandable but misconceived, as foreign policy is now of even greater importance to our political lives than ever before. This is because it is a key site for responsible action, and for democratic accountability in a world where the facts and myths of globalization have obscured the locations of decision-making and confused the debate over democratic participation. The aim is therefore twofold: first to persuade any practitioners and general readers who might pass this way that there already exists a useful frame of analysis which can help them to make sense of particular cases, and problems arising from them, such as the role of the media, or the impact of domestic politics; and second, to make the case to those in the academic world that foreign policy is an area of the greatest political and intellectual importance, requiring a new phase of study.

Broadly interpreted, foreign policy is about the fundamental issue of how organized groups, at least in part strangers to each other, interrelate. The nature of these groups and their interrelations is naturally in evolution, and this book attempts to trace the impact of recent upheavals, but there is great continuity over recorded history around the central question of how societies co-exist, at once separately and together, at times in conditions of great antagonism but also managing to cooperate on a regular basis. There is every reason to suppose that this problem – which is also the defining issue of International Relations more generally – will be at the heart of many of the great dramas, tragedies and achievements of the future, just as it has been, positively, in the peaceful transition from the Warsaw Pact, and negatively, in the Balkans. Until 'global governance' crystallizes into something solid and coherent, with international institutions taking genuine responsibility for the welfare of a real world society, citizens and politicians alike will continue to wrestle with the dilemmas arising from the existence of foreignness, in varying ways and to varying degrees. Indeed, to the extent that international affairs now impinges more on people's everyday lives than it used to, the continuum between the domestic and the foreign is likely to generate more issues than it did in the past, not less.

The task is a daunting one since it involves great breadth at the risk of sacrificing depth. The scope is comparative and world-wide. Yet the same is true of any attempt to write about other major social phenomena, such as war or poverty. The first priority must be to work with a frame of reference which may be applied to all instances of the phenomenon under the microscope, and thereby to analyse the concepts and processes which it necessarily entails – even if that leads us to note more differences than similarities in the way foreign policy is conducted. Indeed, the argument must not escape into too much abstraction; empirical examples are employed throughout, from a wide range of countries and time periods. An historical perspective is indispensable, but the theme of the book is the changing nature of contemporary foreign policy. Thus, while reference is made to events throughout the twentieth century, the main focus is on the period since the end of the Second World War, in which new states have multiplied through decolonization and old states have found new ways of coordinating their foreign policies. The author's area of special knowledge, as well as the nature of the literature, means that examples are often drawn from western Europe and north America, but a conscious effort has been made to do justice to diversity.

Given the breadth of the subject and the gradual drift in International Relations writing away from statist subjects, it is not as surprising as it first seems that few general books on foreign policy have been written since Joseph Frankel's *The Making of Foreign Policy* launched Foreign Policy Analysis in 1963.[1] There have been some excellent texts produced, notably by Jensen in the United States and Clarke and White in Britain, but those who have wanted to reflect at length on foreign policy have tended to rely on the platform of either a country study or a particular 'middle-range' theory.[2] Many perceptive and detailed works have been produced in each category over the last thirty years or so, and the current book draws heavily on them, while not pretending to an exhaustive coverage. Apart from those already mentioned, a long list of scholars has made major contributions to our understanding of foreign policy both in particular contexts and more generally.[3] They in turn have drawn on great social scientists in other disciplines, such as Kenneth Boulding or Herbert Simon.

There are two figures in particular, however, who with Joseph Frankel, represent key reference points for the present work. The writings of Stanley Hoffmann and Arnold Wolfers combine the capacity for penetrating analysis with a humane concern for the often tragic consequences of foreign policy.[4] They naturally see the discussions of power, process and value as inherently linked, and do not allow themselves to be side-tracked by excessive concerns about the separation of facts and values – while at the same time being scrupulously dispassionate in tone. For them, empirical work and political theory are both indispensable to writing intelligently about politics, and accordingly their work resists pigeon-holing. It continues to inspire.

Analysis is the main skill of Hoffmann and Wolfers and it is the key word in 'foreign policy analysis'. By analysis is meant not just the necessary breaking down of foreign policy into its constituent parts, concepts and processes, and the examination of the impact of its various environments. It is also understood in a sense akin to psychoanalysis, whereby an attempt is made to draw out deeper meanings than appear on the surface, and to understand action in terms of the way actors constantly redefine themselves through interaction with others. The interplay, indeed overlap, between the domestic and the external sources of behaviour is central to any modern understanding of what foreign policy does, just as the interplay between the interior and exterior worlds is the way in to understanding an individual's behaviour. The relationships at stake in the world of foreign policy are those between states but also between states and transnational actors of many different kinds, and across a range of issue-areas in what is a multi-level international system with a hugely varied cast. Understanding how foreign policy decisions are arrived at, implemented and eventually changed is not a matter of a single theory, even less of generalizing on the basis of an individual case. It involves doing justice to the richness and complexity of the foreign policy universe, without forgetting the basic premise of social science – that there is order in the world, and it can be systematically observed. This means accepting that there are two sides to the politics of foreign policy – the slow-moving international system, and the darting, sometimes unpredictable movements of the individual players the system contains. It is the interplay between the two which constitutes our large, elusive but fascinating subject.

1

Foreign Policy in International Relations

To the non-academic citizen 'foreign policy' is an uncontentious aspect of the world of politics, albeit one that is generally remote and inaccessible. Most people in most states would have little difficulty in accepting that foreign policy exists and that it consists in what one state does to, or with, other states. To many specialists, however, this conventional wisdom is deeply suspect. As the concepts of state sovereignty and independence have come under attack in recent decades, so the idea that a government might have a discrete set of actions (let alone strategies) for dealing with the outside world has come to seem anachronistic, even naïve. The very division between home and abroad, domestic and foreign, inside and outside has been brought into question from a number of different viewpoints, conceptual and political. In consequence, a serious division has opened up, not for the first time, between the normal discourse of democratic mass politics and the professional discourse of academic commentators. Some attempts have been made at bridging this gap through popularizing such terms as 'interdependence' and 'globalization', but since no scientific consensus attaches to them, the only result has been to obscure matters further. On the other side of the coin various forms of nationalist reaction have taken place against the idea that a given society might have to accept limits on its freedom of action by virtue of inhabiting a common international system, and there are too many examples of groups, even whole nations, believing that survival requires a foreign policy geared to a degree of brutal self-interest barely imaginable even by Thomas Hobbes.[1]

The gap between popular and professional understandings of foreign policy is beginning, therefore, to have some serious consequences. These are compounded by the fact that intellectuals are themselves divided three ways, between the specialists in a given country or area, who still tend to talk the language of normal diplomacy, the academic subject of International Relations, which has become introverted in musings about its own philosophical evolution, and 'public intellectuals' from other disciplines who sometimes feel a responsibility to intervene in the key ethical issues of foreign policy, such as Bosnia, but are all too often innocent of the history and theory of international politics. These various divisions mean at best that debates are conducted at cross-purposes and at worst that in the area of external policy the democratic process is severely compromised.

It is my hope in this book to go some way towards redressing the imbalance caused by people talking past each other. I aim to provide a conceptualization of foreign policy that might stand some chance both of bringing its usefulness back into focus for an academic subject which seems to have lost interest in actions and decisions, and of helping public debate about international affairs to evolve in the direction of understanding the interplay between the state and its external context. For both audiences the aim is basically the same: to break the association of foreign policy with the cruder versions of realism – that is, the assumption that behaviour can only be understood and/or guided by reference to self-evident national interests – and to show that both democracy and efficiency, the twin totems of modern society, require a workable notion of foreign policy if they are not to be lost in a miasma of generalization about 'global governance' and the like.

Foreign policy needs liberating from the narrow and over-simplified views that are often held of it, and International Relations as a subject needs to move forward in reconstituting its notions of agency after the waves of attacks on realism in recent decades, which have established the weakness of state-centric accounts without putting much in their place.

The approach taken here is to rework the idea of foreign policy, not to defend a particular school of thought or appeal to a mythological past of paradigmatic unity and shared discourse. Too many people have doubts about the contemporary function of foreign policy for the issue to be brushed aside. Equally, there is widespread bewilderment as to where we can realistically expect meaningful actions to be taken in international relations, and over the appropriate contemporary roles of states, international organizations, pressure groups, businesses and private individuals. The very definition of international politics is at stake in the questions a reconsideration of foreign policy naturally throws up, that is, 'who acts, for whom and with what effect?'

An Initial Definition

The increased internationalization of much of daily life, especially in developed, commercially active countries, causes problems when it comes to defining foreign policy and what should be studied under that heading. Is the focus to be reduced to the rump of what diplomats say to each other, which would leave out many of the most interesting aspects of international politics, or should it be widened to include almost everything that emanates from every actor on the world scene? This genuine dilemma over what foreign policy includes has led some to assume that its content is now minimal, and that agency lies else-where, with transnational enterprises of various kinds. It has led others to ignore the question of agency altogether, as if in embarrassment, con-centrating their attention on structures – power balances for neo-realists, international regimes for liberals, and markets for the gurus of global-ization. Both of these reactions represent a *trahison des clercs*, as they lead to the neglect of a wide range of activities with the potential for influencing the lives of millions. Foreign policy consists in varied activ-ities, whether Richard Holbrooke's mediation over Kosovo, the conflict with Russia over NATO enlargement, debates over China's entry into the World Trade Organization or Nelson Mandela's intercession for Ken Sara Wiwa in Nigeria. It is not a residual category to be associated with a dwindling number of 'diplomatic' issues.

A brief definition of foreign policy can be given as follows: the sum of official external relations conducted by an independent actor (usually a state) in international relations. The phrase 'an independent actor' enables the inclusion of phenomena such as the European Union; exter-nal relations are 'official' to allow the inclusion of outputs from all parts of the governing mechanisms of the state or enterprise while also main-taining parsimony with respect to the vast number of international trans-actions now being conducted; policy is the 'sum' of these official relations because otherwise every particular action could be seen as a separate foreign policy – whereas actors usually seek some degree of coherence towards the outside world. Lastly, the policy is 'foreign' because the world is still more separated into distinctive communities than it is a single, homogenizing entity. These communities therefore need strategies for coping with foreigners (or strangers) in their various aspects (it should be noted that the word 'foreign' derives from the latin 'foris' meaning 'outside').[2]

Definitions of political activities are notoriously difficult and foreign policy is no exception.[3] To some extent decision-makers themselves decide what foreign policy is by what they choose to do, but now that foreign offices do not monopolize external relations this only pushes the problem onto another level, to the point of deciding which personnel are to be counted as 'foreign policy-makers'. In a world where important international disputes occur over the price of bananas or illegal immigration it would be absurd to concentrate foreign policy analysis on relations between national diplomatic services. Although the latter try to achieve the status of gatekeeper and clearing-house, in practice they have to accept a great deal of parallel diplomacy on the part of colleagues in 'domestic' ministries. It is for the same reason that the once popular distinction between 'high' and 'low' politics is no longer of much help.[4] High politics – in the sense of serious conflict touching on the state's most basic concerns – can be as much about monetary integration as about territory and the threat of armed attack. Conversely low politics – in the sense of routine exchanges contained within knowable limits and rarely reaching the public realm – can be observed in NATO or OSCE multilateralism as much as (perhaps more than) in discussions over fish or airport landing rights. Thus the *intrinsic content* of an issue is not a guide to its level of political salience or to the way it will be handled, except in the tautological sense that any issue which blows up into a high-level international conflict (and almost anything has the potential so to do) will lead to decision-makers at the highest level suddenly taking over responsibility – their relations with the experts who had been managing the matter on a daily basis then become a matter of some moment, which can be studied as a typical problem of foreign policy analysis.

The idea of foreign policy also implies both politics and coherence. Everything that a given actor generates officially at the international level is grist to the mill of foreign policy, but when we are asked to say what foreign policy consists of we usually refer to the more centrally political aspects of the activity, that is, actions, statements and values relating to how the actor wishes to advance its main objectives and to shape the external world – a version of 'the authoritative allocation of values', except that what connotes 'authority' is precisely what is at issue in international relations. It is natural that foreign policy should be seen as a political activity, given the at best informally structured nature of the international system, but as we have already seen, it is difficult to predict in advance what is likely to rise up the political agenda.

There is a similar issue with coherence. The very notion of a 'policy' in any field implies conscious intentions and coordination. It is the umbrella term under which huddle the myriad particular 'decisions' and routinized outputs of an actor's behaviour. That very often the system of policy-making fails to live up to these aspirations is beside the point; the pursuit of a foreign (or health, or education) policy is about the effort to carry through some generally conceived strategy, usually on the basis of a degree of rationality, in the sense that objectives, time-frames and instruments are at least brought into focus. Thus foreign policy must always be seen as a way of trying to hold together or make sense of the various activities which the state or even the wider community is engaged in internationally. In that sense it is one way in which a society defines itself, against the backcloth of the outside world.

Foreign policy is therefore both more and less than the 'external relations' which states generate continually on all fronts.[5] It attempts to coordinate, and it is the way in which – at least in principle – priorities are established between competing externally-projected interests. It should also project the values which the society in question thinks are universal, whether through Robin Cook's ethically-motivated foreign policy or less directly as with the Canadian or Swedish commitment to UN peace-keeping operations. It is, in short, the focal political point of an actor's external relations.

Competing Approaches

Foreign policy may be approached in many different ways within International Relations. The subject has also, however, been extensively studied by historians, at first via the detailed accounts of diplomatic historians and then through the lens of *'international history'*, which strove to relate diplomacy to its domestic roots, whether political, social, economic or cultural.[6] Indeed, in recent years there has been something of an equal and opposite move towards foreign policy analysis on the part of historians, as IR has moved away from it. The tools of decision-making analysis are readily adaptable to detailed cases, and the opening up of many state archives has made it impossible to avoid evidence of such pathologies as bureaucratic politics or small group dynamics. In the United States in particular, there has been a deliberate encouragement of links between historians and political scientists, with much useful cross-fertilization.[7]

At a half-way house between history and political science lie *country-studies*. There remain many scholars immune to the pull of intellectual fashion who continue to develop their expertise on the foreign policy of an individual state, almost always with the will and capacity to demonstrate the intimate links with domestic society. Area-studies are strong in both the United Kingdom and, particularly so, in France, as any reading of *Le Monde* will demonstrate. United States foreign policy naturally generates most analysis, although from regrettably few non-Americans.[8] The other permanent members of the UN Security Council also continue to be studied in some depth, while there has been a notable upsurge of interest in Italian and, particularly, German foreign policy. Japan, Australia, Canada, Egypt, India, Indonesia, Spain and Brazil figure quite prominently in the literature, while other states are usually dealt with in groups, as with 'African foreign policies' or 'European foreign policy'.[9] There is a need to break down some of the larger categories used, such as 'the foreign policies of new states' and in particular to provide more detailed work on important cases such as Iran, South Africa, Syria, Turkey or Pakistan.[10] It will be a pity, however, if those who remain convinced of the importance of states in international relations are confined to studying single cases. Unless welcomed by IR in general they will inevitably be forced into the camps of either history or comparative politics, which will be to the gain of the latter but much to the detriment of International Relations.

Realism is the best known approach in IR, and the most criticized. It is the traditional way in which practitioners have thought about international relations, emphasizing the importance of power in a dangerous, unpredictable world. Realism became the orthodoxy in academic writing after the discrediting of the 'legalistic–moralistic' approach of the inter-war period, and in the Cold War it seemed self-evident that states, and military force, were the main features of the international system. Much realist thought was more subtle than this summary allows, as any encounter with the work of E.H. Carr, Hans Morgenthau, Reinhold Niebuhr, Martin Wight and Arnold Wolfers soon reveals.[11] What realism did not do, however, was probe into decision-making or other domestic sources of international behaviour.

In recent years foreign policy analysis has often been seen as realist on the grounds that it is 'state-centric'. This is ironical given that FPA grew up in reaction to the assumption of classical realism that the state was a single, coherent actor pursuing clear national interests in a rational manner, with varying degrees of success according to the talents of particular leaders and the constraints of circumstance. The work done in FPA invariably challenged the ideas of rationality, coherence, national interest and external orientation – possibly, indeed, to excess. As will be shown below, it is fundamentally pluralist in orientation. It is true that states remain important to FPA, but its methods may be used

Actors + Agency ; ≠ single coherent rational nat unity etc

to study all types of actor in international relations, and indeed this book focuses on actors and agency rather than limiting itself in principle to states.[12] The only way that the label of realism can be justified is if all those who believe that states are of continued significance in international relations are deemed *eo ipso* realists.[13] This is an indefensible proposition, as the large body of liberal thought about states and international society indicates.

Life was breathed back into realism, despite the attacks from foreign policy analysts, students of transnational relations and others, by Kenneth Waltz's formulation of *neo-realism* in the late 1970s.[14] Whereas realism was not clear about where the drive for power originated – in human passions, in the state itself, or in a world which lacked rules – Waltz was clear and systematic. His view was that the international system was dominant in certain key respects. It represented a balance of power with its own logic, so that if one wished to explain war or other major features of the international system as a whole the only resort was to a parsimonious theory such as his which stressed 'the logic of anarchy'.[15] Neo-realism captured the heights of IR in the United States both because of its scientific set of propositions and the appeal of balance of power theory to the system's hegemon. By the same token it has had less appeal elsewhere.

neo-realism int sys key focus

In neo-realist theory, foreign policy, with its associated interest in domestic politics and in decision-making, was simply not relevant, and indeed barely discussed. Waltz can be accused of inconsistency, since his previous book had been about the differences between US and UK ways of making foreign policy, concluding that the more open American system was also the more efficient.[16] Yet he has a broadly integrated view which allows for a discussion of agency through foreign policy, so long as it does not pretend to explain what inherently it cannot explain – for example, by taking a 'reductionist' approach to the study of war in general, as opposed to the origins of a particular war where it may have a great deal to contribute.

Neo-realism therefore deals in levels of analysis, with foreign policy analysis operating at the level of the explanation of particular units. This is not the place to debate the overall value of neo-realism in IR. It is important, however, to show that it is unsatisfactory – because highly limiting – as an approach to foreign policy. In Chapter 2 I shall discuss the underlying issues of structure and agency. For the moment, it is worth stressing how few interesting political and intellectual problems are left for an actor in a system which operates in the top–down manner envisaged by Waltz and his colleagues. Given the historical debates which have taken place on the role of German foreign policy in the origins of two world wars (with special reference to Prussian culture and Nazi leaders respectively), on the international impact of the differences between Soviet and Chinese communism, or on the domestic politics of US policy in Vietnam, to take only the most dramatic examples, it seems self-defeating to assume the predominance of the 'pattern of power' in determining great events in international relations. For neo-realism has a deterministic quality which is at odds with the tendency of FPA to stress the open interplay of multiple factors, domestic and international.[17] It also assumes that states are primarily driven by the need to maximize their security, largely through the exercise of power and independence. Most students of foreign policy would see this as excessive generalization, doing less than justice to the variety of states' actual positions and goals.

An approach which has so far had little particular impact on the study of foreign policy, although it is widely disseminated elsewhere in political science, is that of *rational choice*, or public choice in some recent incarnations. This is partly because FPA grew up attacking the assumption of rational action on the part of a unitary actor with given goals (usually power maximization) which was associated with realism. It continues to be the case because few IR scholars of any persuasion believe that the explanation of international relations can be reduced to the individual preferences of decision-makers seeking votes, political support, personal advantage or some other kind of measurable currency. Rational choice has grown out of the individualist assumptions of economics, and in its stress on power as currency and on the drive towards equilibrium it is closely related to neo-realism. Yet the collective action problems are particularly acute in international relations. As David Lake has pointed out, 'there is no necessary reason why the interests of self-seeking politicians should coincide with the national interest'.[18] This is hardly news to any foreign policy analyst, but there is a real issue in relating the motives and behaviour of individual decision-makers to the collective ends of foreign policy, particularly when mistakes are only likely to be punished occasionally, and *in extremis*, unlike much of domestic politics where politicians are afraid to raise taxes by one per cent for fear of defeat at the next election.

Public choice theory addresses this very problem of collective action, and the converse, that policies agreed jointly (often bipartisanly) may be remote from the actual preferences of individual politicians – let alone those of the voters. It therefore offers some possibilities for foreign policy, particularly in relation to foreign economic policy, to the environment, and to alliance politics, where pay-offs, free-riding and the like may be more evident. Even here, however, the necessary assumption that states are unified actors is difficult to sustain empirically. More generally, the economic formalism of the public choice approach and the contortions it must perform to cope with such matters as competing values, geopolitics and conceptions of international society limit its ability to generate understanding. Like game theory, public choice can be of considerable heuristic use, but to start from an assumption of unitary decision-making optimizing given preferences, with the influences which shape preferences bracketed out, limits the applicability to actual cases.[19] Moreover, contrary to some globalization theory, as well as to public choice, international politics is about much more than adapting to the market.

In recent years the wave of *post-positivism* has brought a new perspective to bear on foreign policy. Post-positivists are another broad church, but in general they reject the fact–value distinction most prominent among realists and behaviouralists, and consider that there is little point in attempting to work scientifically towards a 'truthful' picture of human behaviour. This is because politics is constituted by language, ideas and values. We cannot stand outside ourselves and make neutral judgements. That this view has incited considerable controversy is not the issue here. More relevant is the extra dimension it has given to foreign policy studies – another competing approach, but one which confirms the importance of the state. Writers like David Campbell, Roxanne Doty and Henrik Larsen have examined the language of foreign policy and what they see as its dominant, usually disciplinary, discourses.[20] These are, however, still national.[21] Language is seen as crucial to national identity, on which the representation of outsiders ('the Other') will be a significant influence. Indeed, foreign policy is important precisely because it reinforces (undesirably, in the views of Campbell) national and statist culture. If this approach can be linked more effectively to the analysis of choice, and can confront the problem of evidence, then it may yet reach out from beyond the circle of the converted to contribute more to our understanding of foreign policy. Language, whether official or private, rhetorical or observational, has a lot to tell us about both mind-sets and actions, and it is a relatively untapped resource.

All the approaches listed above have something to offer the student of foreign policy – and they need not be seen as 'competing' in every respect. History and country-studies are an indispensable part of any analyst's armoury, while it would be pig-headed to ignore the ideas generated from realism, public choice and post-positivism. Nonetheless, there are limits to eclecticism, and the present book is rooted in the particular tradition of writing known as *foreign policy analysis* (FPA), albeit with a concern to extend the subject well beyond decision-making, and in particular to ensure that foreign policy is seen not as a technical exercise but as an important form of political argument. Since the chapters which follow apply FPA in some detail, there is no need to describe its approach here in more than summary form.

FPA enquires into the motives and other sources of the behaviour of international actors, particularly states. It does this by giving a good deal of attention to decision-making, initially so as to probe behind the formal self-descriptions (and fictions) of the processes of government and public administration. In so doing it tests the plausible hypothesis that the outputs of foreign policy are to some degree determined by the nature of the decision-making process. As the language used here suggests, there was a strong behaviouralist impetus behind the rise of FPA, but the subject has subsequently developed in a much more open-ended way, particularly in Britain.[22] The Comparative Foreign Policy school which was dominant in the United States for so long did not probe the politics of foreign policy, internal or external; it was interested in finding correlations between the factors involved in foreign policy over as wide a range as possible.[23]

This is a world away from the kind of FPA which has developed in alliance with the more theoretically-minded historians, and which is the basis of the present book. This approach employs 'middle-range theories' to examine particular areas of human activity such as perception or geopolitics, and is sceptical that an overarching single theory of foreign policy can ever be achieved without being bland and tautological.[24] The Scandinavian attempt to promulgate 'weak (general) theory' to cope with the problem of integrating middle-range theories might succeed – but it is difficult to see what it would look like in practice.[25] A great deal of high-quality scholarship has already come out of FPA's middle-range theories and the challenge is to build on that rather than to start again. They are already integrated in the sense that foreign policy analysis is underpinned by systems theory, even if there are still many creative interconnections to be explored.[26]

The approach taken in this book is based on the assumption that Foreign Policy Analysis can and should be open, comparative, conceptual, interdisciplinary and range across the domestic–foreign frontier. It should be analytical in the sense of detachment, of not being *parti pris*, but it should not be positivist, in the sense of assuming that 'facts' are always external and disconnected from actors' perceptions and self-understandings.

What is more, it should always attempt to connect its analysis to the underlying questions of all political life, such as 'who benefits?' 'what is the right course of action?' and 'which institutions best serve our desired ends?' Like much American International Relations, FPA strove at first to earn the status of science, only to suffer in range and reputation as a result. It is time to move on.

The Changing International Context   *Systemic*

The politics of foreign policy are perpetually changing, depending on the country or the region, and by no means always in the same directions. This is why case and country-studies are so important. There is no point in lofty generalizations if they seem beside the point to experts on Guyana, or Germany, or Gabon. Yet as the result of imperial expansion, world war and economic integration we have had to get used to seeing the world, and the international political system, as a whole. Changes in the whole are thus real and of great significance for the parts. Conversely, changes in a particularly important part may lead to upheaval in the system as a whole. We have had a strong sense of this since the implosions of communism, the Cold War and the Soviet Union in the dramatic events of 1989–91. When the phenomenon – or perhaps the idea – of globalization is added to the equation it is natural to conclude that we are living in dramatic times which cannot but have a transformative effect on foreign policy as an activity, and on individual states' foreign policy problems.

There are three elements of the contemporary international context which can be taken to represent major change: the end of the Cold War; the process of globalization; and the challenge to the Westphalia state system represented by the doctrine of humanitarian intervention (*le droit d'ingérence*). Each of these great issues will be examined in turn, but only in terms of the implications for foreign policy.

The end of the Cold War with the collapse of the Warsaw Pact in 1989 is seen by some as a revolution in international affairs in itself.[27] Alternatively, it can be viewed as involving 'only' the collapse of a particular state/empire, with large consequences for the balance of power but no different in kind from the end of Napoleonic France or Wilhelmine Germany. This second position seems more convincing, but when one bears in mind the causal interconnections between the end of the Cold War and globalization (possibly accelerated) and the extent of the current challenge to the principle of non-intervention (not feasible in the era of the Brezhnev doctrine) then the contrast between the two becomes rather less sharp.

The end of an empire always alters the outlook and calculations of the other members of the system, and not only at the end of major wars. The dismantling of the French and British empires between 1945–64 created many new states and seemed to have weakened the two metropole powers. Yet adjustment soon takes place. By 1973 it had become difficult to remember the world as it was before decolonization, while the position of France and Britain remained remarkably unchanged. Even to this day their permanent seats on the UN Security Council are not in real danger. On the other hand, both decolonization and the end of the Cold War signalled the death of a set of particular ideas, and the arrival of new possibilities. The nature of a new order may not be immediately apparent, but it can be immanent. In the case of 1991 and after, what happened was not only the humiliation of a superpower, and the folding up of a set of international institutions, but also the destruction of a major transnational ideology.

This ideology, coupled with the power of the Soviet Union, had acted as a straitjacket for the foreign policies of many different states, not just those in eastern Europe. Poor states needing Soviet aid, or looking for reassurance against American power, all found themselves defined by it. Opponents, likewise, either turned directly to the US and its allies for fear of international communism, or self-consciously adopted a strategy of non-alignment in the hope of escaping the bipolar trap. Some states found themselves the victims of various kinds of intervention in any case. Large resources were consumed by those who saw themselves (rightly or wrongly) as threatened by Soviet communism.

All this has now disappeared. There is no communist aid or interventionism. There is no anti-communist excuse for western interventionism. There is no need for neutralism or non-alignment, even if, like the Cheshire cat's grin, something always remains in the ether. Resources are (or should be) released for other purposes, domestic and international. Internal politics have, in many cases, been reconfigured as the result of the ideological straitjacket being removed. Indeed, for some states the very relationship between foreign and domestic politics has been cast into the melting pot. In some rather unpredictable states, politics has been shaken up by the removal of the old orthodoxy. France has found it easier to move into a working relationship with NATO, and Italy has begun to develop a more confident national foreign policy. In both countries the domestic environment has become more fluid as the result of the demoralization of what were previously strong communist parties.[28]

The end of the Cold War has thus introduced qualitative changes to international politics, which foreign policies have to take into account, but which do not amount to a challenge to foreign policy as such. *Globalization,* by contrast, is seen by many as having rendered foreign policy redundant. At least, the large numbers who write about globalization give this impression by the simple fact of ignoring it.[29] In part, foreign policy is a sub-set of the problem of what is happening to the state in an age of globalization, understood as the creation of an integrated world capitalist market, and the putting in place of some of the sinews of a global civil society, through developments in information technology, travel and education. Globalization in its turn has been boosted by political change, notably the emergence of the confident states of east Asia in the wake of the Vietnam war, and the collapse of the communist bloc in Europe.

At one level the problem of globalization is just the latest episode in the long-running debate about the impact of economics on politics, which began with Richard Cobden in the 1860s making a linkage between peace and free trade, and has had at least one other active phase, during the 1970s discussion of interdependence and détente. It is always a bad mistake to assume that the present will resemble the past, but in the case of foreign policy and globalization there seem to be good reasons for supposing that the death of foreign policy has been forecast prematurely.[30] If foreign policy is essentially the political strategy conducted by independent units in relation to each other, indeed, then this could only happen with the *de facto* disappearance of independent units. Discounting the possibility of world government, this could conceivably come about by stealth, through the emergence of global *governance* in the form of a net of issue-based regimes, in which units took up positions on the merits of a problem, without concern for community-based linkages. This seems improbable for three reasons: states would become unviable as devices for satisfying their citizens, who expect the use of linkage in order to achieve priority goals; there would be a significant danger of partial interests capturing the policy of the state as a whole, and subordinating the notion of the 'common good';[31] the overall relationship between goals, resources and institutions could not be effectively managed – issues can never be kept in neat compartments.

Much more significant in terms of the impact of globalization is likely to be a reshuffled relationship between foreign policy and foreign economic policy. The two things should be considered in tandem, but rarely are because of the intellectual difficulties of keeping such a wide range of activity in focus at the same time – and because of scholastic habit. In times of stability, as the post-1991 period seemed at first likely to be, it is natural to expect that economics will occupy a central place in foreign policy. Modernity heightens this expectation. Although Europe at least seems to have exchanged a period of grim stability in the Cold War for one of mixed hope and turbulence, this trend need not be denied. Much of foreign policy for modern states is about promoting prosperity as much as security, and indeed about blurring the two concepts together. In some areas of economic and social life governments' role may be extremely limited as they bend the knee before the efficiency of the market principle, but this does not mean that it is non-existent; far from it, in fact. Governments simply become subtle and varied in their strategies for protecting the welfare of their citizens, sometimes working together with other states, sometimes intervening indirectly (even illegally) to win contracts, and sometimes using traditional means, such as defence expenditure, for reasons of economic policy. Of course handling instant financial transfers, multinationals' tax avoidance and the fast-changing nature of innovation means that the decision-making system for external policy cannot remain unchanged. Foreign ministries have no choice but to accept the direct involvement of many more ministries, while trying to reposition themselves as coordinators in some form, and experts on 'the international' as a whole. This does not make any fundamental difference to the fact that states need some form of external strategy, and machinery, for managing their external environment. That it now contains many more events of importance, which press directly onto the domestic, makes the conduct of foreign policy more important, not less.

The third major contemporary development in international relations could well in the long run turn out to be the most significant. The emergence of serious support for the idea that the right of a state to determine its own internal affairs should be qualified so as to prevent serious human rights abuses has the potential to precipitate moves towards a different kind of system, in which superordinate law and institutions set limits to both internal and external behaviour – in short, towards an embryonic international constitution. Foreign policy has always, of course, been constrained from the outside, but the inhibitions have come from fear, or concerns about practicality, or from internal value-systems. If a *law of humanitarian intervention*, or what Tony Blair has called 'the doctrine of international community', becomes established, the constraints will become more systematic, transparent and institutionalized.[32] The trial of Slobodan Milosevic at The Hague is an attempt to begin this process.

Even if the trend continues, it is clear that any challenge to the 'Westphalian system' of sovereign states possessing the ultimate right to determine their own law and political system will be a long-drawn-out and difficult business. The United Nations Charter flagged the tension between human rights and sovereignty over 55 years ago, but left the issue hanging in the air. The Universal Declaration of Human Rights in 1948 was little more than a hopeful signpost, with no capacity for enforcement. The move towards greater consensus on the value of human rights, and indeed liberal democracy, since 1991 means that if powerful states are prepared to sponsor change, it might begin to have more practical meaning – as arguably it has already begun to do.[33] For the present, the most that can be said is that we have entered a long period of transition with respect to the foundational principles of international order, and that this will have inevitable consequences for foreign policy.

These consequences will mean uncertainty about rules and norms, and particularly about their implementation: it is highly probable that the 'double standards' problem will become ever more evident, with intervention – even for the best of reasons – occurring on a patchy and discriminatory basis. To some degree all states will have to take on board new considerations and obligations as they formulate foreign policy, but for many of them, having just become used to the notion of sovereignty, it will be disconcerting to see new principles introduced in parallel. This is particularly true of regimes in new states, which are often the most passionate defenders of independence and non-intervention. The new possibilities will be twofold: interference in one's own affairs if they draw the hostile attention of the 'international community', usually in the form of the more powerful democratic states; and being drawn into new international commitments, including what might be actions with both high risks and high costs. In either case, domestic society would become more exposed to external developments, with potentially significant consequences for the citizenry. As the external environment becomes more complicated, with law, organizations and transnational human rights groups all protruding more into states, or engaging their support, so foreign policy will be a more critical site for political decision-making, not less.

The Challenge to Foreign Policy Analysis

Change is a perpetual challenge to social science, and Foreign Policy Analysis is no exception. It has faced, for example, the problem of how to integrate transnational actors into its framework since the early 1970s. The changes in the international context described above – themselves with longer roots than just the past ten years – represent the current challenges. As I have argued, none of them poses the kind of threat to the very purpose and existence of foreign policy which is often rather unthinkingly assumed. Each of them, however, is having a significant impact on the nature of contemporary foreign policy, on its relationship with domestic society and on the means by which it is conducted. The details of these changes – and the elements of continuity – will become clear in the chapters which follow. Beneath the detail, however, lie certain key questions, theoretical and practical, which provide the rationale for the book as a whole.

In theoretical terms the main issue FPA faces is whether foreign policy remains a key site of agency in international relations, or whether it is being steadily emptied of content. This in turn depends on views about the nature of agency and its relationship to structures in world politics. Part of the answer may be given through theorizing the state, evidently still a major source of political life, but not all of it. The state is one of a variety of different international actors, whose positions relative to each other and to structures need to be traced.

Another dimension of the problem is the extent to which actors, and the communities they embody, can still be said to have distinct 'foreign' and 'domestic' environments. If they do, then it follows that they will need some form of means of coping with the particularities of the foreign. But if the environments are blurring into each other so as to become functionally indistinguishable, do they not need to integrate policies and mechanisms accordingly? If one allows the more modest proposition that any entity with the capacity to make decisions has an 'inside' and an 'outside' (associated with the universal notion of 'minding our own business') does this mean in the international context that dealing with the outside is another way of describing foreign policy, or is it rather an administrative boundary, with no qualitative shift?

The third aspect of the theoretical challenge facing the study of foreign policy concerns the category of 'external relations'. If we do conclude that inside is not the same as outside, and in particular that policy-makers have to operate in differing kinds of environment, does this mean that everything which a system projects outwards is foreign policy? Conversely, how do those activities which are conventionally labelled 'foreign policy' relate to the multiple strands of a society's interactions with the world, private and public? This issue is closely related to that of the very definition of foreign policy, on which a provisional answer has been given earlier in this chapter. Yet, as with other large political concepts such as democracy, analysis and definitions are in a constant dialectical relation with each other. This means that no position on the relationship of external relations to foreign policy will convince until the problem has been broken down into its component parts – as it will be in subsequent chapters through the discussions of bureaucratic politics, transnational relations and domestic society.

Finally, Foreign Policy Analysis must also face the normative issues which its positivist roots have tended to obscure. If it is an area of serious enquiry then it must confront – if not be dominated by – the possibility that it might contain built-in normative biases. More prosaically, it just might not address certain important value-based questions. It is certainly true that many of the interesting questions about foreign policy are not technical but involve issues of value or principle. One such is how far foreign policy may be effectively harnessed to an ethical cause, without damaging other legitimate goals. Another is the long-debated issue of how far foreign policy can or should be accountable to citizens who are probably ignorant of the issues but who may ultimately be asked to die in its name. The tension between efficiency and democracy, and the need to trade them off, is particularly sharp here. The changing contemporary environment, however, has given extra force to one particular normative issue which has always existed between the interstices of foreign policy, namely how much responsibility to take for shaping the lives of others outside one's own society, and for the international milieu as a whole. Although states vary in what they can do, and view the matter through the lens of self-interest, this is a perpetual ethical challenge for every foreign policy. The broadening of horizons enabled by technology and the pace of economic growth since 1945 have brought the issue of wider responsibilities to the forefront of policy-makers' concerns.

This brings us to the practical questions facing Foreign Policy Analysis. The first links theory to practice by asking what expectations is it reasonable for citizens to have of policy-makers, and for policy-makers to have of themselves? How much of what may be deemed desirable is also feasible? There are naturally limits to the extent to which a general answer can be given, but it must surely be the task of any analyst to clarify the nature of action in relation to the outside world by relating the complexity of the environment to the needs and circumstances of particular actors. On that basis realistic expectations may be constructed about both instrumental gains and shared responsibilities. Capabilities can be the better brought into line with expectations, if some sophisticated understanding exists of the degree to which choices are constrained, and of the margin there might be for initiative. Only by analysing actors and their milieux in conjunction can this be done.

How far can we generalize about foreign policy? The assumption of this book is that there are many common features and dilemmas which can be anatomized. Yet states clearly vary enormously in size, power and internal composition, to say nothing of non-state actors. In the post-1991 world this argument can be extended to the point where it might seem that the foreign policy of the world's only superpower is in a category of its own. Indeed, the United States shows few signs of angst about whether foreign policy exists or counts in the world, unlike the middle-range states. It is revealing that in the American study of International Relations, the state and its power is still a central theme, whether through the successful policy journals like *Foreign Affairs* and *Foreign Policy*, or through the dominant academic school of neo-realism. Globalization theory, and constructivism, which tend to stress the impact of international structures, have made far less ground than in Europe, or neighbouring Canada. Where you sit really does influence what you see.

'The changing politics of foreign policy' is not, however, only about perception. Even the USA has to cope with limitations on its freedom of action, despite its apparent hegemony after 1991. It is also just as subject to decision-making pathologies, and to ends–means problems as any other actor. What is more, the interpenetration of foreign with domestic politics is universal, and varies only in degree. Different societies, perhaps different kinds of society, produce different sorts of domestic input into foreign policy, including conceptions of a desirable world and expectations about what can be done to improve it. It is commonplace to observe that the United States, for example, has consistently believed that its own values should be exported, whereas China has never felt the need to proselytize, despite its own conviction of superiority. The nature of variation and the possible links to foreign policy are themselves things to be charted, whether between democracies and autocracies, rich states and poor, ancient cultures and new states engaged in nation-building.

The principal practical challenge for any foreign policy analyst should be to make transparent and help spread to a wider public the often arcane processes of foreign policy-making. In the present environment that means debating the evolving character of foreign policy – is it more than what foreign ministries do? – but ultimately identifying the sites of decision and meaningful action. Both accountability and efficiency depend on a prior knowledge of how choices get formulated, who has most influence on them and how their feasibility may be evaluated. As any specialist knows, the answers to these questions are by no means always close to those which even an intelligent reader of a good newspaper might infer. In particular, FPA has the capacity to indicate the extent to which the nature of the decision-making process determines the outcomes of foreign policy, in terms of both the intrinsic quality of a decision and its effective implementation. Too often public discussion oscillates between fatalism about the impossibility of affecting international affairs, and the personalization of policy through the high expectations held of individual leaders.

Argument and Structure

In summary, the study of foreign policy faces perpetual challenges of both an intellectual and practical kind, as with any branch of social science. Equally, the exponents of foreign policy have to cope with a confusing, mixed-actor international environment where obstacles and opportunities are by no means clearly delineated. Lastly, citizens face a mass of events, information and competing interpretations which leave many confused. It is the task of FPA to try to resolve some of this confusion by clarifying basic concepts as well as by showing how agency may be understood in the modern world. This does not mean either reasserting traditional notions of the primacy of foreign policy, or accepting the common tendency to downgrade states and their international relations. The challenge is to reconstitute the idea of political agency in world affairs, and to rethink the relationship between agency and foreign policy.

Accordingly this book has begun with an examination of where foreign policy stands, in the world and in the academy. It continues with a more detailed discussion of the politics of foreign policy – that is, the problem of acting in international affairs, through the state and other actors, and of balancing the competing pressures and expectations which beset any foreign policy-maker. There are some difficult theoretical issues at stake in terms of the relationship between foreign policy and the state and its meaning in the context of the 'agency–structure debate' so prominent in social science during recent decades.

In the main body of the book the argument is divided into three sections. The first deals with agency itself, that is the ways in which actions are generated and conducted, and by whom, under the general heading of foreign policy. The main 'actors' are conceived not as abstract entities but as the decision-makers who are formally responsible for making decisions for the units which interact internationally – that is, mainly but not exclusively states. These actors do not always manage to achieve unity of purpose. In principle the 'agents' of responsible decision-makers are civil servants and other hired guns, and their important discretionary powers are given separate attention in Chapter 3. A fourth chapter deals with the problem of acting rationally, which has exercised all policy analysts since the 1950s; the usefulness of 'rational actor' and 'rational choice' assumptions are examined in the context of the extensive literature on psychological factors in decision-making and on the difficulties of handling information overload. The ineluctable process of 'learning from history' is also central here. Finally, agency has to be understood in the context of the capabilities and instruments at policy-makers' disposal, and the difficulties of using them to achieve stated goals even where they appear to be extensive and efficiently organized. 'Implementation' is now generally recognized as a distinct and difficult dimension of acting in foreign policy.[34]

The second section of the book shifts the focus not so much from 'agency' to 'structure' – since actors and agents are partly themselves structures – as to the international context in which action is played out. This is seen in classical terms as providing *opportunities* for initiating change and for promoting particular concerns, as well as *constraints* on what can be done. A crucial theme will be the limits to determinism: that is, states and other decision-generating entities always possess the suicide option, or the capacity to fly in the face of pressures to be realistic. They may take this option only rarely, but its very existence helps to define what it is to be an actor. The right and the ability to make one's own mistakes is what makes us as individuals responsible adults, and it is worth the risk of anthropomorphism to make the point that collective entities also have on occasions to be able to defy fate, whether in the form of logic, the inevitable, the international political system or some deeper 'structure'. When they cannot even make their own decisions, as with Lebanon in the 1980s, or a purely intergovernmental organization like the Western European Union (WEU), they lack, indeed, both political and legal 'personality'.[35]

The international context is treated in two chapters which analyse the diverse forms of constraint and opportunity that actors experience. The international political system – Hedley Bull's 'anarchical society' – is examined with a view to identifying how far international law, organizations and norms bear down on states and other actors and also to what

extent their values have been internalized through a process of socialization. By contrast, geopolitics is treated as a more 'enduring framework' in the sense that the very existence of separate territorial units on
the face of the earth creates issues of 'foreignness', of regionalism and
of variable vulnerability to outside interference. Even if boundaries are
in a process of continual historical flux, the fact of the uneven distribution of the world's resources among disparate communities cannot help
but create problems of choice over security, friendship and political
economy. This Waltzian perspective need not, however, be treated in
a Waltzian way. Geographical and historical specifics are taken to be
more important than abstractions like bipolarity or multipolarity, while
geopolitics produces great variation around the notions of threat and
'otherness'.

The second chapter in this section deals with the extent to which such
choices have become complicated by transnational forces which might
simultaneously be making geography less significant and undermining
the sense of a distinctive community. Foreign policy might be becoming, in Walter Bagehot's terms, a 'dignified' rather than an 'efficient'
political institution if the world it purports to be dealing with is in fact
less that of governments than of cross-national social, economic and
political movements.

The third and last part of the book picks up on one further possible
consequence of transnationalism, namely that it might have a solvent
effect on the separate community which a given foreign policy is supposed to serve. Given the moral claims that can be made on behalf of
'duties beyond borders', decision-makers are thus faced with the potential problem of serving competing constituencies, while conversely having other states taking a more direct interest in their 'domestic'
environment.[36] Bearing this in mind, the section's theme is that of
'responsibility', or the sense of beholdenness which decision-makers
have to the community on whose behalf foreign policy, in the first
instance, is conducted, but also possibly to a perceived community of
a much wider ambit.

The examination begins with the general issue of how domestic
society relates to foreign policy, and which elements represent the most
significant 'sources' of foreign policy, in the sense that actions 'begin
at home' even if they must be conducted abroad. Foreign policy is about
mediating the two-way flow between internal and external dynamics.
An attempt is made to grapple with the issue of comparative foreign policy studies, of how far certain kinds of society produce distinctive kinds
of foreign policy. The 'democratic peace' hypothesis, that democracies

do not fight wars against each other, is obviously the starting-point here, but there are many other things to say about the impact of domestic structures (for this too is a form of structural explanation) on external behaviour – for example, the impact of revolution and turmoil, or levels of economic development, both of which can be seen as at least as important in defining an actor's external strategies as geopolitical position or formal capabilities.

The second chapter in this section deals with the basic problem of democratic communities in international relations: that is, how to reconcile the need for freedom of action in dealings with intractable outsiders with the requirements of popular consent and parliamentary scrutiny. This involves also considering the ever-increasing interest of public opinion in international relations, to the point where many groups and individuals have lost patience with the governments that formally represent them and have begun either to agitate more loudly for changes in foreign policy, not accepting the classical arguments for national unity over 'national interests', or themselves to engage directly in international relations.[37] The 'no-global' protests at Seattle, Göteborg and Genova during 2000–01 were a dramatic case in point.

As the tripartite survey of agency, the global context and the constituencies of foreign policy moves to its close, the book's last chapter takes stock by looking at the problem of responsibility in a wider frame. It considers whether foreign policy in modern conditions can deliver what is expected of it, whether by citizens, decision-makers or academics. It argues that meaningful and intentional actions are still possible under the heading of foreign policy so long as they are based on a good understanding not just of external constraints but also of the various kinds of interpenetration to be found between structures at home and abroad, and of the limits of unilateralism. While it accepts that 'responsibility' is (and should be) increasingly felt to people outside the immediate foreign policy constituency (indeed, in some respects to humanity as a whole) it does not seek to resolve the ethical dilemmas arising from the notion of duties beyond borders. It does, however, delineate the parameters of responsibility within which all foreign policy-makers have to work, and for which the term 'national interest' is now a wholly inadequate characterization.

* * *

The argument of this book is that foreign policy is a central part of our understanding of international relations, even if it is far from being the whole story. It is currently neglected, for some good reasons, but many bad, and it needs bringing back into focus. It must play a major part in filling the current hole in accounts of international relations with respect to 'agency', which is much discussed at the epistemological level but insufficiently operationalized. As Valerie Hudson has recently pointed out, 'IR requires a theory of human political choice ... one area within the study of IR that has begun to develop such a theoretical perspective is foreign policy analysis'.[38]

Foreign policy is at the hinge of domestic politics and international relations. Raymond Aron said that ' "the problem of foreign policy" ... [is] the double problem of individual and collective survival'.[39] If we substitute the word 'development' for the Cold War stress on 'survival', we see that foreign policy is still central to the human predicament. Its study represents a wealth of possibilities for those not blinded by prejudice against 'state-centric' approaches or by stereotypes about FPA as a branch of realism. Fred Halliday has argued that FPA needs to develop a theory of the state which connects its inherent functions with those of external action without falling back on realism, and this is an important next step. It can be done partly in terms of the way the twin needs of democracy and efficiency are played out in the international context.[40] On the one hand more and more of society's needs are dependent on effective action in international relations. On the other hand, democracy has the potential both to turn a state inward and to press it into external crusades on the basis of what are perceived as universal values. Each of these tendencies means that foreign policy becomes crucial both as an expression of statehood, and as a means of brokering what is now a simultaneous stream of internal and external demands upon government. As a crucial form of agency in international relations, foreign policy helps to shape the domestic and foreign environments in which it operates, just as it must perpetually adapt to be effective in them.[41]

There is, after all, a serious problem of *multiple responsibilities* now facing decision-makers. They are responsible to, variously: voters, special interests active abroad, allies, expatriates, humanity as a whole, future generations, the like-minded, linguistic cousins, international law and principles of order, the United Nations, peoples requiring emergency assistance, those with historical claims. The list could be extended. No foreign policy can hope to reconcile so many competing claims; equally, each single one is overlooked at leaders' peril. Foreign policy is the channel by which external action and responsibilities have to be addressed, even if we do not use the term. Public policy has somehow to be related to outsiders and if necessary raised to the higher level of international institutions. Foreign policy therefore faces a major challenge, needing to be purposeful but not deluded, democratic but not paralysed, ethical but still grounded in a particular society. If the gauntlet is not picked up it is difficult to see where the initiatives and coordinating capacities which international society increasingly requires are going to come from. International cooperation is hardly, after all, self-executing. What follows in this book is based on the knowledge generated by Foreign Policy Analysis thus far; it attempts to assess what may be feasibly expected of foreign policy, and what may not.

2

The Politics of Foreign Policy

The subject of this book is the politics of foreign policy in the broadest sense – who gets what out of foreign policy actions, and what happens when the values of separate communities collide. The main themes, of agency, the international and responsibility illustrate the dilemmas faced by states and other actors, and their consequences for the international system as a whole. This, however, requires a certain theoretical ground-clearing, in relation to key problems such as the nature of action and actors, the limits to choice, and the varying hopes and political strategies which attach themselves to the vehicle we call 'foreign policy'. Accordingly, this chapter attempts to establish the starting point of the analysis in relation to what kind of action is possible within the structures we observe in international politics. It moves on to analyse the intimate relationship between the state and foreign policy, dealing in passing with the distraction of sovereignty, and then tackles the fundamental difficulty of how far the distinction between the domestic and the foreign is evaporating. The chapter finally moves on to the issues which are political in the more overt sense of whom and what foreign policy serves and is expected to serve. Readers of a practical bent may wish to move directly on to Part I, but this chapter is not intended as a mere scholastic prelude; since no discussion of foreign policy can avoid the inherent conceptual problems, it is best to confront them at the earliest opportunity.

Agency and Structure

One of the most interesting but inaccessible debates in social science during recent years has concerned the relationship between 'agency' and 'structure'. At the simplest level the debate has been about whether agents (those who are capable of action) are shaped by structures (whatever they may be) or vice versa.[1] In one sense the agency–structure debate has been good for foreign policy analysis. It has returned the perennial issues of causation, freedom and determinism to the agenda of International Relations and it has led to a sharper examination of the rather unsophisticated conceptual basis of some foreign policy studies. On the other hand, it has been for the most part a highly abstract debate, focusing on meta-ontology and epistemology.[2] It has also often been presented as the agency–structure 'problem', which by extension should admit of a 'solution'. This is not the approach taken here, where the mathematical analogy is seen as inappropriate to the immense political and historical complexities facing all those who wish to understand foreign policy. Rather it is assumed that causation always involves both structures and agencies, and that – as a number of authors have pointed out, following Anthony Giddens – the two kinds of phenomena help to constitute each other in a perpetual process of interaction.[3] This means, by definition, that it is impossible to come to fixed conclusions about the limits to agents' freedom of choice or their capacity for impact (two different things). We may analyse the parameters of choice, constraint and change but human beings will always have the 'wiggle room' of specific historical circumstances in which to remake at least some of their world.[4]

Structures, broadly speaking, are the sets of factors which make up the multiple environments in which agents operate, and they shape the nature of choices, by setting limits to the possible but also, more profoundly, by determining the nature of the problems which occur there, by shaping our very life-worlds. Structures exist at all levels, from the family to the international system, and it is an error in foreign policy to suppose that 'structure' refers only to the external environment. The political, bureaucratic and social structures which condition foreign policy-making are of vital importance.[5] Structures are as much conceptual as concrete entities because they often represent processes, or patterns of interaction. It is accordingly difficult to ascertain their existence and all too easy to imagine them into existence. Moreover, since structures are consistently influenced by agents, they are always in flux and should not be regarded as fixed entities like an engineering jig, with precise, limited and determining qualities. The nature of a structure will always be contested because even those at the less abstract end of the continuum, such as states, cannot be reduced to the sum of their visible parts, such as institutions.

If one follows this line of thought the principal intellectual problems which arise in relation to structures are first their identification, second their inter-relations (possibly hierarchical) and lastly their relations with agents. *Agents* for their part are the entities capable of decisions and actions in any given context. They may be single individuals or collectives, and they may be characterized by conscious intentions or by patterns of behaviour which at least in part do not result from deliberation – for example, the armed services may display inefficiency over a period of time while having a self-image of precision. The term *actors* is, in my view, preferable to that of 'agents' given the latter's sense in English of subordination to a higher authority (an 'agent of X or Y'). Thus despite the ubiquity of the 'agency–structure debate' in the academic literature, 'actor' will be the preferred term in this book, with 'agents' used to refer to the bureaucratic entities at least nominally under the control of the primary political actors. This also fits with the common usage of 'states and other actors', in both the academic world and that of practical international politics.

Although the focus here is not on epistemology or ontology, the account given above of the agency–structure question needs some brief contextualizing. In general, I follow the arguments made by both Barry Buzan and Walter Carlsnaes in their comments on structure and agency to the effect that a clear distinction must be made between units of analysis and modes of explanation.[6] This the old 'levels of analysis' model did not do, in and of itself.[7] Individuals, states and the international system are units of analysis, to be described in their own terms; yet they do not necessarily explain outcomes. Conversely, it is unlikely that explanations of political phenomena will be found at one level alone. Rather, they should be looked for in sources such as structures, processes and interactions between units/actors. It is then important to bear in mind four fundamental distinctions, between:

- units and actors. Units are useful ways in which we divide the world up conceptually, so as to calibrate space and time. They may include periods such as the 'short twentieth century', or the component parts of a system, such as the international economy. They will often be contestable. Actors, by contrast, are entities capable of the exercise of independent will and decision-making, and are relatively easy to identify. Actors can always be said to be units, but not all units are actors.
- actors and structures, each of which may exist in many forms and with varying capacities for determining the other.

- positivism and constructivism, as epistemological starting-points for understanding foreign policy; the one seeing 'facts' as things that scientific observation can establish, the other stressing that accounts of the world are shaped by preferences – and often power – so that if truth is possible at all it lies only in understanding how different versions of events have come to be produced and how they compete.
- the notion of free will for sentient beings, and the idea that choice is illusory given the power of historical forces.

It may be worth giving a basic statement of the assumptions which the present book makes on these important issues. Even if the brevity will leave some readers dissatisfied it is better to be transparent and to make it clear that the issues have been taken into account.

As suggested already, the 'levels of analysis' approach will no longer do except in the most basic sense of alerting newcomers to the different perspectives that may be obtained by looking at things from the viewpoints of the individual, the state and the international system as a whole. Ultimately it is not clear whether this 'analysis' can go further to deliver an explanation of causation or prescriptions for change. Accordingly it must be supplemented by the distinction between actors and structures, some of which will be simultaneously actors within a wider structure (such as a foreign ministry, which is an important structure to its employees but also with certain actor-like qualities of its own). Foreign policy-making is a complex process of interaction between many actors, differentially embedded in a wide range of different structures. Their interaction is a dynamic process, leading to the constant evolution of both actors and structures.

In terms of how we might know anything about actors and structures, the approach here takes something from positivism, but it is not positivist. Neither, however, is it relativist, since it asserts that something called empirical knowledge is possible, on the basis of professional scholarship and a constantly critical attitude towards sources – certainly on subjects like the intentions of the British and French governments during the Suez crisis of 1956, but even on more diffuse questions like the changing nature of war. It accepts that some of the painstaking work in foreign policy analysis coming out of the behavioural stable, on crises, misperceptions and bureaucratic politics, is of great use, being suggestive and systematic. On the other hand, the belief that political and social behaviour can be reduced to law-like statements, made on the basis of value-free observations of a whole 'class' of phenomena, is taken to be axiomatically mistaken. Human beings respond to any observation made about them and the complexity of their actions goes far beyond that which can be captured by the correlation of variables or a stimulus–response model. The greater the generalization, therefore, the blander it will be.

On the issue of freedom it is from a broadly pluralist position that I seek to examine foreign policy and its dilemmas. Human beings are seen as always having choices, even if in many circumstances the dice are heavily loaded in one direction or another. Individuals are the original source of intentions, and they make a difference. But they never work in a vacuum, and the pattern of their institutional and political environment will have a big influence on how they see the world. Moreover, at the level of the international system they are rarely prominent. Here agency is multiple and various, with states the most important single class of actors, given their preponderant influence over the means of political mobilization. Pluralism exists mainly in the sense that the system is not highly determined; spaces for action open up often and unpredictably. It is then a question of who is willing and able to occupy these spaces and on whose behalf decisions are taken. Although it is usually the most powerful of states who take the initiative, even they find it difficult to shift the contours of the system, as the history of international communism or nuclear non-proliferation shows. The United States' 'war on terrorism' after the terrible attacks of 11 September 2001 shows both that great states will try to change the whole system and that they face an enormous task in so doing.

On epistemological and methodological issues, it will by now be clear that I do not accept the well-known position of Martin Hollis and Steve Smith that there are always 'two stories to tell in International Relations' – that is, *understanding* why actors take the positions they do, and *explaining* their outputs – and that these two accounts cannot be reconciled.[8] If this were true, a great deal of illuminating historical scholarship would never have been possible. Technically, such work is not scientific explanation in the sense of establishing if–then propositions, but the past thirty years have shown that significant versions of the latter rarely turn out to be possible even using scientific method. Good history or traditional political science 'explains' in the sense of highlighting key factors and the nature of their interplay on the basis of analysis and evidence that most critical but reasonable readers find convincing – that is, they survive the test of the intellectual market.[9] Furthermore, 'understanding' is not just a matter of reconstructing the world-view of actors themselves – one of the limitations of early decision-making theory.[10] It also involves placing their perceptions in the contexts of the myriad pressures on decision-making, internal and external, and of historical change.[11]

As with agency and structure, both explaining and understanding are necessary parts of good foreign policy analysis. We need to account for foreign policy behaviour in a number of different ways, and to be able to analyse complexity sufficiently well to make possible normative statements which are grounded in empirical knowledge. Like most phenomena in social science, foreign policy is both general and highly particular to context. It is not sensible to limit our chances of doing justice to these different dimensions by limiting the approaches employed more than we have to. Our ontology should be wide-ranging (foreign policy involves many actors), our epistemology open-ended (there are so many ways of deriving conventional wisdoms in this area) and our methodologies diverse (middle-range theories, weak theories, history, discourse analysis can all contribute).[12] This is what pluralism means when doing foreign policy analysis.

The State, Sovereignty and Foreign Policy

No serious treatment of international politics can avoid taking a view on the state. Yet foreign policy analysis has rarely attempted to theorize the state.[13] This is a triple failing given (i) that it has been state-centric (but *not*, let it be repeated, therefore realist); (ii) that it seeks to bridge International Relations and comparative politics; (iii) that an increasing amount of attention has been paid to the state in recent decades, including in IR. A theory of what the state does, and what it is for, is necessary in order to clarify the various confusions which arise in terminology. Also, more importantly, it helps us to examine how far the domestic and the international roles of the state gel. If they are at odds, what space does this create for other actors, and what limitations does it impose on foreign policy?

There is a link here to the problem of sovereignty, which has a domestic meaning, as in 'the sovereign people', as well as the external conception of 'the sovereign state'. In the by now extensive and stalled debate on the subject, sovereignty and its meaning have become a battleground between those who wish to see the state dethroned from its position as a central factor in international relations and those who defend its primacy.[14] Although those who study foreign policy can hardly help but be more identified with the latter position, there is no need for them to become trapped in a dichotomized argument.

Sovereignty is a central legal concept in the current international system, and an attribute difficult to acquire – and to lose.[15] Equally, states' capacity to exercise the independent choices implied by sovereignty is often in practice curtailed, while their power varies widely and is never absolute. All too often in the political world sovereignty is merely confused with power, which leads many to believe that relative weakness makes sovereignty meaningless, and some others (for example the Soviet Union) to make the opposite error of assuming that sovereignty depends on maximizing power.[16]

Foreign policy exists in the space created by states' existence and by their very lack of omnipotence. Its rationale is to mediate the impact of the external on the domestic and to find ways of projecting a particular set of concerns in a very intractable world. It depends on sovereignty not being extinguished where it already exists, but otherwise is more linked to the existence of a distinguishable set of domestic interests, which vary independently of the given of sovereign statehood. The formal possession of sovereignty makes it highly likely that a state will have a foreign policy. Conversely, where sovereignty is denied or the capacity to exercise it severely impeded, foreign policy becomes particularly difficult – but not impossible. Ultimately foreign policy rests on the *effectiveness* of the state at home and abroad, which is more a matter of political sociology than of law.

In what different ways may the state be described, and how do they bear on foreign policy? There is now a great deal of literature extant and many competing versions of what the state is about.[17] This is not the place for an exhaustive survey of the possibilities, but it is important to note that the interpretations broadly divide into those which are *outside–in*, where the external role determines the state's internal character, and those which are *inside–out*, where the constitutional nature of the state is primordial and has distinctive effects on international relations.[18] Into the first category fall the view that the state was formed through competitive politics in Renaissance Europe, and the growing operations of an international market.[19] It became consolidated in the Westphalian system, which gradually made possible territorial nation–states, through external recognition and the principle of non-intervention in domestic affairs. A refinement would be the imperialist state whose myths and militarism shape the character of its domestic institutions.[20] Into the second category falls the view that the state is essentially the product of a social contract to engage in common cause, as would variations on the theme that the state is perpetually being fought over by competing classes or elites, at times in a condition of revolutionary struggle.[21] Each of these endogenous versions would have its own particular consequences for the conduct of foreign affairs.

No interpretation of the state which fails to bind the domestic and the international aspects together can be very convincing. The history of the emergence of states shows that they developed very slowly in the crucible of both general forces like the Reformation and particular, internal conditions like the transformation of English government carried out by the Tudors or the centralization of France under Louis XIV. Who can say whether the chicken of engagement in war or the egg of domestic change was the primary factor in producing the history of statehood, and the international power which ensued? It is important to conceive of the state in a way which does justice to its *simultaneous* internal and external roles, and this will be attempted below on the basis of an ideal-type from which, naturally, there is a wide range of deviation in practice.

Before this can be done we need to make it clear what the state is *not*. Notwithstanding the constant slippage even in professional usage, the state is to be clearly distinguished from government, from civil society and from the nation. The very existence of international relations encourages an elision of these terms since from an eyrie overlooking the whole system the distinctions are far less sharp than they seem from within the state. But it is vital to recognize that a government is a temporary holder of power and a state is the set of institutions, dispositions and territory which makes it possible for governments to exist – and to change. It is only extinguished very occasionally, usually in conditions of trauma. Equally, civil society exists separately from the state. If the latter becomes overbearing it erodes the liberties of the people; if it identifies society completely with itself it creates totalitarianism. Lastly, even if the term 'nation' is just as elusive as that of 'state' the two things are very distinct. A nation is a group of people that conceives itself to have a common identity, history and destiny. It seeks statehood, but may exist independently of it, just as the state does not need to be coterminous with any particular nation – although when working well it will usually breed a moderate sense of nationhood delineated by its own borders. The 'nation–state' is an historic compromise which like most such does not display pathological symptoms until an excessive symmetry is pursued.[22]

What then is the state, seen in the round? A brief sketch follows of an ideal-type, in the sense that it is seen as containing the core features of a state that exists simultaneously for its people and in the world, in a condition of some equilibrium. It contains normative elements in that the denial of popular sovereignty and aggressive international behaviour are counted as deviant qualities. States are seen as being of diverse types – indeed with the capacity to change types, as through democratization – but nonetheless revolving around certain essential features which provide us with a baseline against which to measure variance. These features are seen as relating in unbreakable interconnection to both the internal and external circumstances of a given society of people. Whether the society preceded international recognition, or was the product of international events, matters less than whether the state as a whole works well for the people who find themselves living within it, but *who have simultaneously to live in a condition of interdependence with other peoples.*

The first feature of a well-functioning state is the set of institutions representing the *res publica*, or the elements of legitimated power which a government runs in trust for the people (in this era of popular sovereignty). These include the machinery of justice, the police and armed forces, public administration and the institutions of political life. Their purpose is to ensure continuity, order and common purpose, and they are supposed not to fall into the hands of any particular class, party or elite. This can never be guaranteed and at worst the state can become a private instrument – a 'prebendal state' – when the unit created by external recognition and territoriality becomes an empty shell to be filled by those possessing *force majeure*.[23] In that event, however, the sharp contrast between the external status of the state and its lack of public content creates in modern conditions not only domestic tensions but also pressure from the outside to bring things back in line. Less dramatically, states will vary in the extensiveness and dominance of their public institutions, especially in relation to economic life and conscription into the armed services. This is a matter of legitimate diversity, and neither third parties' security needs nor the homogenizing force of human rights and democratization provide any justification for intruding on all aspects of the state–society relationship.

It might be argued that the above is a description of the 'constitutional state', while more common historically is the state as an agglomeration of power, pressing down upon the citizenry.[24] The response to this is that the latter is not a true state but the mere instrument of power of a dominant class or dynasty, even if functional in the international relations sense of a state. This is why we do not describe mediaeval kingdoms as 'states', for there was no machinery independent of the royal household being held in trust for society (which itself would have been an anachronistic concept). Certainly the claims and aspirations of most people around the world, politicians and citizens, now extend well beyond Hobbesian visions of mere order – except in the immediate aftermath of war or other crises. The very idea of the (modern) state requires institutions which are robust enough to remain separate from government and to keep the country functioning in the event of an inter-regnum.[25] This has external as well as internal significance because without such institutions outside powers are drawn to intervene, as in Egypt and Ottoman Turkey in the nineteenth century, or Albania very recently.

Constitutionalism, indeed, is the second defining feature of modern statehood. The state, to acquire legitimacy, has to act as a guardian of civil society, ensuring equity of treatment, including '*la carrière ouverte aux talents*', basic rights before the law, the accountability of those in positions of power, and the protection of public funds. The state must, in a Hegelian sense, be the means through which freedom is enlarged as well as protected, the focal point of public discourse on the basic purposes of society and political organization. If it does not do this, but instead becomes the oppressor and controller of the people, presenting itself as the source of their legitimacy rather than vice versa, then it has become by definition a special interest group exploiting the state. Moreover, where the state partially fails to provide the guarantees outlined above, as it has done in Italy, it falls into disrepute and other solutions are sought (in Italy this means either private 'protection' or, more respectably, 'Europe').

In the early twenty-first century the constitutional state does not exist in a vacuum. It is reinforced by external human rights regimes, the UN system and the power of the western democracies – even if, on occasions, it is undermined by their double standards and by the perceived exigencies of national security. It also has to reinforce its own legitimacy by not ignoring the fate of those in other states where liberties are far from guaranteed. How far to go in that obligation is one of the central dilemmas of foreign policy. It is clear, however, that it is not possible to be insouciant about repression elsewhere without the state itself losing something in relation to the claim of upholding basic rights. The project of constitutionalism is now at least in part a universal one, which is not to say that all states have to follow the same model of democracy, let alone that the United States and its allies have reached a satisfactory level of democratic practice. What it does say is that the notion of the state as the enemy of democracy inside and out, as indelibly associated with the values of *machtpolitik*, is not only outdated but fundamentally wrong. Many individual states have been misappropriated, in both their domestic and foreign contexts. By contrast, statehood itself is an aspect of modernity which, in Weberian terms, inherently fosters the idea of the public good. It needs reclaiming for liberalism, even if *on occasions* liberal states will need to follow the dictates of realism in order to ensure their own survival.

The last major definitional attribute of the state is the fact of its recognition by the international system – the key outside–in criterion. This is indispensable to statehood because if recognition is not forthcoming of the right of the state to exist inside its territorial boundaries, the way is opened for other states to contest its position, with invasion, civil war and chaos – or mere resentment and uncooperativeness – the possible consequences. What is more, the consequent absence of diplomatic recognition and membership of international organizations deprives the state of a standing in international law and of an effective personality in international political relations. It is the grossest handicap, which is why the breakaway Yugoslav republics sought recognition in 1991 so keenly. Accordingly recognition is not awarded indiscriminately. Although states vary in their attitudes, thereby often creating conflict, the usual minimum conditions now are internal legitimacy, effective control over a given territory which does not derive from conquest in the recent past, and the capacity to enter into relations with other such entities.[26] Where the 'international community' does confer recognition by admitting a new state to the UN, it is not on a particular government but on the fact of the state's existence on equal terms with others, sharing the same rights and duties in international law.[27] It is also, more than fifty years on from Article 2.7 of the UN Charter, not a *carte blanche* for statehood to develop inside the citadel of sovereignty in whatever way a dominant elite might wish. The growing presumption of humanitarian intervention means that the worst excesses will draw external condemnation and quite probably some form of pressure for change. That this tendency is inconsistently and often inadequately felt is not a reason for discounting its arrival as an important new factor in statehood.

Thus the essential features of modern statehood all involve both internal and external aspects and it is not sensible to privilege one side over the other. The definition given here of the state has certainly been a liberal one, but liberalism has its variants, such as that of the minimalist state dedicated to facilitating free economic enterprise. History helps to explain these varying manifestations, but for an understanding of the relationship between foreign policy and the state we need more. What a theory of the state does is to provide an account of the state's distinctive functions, inside and outside, and of the links which connect them.

It may well be that the state is a transient historical phenomenon – what is not? – but its demise as an institution of world politics cannot but be a slow and complex evolution in which conscious choice and agency will not figure prominently. Ultimately, the multiple decisions of millions over many generations will decide what kind of successor institution we end up with, and public policy will only grope its way slowly towards new dispositions – as in the case of the European Union, where a single European state is still a remote possibility nearly half a century from its launch in that direction.

Bearing the fog of history in mind, there are two possible answers to the question of what functions states perform, one foreign policy-related and one domestic. The combined answer they provide is closely related to the formal definition of statehood given above, but it is not the same; it engages directly with the political and normative question of the values attaching to statehood and the issue of whether scepticism about the usefulness of the state is justified.

The foreign policy answer has three parts, and amounts to the argument that welfare in a global system of (patchy) interdependence requires socio-political units which are both manageable and accessible to their citizens. For: (i) the world is not yet so secure that we can trust in international organization to ensure our physical and political survival; at some level 'we' therefore need to look after ourselves by taking out an insurance policy against damaging exogenous change; (ii) the international system, political and economic, is sufficiently large and complex that without some vehicle in which to travel it is easy to get lost; states provide identity, direction and agency; (iii) without states a given society would have no 'private space', that is, the capacity to regulate social behaviour in a particular way, to manage admission and to cherish particular traditions (if these things are anathema to some, then they must be balanced against the costs of global openness).

The domestic answer is that the state is there to provide the conditions of peace, order and organization required for individuals to flourish. This is not just a matter of a Hobbesian concern over the war of all against all, but how an industrialized or industrializing society can so arrange itself that chaos is averted and the weak do not go straight to the wall. Vital services like energy supply, air traffic control, policing and transport cannot simply be provided by the free market, let alone by a combination of local and global governance. They require an effective *intermediate* level of political organization to regulate, facilitate, lead and underwrite. This we currently call the state and something like it would have to be invented if it did not exist.

If we combine these two answers it can be seen that the argument is really about three things: manageability of scale, protection and democracy. If these values are important we must acknowledge both that they cannot be provided without some balance being struck between domestic and international goals and that the alternatives to the state are themselves shot through with problems. The approach presented in this book is thus one of liberal realism, which acknowledges the contingency and insecurity of world politics while being convinced that existential choice is possible, that human agency continually displays the capacity to make a difference and that the state is not necessarily the defensive, paranoid military fortress that is often described.[28] Liberal realism wishes the democratic state to survive but also to grow and to promote constitutional values internationally, so that inter-state, and also inter-societal relations can be conducted on a basis of secure and cooperative diversity, with the state as an important source of order held in common, not least because of a converging understanding of what statehood entails.[29] If the argument holds, then there are clearly still a number of important functions for foreign policy to perform, and the identity of those acting on behalf of the state becomes a matter of some importance.

Between Home and Abroad[30]

The argument so far has stressed the interconnections between the domestic and the foreign. Foreign policy can never be abstracted from the domestic context out of which it springs. Without domestic society and the state there would be no foreign policy. This is not wholly to dismiss the realist perception that the nature of international politics tends to discipline foreign policy and to reduce its degree of variation – in other words, that to play the game you have to stick to the rules. It is, rather, to argue that foreign policy cannot be reduced to a game like chess, with set rules, a single dominant value, and a unitary, optimizing decision-maker. Robert Putnam has pointed out that foreign policy is at the least a two-level game, but the diverse manifestations of domestic society make interaction much more than a game.[31]

This is not to say that either the domestic or the foreign represents a hard and fast category. Writers like R.B.J. Walker and Cynthia Weber have challenged the very distinction between 'inside' and 'outside' and there can be little doubt that in many countries there is a noticeable grey area between what is regarded as distinctively 'home affairs' and what is international, or mixed up with the domestic environment of another state.[32] Ireland, with its large cultural overlap with the United Kingdom, widespread diaspora and heavy dependence on EU programmes, is a good example. Nonetheless, palpable domestic communities still exist, usually supported (and limited) by the state, while their constraints and advantages are keenly felt by their citizens. This is not a matter of nationalism, although in many places the latter strengthens feelings of distinctiveness. Rather, shared historical experiences, myths, culture in the widest sense, including food, language, architecture, jokes, music, sport and newspapers all help to create the emotion of 'belonging' primarily in one society. This is true for all those except the international elite which dominates writing about international relations, and which understandably tends to project its own experiences onto the mass.[33]

The domestic and the foreign are two ends of a continuum rather than being sharply demarcated.[34] Yet it is still possible to use the idea of domestic society at both practical and theoretical levels. Indeed, it is almost impossible to do without it. The world cannot be explained only in holistic terms, and even writers like Susan Strange who resist the conventional categories are forced to include states and security in their system of interpretation.[35] In terms of policy, international institutions and summits are geared almost wholly to intergovernmental compromises, and the most powerful figures in world business have to acknowledge the difference made by a particular political context – as Rupert Murdoch has done assiduously in China, and the world's airlines have had to do since the attacks on New York and Washington of 11 September 2001.[36]

The idea of the domestic is particularly indispensable when we confront the issues of democracy and accountability.[37] How are popular concerns to be expressed and protected if not through the mechanisms of specific societies and polities? Internationally, the issue of democracy largely relates to the artificial issue of equal rights between states of differing sizes and power, as over voting in the UN. In the European Union, the only serious supranational entity, there is an acknowledged 'democratic deficit' due to the weakness of the directly-elected European Parliament. Even at the national level in established liberal states, democracy is often all too rudimentary (particularly in the area of foreign policy), but at least the structures and presuppositions exist for asserting the rights to representation, scrutiny and due process. This is not the case with such entities as pressure groups, opinion polls and phone-ins, however desirable in themselves, while their transnational manifestations are even less substantial.

A focus on foreign policy is therefore the most feasible way of addressing the question of how democracy works (or not) in the global context. Through foreign policy one can measure how far the needs of a particular society are being protected or advanced in the context of the outside forces which affect them. This is most obviously true in the area of defence, but also in the wider categories of security and welfare.

There may be limits to what governments can do to promote these values, but citizens expect them to be able to do something, given that in most cases there are no alternatives. Companies' obligations are to their shareholders, and international banks' to principles of good finance (if not to certain powerful governments).

Through foreign policy one can also raise questions of morality in international relations.[38] To a certain extent this can be done by reference to individual responsibility and to the functions of the United Nations and its specialized agencies, but mostly it comes down to what should be expected of national governments – not least in the UN, which is almost wholly dependent on foreign policy decisions taken by states. It is just as difficult at the practical as at the philosophical level to decide on the extent of one community's obligations to others, and to the principles of international order. Without reference to foreign policy and its instruments, however, it becomes impossible.

Both the practitioner and the analyst of foreign policy must take notice of the two-way flows which arise from the distinction between the foreign and the domestic: foreign policy has its domestic sources, and domestic policy has its foreign influences.[39] It is important to trace the pattern of forces, to distinguish them and to be aware that there is a great deal of variation, spatial and historical. But the basic distinction cannot be ignored. Although there are some elements of domestication evident in the international system, with challenges to the rule of non-intervention, and many avenues through which public policy is coordinated, no serious observer would argue that this is anything but tentative and patchy. Conversely, although all states have to factor international considerations in their decision-making on issues from education to waste disposal, this is not the same as saying that their internal policies are determined by interdependence or globalization. Their own structures, paths of development and political will represent crucial intervening variables between external trends and policy outcomes.

Thus the domestic and the foreign are distinguishable both in degree and in kind. What is more, every country fits the general model. The greatest powers may be dislocated by faraway events, as the United States found with the Vietnam War, while the smallest states may have their international position shaped by domestic inputs, as when Malta rejected the offer of a place in the queue for EU membership after the result of a General Election.[40] Every society has its particular cluster of traditions, groups, procedures and needs, just as it has a peculiar geopolitical position and place in the World Bank's league tables. All have a practical as well as emotional sense of the distinction between home and abroad.

The interplay between these two sets of characteristics, overlapping but not identical, shapes not just the country's foreign policy but also its general development. It therefore merits serious intellectual attention.

Foreign Policy for Whom?

Siamese twins

States and foreign policies are nearly Siamese twins, but not quite. There are other actors which generate activities resembling foreign policies, and this complicates the conventional domestic/foreign divide further. It is not always clear who is representing whom in international relations. Some unrecognized states effectively conduct independent external strategies, even if the lack of normal representative facilities and/or dependence on what is often an overbearing supporter makes them difficult to implement. Taiwan and Northern Cyprus since 1974 are prominent examples. Hong Kong has maintained extensive external relations in the sphere of political economy since becoming a Special Administrative Region of the People's Republic of China in 1997, including becoming a member of the WTO before China itself. It does not assert a profile on traditional foreign policy issues, but civil society's views on human rights and democratic governance seep out into the world through the still relatively free media. It thus has something like a partial foreign policy, even if it would never dare to use the term. There are also cases of dispossessed peoples without any clear-cut territorial base, such as the Palestinians before 1994 and the African National Congress, representing most black South Africans, between 1961–91.

Most of these cases are relatively straightforward, since they represent actors wanting to be states and trying to emulate state foreign policies. More problematic are the global strategies of transnational companies. Few would pretend that News International, Microsoft and Nestlé do not involve themselves in politics. But whether their political activities can be described as foreign policies is another matter. They do have global strategies, which go well beyond mere marketing or even production. Rupert Murdoch's activities with satellite television make him a major player in the international politics of Asia, just as his TV and newspaper interests have made it necessary for the last three British prime ministers to keep him onside. But businesses do not represent societies and they have little ability to participate directly in the evolution of the general international order through institutions, law and security arrangements. Their interest in international politics is intensely narrow, focused on maintaining a small number of variables within tolerable limits.[41] It is not even clear that businesses have a clear interest in peace over war, or vice versa, either of which might lead them to greater political interventionism. War will bring profits to some, and bankruptcies to others.

On the other hand, in their diversity and egoism, transnational companies are no different from most states. States and businesses both have their internal environments, even if the companies are geographically dispersed. Both have to compute the best ways to survive, and with luck prosper, in an increasingly intractable external environment which only a few actors seem to have the capacity to shape. As Stopford and Strange observe: 'World-class firms almost need a kind of foreign ministry and a cadre of corporate diplomats that combine local expertise and broad experience of dealing with governments in other countries.'[42]

On the wide definition of foreign policy introduced earlier, there is no reason to restrict foreign policy analysis to states, even if there will be more to say about the latter. The same is true of cities, regions, churches and transnational pressure groups, all of which are increasingly taking a direct role in international relations. The problem here is whether they truly qualify as independent actors. The Vatican clearly has a foreign policy – it is a micro-state as well as the possessor of formidable financial and ideological resources. Other churches, by contrast, are either more diffused and divided or dependent on states for assistance in the process of global projection.[43] Yet sects like the Mormons, Hamas or Opus Dei have had the capacity to pursue strategies across state lines, often with political consequences.[44] Regions, especially in federal systems, are also capable of using the spaces created by democracy and free trade to take initiatives on commercial matters, and the activities of Greenpeace, Amnesty International and Oxfam all have political as well as humanitarian dimensions.[45] Thus, even where an actor is not wholly independent of states, lacks a clear constituency and has only a limited range of concerns, it may still be worth viewing in terms of foreign policy. The Al Qaeda terrorist network has demonstrated this with chilling consequences. Sovereignty, and even identifiability, may be lacking, but the entity concerned may still have scope for autonomous decisions which affect others – in short, a degree of actorness. These transnational actors represent a significant form of agency in inter-national relations, and they should not only be discussed at the level of the system, in terms of interdependence or global civil society.[46] Their aims, policy-making processes and impact need serious analysis.

The transnational aspect is, however, marginal by comparison to the traditional meaning of the question as to whom foreign policy is for.

This relates to the relationship between elite and mass which has pre-occupied commentators since the First World War, when the pitiless sacrifice of millions led to the rise of the Union of Democratic Control in Britain and Woodrow Wilson's rejection of the old order from his position as President of the United States – and then leader of his country's delegation at the Paris Peace Conference.[47] The basic issue here, on which so far there has been little progress, can be put in the form of another question: if democracy and popular sovereignty are to be the hallmarks of modern statehood, is it acceptable for foreign and defence policies to be delegated almost wholly to a small elite, on the grounds that dealings with other states require secrecy, continuity, experience and personal contacts? Most people would reply in the negative, but striking the right balance between democracy and efficiency in this context has so far proved an almost impossible task. The 'open diplomacy' aspirations of Wilson soon proved unworkable, and even today few liberal democracies have procedures for accountability in foreign policy which come near those that apply in domestic areas. The United States has the most developed system of legislative participation in foreign affairs, but the executive also found many ways to get around the Congress during the Cold War – being able to appeal to a present danger is a powerful weapon. This has not stopped other states complaining bitterly that the United States has gone too far in the direction of obeisance to the Congress, making its foreign policy irresponsible and inconsistent.

Foreign policy may be 'for the people' in a fundamental sense, but it is largely still made on their behalf by cognoscenti who complain about having their hands tied by public opinion yet evince little evidence of constraint in practice. What is more, these experts increasingly form a transnational class underpinned by personal relations, intermarriage, subsidized conferences and multilingualism – all of which tend to distance them from their own domestic constituencies. This is reminiscent of the aristocratic world of the eighteenth and early nineteenth centuries – the 'freemasonry of diplomacy' – but it extends much further to include business, academe, interest-groups, the media and all forms of international organizations and para-organizations. What is more, the international human rights discourse, steadily growing in importance since 1945, has put the needs of the citizens of other states on the foreign policy agenda of most democracies, thus further confusing the question of whose interests foreign policy is supposed to be serving.[48]

The growth of an international middle class has, on the other hand, stimulated an impatience in many states with the torpor of their legislators, and there are now signs of an awakening interest in international elations, if not at the mass level then at least among younger and more educated citizens. The number of pressure groups is rising and the notion that governments cannot be criticized on foreign policy matters without endangering the national interest has almost disappeared. The interconnections between domestic and foreign affairs are more widely understood, especially within the European Union. There is thus a need to reassess the relationship between foreign policy and democratic politics, from both an analytical and a normative viewpoint. The foreign policy of a state is now a complex balance between: concerns for the overall welfare of society, as interpreted by governments in debate with various particular stakeholders; concerns for general principles of international order and justice; and concerns for selected groups of foreigners designated as friends or as especially deserving of help. How these criteria are related to each other, and by whom, should be a key concern of contemporary foreign policy analysis and a start will be made later in this volume.

Expectations of Foreign Policy

Domestic politics produces pressures for more democracy in foreign policy, but this does not mean that 'efficiency' is any less valued. Indeed, most citizens probably rank efficiency higher in the sense that they want their government to defend their interests effectively abroad, and only want to get involved at times of crisis. Yet efficiency is not a value-neutral term, and since it applies as much to the content of policy as to its process, normative issues arise all the time, not least in terms of pursuing measures which will lead the country into avoidable crises in the first place. This problem means that even among the relatively small elites which follow foreign affairs, there are varying expectations of what a successful foreign policy will entail. Although in the nature of things such competing views cannot be reconciled by mere analysis, the field can be narrowed by a consideration of what might be feasible, given the current international system, as well as broadly desirable. What follows is a brief attempt to identify the principal expectations which most citizens, and indeed policy-makers, will have of their country's foreign policy.

To some extent this is a similar exercise to that which used to be conducted by those who believed in immutable national interests. But there are fundamental differences. In an era in which the intellectual and moral shortcomings of realism have been exposed it is difficult to believe in self-evident objective interests.[49] It is much more convincing to focus on the functions of states as mechanisms for relating the expressed wishes of the domestic constituency, the demands of the external milieu, and (indeed) the basic needs of the state qua state. This allows us to bring in the subjective element arising from domestic politics, decision-makers' own perceptions, and the evolving nature of international politics, where the pursuit of empire is no longer a vital interest and a conception of 'planet earth' has quickly become part of the mental furniture of even cynical politicians.

There are seven main expectations which we tend to have of foreign policy. They apply to states in the first instance, but can, *mutatis mutandis*, be adapted to non-state actors. They naturally vary over time and place, and certainly in their detailed manifestations. Nonetheless, it is not unreasonable to see them in broad terms as being held in common by the inhabitants of all but the most unstable or inward-looking states. They are listed in broad order from the most particular to the most general:

- *Protecting citizens abroad*: foreign policy has both to work towards achieving the general conditions in which expatriates will be secure to pursue life and work abroad, and to help them when they get into trouble. This can range from prison sentences for the possession of drugs, through the exploitation of cheap labour to the taking of hostages by a hostile government. At none of these levels is it sufficient – let alone seen domestically as being sufficient – to leave matters in the hands of the international lawyers.

- *Projecting identity abroad*: this is a problematic function as in many states there would be a strong reaction against the government acting as gatekeeper to the cultural activities of its own citizens. Culture is rarely best served by the dead hand of public bureaucracy. Nonetheless, countries cannot have good mutual relations without such things as state visits and subsidized exchanges, while intelligently run short-wave radio stations or language acquisition programmes can overcome the natural suspicion of propaganda and create significant increments of goodwill, even new business.

- *Homeostasis*, or the maintenance of territorial integrity and social peace against external threats. Challenges which come from inside, such as demands for regional autonomy, are not the proper business of foreign policy until they become connected to outside pressures, when decision-makers have to be careful not to be drawn into confusing 'enemies' within and without.

- *Advancing prosperity*: despite the advance of monetarism and privatization there is still a heavy expectation on governments that they will act internationally to promote the country's economic well-being. The formal side of foreign economic policy includes trade negotiations, trade promotion and monetary diplomacy. Less visible are the benefits deriving from public–private cooperation over export credits, aid programmes, defence spending and cultural diplomacy. In this context in particular it is an important function of foreign policy to ensure that state resources do not fall into the hands of vested interests, and that a clear sense of *public* good prevails.

- *Making decisions on interventions abroad*: this is partly a matter of judgements on what the country's security requires – is deterrence or military action required to protect energy supplies or to stop a distant state from acquiring nuclear weapons? – and partly a matter of the moral calculus required to know whose suffering deserves a particular humanitarian commitment. On both counts the contemporary tendency is towards multilateral action legitimized by international law, but national decisions are always required about entry into a coalition in the first place, or the possibilities of going it alone if one does not materialize.

- *Negotiating a stable international order*: at both political and economic levels foreign policy should not just be looking to protect narrow and often short-term national concerns but should also be working towards a more secure global system, from which threats will emanate less often and less unpredictably. International organizations and regimes are prime sites for work on these 'milieu goals'.[50]

- *Protecting the global commons*: this is not something that would have been expected of foreign policy until the past two decades, but now it is of crucial importance that certain aspects of environmental degradation be halted. Paradoxically, this can only be achieved by both universal agreement and national action. There are no other mechanisms available than states negotiating in the forum of international organization if cooperative agreements are to be reached on the things which go beyond the concern and the power of individual states, such as CFC emissions or over-fishing. International agreements are painfully reached and often represent only lowest common denominator outcomes, but the alternative, of no agreement and leaving matters to the private decisions of responsible citizens and businesses, is hardly more promising.

One could add more detail on the expectations that are held of foreign policy, whether by decision-makers or citizenry. It should be borne in mind that it is common to have exaggerated political expectations of what can be done with foreign policy (witness the demands for 'solutions' in Bosnia and for 'victories' against terrorism), just as there is an academic trend towards expecting too little. Foreign policy is the way in which most political action in international relations occurs, albeit often through coordinated strategies, and, with all its problems, people still look to it for both protection and change.

All those involved in the processes of foreign policy and international politics, including the relatively detached analyst, have expectations of foreign policy. To the extent that they relate mostly to issues of content and 'efficiency' they should be (but often are not) kept in harness with the requirements of democratic process. Equally if they are allowed to get too much out of sync with the levels of available capabilities, fatal misunderstandings may arise as to what a state is able or willing to do. Failing to deliver on implicit promises, or conversely (as with the People's Republic of China) having immense resources which outsiders do not expect you to use, are recipes for misunderstandings which can lead to conflict both inside a state and with others. In practice it is difficult to live up to this injunction, and it is part of the task of the foreign policy analyst to trace diverging patterns of expectations and to measure any capability-expectations gaps which may arise.[51] This cannot be a matter of scientific exactitude, but it can be done comparatively and with a theoretically-derived sensitivity to the interaction of domestic and international political forces. If articulated, expectations will also lead to debate over normative preferences, since by their nature they join practical outcomes to underlying principles.

The Diversity of States

In this chapter we have looked at the problems which lie just beneath the surface in any discussion of the politics of foreign policy – the nature of action and constraint; the role of the state; the demarcation of the domestic and the foreign; the nature of the constituencies of foreign policy; and the problem of purpose and expectations. All this has involved a good deal of generalization. Just as in the book as a whole, however, the issue is less that of the fact of generalization than of its extent. The aim is to establish the parameters within which foreign policy-making takes place, rather than to assert broad truths which would quite properly be contested by others and subjected to qualification on the basis of context. The aim is to reveal the dialectical relationships between shared and distinctive experiences, between the common dilemma and the specific response.

Each category that we use in social science is a generalization, whether it be large, as with types of international system, or relatively small, as with the impact of physical illness on leaders' performance. Each will be subject to scrutiny and debate, and it is through that very process that we are getting as near to the 'truth' as we are ever likely to. In the study of foreign policy the central category is that of actors, and we have already suggested that this includes various kinds of non-state actors. Yet states represent the main source of foreign policies, and it is important to acknowledge at the outset that they too include a range of different types. In saying this we are referring to both internal and external characteristics, welded together in a particular constellation – of position, size, borders and physical patrimony on the other hand, and political system, culture and level of development on the other. All of these dimensions may be used to generate statements about differentiated behaviour. Separate literatures exist, for example, on the foreign policies of small states, developing countries and middle range powers.[52] The 'democratic peace' debate essentially concerns the impact of political systems on foreign policy, and there has been much speculation about the external performance of 'strong' and 'weak', corporatist or decentralized states.[53] The latest round of theory concerns 'post-modern states' and their supposed commitment to multi-level systems of international governance.[54]

These ways of breaking down the broad category of 'state foreign policies' are useful and suggestive, even if they are all also inherently contestable. They can become obstacles to understanding, however, if used as means of generating mere correlations between outputs and national attributes, as in the old behaviouralist interest in whether 'closed' regimes produced inflexible or unpredictable policies. Such questions are only the beginning. If, as with the democratic peace debate, they lead us to probe into the nature of the subtle interconnections between domestic structures and foreign policy positions, all well and good. But they are unlikely to be able to do that without an understanding of decision-making, choice, and internal politics on the one hand, and the dynamics of the international system on the other. We now turn to the first of these two fields of analysis, with a view to observing foreign policy in action.

Part I
Agency

[handwritten annotations: Agency — individual taking decisions/implementing them on behalf of (state)]

3

Actors: the Responsible Decision-makers

[handwritten: Decision-making → acting/ agency.]

Decision-making must be the starting-point if we wish to understand the dilemmas of acting in the international system. Agency entails individual human beings taking decisions and implementing them on behalf of entities which possess varying degrees of coherence, organization and power – of which the most effective are generally states. Any analysis of this activity needs to focus in turn on the political dimension, where named individuals have formal responsibility for foreign policy, on the associated bureaucracies, which provide so much of the continuity and expertise which make action meaningful, and on the problem of rationality, or the capacity to pursue objectives in a logical, intentional manner in what is a particularly inchoate environment. Finally, foreign policy actions cannot be understood without an appreciation of their implementation phase, which is at least as important as that of decision-making, given that outcomes are so often markedly different from original intentions. This first section of the book tackles these four aspects of agency in sequence, beginning with the most visible, political level of activity. *[handwritten: POLITICAL LEVEL]*

When the level of discussion is that of the international system, states or other entities can perfectly well be treated as unified actors. Although short-hand, it still makes sense to say that 'Iraq invaded Kuwait', or 'Japan wishes to become a permanent member of the UN Security Council'. That is, after the processes of decision-making appropriate to the countries concerned, the state took up an external position which was acknowledged as a move in international relations by other states, which then reacted in their turn. Tracing these various moves gives us many of the events of international politics and we can attempt to analyse the patterns they produce.

1) international position
2) domestic context
3) nature of decision-making process

Realists generally believe that the information thus generated can explain a good deal of international relations, including the behaviour of individual states. That is not the position of foreign policy analysis, which is premised on the belief that we can only fully understand what states do by looking at two interactions: between their international position and their domestic context; and between the problem being faced and the nature of the decision-making process employed to handle it. Further, we must now accept that there are other international actors than states, including some based in particular societies but in competition with their own government, and that the border-zone between the external and the internal, often termed 'intermestic', is now both wide and fuzzy.[1] Nissan's support for the single European currency project, or Greenpeace's opposition to nuclear testing, are just as much international actions as those of Iraq and Japan cited above.

inter-mestic.

It soon becomes indispensable, however, when trying to understand an international event or a particular actor's behaviour, to break down the action into its various levels and components. Was Iraq's decision to invade Iran really Saddam Hussein's alone? If it was, did he nonetheless have the broad support of his populace? What was the thinking behind the calculations that must have gone on inside the Iraqi military establishment? Similarly, with the less dramatic case of Japan, how far was the change in policy on the Security Council the product of painful consensus-building, and how far the result of leadership? What were the positions held in the various ministries which might be differentially affected by an increase in the country's responsibilities for international security? These are questions which need regional specialists to give answers, but their effective formulation depends on the body of theory and analysis which has been built up in the comparative study of foreign policy.

Those who are formally responsible for taking decisions in foreign policy, and who therefore carry the can at home and abroad, are politicians of various descriptions. Their precise titles and locations in the political structure will vary a great deal according to the type of state or other international actors they represent. The heads of multinational corporations, or financiers such as George Soros, may resemble more the strategic players of game theory, working to a limited number of concerns, than true politicians. But they share the high profile and vulnerability when things go badly wrong, in contrast to the much larger number of bureaucrats behind the scenes. The delineation of the roles of responsible decision-makers will involve a discussion of the various institutions which tend to be involved, such as executive councils, inner cabinets and the providers of intelligence. The aim is ultimately to

responsibility .

uncover the practical meaning of 'responsibility' for those conducting foreign policy at the highest level.

Who Governs, in Foreign Policy?   DAHL – "who governs"

If the application of Robert Dahl's famous question to foreign policy is one of the main purposes of this book as a whole, a short answer can still be given at this stage. In most states the formal office-holders dealing with foreign policy questions are limited in number, although the growing scope of foreign and intermestic policies is bringing more people into play by the year.

The nominal chief of foreign policy operations in most states is the foreign minister, whatever his or her precise title (for example, 'Secretary of State' in Washington, DC). Foreign ministers are still of considerable importance by virtue of specializing in external policy but they struggle to keep control of their vast portfolio, increasingly invaded as it is by colleagues running other ministries, and they are always likely to be trumped by a head of government who decides to take a direct interest in foreign affairs. Their relationship and activities are discussed in the next section; for the moment it is enough to stress that heads of government, whether they intend to or not, are invariably drawn into foreign affairs, and a large proportion of their time is spent upon it. Conversely, outsiders rarely assume that a foreign minister has full powers and often prefer to open up direct channels to the head of government. A further potential confusion is opened up by the fact that some heads of government are also heads of state (as in France, the United States and South Africa), and therefore have ceremonial as well as executive functions which place them on a higher level of protocol, with more weight but less accessibility than a simple head of government.[2] In most states the functions are separated between two individuals. The separate head of state, whether dynastic monarch or elected personality, has some function in foreign relations, but is much less of a figure than the chief executive. Most informed outsiders, for example, would know that in 2001 Silvio Berlusconi was the Prime Minister of Italy. Only a small proportion would also identify Carlo Azeglio Ciampi as the Italian President. Nonetheless, a figure such as Ciampi can have real influence in improving relations with other countries, and with symbolizing the state's outlook in a way that is above factional politics. After Berlusconi's gaffe in talking about a clash of civilizations after the attack on the World Trade Center, there were calls for the President to

Powell
v.
Bush,
Rumsfeld
Cheyne

speak for the whole country on the matter. Richard von Weizsäcker was very successful in this role for the Federal Republic of Germany between 1984–94, embodying its democratic and pacific values and making it clear that his compatriots accepted responsibility for their past.[3]

The other members of the political foreign policy elite vary more widely from country to country. Where there is some form of cabinet government the foreign minister will have to keep all colleagues informed on the main lines of policy and get their active support on an issue of high significance. Some will be continually involved in aspects of external relations by virtue of their own responsibilities (such as agriculture ministers inside the EU) and their actions will need coordinating, both with each other and with the foreign ministry. In general more and more departmental ministers are discovering an external dimension to their job, but it would be wrong to suggest that many of them make it their priority or indeed that they have an international conception of public policy. This is still a matter of great variability. The key colleagues for a foreign minister will normally be the ministers of defence, economics and trade, in that order.

A few other key individuals should be included in any description of the top office-holders in the area of foreign policy. The chief of the foreign intelligence service could be a visible political figure but equally he could be a bureaucrat operating in the shadows. Either way he (exceptionally she) will be answerable to the head of government and/or the foreign minister, and will be a central figure in any high-level discussions on policy. Similarly the chairman of the chiefs of staff, on one definition strictly a bureaucrat, is likely to have permanent and direct access to the highest circles of foreign policy-making, particularly where armed conflict is a possible outcome. In a completely different vein, the chair of the parliamentary foreign affairs committee, where one exists, may sometimes be drawn into top-level consultations where the need for wider political consensus is particularly strong. Such a figure can certainly be used as a mouthpiece, with a useful ambiguity as to authenticity built in. Where there is actually a formal division of power on foreign policy as in the United States the key chairs and senators become almost parallel foreign policy-makers to the President, and have to be courted assiduously by the White House so as to avoid embarrassing divisions in relations with other states.

In the case of transnational enterprises the responsibility for international strategy is less clear. Normally the chief executive of a multinational company will be party to any decisions with political implications – that is, which involve dealing with governments. There may also be a director or vice president with special responsibility for an international division, only loosely responsible to shareholders.[4] Globalization has involved much integration of transnational production and communication networks, although 'the emergence of the truly "placeless" global corporations is still a long way off'.[5] For an international pressure group or political party the situation is different. The former run on small budgets and cannot afford to have many executive officers flying the world on diplomatic business, even if the need for negotiations with governments is more pressing than it is for companies. What is more, they tend to prize the collective nature of their decision-making. Nonetheless, the two or three individuals at the top of organizations like Amnesty International become very well-known and engage in much para-diplomacy.[6] Political entities are usually more directly imitative of state structures, because they wish ultimately to acquire them. Thus Oliver Tambo was the foreign secretary in exile of the African National Congress (ANC) for all the time that its president, Nelson Mandela, was in prison, and he ran an extremely effective international policy – albeit reliant on the political and logistical support of sympathetic governments.[7] Similarly the Palestine Liberation Organization (PLO) ran a foreign policy in all but name for many years under the leadership of Yasser Arafat. The latter has not become noticeably better known (or more powerful) since he has become a legitimate head of government in a (semi-) sovereign state. These revolutionary movements did not survive, however, by relying on one man for their strategy. They usually rested on a tight-knit cell of leaders operating in a disciplined but collective way. Otherwise arrests and deaths would have decimated the movement. Osama bin Laden's Al Qaeda network has skilfully exploited its leader's wealth and charisma while remaining diffuse and horizontal in structure.

The issue of who holds formal office is not the trivial question that some behaviouralist writers, critical of the aridity of the public administration approach, once thought. Although it is crucial to distinguish between formal and real power, and never to assume that decisions are made as the official flow charts would have it, those who occupy the highest positions in a state have the opportunity to dispose of a great deal of influence. In foreign policy they have at their disposal the resources of the state, and – because external policy requires relatively little legislation – a fairly unstructured decisional environment to exploit. They can also, even today, often work away from the public eye. This provides a considerable opportunity for the relatively small group of men and women who are the formal, political decision-makers to

exert leadership in foreign policy and to personify the state in their
actions. At this level individuals have considerable scope to influence
events. How they do so depends, as we shall see, on a mix of factors:
the personal and political qualities of the personalities involved, the
nature of the issue being decided, and the political structures of the state
in question.   *individuals*

The Foreign Policy Executive

In most political systems any given area of policy will be conducted at
the highest level by a combination of the head of government, free of
any particular portfolio, and the departmental minister, the specialist.
This is particularly the case with foreign policy, where the expectations
of head of government involvement, from inside and outside, are high
and where it is difficult for others to develop an equivalent level of
expertise. On the other hand, some of what goes to make up foreign
policy in a developed state is handled by economic ministers who themselves participate directly in international meetings on finance or trade
and therefore possess a knowledge which the foreign ministry general-
ist will struggle to match. Insofar as foreign policy, therefore, seeks to
integrate the various strands of external relations, it will be conducted
by what can be termed the 'foreign policy executive', consisting in the
first instance of the head of government and the foreign minister, but
often widened according to circumstances to include defence, finance,
economics and trade ministers. There may often also be other ministers
without particular portfolios, close to the head of government, whose
job is to help on matters of high politics (in the sense of something conceived of as involving the government's central values and objectives).[8]

The reason why foreign policy, even on a wide definition, is particularly susceptible to being made by an inner executive, is twofold: on the
one hand most politicians spend much time looking over their shoulders
to their domestic base, and do not wish to 'waste' time on cultivating foreign contacts from which there might be little return. On the other hand,
the international environment still presents a long and steep learning-
curve for any politician wishing to feel at home in it. Consequently,
when that curve has been surmounted, a minister is usually on the cir-
cuit for life, since their hard-won expertise is valued if not at home then
in the various IGOs and INGOs where openings can be found – witness
the careers of David Owen, Javier Solana and Mikhail Gorbachev.[9]
Moreover, in foreign policy the number of unforeseen issues which

arises is disproportionately high, giving the advantage in policy-making to those who hold the power of initiative and response. Foreign policy problems are also often unstructured in advance, in the sense that there is no obvious framework or timetable for their consideration in the way that a domestic issue, often based on a manifesto commitment, expert report or parliamentary legislation, tends to be. Once again this means that responsibility falls onto the shoulders of the small number of politicians with the special knowledge and flexibility to respond.

There is a degree of overlap between the kinds of issues I have described and the nature of crisis. But the argument is not that foreign policy is mostly conducted in conditions of crisis, or that crises tend to be run by a few individuals at the top. Foreign policy is almost as much a matter of routine business as is domestic policy, and crisis is comparatively rare.[10] Furthermore, even crisis does not automatically produce a highly personalized decision-making system – examples can easily be found of deliberate attempts to build consensus and to spread responsibility around a wider group than the foreign policy executive, even if purely operational matters have a restricted circulation list. In fact, crises sometimes heighten the desire not to risk going too far out on a limb from the domestic political base, as can be seen with John Kennedy's careful consultations during the Cuban Missile Crisis of 1962 and the Soviet vacillation over the Czech problem in the summer of 1968.[11] The point is, rather, that even non-crisis foreign policy issues are often only loosely structured and represent something of a blank canvas on which it is difficult for a committee to work collectively in sketching the way forward. Thus the foreign policy executive tends to take the initiative, to outline proposals and to invite responses from colleagues which will inevitably deal more with matters of detail than with fundamental direction. An autocratic political system exacerbates this tendency, but even in democracies the political structure is usually canted towards making foreign policy a special area, with maximum freedom for the key elite. In France, for example, foreign policy very much gravitates towards the president and the Elysée Palace, and the foreign minister may be forced to work more with the president than with his own prime minister.

On a minority of occasions a foreign policy issue will turn out to be highly structured, with a clear issue, documents on the table and a reasonably long time period for consideration. In those circumstances the foreign policy executive will either choose, or be forced, to allow wider participation from Cabinet colleagues, or whatever the relevant political group might be. Examples of the kind of issue in question are treaty negotiations, such as the Anglo–Soviet negotiations over an alliance in the spring of 1939, when prime minister Neville Chamberlain was forced to make concession after concession to Cabinet colleagues more eager than he was to see an agreement. This could happen because concrete proposals were being taken line by line by a Cabinet committee, and the full Cabinet was able to monitor progress with some precision. It was also perceived by most ministers to be an issue of the highest importance.[12]

A similar issue would be the application of any state to join the EU. This is not something that can be rushed through by sleight of hand. Poland, Hungary and the Czech Republic, the front-runners, have had a huge range of legislative issues to consider in detail, and the question of accession penetrates deep into domestic society. No small foreign policy executive could manage all this alone, or would be allowed to. Conversely, from the EU side the creation of policy on enlargement was a classic case of a fluid, general and creative process in which leaders holding the initiative set the parameters for everyone else and pushed the policy on, while leaving the ramifications and details for later.[13] It is also true that even when the issues are clear from the start, some detailed negotiations, like those in the framework of the General Agreement on Tariffs and Trade (GATT) and the World Trade Organization (WTO) are usually so specialized and long-drawn-out as to induce terminal boredom in all those trying to follow from the margins. There is a powerful tendency to leave things in the hands of the two or three ministers who have to deal with them. This can be resisted but it does represent the default setting.

This means that an individual personality, particularly in the two positions of head of government and foreign minister, can have a significant influence on policy. The psychological dimension of such influence is considered in Chapter 5, but here the need is to show how and to what extent this impact takes place.

The foreign policy executive always gathers around it an inner coterie of trusted colleagues, security advisers and *éminences grises*, but without strong personalities at the helm little may happen. Prior knowledge of foreign affairs is not even necessary. Motivated leaders learn on the job, as with Mrs Thatcher as Prime Minister of Britain. For most of her first term of office (1979–83) she was dependent on the expertise of her Foreign Secretary, Lord Carrington. After his departure over the Falklands invasion the Prime Minister quickly became one of the most active and notable figures in world diplomacy. Thatcher undoubtedly made her mark on Britain's foreign policy, most obviously in relations with the EC, but less predictably in reviving policy towards eastern Europe and in creating a special relationship with Mikhail Gorbachev. Leaders of her type often hanker after a place in history, and it is obvious that this is more likely to be achieved by influence at the world level than by actions inside one country.

For better or for worse, therefore, many heads of government end up by having a distinct impact on their country's foreign relations. This is true for both big and small states, as a list which includes Chou En lai, Ronald Reagan, Nikita Khrushchev, Menachem Begin, Lee Kuan Yew and Georges Papandreou easily demonstrates. It follows that changes in government can have a disruptive effect on foreign policy depending on whether a major personality is leaving or entering office – and in the latter case it is rarely evident in advance. When François Mitterrand became President of France in May 1981 he arrived as a shop-soiled character who had been twice defeated – by de Gaulle and Giscard d'Estaing – and seemed desperate for power at any cost. By the time he left office in 1995 he and Helmut Kohl were the acknowledged architects of the new European Union. Likewise Harry Truman in 1945 seemed a provincial figure in comparison to his predecessor Franklin D. Roosevelt. Yet by 1949 Truman was the dominant influence over the West's role in the emerging Cold War.

The ability to lead is dependent on circumstances being ripe.[14] Conversely, some apparently influential figures are more significant for their ability to embody either the wishes of a particular political movement or the *zeitgeist* than for a sharp personal contribution. Ronald Reagan is the best contemporary example. His grasp of detail was notoriously weak, but he brilliantly articulated 'a cultural narrative of American myths' in the interests of restoring confidence and assertiveness to the foreign policy of the United States, particularly in relation to dealings with the Soviet Union.[15] As the leader of Russia, Boris Yeltsin was less slick than Reagan, but came to be regarded (especially abroad) as being of vital importance, less for what he did than for the way he symbolized reform and forestalled the arrival in office of potentially more dangerous individuals. Such types can come to personify their country's international position, which is a potentially dangerous development given the narcissism this then encourages.

If heads of government have a natural tendency to get drawn into foreign policy and to become their own foreign minister, there is no iron law that they will end up in a dominant position. This is not only because the summits at which leaders are most visible are relatively infrequent or because not all possess the personal capacity for statesmanship.[16] Just as important is the fact that some political cultures are more resistant to the cult of personality than others (the Scandinavian states have generally produced neither dramatic foreign policies nor charismatic leaders), and that many governments simply do not last long enough to provide the time an individual leader needs to make a major impact. Even if there is some continuity, and the will to be assertive, over-work, illness or political distractions can prove serious impediments. Georges Pompidou struggled as French President with the illness that was to kill him in 1974. The Soviet Union had sick or otherwise incapacitated leaders for perhaps eighteen of its sixty-seven years of history before Gorbachev.[17] The arrival of Yeltsin in 1991 simply meant nine years more of the same. In terms of mental strain, Richard Nixon, generally thought of as a foreign affairs expert and highly innovative in diplomacy, was reduced to virtual hysteria by the Watergate crisis. On one night at its height, he made 51 phone calls between 9 pm and 4 am. His image, and his position, thus soon became irretrievable. As for foreign ministers, they suffer notoriously from an excess of work and travel. In 1991 American Secretary of State James Baker travelled 235 000 miles in visiting 35 countries. Over 30 years before, the British Cabinet had commissioned a report on the subject from former Prime Minister Lord Attlee, who concluded that the Foreign Secretary and the Chancellor of the Exchequer were over-burdened in comparison to all other ministers, including the premier.[18]

The Nixon–Kissinger period demonstrated the vital importance of the relationship between chief executive and foreign minister. Kissinger had been National Security Adviser in the first Nixon administration from 1969–73, but this had undercut the State Department and he was more than willing to take on the position of Secretary of State himself the second time round. The trust which he and Nixon shared was of vital importance in allowing these two assertive foreign affairs specialists to work together, and permitted Kissinger to run US foreign policy more or less effectively during Nixon's final crisis. The famous move towards China, from 1969–71, was in the first instance Nixon's doing, but it only went forward so successfully because Kissinger respected the limits of his own position. While his diplomatic skills were indispensable he did not engage in the kind of competitive leaking that often damages US diplomacy.

There are, broadly speaking, three possible models of the relationship between head of government and foreign minister, each with its strengths and weaknesses depending on how the personalities involved handle the situation and how they interact with events. Table 3.1 sets out the possibilities.

▸ how Condi went from NSC/A to sec/state/dept.

Table 3.1 **Head of government–foreign minister relations: three models**

1 **Equality:** trust, ability and matching reputations can create a strong team and continuity. The weakness is the danger of becoming detached from other colleagues and of appearing too dominant. Examples of effective partnerships: Truman and Marshall (US, 1947–9); Truman and Acheson (US, 1949–53); Nixon and Kissinger (US, 1973–4); Geisel and Azereido da Silveira (Brazil, 1974–9); Bush and Baker (US, 1989–93); Gorbachev and Shevardnadze (USSR, 1985–90); Andreotti and De Michelis (Italy, 1989–92). Alternatively equal strength can lead to antagonism, as with Churchill and Eden (see below), Mitterrand and Cheysson in France (1981–3) or Kohl and Genscher (FRG, 1982–92), where their different political parties exacerbated personal tensions, and blindness, as with Galtieri and Costa Mendez (Argentina, 1981–2).

2 **Subordinate foreign minister:** where a politically or personally weak individual is appointed, often deliberately, it gives the head of government a free hand and turns the minister into a functionary. The weakness is the danger of an excessive concentration of power and an increasing arrogance of judgement. Examples: Eden and Selwyn Lloyd (UK, 1955–6); Khrushchev and Gromyko (USSR, 1957–64); Saddam Hussein and Tariq Aziz (Iraq, 1979–); Nehru (India, 1947–64) who held the position of foreign minister himself.[19]

3 **Established foreign minister:** this can work surprisingly well where there is a clear division of labour and excellent communications. It works badly where there is less a lack of interest on the part of the head of government than a lack of competence, and/or where political rivalry develops between the two figures. Examples of the former: Attlee and Bevin (UK, 1945–51); Reagan and Schultz (US, 1981–5). Of the latter: Eisenhower and Dulles (US, 1953–8); Chernenko and Gromyko (USSR, 1984–5); Kohl and Genscher (FRG, in the early part of Kohl's Chancellorship, when his main concerns were domestic); Clinton and Warren Christopher (US, 1993–7).

There seems to be surprisingly little self-consciousness about this crucial relationship. Pairings arise more out of the need for political balance, or from the whim of the head of government (who possesses the crucial power to hire and fire) than from any attempt to meet the demands of the situation. In the first Blair administration in Britain for example, Robin Cook rather unwillingly took on the post of Foreign Secretary as the only one available at a suitable level of seniority. As a result he and the Prime Minister did not make up so happy a team as that between Blair and Gordon Brown (Chancellor of the Exchequer) on economic affairs, where the bases of agreement and a division of labour had clearly been established in advance.[20] Two strong personalities inside the foreign policy executive can cause serious problems. Anthony Eden regarded himself as more expert than the ageing Winston Churchill by the time the latter formed his second administration in 1951, and his reluctance to accept interference with his duties as Foreign Secretary caused personal tensions and errors of policy.[21] Where personal differences reinforce political divisions, as within a coalition government, the clashes can be savage and burst into the public realm. This was the case with the relationship between Prime Minister Felipe Gonzalez of Spain and his Foreign Minister Fernando Morán (who eventually resigned). On one occasion Morán was so upset by a pro-NATO speech made by Gonzalez in Germany that he left the official entourage and returned home.[22] In September 2001, during the crisis after the World Trade Center attack, Israel's Prime Minister Ariel Sharon vetoed the meeting Foreign Minister Shimon Peres had arranged with Yasser Arafat, pushing their relationship near to breaking-point.[23]

Foreign ministers are vulnerable to removal in the early phases of their tenure, in particular being made scapegoats for failure, but the longer they survive the more vital their experience and contacts become. Maxim Litvinov was sacrificed readily by Stalin to his change of policy towards Germany in 1939; Alexander Haig paid the price in 1983 for pressing too hard and too quickly to run foreign policy by himself. Antonio Samaras of Greece was dismissed by Prime Minister Mitsotakis of Greece for being excessively nationalist over the 'Macedonian' problem, and responded by setting up his own political party to prolong the dispute.[24]

On the other side of the coin Molotov survived for ten years (and returned for three more after Stalin's death), Gromyko for 28, and Hans-Dietrich Genscher for 17, becoming steadily more indispensable. Sheikh Yamani, as the oil minister of King Fahd of Saudi Arabia, performed much the same vital function of continuity for nearly two decades. The position of these individuals was strengthened by the fact that they had become important not just to their own state but to the network of international relations as a whole. So long as they are not perceived at home as having 'gone native' (as Sir Geoffrey Howe was by Mrs Thatcher and her circle) then the way they have come to embody international society and diplomacy makes them difficult to sack. If they resign on a point of principle, as Anthony Eden did from Chamberlain's government in 1938, Cyrus Vance did over President Carter's approval of the hostage rescue mission in his absence in 1980, and as Ismail Fahmi did in protest against Egyptian President Sadat's personal decision to go to Jerusalem in 1977, the consequences can ultimately be very damaging.[25] Even Howe had his revenge; Mrs Thatcher was brought down by an undeclared and subtle coalition of opponents from her own Cabinet and other European leaders, all of whom saw Howe's humiliation as the last straw.[26]

Howe ?

Cabinets, Security Councils and Politburos

Although it is sometimes easy to get the impression that the foreign policy executive monopolizes key decisions – an impression the individuals themselves often do little to discourage – the government as a whole rarely becomes completely detached from foreign affairs. In times of war and crisis the issues cannot be avoided; in times of peace the external dimension of economic policy broadens ministers' perspective.

Most leaders use what is conventionally called a 'cabinet', even if it sometimes bears little resemblance to the British original. The United States pioneered the idea of a National Security Council on foreign and defence matters in 1947 and by 1950, boosted by the Korean War, this had become a more significant body in its area than the routine Cabinet.[27] In the states of the Soviet bloc the key hierarchy was the Communist Party, not the formal government, and the top decision-making unit the Party's Politburo, not the state's Council of Ministers. In other types of states other designations have been used – in Colonel Gaddafi's Libya it is the Revolutionary Command Council, in Taliban Afghanistan it was the Interim Council of Ministers. The fact remains that all but the most tyrannical leaders need some forum in which to bring together senior colleagues, so as to share ideas and coordinate strategy.[28] These can be generically referred to as cabinets.

On various occasions leaders will convene ad hoc inner cabinets to deal with particularly difficult problems, especially in war-time. Prime Minister Blair, notably dismissive of cabinet government, was persuaded of the value of a war cabinet four weeks after the attacks on New York and Washington in 2001. It can happen in more routine times that an informal inner cabinet congeals around the foreign policy executive, dealing with what are perceived of as the highest matters of state. This can be related to what R.A.W. Rhodes has called the 'core executive' in a state – the 'final arbiters of conflict between different parts of the government machine' – key political figures and their advisers.[29] But such arrangements are rarely fixed; formal arrangements always create problems as to who is in and who excluded from any given special committee. It is much better for the leadership, although not for cabinet accountability, to encourage a certain amount of uncertainty as to the extent of informal consultations in those private meetings which in any political system have the capacity to decide the outcome in the larger forum.[30]

To some extent the membership of such groupings on foreign policy questions is self-selecting. There is usually only a small number of senior politicians who are familiar with foreign leaders and can be trusted with intelligence information. This self-perpetuating process was particularly evident in Italy between 1960–92, when the same names appeared and reappeared as either prime minister or foreign minister. In the 33 governments formed during that period, Aldo Moro was prime minister five times and foreign minister nine. Mariano Rumor was prime minister five and foreign secretary three; Giulio Andreotti was prime minister seven times and foreign minister on five occasions.[31] In Britain the circulation of the elite has been more vigorous but a restricted access on matters of state is formalized in the title of Privy Councillor, which is conferred for life on current and former ministers of the Crown and other 'distinguished subjects' including the leader of the Opposition. Councillors have to swear an oath of secrecy, which allows consultation on a highly confidential basis in 'the national interest'.[32] Michael Foot, Leader of the Opposition in 1982, famously refused confidential information on these terms so that he would remain free to criticize the government over the Falklands War.[33] In France, because of the preeminence of the Elysée Palace in the Fifth Republic, it is even easier to draw certain key figures into decision-making informally. By the same token systematic coordination on important matters becomes very hit-and-miss, with the prime minister and some of his colleagues often out of the loop. It is for this reason that discussions began in the early 1990s on whether France should follow the US lead and set up a formal National Security Council where all the major security and intelligence players would sit.[34]

Full cabinets remain in the background on routine foreign policy matters. They can easily become pro forma institutions, with the real work being left to a small number of relatively expert politicians, usually in a standing sub-committee. This is more due to the weight of documentation to be digested in a short time than to manipulation on the part of the foreign policy executive; most ministers are more concerned to make sure they do not drop the ball in their own area than to trespass on those of others. Moreover, given that trade and monetary questions are even more arcane than security problems, it is an illusion to suppose that the changing nature of diplomacy has broadened the base of cabinet discussions on international questions. Instead, it has simply created a new problem of coordination, between different kinds of externally-oriented responsibilities – for defence, finance, trade and development. Foreign ministers, and heads of government, naturally want to take on this role of coordination, but the atomization of the process is difficult to resist.

Despite the weight of specialization the full cabinet (or politiburo, or security council) can never be taken for granted. It can come to life unexpectedly, and if united can even threaten the political survival of the head of government. This was the case in Britain before the fact, when a rumbling cabinet rebellion may have headed off Chamberlain and Halifax from further appeasement after Hitler's invasion of Poland on 1 September 1939, and after the fact over the Suez crisis of 1956, when the way in which Prime Minister Anthony Eden and Foreign Secretary Selwyn Lloyd had committed the government to a disastrous invasion of Egypt without consultation, led to a quiet revolt that ousted both within six months.[35] The fact that this can happen, admittedly most often during crises, makes the foreign policy executive more cautious about overlooking colleagues than they might otherwise be. In the case of P.W. Botha, last President of apartheid South Africa, the reverse was true. The failure of Foreign Minister Pik Botha and heir-apparent F.W. de Klerk (the Education Minister!) to consult Botha over their decision to visit Kenneth Kuanda in Zambia forced him into open protest and resignation.[36]

This uncertainty does not amount to a real system of checks and balances. Two ministers resigned from the British Cabinet in August 1914, but it was not enough to stop the war proceeding.[37] Stalin was in shock for three days after the German invasion of 22 June 1941, but no-one dared replace him, and when he recovered his control became even more absolute.[38] More important is the political culture in which the institution exists. By 1964 the Soviet system had become resistant to Stalinism, and ironically one of its main critics, Khrushchev, fell partly as a result of losing colleagues' confidence over his handling of the Cuban missile crisis and preceding foreign policy problems.[39] In Japan, by contrast, no nail ever sticks up from the floorboards for too long, and foreign policy decisions, like cabinet government in general, tend to be by consensus. In 1986 the then Prime Minister Yasuhiro Nakasone was criticized for departing from this tradition, partly through a minor cult of personality (he established the 'Ron–Yasu' relationship with Ronald Reagan) and partly for daring to sack – under foreign pressure – the education minister who had denied in public that Japan had committed war-time atrocities against China. Nakasone did not have, subsequently, the prominent career he expected.[40]

Thus, if we consider together the foreign policy executive and the 'cabinets' to which it is answerable, rarely a group of more than 20 in total, we can see that the political office-holders enjoy a good deal of freedom in which to make decisions. The foreign policy executive in particular holds the powers of initiative, information, convening meetings and (in the case of the head of government) also the appointment of colleagues. This means that much foreign policy business is handled by a small number of specialists. Only when a problem is both of high priority and structured in such a way as to make it possible for a committee to follow the issues does the balance of advantage swing to the larger group. This is sometimes the case in crises, when what is at stake is well known, but often crisis simply exacerbates the tendency to rely on the foreign policy executive for rapid and creative responses. It is, therefore, not wholly surprising if the executive is seen from outside as personifying the state. Individual leaders have a range of opportunities to be real foreign policy actors.

Intelligence: a Special Case?

One of the key elements in foreign policy-making is the use of intelligence material, gained from both foreign operations and domestic counter-intelligence.[41] It raises interesting questions about how information is assessed and about a particular kind of bureaucratic politics, but in this context the issue is whether the intelligence services are capable of running an alternative policy to their political superiors, under the cover of official foreign policy.[42] The relationship between intelligence and politics is of crucial importance to the success of foreign policy, and although much routine information-gathering is a low-level business, ultimately the issues are played out at the highest level. Intelligence sits right in the middle of the civil–military relation, which can be crucial even in a democracy, as we saw when General Eisenhower became President of the United States during the Korean War, or when General de Gaulle put a decisive end to the Fourth French Republic in 1958.

Because both the successes and the failures of intelligence are spectacular, the foreign policy executive has to pay the closest attention to the advice of intelligence chiefs.[43] Political leaders can be raised on high or brought right down by the results of their judgements about intelligence forecasts. Jimmy Carter, for example, never recovered from gambling in 1980 on the attempt to liberate the American hostages in Teheran by military means. He was ill-advised by his special forces, and paid the price at the presidential election the following November.[44] Winston Churchill, by contrast, attained his mythical status as a great war leader in part because of his astute and experienced use of intelligence – an area where he constantly wrong-footed Hitler.[45] The key variables in this process are fourfold: the quality of the intelligence, its ability to reach political leaders; leaders' judgements; and the independent actions of the intelligence community. It is the last two which concern us here.

A secure executive has wide discretion whether or not to take notice of intelligence. De Gaulle was sceptical of it and preferred to pursue his own previously thought out *'grandes lignes'*.[46] Moreover, if the official intelligence services cannot or will not follow instructions, it is always possible to set up informal, parallel systems, as did President Reagan with Colonel Oliver North and his operatives in the Iran–Contra scandal, or François Mitterrand with the 'Elysée cell' he set up in dissatisfaction with the state counter-terrorism operation.[47] There is barely any public scrutiny to check these actions except after the fact, when things go wrong and/or illegalities get exposed.[48] The phenomenon of built-in deniability, *à la* Henry II and Thomas à Becket, is a great advantage, although both the Iraqi Supergun and Sierra Leone affairs in Britain have shown that the converse sometimes applies – that mud sticks to everyone, especially those ultimately responsible. The fact that most intelligence services are fragmented between home security, foreign operations and military intelligence (with each of the armed services often having its own branch of intelligence) makes it often difficult to decide on the most useful information amidst all the 'noise', but it also makes it possible for politicians to operate the strategy of divide and rule. The CIA's various failures, for example, have given the White House some leverage over this potential state within a state, while the rival Defence Intelligence Agency is institutionally limited from straying too far into non-military subjects.

The intelligence services naturally have an interest in the carefully-selected information they let out, in playing down their role vis à vis their political masters. This should not lead us to underestimate the degree of autonomy they often enjoy in foreign policy matters. This is partly operational, as with snooping on allies' communications, which could be diplomatically embarrassing, and partly strategic, in that they are able to plant their people inside the head of government's entourage, and in rival sources of analysis, such as research institutes and universities. Most important, their information is fundamentally uncheckable by anyone outside their own circle, unlike that of the academic, journalist or even career diplomat. Few leaders have the time or inclination to look at raw data, and those, like Churchill or Margaret Thatcher, who do have a tendency to be their own intelligence officer have no basis, other than intuition, and a limited capacity for cross-checking, for evaluating it. They all have to rely on human filters.[49]

political culture

A great deal, again, depends on the political culture of the particular country. In Soviet Russia the secret police methods of Stalin, combined with the state's sense of being under perpetual siege by hostile foreign powers, led to the KGB becoming institutionalized as a major force in all aspects of top decision-making. If the Communist Party was the parallel power structure to the state, then the KGB was the parallel structure to the party. Often the most able people would gravitate towards the intelligence services because of the relative freedom, personal and intellectual, which they could enjoy there compared to the ideologically top-heavy party cadres. These were the people with the clearest sense of what life was like in the West and of how far the Soviet Union was slipping behind under Leonid Brezhnev.[50] It was not therefore wholly surprising that their candidates, first Yuri Andropov and then Mikhail Gorbachev, should have found themselves in the position of supreme power in the USSR.[51] After ten years of post Soviet Russia, its current leader, Vladimir Putin, is from the same stable.

This kind of power is less likely to be found in countries with a wider range of effective institutions, although this is not to say that the intelligence services cannot veto the advance of key individuals they distrust.[52] In general, intelligence is a factor which must be reckoned with in any analysis of foreign policy.[53] It is all too easy to skim over the surface of events without asking about the advice top leaders were getting from their 'permanent government', or about the extent to which the latter were engaged in covert operations – with or without explicit authorization – that did not always square with declaratory policy. Clear answers to such questions can rarely be found, but on the basis of the historical record it is not unreasonable to conclude that intelligence services are occasionally pro-active, and intermittently decisive, in a state's foreign relations.[54] By the same token their internal divisions, relatively limited resources and rather narrow range of concerns mean that they should not be seen as the hidden string-pullers of political marionettes. Political leaders usually manage to set their own broad foreign policy parameters, and where there is consensus and continuity they tend to have been determined by deeper forces than the influence of MI6 or the DGSE. Intelligence can become crucial when it is least expected, but most politicians in office have plenty of other things to worry about, at home and abroad, than the machinations of their own secret services. What is more, spectacular failures such as the inability to predict the terrorist attacks of 11 September 2001 do damage to reputations which can take decades to repair.

Leading Responsibly

leaders matter!

Most scholars agree that leaders make a difference in foreign policy. Had Rabin and Peres rather than Begin and Sharon been leading Israel in 1982, says Shlomo Gazit, there would probably have been no invasion of the Lebanon.[55] It is true that Begin and the Likud Party had been elected by the Israeli people precisely because they were more hawkish on security questions, but that still left the prime minister and his colleagues a lot of scope for taking their own decisions. Since Israel is a democracy, they were supposed to lead responsibly, that is, bearing in the mind the wishes of their party and the electorate but still using their own judgement and values to assess what the circumstances required. For 'responsible' is an ambiguous word, referring on the one hand to behaviour which is generally sober and sensitive to context, and on the other to a person's answerability to specified others. This is the Weberian ideal-type of modern, legal–bureaucratic leadership.[56]

Political leadership in every area of policy involves quite a small group of people – cabinets rarely number many more than 20. In foreign policy this elite is generally even smaller, because of the nature of the issues, at once specialized and overwhelmingly comprehensive, which sets limits on those who can or wish to participate. The circuits of those who operate at the highest levels of international politics are still surprisingly restricted in numbers. This makes it possible for the foreign policy of the state to be 'captured' by a coterie of individuals, circulating over many years, with a particular perspective or even set of private interests. This is what the isolationists said, not wholly without justice, about the east coast WASPs who committed the USA to the defence of western Europe after 1947. It is more obviously true (but not just of foreign policy) in the sheikhdoms of the Persian Gulf.

Yet even when a small elite monopolizes foreign policy, it does not follow that they are able or willing to exploit the state in the narrow sense of venality. More likely is that they come to identify themselves with the state, holding strongly to a particular image of what foreign policy should be doing and seeing their own line of policy as so much more 'responsible' than the alternatives. For it is all too easy both for insiders and outsiders to confuse the personalities of state foreign policy – the visible foreign policy executive – with 'national character' or with the interests of the whole community. The same mistake may be made with INGOs, when the Roman Catholic Church is identified with the pontiff of the day, or the problems of a multinational company are reduced to

→ ≠ confuse FP/DM, personalities w/ "national character"

the dynastic politics of an Agnelli or a Murdoch. It happens less in the 'faceless' corporate environment, but in a world of collective actors, and where states of all sizes enjoy formal equality, some personification is inevitable. Sometimes this is consciously exploited; more often, it leads to confusions on all sides as to who is really speaking for whom, and for which interests. Gorbachev, for instance, revolutionized Soviet foreign policy, but turned out not to be so representative of the country's people as most outsiders assumed. Like Churchill in 1945, Gorbachev was summarily expelled from office at the hour of his greatest fame.

Foreign policy has its peculiarities as an area of public policy. Whereas health, education and transport are always close to the centre of popular concerns, but only rarely bring forth great dramas, foreign policy can run in its own channels unseen by all except the specialists, only to break into the collective consciousness as a *grand guignol*, with the potential to do serious damage to the very fabric of the state and to its citizens' lives. This means that responsible leadership consists in not being lulled into complacency by the lack of daily domestic interest, and in not confusing the processes of decision-making by elites with the structures of multilayered international politics. It has to take the long view, trying to manage affairs so to avoid getting into the dangerous crises (whether military, political or economic) which are inherently transformational and restrictive of choice. It is *crisis-* (not conflict-) prevention which should be the touchstone of foreign policy, given that conflict in some form is inevitable and crisis is not. At the same time, an excessive emphasis on foreign affairs, with a corresponding over-insurance in costly defence policies against notional risks, can bankrupt the state and pervert its values. Both superpowers suffered from this to some degree during the Cold War, and the Soviet Union collapsed as a result.[57]

The responsibility of foreign policy does not always weigh heavily on decision-makers' shoulders, even if it ought to. Some insist on a particular version of 'the national interest' that is little more than a costly bet with history. Either way, there is a good deal of scope for actorness for the individuals and small groups who find themselves deciding on behalf of peoples in international relations. They have quite a margin in which to err or to show wisdom, even allowing for the constraints of the structures in which they are operating, international, transnational and domestic. They *interpret* a society's needs, for security, prosperity and independence, in a long perspective and with some degree of institutional freedom. Yet in so doing, they do not act alone. In the modern era foreign relations cannot be conducted by gifted amateurs with a small number of personal assistants. A formidable bureaucracy geared to international policy has now grown up around most points of decision, and it is to the question of how far these seemingly non-political officials are obedient agents, and how far themselves shapers, or actors, that we now turn.

US now
USSR before

4
Agents: Bureaucracy and the Proliferation of External Relations

All modern leaders are heavily dependent on their professional staff, from the *éminences grises* who participate in summits, like Chancellor Kohl's Joachim Bitterlich, to the desk officers hidden away in ministries who follow day-to-day events in the Gambia or the Food and Agriculture Organization. This is true even of autocrats like Saddam Hussein; they may ensure obedience by terror rather than by legitimacy, as in democratic states, but they cannot run a complex set of external relations and social control solely through the clan-members of their power-base. Every system requires its janissaries to run embassies, manage the armed forces, gather and assess the mountains of information now available and not least assist in the many technical negotiations which constitute contemporary international relations. Policy-making works on the basis of formal operating rules, but also through trust and informal job-sharing.[1]

The importance of these cadres in foreign policy-making has long been recognized by scholars, and much literature now exists on the political impact of bureaucrats and the extent to which foreign policy is really in their hands. This chapter will examine the hypothesis of bureaucratic control by comparing the Weberian ideal-type with practice across different systems of society and government, with the help of the theories of 'bureaucratic politics' which have been developed by political scientists and students of International Relations. It will also discuss the way in which the foreign policy bureaucracy is no longer confined to ministries of foreign affairs, but extends horizontally across most governmental departments, provoking new problems of coordination and control.

72

Agents not Agency

The arrival of industrialization and a complex division of labour in nineteenth-century Europe fostered existing developments towards modern systems of government and administration. In particular the twin doctrines of democracy and meritocracy began to shape the expanding apparatus of the state. So far as foreign policy-making was concerned the impact of the new meritocratic thinking was evident rather earlier than that of democratic philosophy. Both had been present in the great symbol of modern upheaval, the French Revolution. Napoleon's revolution in French administration, with its key notion of *la carrière ouverte aux talents*, had been made possible by the sweeping away of feudal privileges between 1789–93, just as the great idea of popular sovereignty had been unleashed on the world by the Revolution. However disappointing its practical application in the Paris of Jacobins, Bonapartists and then restored Bourbons, there was to be no going back in terms of the discourse of European politics. But whereas even the aspiration for a democratic foreign policy, in the form of the policies of Woodrow Wilson, would not reach the political agenda for more than another hundred years, the pressure for greater efficiency and the mobilization of more state resources meant that the introduction of meritocratic measures into the official class began to take place around the middle of the nineteenth century.

In Britain, for example, the Northcote–Trevelyan report of 1854 led eventually to the civil service reforms of 1871 whereby formal grades of administrative and executive service were introduced as part of the move against corruption and incompetence. The army and navy reforms begun in the 1870 were designed to the same general end, so that position could no longer so easily be gained on the basis of birth and connections. This was partly the consequence of demonstrable incompetence during the Crimean War of 1854–6. Similarly in France, the devastating defeats of 1870–71 led to a reconsideration of many aspects of state policy, including education and the armed forces. The subsequent reforms meant that the country was to provide a far more formidable adversary for Germany in 1914. For its part, the newly unified Germany, with Prussia at its core, was proving a model of new administrative practice for other countries, even if the element of promotion on merit was still circumscribed by the powerful presence of the Junkers' elite in both army and government.

The ideas of rational conduct and a clear chain of command/authority were important to the new German model of administration, but they were by no means unproblematical, as the foremost theorist of modern bureaucracy, Max Weber, was subsequently to make clear.[2] A modern system had to go beyond the notion of unqualified obedience to the next rung in the hierarchy; this had, after all, been the *motif* of absolutist forms of government. The ethos of democracy increasingly demanded a system in which obedience was owed only to legitimate government, and where legitimacy derived from the popular will. Moreover, obedience had to go hand in hand at all levels with accountability: politicians were to become ever more accountable to electorates, and to the press, while their subordinates were accountable both to their immediate superiors and to a growing corpus of written rules, necessary to systematize an ever more complex administration of interlinked parts. Finally, it was slowly becoming clear that both bureaucrats and their masters needed to be sensitive, and to some extent open, to inputs from mass society, from whom they took their rationale.

In pre-modern days, the clerks and secretaries who were the forerunners of today's 'secretaries of state' were judged by a particular form of efficiency – their ability to perform the prince's will, or at most their ability to persuade him to do what he surely would have wanted to do in any case. Until the age of mercantilism, there were no abstract indicators, whether economic or relating to 'power', against which performance could be measured. With the arrival of meritocratic thinking, however, in the wake of the enlightenment, came a sense of loyalty to the *res publica*, independent in the last analysis of the orders of any politician. This was a reworking of the classical distinction between the private and the public spheres in the light of notions of popular sovereignty.[3] By the late nineteenth century it was becoming accepted that an official should serve both legitimate political authority and some higher notion of the national interest in the event that the former proved corrupt or particularly inept (as in the case of those officials in the 1930s who leaked information on Britain's weak defences to an out-of-office Winston Churchill). It was, of course, to be hoped that such a fundamental conflict of loyalties would arise only rarely. For the most part the new breed of civil servant was to be loyal, professional, clear-sighted and non-political. The ideal-type of the modern official as articulated (but not invented) by Weber was that of someone who had been trained to implement policy decided upon by those engaged in politics, without themselves becoming politicized.[4] The human temptation to play politics was to be neutralized by the provision of proper job security and salaries, as well as by an ethos of responsibility and *esprit de corps*. More negatively the incentives to use office in the traditional way for the pursuit of personal wealth and advancement were diminished by supervision and by the fear of denied promotion or even dismissal.

This new class was to consist of reliable *agents*, in the sense of acting on behalf of others. But in today's terms they were not themselves either the repository of *agency* or independent foreign policy actors.

This was the theory. Certain states, like Britain, started to implement it much earlier than others, and it is in any case a job, like the painting of the Forth Bridge, which can never be completed. Arguably some states, even developed ones, have still not made much progress on it today. But wherever one looks, foreign policy was almost the last area to be reformed. The association of foreign policy with international elite networks meant that the impact of democratic and meritocratic thought fed through slowly, sometimes on the basis of two steps forward, one-and-a-half steps back.

Bureaucracy and Foreign Policy

The 'age of the masses' affected diplomacy in only piecemeal fashion, even if the two world wars caused major upheavals. Woodrow Wilson articulated the principles of 'open covenants, openly arrived at' in 1917, with its assumption that the old 'freemasonry' of international diplomacy had been responsible for the disastrous errors leading to the Great War. Efficiency, merit and democracy were conjoined in a new philosophy of foreign policy as a form of public service. As it happens, the values of professionalism had already begun to creep into the British, French, Japanese and American foreign ministries by 1914, with a gradual acceptance that intellectual ability was as important as social connections. After 1918 further changes were seen in Soviet Russia (where, however, one form of caste soon replaced another in the diplomatic corps), and Germany, although the highly turbulent and ideological thirty years which followed made this a period in which the advancing role of civil servants was inevitably stalled.[5]

Diplomatic dynasties continued to survive in the twentieth century – but the era of the gentleman diplomat was steadily giving way to an order in which officials were seen as both indispensable and wholly subordinate. This was as true of the United States, where state service enjoyed only moderate prestige and where each presidential election produced a new raft of political appointees to control the higher echelons of the State Department, as it was of the Soviet Union, where the organs of the state soon came to be infiltrated and controlled by the Communist Party – as late as 1956 Khrushchev could boast that 'Gromyko only says what we tell him to'.[6] In Britain, the ideological hostilities of the 1920s, when the Foreign Office barely concealed its lack of trust in the first Labour government's ability to defend the national interest, were put to rest – at least so far as the leadership was concerned – during Labour's first full term (1945–50) when the prime minister and foreign secretary worked closely with senior officials to construct a new order in Europe. With France finally settling down under the Fifth Republic to an era in which respected presidents were served by able, loyal functionaries from the *grandes écoles*, the second half of the twentieth century seemed to have established bureaucracy as the neutral buffer in the political process, responsible for logistics, implementation and advice, but always subject to the decisions of the people's elected representatives.

Ironically it was just at this time, the 1950s and 1960s, that academics were beginning to question the truth of such a neat model, and to see bureaucrats themselves as powerful players in the policy process. Individual officials had already drawn attention to themselves, like Sir Eyre Crowe and his famous memorandum on British foreign policy of 1907, or André François-Poncet, the influential French Ambassador in Berlin from 1931 to 1938.[7] More common was the tendency of ad hoc personal advisers, such as Woodrow Wilson's Colonel House, or Tsar Nicholas's Rasputin, to come to public attention as svengali figures. Thereafter the steady growth in size of bureaucratic apparatuses, the increased number of states in the international system, and with them diplomatic representations, plus the remarkable economic expansion of the post-war years, all served to highlight the changing balance of power, in terms of numbers, resources and information (expertise), between politicians and officials.[8]

In the area of foreign policy the loyal 'agents' seemed from the outside to constitute a particularly compact and manageable body, with a readily identifiable foreign ministry and diplomatic service at the service of each state. Moreover, the strong sense of elite status and *esprit de corps* of diplomats, many of whom naturally served far from the supervising eyes of their domestic masters, made them obvious candidates for study as the real authors of foreign policy.

The Ministry of Foreign Affairs

As we shall see, the past fifty years have seen the emergence of many rivals to conventional diplomats from within the bureaucracy. Nonetheless, the foreign ministry and those serving abroad (who have increasingly come under the ministry's control) represent a formidable engine in the making of policy. The ministry still performs three vital functions:

- *Routine information-gathering*: no state can manage without the means to collect and analyse information on the range of issues in which it has interests. Although journalists now have better and quicker sources on developments in wider society, there is no substitute for the first-hand knowledge of their interlocuteurs in host administrations which good diplomats possess. In conjunction with the intelligence services they can also monitor policy-implementation in detail, when journalists have long ago moved on to other stories. This is why one of the first steps of the British government after the fall of Kabul in November 2001 was to re-establish the embassy and to send the Head of the South Asia Department of the FCO to run it.
- *Policy-making*: politicians formulate their foreign policies in opposition and have the assistance of their party machines in government. But they still rely heavily on the experts in the foreign ministry to sift the vast quantities of incoming information, to interpret and predict the actions of other states, and to formulate policy options on the thousand and one detailed questions which never come to public attention. Only in one-party states can the party machine represent an alternative to this concentration of specialized advice, as in the Soviet Union or China, where the International Departments of the Communist Party became surrogate foreign ministries.[9]
- *Memory*: every system needs continuity in its external relations, and career diplomats institutionalize it by serving as the system's collective memory, with the help of their record-keeping system. Without the capacity to relate myriad past commitments and treaties to the present, and to each other, decision-makers would be left floundering in chaos, given the complexity of the contemporary international system. Alternatively they would turn inwards, as with countries like North Korea which have been too paranoid to permit the development of civil service expertise. Conversely, the possession of this institutional memory does produce pressures for conservatism in foreign affairs. If *pacta sunt servanda*, as diplomats and their legal advisers usually believe, then it is difficult to strike out in new directions, and domestic radicals of various colours easily become frustrated with what they see as the inertia and obstructionism of their own foreign ministry. This is exacerbated by the uncertainties

of the external environment and the tendency of the experts to rely on the 'lessons' of the past.

Apart from these broad functions, in most cases where foreign ministries are not demoralized and deliberately emasculated, they develop certain institutional strengths. In the first instance they usually attract high-quality personnel, selected in the modern era by competitive examinations. The social and intellectual sources of recruitment may still be narrow – history and law graduates from comfortable backgrounds for the most part – but the meritocratic principle is now dominant: the diplomatic service represents an elite of ability as well as ethos. In 1984, 28 per cent of all French ambassadors had been educated at the top-ranking Ecole Nationale d'Administration (ENA), while 75–80 per cent of ENA's own recruits came from Paris's Institut des Etudes Politiques ('Sciences Po'). And there is no doubt that both ENA and Sciences Po and their equivalents elsewhere are funnels for students of the highest calibre. Even in very small countries like Ireland and Luxembourg, the quality of their officials is perceived abroad as being high – in the two cases cited running the six-month revolving presidency of the EU has never proved a technical problem, even if at times the volume of work has been excessive.[10]

Secondly, where they do enjoy trust, foreign ministries will have a considerable degree of autonomy, virtually constituting a sub-elite within the machinery of government. Their control over external representations, their privileged contacts with foreigners and the continued mystique of international affairs gives them a certain carapace which protects against interference by other parts of the domestic administration. In the long run this can attract resentment and hostility, as with Truman's often-expressed view of foreign service officers as 'the striped pants boys', or the Nazi Party's determination to control its too-reasonable diplomats by compelling them to become members of the Party.[11] Still, for countries as diverse as Argentina, Egypt, Norway and Canada the foreign ministry and its diplomats constitute a distinctive and high-status profession without which the state would be significantly disadvantaged in the international system.

Lastly, foreign ministries have adapted during the current century to the vastly greater range of business which confronts states by organizing themselves on both geographical and functional lines. At various times each has been in fashion; for example, the European Commission, which in one respect is a proto-European foreign ministry, has had three reorganizations in less than a decade, swinging back and forth between the geographical and the functional principle.[12] The Dutch foreign ministry has dealt with the problem by consolidating its regional directorates: political, economic and aid-related.[13] In general, however, it is now generally recognized that a foreign ministry needs both area specialists and experts in functional questions like energy and the environment, themselves partly reflecting the emergence of ever-more specialized international organizations.[14] Foreign ministries are increasingly stretched thin in the attempt to cater for this range of knowledge, but only they possess the *combination* of the different skills required.

Naturally these continuing strengths are only part of the story. Indeed current conventional wisdom tends to see foreign ministries and their employees as dinosaurs being supplanted by home-based experts and non-governmental para-diplomats. Let us examine the reasons why diplomatic services are under challenge, in the very era when they have finally become modern, professional organizations:

- *Technical incompetence*: diplomats are seen as over-generalist and over-stretched, incapable of discussion on equal terms with economists, scientists and businessmen. Even the 'specialism in abroad' counts for less now that travel is so easy and so common. Typical was the day trip made by British Foreign Secretary Robin Cook to Ankara in May 1998.[15] Mr Cook was also particularly aware of the 'infomatic' challenge. He introduced a secure electronic mail system, since his officials were receiving hot information later than the foreign editors of most newspapers.

- *The spread of mini-foreign offices*: most domestic departments now engage directly in international relations by sending their own experts out to meet their equivalents in another state or to participate in a specialized international organization. This is particularly the case in the European Union, where the Council of Finance Ministers (ECOFIN) is now a serious rival to the Council of (Foreign) Ministers as the working 'Cabinet' of the EU. In Japan the Ministry of International Trade and Industry has more prestige than the foreign ministry, together with its own network of external contacts. In the 1980s it caused problems by encouraging Toshiba, for commercial reasons, to break the rules of the CoCom (the Coordinating Committee associated with NATO from 1949–93 to control the export of strategic goods to hostile countries) by selling computers to the USSR. This was obviously within the purview of classical foreign policy. In Mexico 'almost every Ministry has a *Dirección General de Asuntos Internacionales*'.[16] These days hardly any government department anywhere can be regarded as wholly 'home' in its remit. Between 1960 and 1980, for example, the number of domestic ministries with their own international units in Finland and Sweden rose from two in each case to six and ten respectively.[17] Similarly, as early as 1975 the US's Murphy Commission investigating 'the Organization of the Government for the Conduct of Foreign Policy' found that of more than 20,000 civilian employees working full-time on foreign affairs (excluding the many in support agencies and in intelligence) only about 4000 worked in the Department of State. Abroad, in 1982 there were 126,520 civilian employees of the Executive branch, from 25 departments and agencies. Of these, 15,339 worked for the State Department, including foreign nationals.[18]

- *Poverty of resources*: foreign ministries use up very small amounts of public expenditure – in general less than 1 per cent of the total. The State Department's budget is rather less than the Pentagon's jet fuel bill. Yet far from strengthening their position, not being a burden turns out to be a political disadvantage. It is one of the paradoxes of modern government that those departments which use most resources, and cause most headaches, such as education, health and social security, seem most able to protect their budgets, while the foreign ministry, whose outputs are less tangible but far less expensive, is constantly vulnerable to cut-backs and bad publicity.[19] What is more, cuts here mean the loss of trained manpower, whose effects cannot quickly be reversed.[20]

- *Lack of domestic constituency*: following on from the above, foreign ministries have few natural supporters within their own societies. Foreign policy requires little domestic legislation and in consequence few members of parliament are drawn into policy-making, with the potential to become allies of the department. Whereas defence ministries can look to those manning bases or employed in the arms industry, and finance ministries always find allies in those who wish to cut taxes, the foreign ministry easily becomes labelled – as by Margaret Thatcher in Britain, and Jessie Helms in the USA – as the department for foreigners. Indeed it is all too easy for diplomats to get out of touch with their domestic base. Even when they return home for a period, they only serve in the nation's capital. In recent years, moreover, diplomacy has acquired a stuffy image, the opposite of street and business credibility, not least as relative salaries have declined, with the result that many of the best and the brightest have gone elsewhere. Even French 'enarques' were attracted away to private industry. This trend has begun to be reversed, as awareness has grown of the limits of a business vision of the world.

These foreign service weaknesses are real. It is not beyond the bounds of possibility that the formal, separate diplomatic apparatus as we know it might disappear over the next few decades to be replaced by what Britain's Berrill Report envisaged in 1977 as 'a foreign service group' within the wider civil service – in other words, a bureaucracy in which service overseas at some point becomes normal for most staff, and where 'external' policy is simply one aspect of policy in general. On the other hand, a terminal prognosis misses some important vital signs. For instance on the issue of technical competence, the more effective foreign ministries have adapted by increasing training in economics, and by allowing some staff to specialize. Furthermore, the greater diversification of external relations has created new needs for coordination and synthesis that foreign ministries, if they can escape the more traditional elements of their mind-set, are well-placed to meet. It is by no means obvious in any case that specialized currency issues are best negotiated by monetary economists, or chemical weapons questions settled by natural scientists. The ability to understand political and historical context is vital, together with the ability to keep experts 'on tap and not on top'.

To the extent that a foreign ministry can do this without falling back on the spurious justifications that only diplomats understand foreigners or the processes of negotiation, then they will maintain the high status that even today attaches to their profession and to the post of minister of foreign affairs. Despite their domestic vulnerabilities diplomats continued to be valued by the members of a formidable network, national and international, of influential figures, not least those politicians (and journalists) who lean on their skills in daily life, and who have seen at close hand how the profession has become more stressful, demanding and often physically dangerous since 1945. Diplomats have been held hostage and sometimes killed in many postings as a result of embodying their countries' policies and being the most obvious point of national weakness. The four-month siege in the Japanese embassy in Lima in 1997, and the killing of American diplomats in bomb attacks in Kenya and Tanzania in August 1998 are vivid recent examples. The G8 summits may take all the headlines, with political advisers, 'sherpas' and flown-out domestic officials to the fore, but behind all the fanfare is a great deal of indispensable routine daily grind in which foreign ministries have a prime role. Few presidential or prime ministerial offices, even in the most prominent cases of Washington, Bonn and Paris, would wish to do without the extensive diplomatic machinery that is also at their disposal. Even Henry Kissinger, who was very hard on American diplomats, dedicated a major book to 'the men and women of the Foreign Service of the United States of America, whose professionalism and dedication sustain American diplomacy'.[21]

Proliferating Rivals

Outsiders dealing with a particular state are always thrown into a quandary when they have to deal with a range of different departments or agencies. Is the adversary playing a strategic game by speaking with competing voices, or is there a genuine problem of fragmented decision-making? There is clearly a great deal of room for misunderstanding when many states are incapable of speaking with one voice.

This happens increasingly because foreign ministries now find themselves in a situation of structural rivalry with domestic competitors and because they do not always succeed in rising to the new challenge of coordination. Whether it is because of the international phenomenon of 'complex interdependence' or because of endogenous changes in the state (and the two processes are difficult to separate out) many states are now facing what has been termed the 'horizontal decentralization' of their foreign relations, or the foreign ministry's loss of control over many external issues to other parts of the state bureaucracy. From the wider perspective of the interests of state and society the problem of unitary action means that opportunities for linkage may be missed in international negotiation, that outsiders will be able to play on internal divisions or confusions, and that long-term strategic planning becomes almost impossible.

Who are the rivals to foreign ministries which have been proliferating in recent decades? They may be listed in four categories, three with substantive concerns and one with a procedural mission. First is the military, which can act as an ally to the foreign ministry, but which has its own sizeable vested interests and direct links with its equivalents overseas. Its actions can, not always intentionally, constitute a form of parallel foreign policy which then boxes in the official version – as did the Anglo-French military conversations of 1905–14, with their growing presumption of an automatic alliance between the two countries.[22] Since the military possesses considerable physical resources, a domestic constituency and its own network of attachés and intelligence sources it clearly has the capacity to embarrass conventional diplomacy. This is to say nothing of the numerous countries in which at one time or another the military has played a disproportionate part in government, and therefore been able to invert the normal servant–master relationship of defence to foreign policy. In the United States the military was not hindered by having General Eisenhower as President for eight years, even if General MacArthur's attempt to subvert democratic policy-making during the Korean War had been rebuffed by Truman, and his successor was aware of the need to tread carefully in civil–military relations. In the Soviet Union the military remained cowed until the death of Stalin by its losses in the purges of 1937–8, but thereafter soon became a massive force for over-insurance in the arms race which eventually brought their state to its knees. The Third World continues to produce examples of military dictatorships which are often cautious in their foreign policies but almost always lacking in the finesse and cooperative capacity which experienced diplomats bring to bear.[23] Brazil in the 1960s, Greece in the 1970s, Turkey in the 1980s, Nigeria and Burma in the 1990s, are all cases in point.

The second category of rival to the foreign ministry is that of the economic ministries. These will vary in number and title according to the state, which might possess one or more departments dealing with foreign trade/commerce, finance, development/foreign aid, industry, agriculture, fisheries and shipping – to say nothing of central banks, an increasing number of which are constitutionally independent of political control, although the other side of their lack of malleability is that their strict monetary remit usually makes them conservative and predictable. These entities are the basis of the hypothesis that interdependence is dissolving foreign policy and replacing it by a mosaic of functional, transgovernmental networks. The important roles of finance officials in IMF and EMU meetings and of trade officials in GATT/WTO negotiations seems to bear out the argument. Karvonen and Sundelius, however, have made a detailed empirical study of this question, largely in relation to Finland and Sweden but also carefully located in a comparative frame of analysis.[24] They conclude that although the picture is inevitably variegated, given the variety of state cultures and the genuine uncertainties about the best way to proceed, foreign ministries have often reasserted their central role in the 'management of interdependence'. Indeed, in 1983 the Swedish Commerce Ministry was dismantled and its international trade functions transferred to the foreign ministry. On the other hand, there is no doubt both that 'domestic' parts of the machinery of government have grown at a faster rate than the 'international' part, through their very expansion into the latter's territory (as we saw above with the notion of 'mini-foreign offices'), and that problems of coordination and control have consequently increased.[25]

The third form of rival is the intelligence services, whose role we have already surveyed in Chapter 3. These are at once the most difficult to keep in line and the least able to participate in routine policy-making and international negotiations. They are to some extent hamstrung by their own strengths. Nonetheless, when western states are at a loss to decide which branch of Syrian intelligence might have been responsible for a bomb attack on a jet airliner, as with the Hindawi affair of 1986, it is clear that a state's foreign policy can at times be splintered by powerful internal elements running their own line – or it can appear to be so, when it suits various parties not to assume a single locus of responsibility within the acting state. Conversely, in a democratic state the leadership can sometimes be forced to take responsibility for a policy failure which was really that of an importunate intelligence service. John Kennedy and the Bay of Pigs operation against Cuba of 1961, and Robin Cook and the Sierra Leone affair of 1998 are two prominent examples. Few intelligence agencies can resist the temptation to move on from information collection to assessment and action, as the role of

Pakistan's Military Intelligence in supporting the Taliban in the war of 2001–2, despite President Musharraf's support for the United States, demonstrated.

The consequences of proliferating external relations leads us to the last, and rather different, set of rivals facing the modern foreign ministry – those who think they can pull the threads of complexity together rather more effectively than can the diplomatic generalists. These people reside either in the prime minister's office and/or cabinet secretariat (in a parliamentary system), in the president's personal 'cabinet' (in a presidential system) or in the party machine in a one-party state. They have the advantages of being close to the head of government and being free of departmental bias, with an overview of the whole system. They often also control high-level appointments across the bureaucracy. All this makes for formidable rivals to the foreign ministry as it seeks to reconcile the many different strands of external relations. Yet the latter is not without its own advantages. A prime ministerial or presidential office can set the main outlines of policy, but it can easily get out of touch with detail, expertise and implementation. The concern with public policy as a whole can lead to the external dimension being unjustly neglected, manipulated for purely political reasons or distorted by ideological pre-occupations, with unpleasant surprises the eventual result. The challenge for foreign policy-makers today, therefore, is to build on the foreign ministry's unique capacity to understand how a state's activities look from the outside, and to judge how much of a united front is actually desirable, while ensuring that no gap arises between classical foreign policy and the various international dimensions of domestic policy. Striking the balance, and keeping the major departments of state in harmony with each other along the way, is one of the great tests of modern government.

The Theory of Bureaucratic Politics

So far theory has hardly entered the discussion. Yet if we are fully to understand the simultaneously fragmented and unitary character of foreign policy-making, we need theories which address the roles of bureaucracy, of choice and of government. Fortunately a rich literature of precisely this kind has grown up over the past thirty years under the general heading of 'bureaucratic politics'.

The theory of bureaucratic politics was introduced thirty years ago by Graham Allison, building on previous work done by Charles Lindblom, Richard Neustadt, Herbert Simon and others.[26] It has been developed since by Allison himself, Morton Halperin, Robert Gallucci and others, and applied in numerous case-studies.[27] Although it has also been subject to healthy criticism it is in ever-wider use empirically, not least among historians. Outside academe, however, things are rather different. Although practitioners would not quarrel with the model, and often live up to its predictions, they are barely aware of its propositions, let alone its implications for the wider issues of choice, democracy and responsibility. *A fortiori*, the citizenry has little clue that foreign policy decisions might be being made in the less than ideal way described by the theory of bureaucratic politics. They have a healthy sense of the self-interest and incompetence of individual politicians, but probably assume that in foreign policy it is not too much to expect the major departments of their country's bureaucracy to pull broadly in the same direction.

Yet this is precisely what does not happen, according to the theory. Allison's two models, soon collapsed into a single theory entitled 'governmental politics', are well enough known by now not to need recounting in detail.[28] Put baldly, the hypothesis, worked out in a case-study of superpower behaviour during the Cuban missile crisis of 1962, was that ministries and other bureaucratic units pursue at best their own versions of the national interest and at worst their own parochial concerns, so that foreign policy-making becomes an inward-looking battleground in which decisions are produced by horse-trading more than logic. But the fundamental assumptions of the argument should be examined, not least because they have been sharply criticized and because they have important implications for any attempt to address the problem of action in foreign policy. If we wish to know where agency lies in modern international relations, we must consider the proposition that the state tends to decompose into its various separate parts, and the degree to which the fissiparous tendencies of bureaucracy might be countered through intelligent leadership or constitutional provisions.

The bureaucratic politics approach has two general consequences for the study of foreign policy: it reinforces the whole domestic politics approach, against the scepticism of realism, neo-realism and some forms of historicism, and it presents a picture of decision-making in which 'foul-ups', as opposed to either rationality or inevitability, are very prominent. In both these respects it is thus central to the subject of foreign policy analysis, which came to the fore precisely because it has forced the domestic environment onto the agenda of International Relations and because it has subverted the claims of decision-makers always to be acting intelligently and/or in the public interest. For our purposes, however, although the bureaucratic politics model highlights the importance of agency, it also complicates the question significantly.

This occurs for one fairly self-evident reason and two more subtle ones. The basic reason is that bureaucratic politics insists that clear, rational decisions dealing with the merits of a problem tend to be supplanted by the mere 'resultants' of an internal process of bargaining and manoeuvring, in which, as Lamborn and Mummie have pointed out, the outcome will probably not correspond to the initial preference-orderings of any particular actor.[29] In other words, internal dynamics invariably shape policy to produce compromises that are unsatisfactory in terms of their external competence. This is, in practice, another version of the view that democracies are at a disadvantage in their dealings with autocratic states, which we shall encounter in Chapter 11, but it adds the problem of competing foreign policies being run from the same state, with no certainty for outsiders or insiders as to which might prevail.

The agency problem is more tangentially affected by a second aspect of the bureaucratic politics theory, namely that of its assumptions about the place of rationality in the calculations of what Allison calls 'the players ... men in jobs'.[30] Are they mostly acting irrationally, or just sub-optimally? Are they, conversely, acting in the same way that is described in the famous 'rational actor model' of the first part of the book, but at the level of individuals and departments rather than unitary states? Either way, does it make a crucial difference to foreign policy outcomes, and the location of responsibility for decisions? These questions touch on the biggest weakness of the theory: that the springs of choice are left unclear. If policy-makers, instead of trying to liaise in the best way possible to construct an effective, united national position, prefer rather to pursue the interests of their own ministry, department or office, why should this be so? In what way might they profit (for at base, the analogy is an economic one) if the state as a whole is served less well than their parochial departmental loyalty? Why, indeed, is it obvious that separate administrative units have competing interests, beyond the trivial level of finance and survival? One can argue that the same problem of rational actorness applies at both levels, the unitary state of Model I and the bureaucratic entity of Model III: that is, are human beings really desiccated calculating machines who optimize on the basis of as much information as they can gather, without much regard for political beliefs, moral values, personal loyalties or sense of identity? It seems very unlikely, even if, to turn Allison on his head, they are more likely to make the effort in the service of a collectivity like the state, whose very survival might be thought to rest on their ability to relate ends systematically to means. It would be almost bizarre to deploy the same resources in the interests of a sub-unit.

If the bureaucratic politics model is correct it does have profound implications for our notions of foreign policy action. It would make it very difficult to rely on a notion of state-as-actor in international relations. States would become less important, not because of the familiar forces of interdependence but because the state apparatus would have become little more than an arena in which competing fiefdoms fought out their inward-looking games. Foreign policy in this perspective either gets made by accident, or it is captured unpredictably by different elements at different times. This was, indeed, the line taken by Allison and Halperin, particularly in the latter's book on the US Anti-Ballistic Missile System decision of 1967.[31] Here he showed that a system originally designed to protect against the USSR was described as being deployed against China, with all the obvious consequences for relations with Beijing, largely because of the battles which had been fought within the government, particularly between Secretary McNamara and the Joint Chiefs of Staff. [HALPERIN]

If this is a true description and one of general applicability then we have to live with the fact. But as Jerel Rosati once pointed out in a famous attack on the theory of bureaucratic politics, it makes the idea of responsible, democratic decision-making difficult to sustain.[32] Rosati made a category error in presuming that because bureaucratic politics undercuts the constitution and presidency of the United States the theory must be mistaken. It may describe something which is undesirable, but that does not make it fanciful. On the other hand Rosati has certainly happened upon an important issue. If policy-making is a seething mass of intertwined bureaucratic conflicts, then the formal responsibility of office-holders for final decisions becomes more nominal than real. Moreover, if the culture permits individuals and units to behave in this way then it must signify that a sense of duty to the government of the day, and to the public behind them (to say nothing of wider societal or universal values), has not been widely disseminated.

Bureaucratic politics and agency are mutually entangled for one final reason. One of the key ideas underpinning the theory is that of role-socialization – even if Allison does not put it in quite these terms. By this is meant the presumed ability of an organizational context to socialize its staff into a particular set of values attached to that unit, over and above apparently superordinate value-systems such as the 'national interest'. Thus foreign ministry personnel will pursue concerns which are very different from those of the military. Even more obviously, inter-service rivalry will be a fact of policy-making life, as the navy is never going to agree that boats should be mothballed while more tanks are bought, and so on. The trouble with this all too plausible picture of how individuals become 'organization man' (or woman – it is often forgotten that in Margaret Thatcher's first Cabinet post as Secretary of State for Education, she was a high-spending minister in favour of state schools!) is twofold. Firstly, it is by no means clear what the 'unit' is that has such determining effects on a person's behaviour. Is it, for example, in the case of a high-ranking defence official, the department as a whole, the minister's inner group, or the particular armed service/ functional division for which he or she happens to have responsibility? And do lower-level functionaries only identify themselves with their immediate unit, or with all the divisions which are on top and around them? Secondly, even if we can identify stable units for given 'players', what is the 'line' which they are supposed to be pushing, and how do they know? Such suppositions as 'the military are hawkish' or 'diplomats tend to appeasement' do not withstand a moment's serious scrutiny.

If there is a relationship between organizational context and substantive policy preference, then it is a more subtle affair than this. Martin Hollis and Steve Smith have been the most effective critics of this part of the bureaucratic politics model, and their amendments make it much more useable.[33] Instead of a mechanical system which either reproduces the problems of rational action or depicts decision-makers as robots wholly programmed by their position in the administrative order, they suggest that the roles individuals take on when they become part of an organization should be regarded as both constraining and enabling. Bureaucratic animals are constrained by their terms of reference, their superiors and the culture (or 'expectations') of their group, and they also have opportunities to interpret their given roles in new ways on the basis of their own personalities and particular circumstances. This description does justice to the evident fact that we are all shaped profoundly by the goals and values of the work we do, while allowing for change and an important element of indeterminacy.

A key question in social science is 'where do preferences (values, ideas, and so forth) come from?' – a question which pinches sharply on the theory of bureaucratic politics, given the assumption that roles are the source of key preferences. In practice, there is no substitute for empirical flexibility on this: that is, being aware when it comes to the analysis of particular cases and countries that outcomes may well have been strongly influenced by bureaucratic competition, while at the same time not falling into the trap of using the model in too rigid or exclusive a manner. There are, after all, many key variables involved in the making of foreign policy, and the theory of bureaucratic politics deserves the status of single-factor explanation no more than any other.

Assuming that bureaucratic roles condition preferences to some degree – if only by making it difficult to change positions radically when new political bosses arrive – there remains the question of interaction between the separate agencies responsible for external relations, and how far competition between them undermines an effective foreign policy. The theory has problems here too, notably in taking an overly narrow view of what constitutes 'politics' within the policy-making system.[34] The tendency to assume that bureaucratic units are characterized by the pursuit of power in some form of micro-imperialist scramble does less than justice to the evident differences of formal responsibility (it is a treasury's *purpose* to try to ensure sound finances) and modes of understanding the world that exist between, say, career diplomats and those who make their living from working in the field on development aid projects. These different groups will engage in politics, but usually at a rather more serious and elevated level than that of mere pork-barrelling. For example, it is clear that in Japan at the present time most officials in the foreign ministry are in favour of Japan becoming a permanent member of the UN Security Council because it will enhance the ministry's domestic position vis à vis rivals such as MITI. On the other hand, there are plenty of officials outside the foreign ministry who favour the move for broader reasons to do with Japan's future place in world politics, and few who would oppose it just so as to scupper the diplomatic corps.

This means that the bureaucratic politics theory must be used in conjunction with an understanding of both wider conceptions of politics and the roles of the formal *political* actors. Through their power of hiring and firing, but also through the manifesto commitments which they embody, the agreements they reach with foreign leaders and the sheer capacity for heroic transcendence of routine which all powerful leaders enjoy, a head of government can change the rules of the bureaucratic game and start the whole dance off again to different music. This happens most obviously in the United States, but there are plenty of examples from other systems, as we saw in Chapter 3. It must also take account of the variability of contexts in which bureaucratic politics are played out – there are many different levels of state power and economic development – as well as varying particular circumstances, historical periods and political cultures. Halperin was myopic when he wrote that 'as we believe, all Governments are similar to the US government as we have described it here'.[35] Most observers have concluded that although the United States system is indeed beset by bureaucratic infighting (which is why the literature originated there) the degree and quality of the problem are unmatched anywhere else.[36] Some other cultures, indeed, display some of the opposite pathologies, as with Japan, where there is an obsessive concern with consensus ('*ringi-sei*') and to a lesser degree the centralized states of France and the United Kingdom, where the structure favours the forces of coordination over those of fragmentation. Moreover, most systems have informal networks which cut across the nominal interdepartmental divisions and produce elites with a strong sense of overall direction and/or common interest.

It is also important not to exaggerate the importance of officials. Some foreign policy disasters have less to do with decision-making fiascoes – whether bureaucratic or otherwise – than with more 'structural' forces such as geo-politics, ideological conflict or the configuration of classes. As Fred Halliday pointed out in relation to the Iranian revolution, 'had there been dozens of wise Persian-speaking C.I.A. and State

Department officials, or had the Shah not been admitted to the USA in October 1979, these broader problems would have remained'.[37] Officials themselves, in memoirs and interviews, naturally tend to highlight problems of resources and coordination, but a different vantage-point, and in particular a longer historical perspective, may well make their concerns seem more ephemeral.

This raft of qualifications is only worth making because the theory of bureaucratic politics has at its core a set of insights which is both strong and parsimonious. In the next section I want to show that the most useful of them derive less from the idea of interdepartmental conflict than from that of organizational process, but there is certainly much empirical evidence to suggest that the former is also a common and influential phenomenon. Allison argued that if he could show that governmental politics occurred even in conditions of extreme crisis, it must be endemic, and even after accepting the more pertinent criticisms of the historical basis of his case study enough remains to make the point plausible. On the Soviet side, recent documents have suggested that there was confusion between Moscow and its military in the field as to who was supposed to be in control of the anti-aircraft batteries on Cuba which shot down an American U2.[38] As for the United States, the navy was certainly reluctant to pull back the blockade line so as to create more time for diplomacy, and some air force chiefs (notably Curtis LeMay) pushed so hard for air-strikes, even after a deal had been done, that President Kennedy had to exert maximum authority to ensure control over events.

In more normal times, budget allocations invariably produce interdepartmental rivalries of an intensity that can leave foreign policy the victim. This was the case with the Navy vs Air Force dispute of the early 1960s which led to the cancellation of the Skybolt missile programme despite the fact that the system had already been offered to the UK.[39] Outside the US there are also many examples of at least intermittent bureaucratic politics. In the Soviet Union after 1978 the newly created Department of International Information provided yet another rival to the Foreign Ministry, and Gromyko complained strenuously about the existence of parallel systems.[40] The Israeli secret services are known to have put agents into their own prime minister's office, while the Coalition's war in Afghanistan in late 2001 saw the Italian foreign ministry at odds with the more cautious officials of the defence ministry.[41] Less dramatic have been the tensions inside the German state between the Chancellor's Office, the foreign ministry (often feeling itself excluded) and the economics ministry – to say nothing of the fiercely

independent Bundesbank in its heyday. At times the German position on
a future European monetary union oscillated wildly according to which
institution was briefing the press.[42]

Thus any bureaucracy which is big enough to have a normal division
of labour between ministries is likely to have a *tendency* to bureaucratic
politics, however much the culture encourages solidarity. In complex
systems, decisions are almost always the result of inter-agency compromises, and therefore in strict terms are sub-optimal, although as we shall
see in the next chapter the checks and balances involved can turn out to
be valuable.[43] If decision-making matters at all in terms of affecting
outcomes, and of providing choices over different courses of action,
then relations between politicians and their officials will matter too, and
a theory of the politics which occurs between them must be taken seriously. It is just as important, however, to look at the characteristics of
bureaucracies which are not strictly political at all.

The Heart of the Matter – Organizational Process

There is a great tradition of writing about bureaucracy which long pre-
dates the work of Allison. From Weber, Michels and Ostrogorski
through to Herbert Simon and Chester Barnard a body of thought has
built up from which the pathologies of modern organizational life have
become clear. These general theories of organization focus particularly
on the routines of bureaucratic procedure and on the handling of information. What they have to say about the problem of rationality is of
great interest, and this will be dealt with in the next chapter. The main
point of interest here is the way in which officials shape policy by their
quiet but ubiquitous presence. As Richard Betts noted in relation to the
power of the military, 'the real problem ... is indirect influence and the
extent to which it may condition the decision-makers' frame of reference'.[44] There are at least five ways in which this happens, independent
of any bureaucratic politics:

- Administrative systems 'factor' problems so as to be able to deal
  with them more efficiently. That is, everything is broken down into
  its component parts and classified into headings and systems that
  suit the pre-existing organizational structures but may not suit the
  problem itself. This is a partly rational, partly historical process and
  it militates against seeing the problem in the round, strategically.
  Where competence exists, the problem will be dealt with well, but

the converse is also true. Thus, US diplomacy on the law of the sea in the late 1970s and early 1980s was hampered by the fact that the State Department's 'Bureau of Oceans and International Environment and Scientific Affairs' was evidently inadequate.[45] If it had been stronger it would surely have led the United States to take a more pro-active, and perhaps constructive, role in the negotiations over a Law of the Sea Treaty. Even where knowledge is not the issue, factoring can cause severe problems. From 1984 the CIA had critical data on Iraqi stores of nerve gas, but it failed to ensure that the US troops who blew up the bunker in Khamisiyah in 1991 were warned about their possible exposure to toxic agents.[46]

- Bureaucracies cannot work without 'standard operating procedures' (SOPs – a key concept in *Essence of Decision*). That is, they need to have formal rules, almost always written down, which individuals are extremely reluctant to over-rule. Personal initiative is discouraged precisely because the *system* is seen as the source of efficiency. The rules usually only get changed under the pressure of a catastrophe which has already happened. Thus the Soviet Union's eastern air defences shot down the Korean civil airliner KAL007 in 1983 without proper reference to Moscow because they had orders not to allow hostile incursions which could be a missile attack on pain of their jobs (and possibly their lives).[47] It was easier to 'obey orders' than to take initiatives and to act on the basis of lateral thinking. It may have been a similar problem which led the US Navy ship *Vincennes* to shoot down an Iranair airbus in 1988, also with complete loss of life. The most famous SOPs are sometimes said to have had even more serious consequences: the Austrian need in 1914 to get the harvest in before calling up their reserves for war, together with the German Schlieffen Plan which led rigidly to the invasion of Belgium in the event of war with France, may between them have ensured that a limited conflict turned into a continent-wide disaster.[48] Greater flexibility would at least have created more contingency plans and more political room for manoeuvre.

- Conservatism is another iron law of bureaucracies. Even at the level of basic competences, decision-makers often do not take measures to change the existing order of things. Thus the administration of EU development policy continued unreformed throughout the 1990s, despite its evident inability even to spend the funds allocated.[49] When problems are anticipated, change – in the form of retraining or new recruitment policies – takes decades to implement. The 'young turks' in the Italian foreign ministry demanded reform for years before the measures announced in 1998 which have begun the slow process of modernization.[50] In actual foreign policy behaviour conservatism usually takes the form of being 'risk-averse', in Allison's terms, and of over-insurance. That is, not wanting to be exposed as having failed to do the job, bureaucrats tend to stick to what they know has worked in the past and to err on the safe side. They often see their job as holding on to politicians 'by their coat-tails' to prevent fanciful initiatives. It is of course thoroughly desirable to think things through and not to take stupid risks, especially with other people's lives and taxes. But it can also be a fatal error not to change in time, as the French armed services found with their attachment to the Maginot line in 1940 and the entire communist bureaucracies of the USSR and eastern Europe discovered in 1989.[51] Margaret Thatcher was disdainful of 'the Foreign Office where compromise and negotiation were ends in themselves' and even more of ministers who could not break free of its 'spell'.[52]

- The quality of bureaucracy most prominent in the public mind – not without justice – is pettiness. Most citizens associate their state with administrative nightmares to do with long queues, unnecessary paperwork and 'officious' behaviour. In the area of foreign affairs the image is bad because of problems getting visas, passing through border controls and getting consular assistance (despite the fact that the first two of these are in fact not the responsibility of the foreign ministry). Behind the scenes the reality does sometimes live up to the stereotype. The small-mindedness of the British officials who refused to accept the evidence before them of genocide against the Jews was staggering, rather like the wall of unseeing which characterized so many of those in the service of apartheid in South Africa. 'I was just doing my job' – the definition of the reliable bureaucrat – has unfortunately become a synonym for lack of imagination and humanity.[53]

- The comparative study of organizations tends, lastly, to highlight the inherent tendency of bureaucracy to expand when not positively checked. This can also be termed elephantiasis. As Kissinger observed, 'the vast bureaucratic mechanisms that emerge develop a momentum and a vested interest of their own'.[54] Problems of coordination abound, particularly given the steady expansion of external relations and the information overloads evident in the second half of the twentieth century. The sheer technical problems of filing, copying, and personnel management present formidable obstacles to efficiency in the biggest systems. Information technology has simply increased the amount of transactions, while the need for encryption and other problems of secure communications are other factors which make size and sophistication to some extent a disadvantage. Nor does privatization reduce the size and unwieldiness of bureaucracy. Although some ideas have been floated about sub-contracting embassy work (as with some prisons), it is not really feasible to expect that a society as a whole can be represented abroad, often in highly political negotiations, by private interests. Whether centralized, like China, or federal, like Germany, the administration of foreign relations is complex and growing in proportion to the increased number of states, international organizations and private transactions that a foreign policy process has at the least to track and quite probably relate to. At the extreme this can have dire consequences: the CIA is said to have received advance warning in 1981 that President Sadat of Egypt was going to be assassinated; there were, however, so many pieces of information to process that the warning was not read until after the murder had taken place.

Politicians and Officials: Can the Dog be Separated from his Tail?

Given the theory of civil service responsibility and obedience to elected politicians, but the evident reality of the former's monopoly of expertise, detail and continuity, the question inevitably arises of whether the tail wags the dog. The theory of bureaucratic politics and its empirical follow-ups have shown convincingly enough that in certain circumstances an administration can indeed have a mind of its own. It is, for instance, notoriously difficult for politicians to intervene in the processes of weapons development and procurement.[55] More interesting, however, in the light of the equally clear weaknesses of this approach, is to ask whether in the complex circumstances of modern foreign policy-making, the dog can be sensibly considered separately from its by now extremely bushy tail. The American use of the term 'official' to cover both politicians and bureaucrats is revealing, placing both sets of people in the category of accountable public servants, and with the implication that it is naïve to look upon professional administrators as being in some sense apolitical. Nor is this any longer a phenomenon peculiar to the United States. The past two British governments have tended to look sceptically on the notion of neutral advice from their top civil servants, and some personnel changes have been made accordingly. The Mandela government in South Africa was understandably keen to get blacks into senior positions in the Department of Foreign Affairs and other ministries, at the same time as it acknowledges the importance of not alienating the existing white cadres.

The ideal-type, whereby bureaucrats provide the 'permanent government' for transient politicians, while at the same time leaving policy-*making* to the people's legitimate representatives, has by no means disappeared, and indeed there are strong normative reasons for aspiring to it. Still, it is idle to pretend that bureaucrats do not also make policy, and that their discretionary powers over, and impact on, the vital implementation phase of policy are not considerable.[56] The whole thrust of the reaction against dry public administration studies in the 1960s was to frame the 'policy-making process' as an integrated whole. In the context of foreign policy, Roger Hilsman, the archetypal scholar-practitioner, formulated a concentric circles model which accepts that there are different kinds of 'power centres' in the policy process, sometimes competing but also overlapping and engaged in a continuous search for consensus based on shared values. In this process some, both politicians and officials, will be closer to the centre of final decision than others, who orbit the inner group in varying degrees of proximity.[57]

As Hilsman pointed out, 'policy-making *is* politics', and the bureaucrats responsible for high level foreign policy decisions are political animals whether they recognize the fact or not. They are a key element of the elite which runs foreign policy, albeit with ever increasing pressures from the domestic society they represent but are not closely in touch with. Divisions of view and interest within the elite are of central importance, but they must not be mistaken for the more profound forms of politics which arise from the clashes between differing value-systems and sets of social interests. The range and depth of these differences almost always goes well beyond those apparent within the foreign policy elite, whether between bureaucrats and politicians or (more likely) between different departments, including both levels of action. From this point of view the dog and its tail wag in reasonable harmony. Different animals will snap at each other from time to time, but the real problem is the ability of the pack as a whole to take all the juiciest bones for itself. As we shall see in Part III, those excluded from the inner circle still find it difficult to share in the process of setting directions in foreign policy, despite the often grievous consequences for themselves. In terms of causation both politicians and officials contribute to foreign policy agency, but in terms of democracy, they count only intermittently and ambiguously as agents of the people.

5

Rationality in Foreign Policy

Rationality is one of the most central and difficult problems in all social science, and it figured prominently in the study of politics during the twentieth century. Any attempt to understand or prescribe action cannot but make some reckoning with the concept, since it has come to represent an ideal-type for both individual and collective decision-making. Indeed, the very idea of making 'decisions' and 'policies' seems to be a modern notion indelibly associated with the attempt to exert rational control over events – as opposed to allowing destiny, God's will, chance or arbitrary (mere) power to determine one's lot. This said, it immediately becomes controversial as to how far human beings are capable of behaving rationally, how rationality is defined in the first place, and whether what we deem rational behaviour is in any case so desirable. These and other doubts have produced raging debates between, *inter alia*, the profession of economics, where the idea of rationality has undoubtedly been of central importance, and other social scientists, for many of whom the concept looks like a straitjacket imposed on the rich diversity of human motives and interactions, and one which assumes a greater degree of calculation (often quantitative) in the business of choosing futures than is either possible or desirable. At the present time this debate has extended into political science, where rational choice approaches, having made considerable inroads, are encountering stiff resistance from those allergic to the idea that politics is best explained in terms of the interactions between egoistic individuals continually assessing the degree to which their preferences will be served by a given outcome – in short, through game theory and its variants.[1]

Rationality in Policy-making

In the subject of International Relations the same issues are at stake, but there are also some very particular complications.[2] In the first place, the 'rational actor model', described by Graham Allison as the counterpoint to his bureaucratic politics approach, is too often blurred with realism, the historically dominant way of thinking about foreign policy. In fact the two are logically distinct: realism privileges national security as the criterion for state decision-makers, whereas the 'rational actor' refers principally to the idea of the state as unitary decision-maker – what kinds of criteria the unitary actor employs in foreign policy are left open. Conversely, many would challenge the idea that realism operates by rational processes. In the second place, 'rationalism' is well known in IR as one label for the principal alternative to realism as an explanation of international politics. Often termed 'Grotianism', and sometimes 'liberalism', it suggests that states often prefer cooperation to conflict and that in fact they have already constructed 'a society of states'.[3] This too is simply a different matter from employing the idea of rationality to explain decision procedures. Lastly, where rational choice assumptions have made progress in IR, as they have through neo-realism and neo-liberal institutionalism, they have run into not just the predictable opposition from traditionalists and historicists, but a rather specific group of opponents, usually labelled 'constructivists', who argue that interests, preferences and values cannot be taken as given.[4] They vary widely and are shaped by a range of personal, intra-state and international factors. Indeed, the main aim of foreign policy analysis from this viewpoint is to probe 'the deeper questions of the formation of identities and the structural forces at the domestic level'.[5] There is an element of US–European difference in this rationalist–constructivist tension, but again, it tells us little about whether foreign policy-making might or might not be a rational process. Together with the other distinctions in this paragraph, it is outlined so as to clear the ground of the principal confusions which habitually attend the discussion of rationality and foreign policy.

After ground-clearing but before substance comes definition. In this case, however, definitions cannot be separated out from the discussion of policy practice, given the wide scope of problems and possibilities which the term rationality invokes. In what follows, four fundamental tensions will be sketched out – between procedure and substance, the individual and the collective, efficiency and democracy, normative and positive – before the bulk of the chapter is devoted to a more concrete assessment of what rationality means in the context of foreign policy, with special reference to the range of constraints on rationality which have by now been extensively explored in the specialist literature. Although by the end of this discussion it may well seem that any clear-sighted thinking in foreign policy is likely to occur more by accident than by design, the fundamental aim is to show how responsible agency is still possible despite the major obstacles of a complex, uncertain and intensely political environment.

Procedure vs Substance

It was Herbert Simon who first made the formal distinction between procedural and substantive rationality, although it had been present in the writings of Max Weber and implicit in those of Adam Smith and J.S. Mill.[6] It can also be formulated as a distinction between process and outcome rationality.[7] Procedural rationality occurs when an actor engages in a systematic process, including reasoning, to enable him or her to achieve the goals which are already in mind. The focus here is on identifying the best means by which any given value may be optimized – or, more realistically, on avoiding those ways of behaving which seem likely to be counterproductive. Substantive rationality, by contrast, tells us what is the 'correct' outcome, given specified goals. One might argue, for example, that the 'only' rational path forward for Russia in its desperate economic condition of 1998 was to throw itself on the mercy of the International Monetary Fund – other strategies might have been possible, but they would have been 'irrational', just as Czechoslovakia could have resisted Hitler in October 1938 despite the loss of Anglo-French support at Munich, but it would hardly have been rational so to do. The trouble with this kind of proposition is that it is barely distinguishable from a normative statement. Most observers would argue, more modestly, that there is a link between procedural and substantive rationality, in that the former is a necessary but not sufficient condition of achieving the latter, and that an 'action rationality' is necessary to make the connection; that is, proper information gathering and decisional procedures still have to be translated into action before a satisfactory outcome can be achieved.[8] Much of foreign policy analysis is confused because these basic distinctions are elided. An outcome might seem rational but have been fortuitously reached by a non-rational route; procedures might be meticulously rational but still of no use because the view taken of the adversary was fundamentally

not so clean-cut!

flawed. US policy-makers in the late 1960s could simply not understand why they were losing the Vietnam War, when the latest techniques of policy analysis were being used (not to mention an avalanche of weaponry).[9]

The Individual vs the Collective

The issue here is where to pitch rationality; is the unit whose behaviour is under the microscope the individual, or the group? If the latter, which group? Inevitably the answer is that rationality starts with the individual, because the latter is the ultimate source of intentional behaviour, but has to extend to the group, from where the problem becomes that of levels of analysis.[10] In this respect rationality epitomizes the general problem of agency and foreign policy: who is/are the agents producing the decisions and actions? All individuals involved, politicians and bureaucrats, have to be assumed to be facing the dilemma of how to act rationally, in terms of both personal interests and their professional responsibility (roles and reasons). Their pursuit of purely personal interests is only likely to matter for our purposes, however, where they enjoy such seniority as to be able to exercise discretion and have an impact on policy. More significant is the problem of collective rationality. Can a decision-making group, let alone a state or other entity, make calculations, whether rational or otherwise? The point of this chapter is to suggest some answers to this question, but for now it is enough to point out that the field of foreign policy analysis has grown up on the back of research which has blown holes in the notion of policy being made by a unitary collective actor. Theories of bureaucratic politics, of domestic politics and of competing perceptions have all suggested that it is very difficult for a state to aggregate the myriad preferences of the human beings who constitute its 'agency' into a single, consistently pursued set of preferences.[11] Moreover, the inherent problems of any collective action are magnified in international relations by the multiple levels of coordination and decision involved – domestic, national, intra-governmental, regional, international and transnational. If the firm is a collective not always in harmony with the interests of its employees, at least its goals are relatively limited: profit, growth, cohesiveness, and so on. For foreign policy-makers the goals are multiple, complex, and subject to many different opinions on the part of the many participants in the decision-making process. To understand the place of rationality in this context is a challenge indeed.[12]

FPA -
anti-
rationalist

{levels?}

[collective rationality →   :)
decision-making   ]   ;)
group.

Efficiency vs Democracy

In a modern constitutional state there is always a tension between the requirements of efficiency and those of democracy. Sometimes the very security of the state, sometimes merely its established policies, can be perceived as under threat if the people's will is done, or merely if the time is taken to consult them. This was Franklin D. Roosevelt's reasoning as he took every step possible to help a beleaguered United Kingdom in 1940, despite Congressional opposition.[13] Efficiency, in the sense of the ability to achieve one's aims, is closely related to rationality in that most people would regard procedural rationality – or the ability to relate ends intelligently to means – as a precondition of efficiency. Democracy, however, provides a separate set of values which cannot be gainsaid. Clearly the rational pursuit of efficiency could be compromised by the need to follow democratic values; at the least there would be opportunity costs involved. It is indeed a well-established line in writing about international relations that democratic states have one hand tied behind their back when dealing with autocratic states and should make a conscious effort to avoid disunity. Conversely some have argued that democratic debates make for a stronger and more resilient foreign policy in the long run.[14] Probably we should be better off by *including* the need for democratic legitimacy in our definitions of efficiency and rationality in the first place. That is, policy will only be effective if it is seen to serve the general ends of the people as a whole and if it attracts their support. Equally, a policy which does not take into account (in a democratic society for sure, but arguably in any) the factor of legitimacy can hardly be deemed rational, in either the procedural or the substantive sense. This is broadly the position of the present book, although as we shall see, the phrase 'taking into account' begs a great many questions.

Normative vs Positive

We have already seen that substantive rationality is barely distinguishable from a debate over values, and it cannot be denied that the very notion of rationality carries within it a particular, contestable view of the world. To the extent that this view derives from modernity, few are able to opt out of it, but in its emphasis on flexible choices between options which can be ranked in terms of how far they 'optimize' preferences, it is certainly quite alien to societies such as Japan or Egypt, with their very different religious and historical frameworks.[15] This is not to imply that the West has a monopoly on rational behaviour; simply that its procedural rationality is not the universal and self-evident good it sometimes seems. Even in the West there is room for a good deal of legitimate disagreement about how much rational procedure might be desirable in decision-making, and as to how big a risk might be run by neglecting the dicta of rationality. Many – as we shall see below – would regard excessive attachment to information gathering and the weighing of alternatives as counterproductive, and would prefer to rely on assets such as intuition, leadership or 'pragmatism'. At the extreme there might also be occasions when decision-makers wish to employ the 'rationality of irrationality', or convincing an adversary that one is irrational in order to deter them from pressing their case.[16]

One advantage of the idea of rationality is that while few these days pretend that it is adequate as a description of how decisions actually get made, it provides a clear and attractive vision of how they should be made, especially in procedural terms. The 'is' and the 'ought' are clearly separated out, so that if the 'ought' does not appeal it can be clearly rejected or amended. This is not the case with some of the models which have been proposed as an improvement on classical rationality. In giving us better pictures of what happens in real-world decision-making, they blur the distinction between description and their own prescriptions, and do indeed sometimes smuggle in the latter unacknowledged. Let us then turn to the main ways in which the limits on rationality have been interpreted, with particular reference to foreign policy.

Bounded Rationality

The huge problems of uncertainty, information overload and complexity which confront any public policy-maker make it almost impossible to live up to the ideal of rational method, with its clear subordination of means to ends, its stress on a comprehensive analysis of options, and its assumption of what Simon has called 'a preposterous omniscience'.[17] What is more, it takes only a short acquaintance with actual patterns of behaviour to understand that something well short of classical rationality obtains in practice, at both individual and collective levels. We have already observed this with respect to certain bureaucratic pathologies, but it is evident to all those close to the practice of politics that policy-making is predominantly an empirical, pragmatic business in which planning and sustained control of programmes are at a premium.[18]

In foreign policy in particular there is a conscious tradition of avoiding excessive abstraction and attempts at structural change, given the evident difficulty even for hegemons of reshaping entire systems, whether regional or global. Thus the famous metaphor of statesmen as canoeists, following the flow and avoiding the rocks rather than having the existential capacity to set their own direction.[19]

Practical observations and metaphors have been given formal, theoretical shape over the past half-century through various scholars working in the area of administrative studies, first among them Herbert Simon and Charles Lindblom. The former's notion of 'bounded rationality' and the latter's concept of 'muddling through' have now become part of the established vocabulary, not just of academic students of public affairs but even of the more sophisticated practitioners. What is their utility for the contemporary study of foreign policy?

The idea of bounded rationality refers essentially to the futility of trying to 'maximize' one's values. Instead, it is preferable to 'satisfice', or accept the first outcome which approximates to one's preferences. This, in the language of the psychotherapist Bruno Bettelheim, is being a 'good enough' politician (or parent) rather than striving for perfection, which will incur huge costs and in any case be unattainable.[20] We do not know enough about consequences, and we cannot imagine all possible options well enough to optimize, even if there were the time and political space to do so. As Robert Keohane has pointed out, this fits well with the need in politics, but particularly in international politics, to compromise and to agree working 'regimes' through which various issue-areas can be managed and expectations stabilized.[21] Just as with the necessary SOPs of domestic bureaucracies, regimes discourage policy-makers from thinking of their agenda as a *tabula rasa*, on which level surface they might be able to construct great monuments to their own memory. The temptation is always great, as we have seen with the diverse hopes of Woodrow Wilson, Hitler and George Bush Snr, but most are less ambitious and accept the need to pursue rationality within the limits of existing assumptions and institutions. In fact we have little choice other than to go for 'acceptable' levels of, say, security rather than 'complete security'.

Satisficing, however, only takes us so far down the road of how to make policy in an uncertain, intractable environment (which is not a bad definition of international relations). In order to cope with this process over time and change, just as the canoeist has to, many would have recourse to the idea of 'muddling through', or more formally, *disjointed incrementalism*.[22] By this is meant not just changing policy only by small steps, avoiding revolutionary transformations, which has been the traditional gradualist philosophy of English politics since 1689, articulated best by Edmund Burke.[23] It also involves, *inter alia*, restricting the number of alternatives to be considered, using the methods of trial and error, accepting that ends and means are difficult to distinguish, concentrating on fixing problems rather than constructing 'positive goals' and, not least, ensuring that a consensus is reached between the many, disjointed points of consultation that exist in modern democracies. If agreement can be reached, the theory holds, the option chosen must be the best in the circumstances, on the grounds that (i) two minds are better than one; (ii) it will be possible to carry the policy through.

The attractions of this approach, as both description and prescription, are easy to see. There is, however, at least one significant objection to the theory of disjointed incrementalism, and it is one which brings us back to the understanding of rationality, in all its variants, as an essentially contested concept. Lindblom, for example, clearly recommends muddling through as the preferred 'strategy' in policy-making, although one might think this comes close to being an oxymoron. The same is true of satisficing, which Simon represents as a much more realistic, useable notion than that epitomized by 'economic man'.[24] Yet both these models have the capacity to mislead by their very realism. Accepting the virtues of muddling through, for example, can legitimize an unwillingness to ask fundamental questions, and to criticize the general direction of policy.[25] Arms races are incremental, by definition, once they have begun, but few would pretend that they are a sensible way of proceeding. The British stumbled along with an over-valued pound for nearly twenty-five years after the Second World War, without daring to do more than adjust economic policy marginally within a harmful stop–go cycle. When the inevitable crisis came, it had serious ramifications for defence policy as well as for sterling.[26] Similarly, the satisficing approach in foreign policy can, if ill-judged, produce fiascoes like the US invasion of Cuba at the Bay of Pigs in 1961, when the new President Kennedy did not subject the line of least resistance placed before him by advisers to a sufficiently strong scrutiny.

An awareness of these problems has led some critics, including Lindblom himself, to suggest that a middle way be found between the classical and the bounded versions of rationality. The possibility will be considered in the last section of this chapter. But it should also be noted that incrementalism carries with it the opposite danger, of making possible radical change by stealth, out of the visual range of democratic institutions. This will by necessity be a slow process, but because it is broken down into small parcels, the full import of the cumulative change will not be apparent until it is too late. It is not even necessary for there to be an author, with a conspiracy or a grand narrative to follow; certain interests can simply nudge policy along in a direction which perhaps even they do not wholly understand at first. In foreign policy the prime example of this is the development of the European Communities (EC). Although Jean Monnet most unusually combined a highly strategic vision with a pragmatic subtle and gradualist method, never forcing the pace when that might have been counterproductive, most of his successors have usually just denied any move towards federalism while seizing any opportunity to push things marginally in that direction, under the cover of particular practical improvements. In this they have been helped by the prevalent ideology in the EC of neo-functionalism and graduated integration. Accordingly even their fiercest opponent, Margaret Thatcher, found herself supporting the Single European Act (SEA) for its initiation of the Single Market, when the SEA also introduced various institutional changes which ratcheted on the integration process towards the eventual Treaties of Maastricht and Amsterdam, which she found anathema.

Other examples of what might be termed 'deceptive incrementalism' are the creation of Bizonia in post-war Germany and the consequent onset of the Cold War, and the imperceptible start of the US commitment to South Vietnam between 1961–5, by the sending of first advisers, then air support and finally ground troops. This is how undeclared wars come to pass. Just as undesirable, however, might be the less dramatic but more common tendencies towards drift and snowballing, both of which are forms of incrementalism. The first is typified by the apparent inability of the rich states to get hold of the problem of Third World debt, even though the arguments for the status quo are generally accepted to be threadbare. The latter can be seen in the steady move of Japan towards the status of a well-armed state, despite the limits imposed on its defence expenditure by the 1946 Constitution. No one now believes that Japan keeps within the 1 per cent of GNP limit used from 1976–87, but it would be a mistake to believe that successive governments in Tokyo set out deliberately to transform the situation. Their commitments, looked on benignly by the United States, have just steadily drifted upwards, compounding each other.[27]

There is one more important aspect of the theory of bounded rationality to explore, and this too raises the is/ought dilemma. John Steinbruner's theory of cybernetic decision-making has provided acute insights into the way the mind and organizations work, and in the context of foreign policy.[28] Building on the work of other cognitive analysts before him, Steinbruner argued that the human mind cannot cope with the mass of information which flows towards it and thus develops repertoires for monitoring a very limited number of variables, indeed often only one major variable. Nor are abstract calculations made about this factor; rather, ends and means are blurred together and adjustments made on a semi-automatic basis. A good example is the way the brain adjusts to the roll of a boat at sea, so that when we step onto dry land, we feel unsteady until the next readjustment takes place. Similarly, if a tennis player consciously thinks about how to volley when at the net, the likelihood of success is diminished. In collective policy-making, the theory brings us back to organizational process, as when one armed service monitors its own well-being rather than security as a whole, but also alerts us to the fact that allowing those closest to events to make their own, parochial adjustments, may be the only way to get anything done, as with the Berlin airlift of 1948, when the USAF and RAF found ways to achieve what some of their political masters thought both dangerous and impossible.[29]

The difficulty with the cybernetic approach is that it is highly convincing as an account of how the individual mind copes with information overload, but rather less convincing on collective operations. What is more, although there is an implicit seal of approval given to the approach as an alternative for the inadequate 'analytical' (rational) method, it is difficult to find examples of the cybernetic process which are not negative. There have been plenty of foul-ups in history because decision-makers have been one-eyed, as with US Army intelligence being preoccupied with internal sabotage before Pearl Harbor, or the Soviet elite over decades paying too much attention to the texts of Marx and Lenin, but it is more difficult to find successes.[30] Perhaps Churchill's wilful insistence on rearmament in the 1930s, or Konrad Adenauer's determination to locate West Germany within the western alliance, count. But even they were strong individuals, not complex organizations.

Although rational foreign policy-making is certainly bounded by the problems of information-processing, this does not mean that the cybernetic, or the incremental, approaches are the inevitable or desirable replacements. There is a considerable difference between demonstrating that the rational approach to policy is deeply flawed, and proposing a working alternative, particularly when little care is taken to distinguish the descriptive from the prescriptive elements in the theory. We shall return to this problem, but for the moment we can move on to areas of research which are primarily concerned to enlarge our understanding of foreign policy-making, and which leave the improvement of practice to others.

Non-decisions in Foreign Policy

The concept of non-decisions is familiar in political science but little has been done to transplant it to International Relations.[31] This is a mistake as the three possible meanings of the term all have considerable resonance for foreign policy behaviour. Firstly, a non-decision is simply a decision *not to act,* to do nothing, despite considerable temptation, and possibly both the need and pressure to act. An example might be the Arab countries' decisions not to make Israel's invasion of the Lebanon in June 1982 a *casus belli* (although there were long-term responses in other ways, as through international terrorism). Saddam Hussein, conversely, might have been better advised in 1980 to take Anwar Sadat's advice 'not to make war on a revolution'.[32] The failure to make a non-decision, and the inability to resist exploiting Iran's weakness after its revolution led to the devastating consequences for both sides of the war of 1980–8. Secondly, there is *decision avoidance, or the failure to act.* This is associated at the extreme with the paralysis of the decision-making system, as during Richard Nixon's Watergate period, but a more usual (and important) example would be the perpetual inability of countries to formulate clear war aims, either in the approach to conflict or during its evolution. This can be deliberate, in order to increase margin for manoeuvre, but more often it is simply the result of policy drift.[33] Third, and perhaps the most significant theoretical development, given its implicit critique of the pluralism dominant in policy studies, is the idea that *certain options are excluded* from the agenda, at times by sleight of hand but more effectively by what Schattschneider called 'the mobilization of bias. Some issues are organized into politics while others are organized out'.[34] Another way of looking at this is to see it as 'the weight of the existing order of things', which raises profound questions in history and political science, such as why the colonialist countries would not consider the possibility of withdrawal from empire before the Second World War, and why any government in France and Britain even today would find it almost impossible to dismantle their respective nuclear deterrents.

Everything does come to an end, eventually, and it is a fascinating process to observe the 'unthinkable' finally becoming thinkable, often with the more dramatic consequences because the wall of prejudice against change had been erected so high in the first place. This is most clearly true in recent times of the revolution wrought by Gorbachev in Soviet foreign policy, but other examples would be the crumbling of apartheid in South Africa, and the sudden switch of American policy towards China in 1971, after two decades of structural inhibition. The power to ignore is one of the most important of political weapons, but it can rebound decisively in the long term. It should not be forgotten that the apparently conservative attachment to gradual change of Burke, and in our own day Michael Oakeshott, always included an injunction to anticipate events by intelligent adaptation, so as to avoid the eventual need for revolution. Policy analysis should never neglect the importance of time: some historical periods are more open for change, of a general or particular kind, than others. Some policies seem rational at one time, irrational at another. Which is to say, firstly, that rationality is contingent, not just on place and culture, but also on period, and secondly, that history seems to provide certain openings in which major restructuring may be attempted, or at least begun, before events once again begin to congeal into stable patterns. 1945–8, and 1988 onwards, may have been such windows.

The idea of non-decisions has considerable applicability in foreign policy analysis because it takes us beyond mere process to the political and social structures beneath, from which power, in its domestic but also possibly transnational forms, derives. More precisely, it enables us to link process to certain key structures, in the way that another neglected theory, that of elites, also does, but with more purchase on the ideas and on policy itself than elite theory, which tended to concentrate on the identity of those who monopolize office, largely in their own self-interest.[35] When certain ideas are excluded from the policy agenda, or when certain attempts at change are systematically blocked, we need to ask not just the questions 'how?' and 'with what consequences?' but also 'why, and by whom?' It may be that there will be no clear answers to such questions, and more than probable that there will be no conspiracy to uncover, but the serious ramifications of foreign policy decisions make it imperative that we probe beneath the surface of current affairs and at least try to identify the structures that might be shaping agency. The concept of non-decisions is a very useful point of entry.

The Psychological Factor

A major limit on pure rationality, albeit one which has to be located within the kind of historical and social contexts we have just been referring to, is the psychology of decision-making. This has been explored extensively in the context of foreign policy, unlike some of the concepts discussed above, at the level of both individual leader and the group.[36] Most of the attention has been directed towards the *cognitive* aspects of the human mind, that is the intellectual functions, as opposed to the *affective* aspects, or the emotional roots of behaviour. In part this has been the reaction of academic psychologists, as well as political and organizational scientists, to the overwhelming influence of Freud and the notion of the dominant unconscious in the first half of the twentieth century. The work which Simon, Lindblom and Steinbruner drew on dealt largely with the less dramatic but arguably more important subject of information-processing. Nonetheless, the wheel has turned again, and as we shall see below, the emotional aspects of group solidarity and social identity are now well to the fore. The strength of the psychological approach to foreign policy-making is in fact that it fruitfully combines insights into both cognitive and affective processes.

Predating the emergence of foreign policy analysis, and to some extent continuing in parallel with it, has been work which arose from the age of the masses and in particular from the spectre of totalitarianism. The first is of only indirect relevance here, dealing as it does with the psychology of crowd behaviour and such mass hysteria as was evinced in *la grande peur* (of the Revolution, in rural France) in 1791.[37] Given some of the scenes in post-revolutionary Iran, or in the genocide and refugee crises of the African Great Lakes zone in the 1990s, to say nothing of the Nuremberg rallies, it would be imprudent to neglect this dimension of international relations. More central to the understanding of foreign policy action is Adorno's theory of the authoritarian personality.[38] This idea has generated considerable controversy, but some central propositions remain, viz., that certain personalities display symptoms of personal and intellectual rigidity which simultaneously advance them to positions of political power and damage their performance in power. They tend to be hierarchical (that is, dominant, but also uncritical of those above them), ethnocentric and unable to cope with ambiguity and non-conformity.[39] At its extreme this can produce the pure paranoia of Stalin's and Saddam's purges, but even in a more muted form it is likely to distort the decision-making process, as with Margaret Thatcher's impatience with dissent in Cabinet or Lee Kuan Yew's determination to control every aspect of life in Singapore.

A good many 'psychobiographies' have been produced on the lives of key statesmen and women, but relatively few have attempted the serious task of trying to place personality in the context of the process of political

cognitive → intellectual functions
v. affective (emotional)

causation, weighing up the respective impact of individual and contextual factors. One successful attempt was that by Alexander and Juliette George on the life of Woodrow Wilson, whose particular form of self-righteousness was rooted in his experiences with a caustic father and, later, as professor and then President at Princeton University. Wilson's character and idealism turned out to be of particular significance given the 'window' for change represented by the allied victory of 1918 and the subsequent peace.[40] Other attempts – of variable success – have been made to explain the lives of Luther, Hitler, Lyndon Johnson and Margaret Thatcher.[41] In any case the key issue is less the peculiarities of a leader's personality than the political space which might or might not exist to allow these qualities to impact on events. In this respect Fred Greenstein has produced an indispensable analysis of how, in particular, an individual personality has more scope for impact on events in less stable regimes, and/or in more fluid circumstances than normal.[42]

Personality and context can sometimes be usefully connected by using the concept of charisma, formulated by Max Weber to refer to the magical, semi-religious appeal that some leaders can have, in the first place to their own followers, but sometimes, as with Nelson Mandela, much more widely. The leader requires first of all qualities of brilliance, strength, and emotional insight, and then circumstances in which there is some kind of political or emotional vacuum to be filled in mass politics. Henry Kissinger rather disparagingly referred to charisma as an instrument of primitive, Third World polities (perhaps because he did not possess it himself), and at times it is difficult to distinguish from the characteristics of a mere icon, like Che Guevara. Margaret Thatcher, like Gorbachev, was charismatic internationally but not domestically, while John Kennedy's charisma was immeasurably enhanced by his violent death. Nasser and the Ayatollah Khomeini were compelling figures to their own people but somewhat perplexing elsewhere. It is clearly not necessary to have charisma to be an effective leader, let alone in foreign policy, but equally its possession sometimes bestows advantages. De Gaulle, Sadat, Willy Brandt of West Germany and Felipe Gonzalez of Spain would all have been far less influential world-wide, and perhaps have retained power less easily at home, if they had come across in public like some of their greyer colleagues – for example, Mubarak or Kiesinger – or if circumstances had not made them seem something like Hegel's 'world historical individuals'. Of course the use of charisma also risks high costs. When politicians let loose the power of mass emotion, they run the risk of believing their own propaganda, subordinating rationality and alarming outsiders. Colonel Gaddafi and

PUTIN

plays on
this!

world historical individuals

Ariel Sharon are examples from our own time. Peace, security and prosperity usually require less glamorous and more concrete methods.

One of the richest areas of scholarship of foreign policy decision-making has been that relating to perception and misperception. There is not the space here to do justice to all the subtleties of the extensive literature, but certain key points must be made in order to clarify further the limits on rationality and ultimately to advance the argument about the nature of agency in foreign policy.

There is at base with any discussion of perception a set of contentious philosophical issues relating to the way we apprehend the world and the extent to which our subjective understandings of it vary. There is a common view, attributable to R.G. Collingwood and in the present context to Charles Reynolds, which holds that it is not possible to make legitimate statements about human behaviour except through a reconstruction of the views of the relevant individuals themselves: that is, in most cases, through historical enquiry.[43] This is not at all incompatible with foreign policy analysis in principle, but it would rule out the kind of positivist approach taken by much of the American literature, which seeks to test 'if–then' hypotheses just as much in this area as in any other – for example, as Vertzberger concludes, 'a certain level of misperception is inevitable in every decision-making system'.[44] Most commentators fall between two stools, using the notion of misperception, which does imply a 'reality' that an actor might not perceive 'correctly', but largely as a lever to open up particular historical problems, accepting that grand generalization is only likely to lead to bland results. This is the approach taken here, on the assumption that there is a difference, however uncertain, between decision-makers' *psychological environment* (how they perceive the world) and their *operational environment* (events as they happen independent of any one person's perception).[45]

Decision-makers cannot avoid having *images* of others which will be as affected by their own cultural and political baggage as much as by the objective evidence. Images are clusters of perceptions which make us make sense of the world. Once established, they change relatively slowly, as with the two super-powers' images of each other during the Cold War. If an actor has no choice but to change an image overnight, it can be personally and politically catastrophic. After Neville Chamberlain was forced to acknowledge in September 1939 that his image of Hitler had been too benign, he fell from office within nine months, and died of cancer within the year. When the German invasion of 22 June 1941 forced Stalin to recognize that the Nazi–Soviet Pact had been a sham, he was paralysed with shock for three days.

All too often, images harden into *stereotypes*, losing the capacity to evolve and becoming ever more remote from the evidence. Lyndon Johnson held quasi-racist views of the North Vietnamese for which he and his soldiers were to pay dearly. The images held of continental Europeans by some British politicians have verged on the comic over the years, and any bilateral conflict will produce symmetrical prejudices that are very difficult to dislodge. Stereotypes are brittle, inflexible simplifications, and any decision-making system of the slightest sophistication will have built-in mechanisms to challenge them. But if the politics of a country is built on 'othering', or finding its own identity in contradistinction to a feared and hated outsider(s), then stereotypes will persist and compound the existing problems.

Misperceptions may be regarded as the most common form of psychological pathology affecting decision-making. Common as garden weeds, they can either be trivial or of the highest significance, depending on the context and the system's capacity for auto-correction. The passage of time means that not all misperceptions are subject to test, given changing conditions and natural loss of impetus. Those which involve explicit predictions, however, can be exposed as incorrect, just as the domino theory, which predicted the fall of all South East Asia to communism should South Vietnam go down, was falsified by events.

The statement that 'decisions are taken in the psychological environment but implemented in the operational environment' may seem banal, but it is an important insight. Decision-makers have no choice but to take continual bets on how other actors will behave and events unfold. By committing themselves to 'actions', that is, making commitments in the external environment, they find out the fate of their bets and the accuracy of their assessments. The external, operational environment provides relentless feedback. Misperceptions are then discovered to have been of various kinds: of intentions, where it is easy to exaggerate both enmity and alliance, and of capabilities, where an adversary tends to be excessively feared in peacetime and underestimated in time of war; of both friends and enemies; of those well-known and those far away. Action always teeters on the edge of incompetence because of the uncertain nature of the underlying perceptions. For example, the favourable judgements which the West made about Boris Yeltsin and, most crucially, his impact inside Russia, risked severe consequences for both Russia and international order.

Misperceptions can arise from various sorts of problem, affective, cognitive and organizational, and usually a combination of all three. A small number of examples will be given here by way of illustration.[46]

At the affective level, decision-makers almost inevitably display the human tendency to intermittent bias, whether for or against another actor or country. Personal relationships develop – 'sentimental alliances' – that while initially advantageous, can prove obstacles if policy tensions arise.[47] Thatcher and Reagan, Kohl and Mitterrand are the clearest contemporary cases. Conversely, some negative views prove almost impossible to shift, as with a whole generation of Israeli leaders against Yasser Arafat.

Another primarily emotional predisposition is the common tendency to over-emphasize self, so that understanding an adversary proves difficult. This can fall well short of full-blooded narcissism (also not uncommon in powerful leaders) and still do damage to foreign relations. As Robert Kennedy pointed out in the aftermath of the Cuban Missile Crisis, the failure to put oneself in the other side's shoes (empathy) is potentially the most fatal of errors. It will prove difficult to predict or understand their responses, and will mean that you are not capable of giving them ways of saving face in the event of a climb-down.[48] It is all too common to assume that others operate on the same assumptions as oneself – or if not, that they are hostile barbarians, beyond the pale. Nationalism produces this last effect, frequently. One way in which decision-makers try to cope with what is effectively cultural diversity as well as psychological narrowness is to assume universal rationality, and/or realism. If, as it has been said, we are all 'pretty rational', then this may be a good, working principle. If not, it can come spectacularly unstuck, as over Saddam Hussein.[49]

One of the sources of misperception which is both affective and cognitive is tracked thinking, or tunnel vision. This is the difficulty human beings often have in relinquishing a view, or an assumption, once taken up. This is partly because we become emotionally attached to 'our' way of seeing things but also because when a pattern appears in information flows or the behaviour of other people, the human mind grasps at it as a way of reducing uncertainty and providing predictability. This will be reinforced by various organizational SOPs. Thus, when the British diplomatic and intelligence services received warnings about an Argentine attack on the Falkland Islands in March 1982, they did not take them seriously until too late because so many similar warnings had proved barren in the past.[50] Tracked thinking almost by definition prevents creative initiatives. If only the Indonesian elite could have relaxed their assumptions about East Timor being crucial to the security of their state they would have been able to move forward more rapidly on finding a solution to the insurgency in the ex-Portuguese colony.

A similar syndrome is the search for consistency that we all engage in. People feel uncomfortable with contradictions in their outlook and generally try to resolve them – often at the expense of understanding subtlety and complexity. When new information arrives which is at odds with existing views, it causes stress, famously labelled by Leon Festinger 'cognitive dissonance'.[51] This term was used in the House of Commons by Denis Healey in order to characterize Margaret Thatcher as being in need of psychiatric assistance.[52] More scientifically, we can say that this is a normal part of information-processing, and that when it occurs there are three possible responses: ignore the new data and continue with existing beliefs; rationalize the data so that it is incorporated into existing beliefs; adapt the beliefs to take the new data into account. The path taken will depend on the individual and the extent to which the decision-making system is open or closed with regard to new developments. Robert Axelrod has shown that decision-makers operate on the basis of 'cognitive maps' which are not easy to change, and Janis and Mann have stressed the way in which both individuals and systems are 'vigilant' in heading off uncomfortable insights.[53] There is an affective component as well in that decision-makers also display a peace of mind imperative, because the alternatives are often too alarming for their whole belief system.[54] This is why Soviet leaders saw Alexander Dubček's 'Prague Spring' of 1968 as a reactionary plot rather than as a necessary reform to avert crisis in the communist system.

A final source of misperception is the drive for cognitive economy, or simplicity. This is what Steinbruner has called the 'universal tendency to generalize'.[55] Intellectually the desire for manageability is in conflict with the drive to understand complexity, but in a political environment the former is powerfully reinforced at the expense of the latter.[56] Too much detail, or expertise, kills understanding in an over-burdened decision-maker and leads to an hostility to the 'academic' approach. Thus Churchill demanded, even of his high-powered scientific adviser Lord Cherwell, 'action this day' and conclusions on one side of a sheet of paper only.[57] There is also a tendency, which can be seen at work in some of the other sources of misperception cited, for an economy of values, that is, avoiding having to reconcile too many criteria at once, leading to unmanageable trade-offs in one's own mind and across the decisional system. This is probably the origin of the persistent preference for presidential 'doctrines' in US foreign policy from the Truman Doctrine on, although since the same tendency is not evident in most other countries one would have to say that a cultural factor and/or an imitative process is at work here.[58]

When we come to the collective psychology of foreign policy decision-making, we arrive first at the theory of *groupthink*. This concept, introduced by Irving Janis in 1972, represents a major qualification of the theory of rational decision.[59] Although, following Lindblom, we might wish to argue that whatever consensus a decision-making group can reach is in and of itself rational, the 'fiascoes' which Janis analyses suggest that the outcomes produced by groupthink are almost always suboptimal. This is because he shows how consensus is often reached, not by the free discussion of a range of options (that is, close to rationality) but by a mix of fear, hierarchy, conformism and ignorance. Groupthink essentially consists in the tendency of groups to seek rapid internal agreement even at the expense of the merits of a problem, and then to stick to their consensus even when the evidence seems to demand it. Criticisms of the orthodoxy, especially when that is associated with the group's leader, become exceptionally difficult, sometimes because there are actually some members ('mindguards') whose function is, rather like party whips in the British House of Commons, to discipline dissent – even at this level of private debate.

Janis's theory of groupthink, with its associated critical case-studies of some of the worst foul-ups in US foreign policy, has excited a good deal of comment and criticism.[60] Despite the evident facts that (i) not all groupthink causes serious problems; (ii) there are other causes of concurrence-seeking than groupthink; (iii) countervailing pressures – bureaucratic politics for one – exist to unsettle comfortable consensuses; (iv) there are other forms of small group behaviour; (v) small groups cannot be understood except in a wider institutional and political context, there is still a core of truthfulness to the approach. In particular, it is worth emphasizing that if decision-makers wish to avoid *irrationality* then they would be well advised to avoid an atmosphere of clubby back-scratching or, worse, servility in their top-level groups. A certain amount of built-in political and intellectual tension within such groups (too much will cause the opposite problems) is a necessary but not sufficient condition of effective policy-making. The siege mentality of the Johnson 'Tuesday lunch' group does seem to have made changes of direction difficult, just as the British Cabinet in March 1939 did not like to challenge the authority of prime minister and foreign secretary, despite their sudden and bizarre change of policy on Germany.[61] Participation in almost any committee or political group is enough to convince one of the utility of the groupthink insights.

The evidence synthesized above shows that foreign policy decision-making is subject to a wide range of psychological pressures, at both individual and group levels. In the face of this it is simply not possible to maintain that decisions are mostly made on the basis of classical rationality. Even bounded rationality presents severe problems, some of them normative. Expecting decision-makers to act effectively – which means in this context being able to satisfy their domestic constituency that they are being consistently influential over the country's external environment in the pursuit of security and other wider values the society may be attached to – means juggling a vast array of factors with the dexterity of Uri Geller and the wisdom of Solomon. Still, leaders do manage. They take decisions, they act and they often give the impression of managing to take a serious, reflective approach to foreign policy. How is this possible?

Sometimes the answer is luck. The British diplomat Sir Robert Vansittart suffered from a visceral distrust of Germans which made him constantly demand action against Hitler. Despite being promoted out of harm's way he was eventually proved right in his policy prescription, but for the wrong reason.[62] On the other hand, even this might have been less luck than hunch, or intuition. It would be foolish to disregard the importance of this ability – which is essentially a mixture of judgement, experience, imagination and the capacity to empathize – in foreign policy, where no amount of efficiency is going to render everything knowable. Decision-makers at times have no choice but to accept the limits on rationality and to bring other qualities into play, some of them using the emotional rather than the calculating side of the brain. Miriam Steiner has argued, in a brilliant and still unsurpassed article, that 'in a world with important nonrationalistic elements, true rationality requires that nonrationalistic capabilities and skills be appreciated and developed side by side with the rationalistic ones'.[63] Feeling and intuition are just as vital attributes of decision-makers as thinking and sense-based observation. Thus the overwhelming mass of impediments to rationality are not quite the obstacles they seem; some, indeed, cry out for a-rational, if not non-rational, techniques, and concepts like judgement, leadership, empathy and charisma always imply at the very least a combination of the intellectual and emotional sides of personality. Ultimately, both cognitive psychology and psychoanalysis have a lot to contribute to our understanding of how foreign policy decisions are and should be made.[64]

The Power of Historical Thinking

History provides politicians with a welcome form of structure amidst uncertainty, as well as a way of mobilizing public opinion behind the government. As individuals they have personal memories, as representatives of a political class they inherit certain dominant myths, rituals and pieces of conventional thinking which they use and abuse but are also themselves trapped within.

It is a common phenomenon for decision-makers to assume that there are 'lessons' to be drawn from history and indeed most human beings constantly refer to the past, so as directly or indirectly to measure their current situation against it. Historical thinking in this sense is inevitable, and not a matter of choice. Social scientists in particular spend their lives analysing history and seeking to discern patterns in it. Those who literally have no sense of the past are amnesiac and as severely disabled as it is possible to be. Despite this, International Relations scholars in recent years have been at pains to stress that there are no clear lessons to be drawn from history and that, as Hegel said, 'we learn from history that we do not learn from history'.[65] This is for a number of different reasons, some philosophical, some practical. Chief among them is the evident tendency of decision-makers to use simple historical comparisons and analogies, and then to end up in difficulty.[66] In particular the crude use by British and American leaders of the spectre of 'appeasement' has been amply documented, with anti-Soviet policies justified (and probably genuinely inspired) by a fear of repeating the mistakes of the 1930s in expecting reasonable behaviour from dictators. Similar instances, however, can be found in relation to the 'lessons' often cited of the Versailles Peace, of the Great Crash, of the Berlin airlift, of the Suez and Bay of Pigs debacles, of Vietnam and of the Rwandan genocide of 1994. And indeed it would be perverse not to draw some conclusions for the future from these and other traumatic events.

The need is to look on history not as a store cupboard of the off-the-shelf possible solutions, but as something integral to ourselves and our sense of identity in both time and space. If history is looked upon as perpetual flux, with familiar objects bobbing up regularly in the stream of change, the present becomes intimately connected to both past and future. It becomes possible to be aware of both difference and similarity without attempting to follow a particular model. Richard Neustadt and Ernest May have provided detailed and intelligent guidance for decision-makers on how to be critically aware of history without falling into the traps of simplistic analogy and teleology.[67] Even if it has to be doubted that leaders will often sit down during weekends at Camp David or Chequers to read their manual, there is a chance that its philosophy will filter down through education, staff training and generational change.

recourse to histr

Much of the time decision-makers refer to history naturally and unselfconsciously. Some of the time, however, they exploit it knowingly, to make a point in foreign relations but more often to mobilize domestic support by wrapping themselves in the national past, as it were. Pageantry, anniversaries and history teaching in schools are all grist to this mill and public opinion is a fairly passive recipient of what is a form of propaganda. Defeats and crises, victories and revolutions, imperial pride and imperial guilt all provide fertile ground for connecting current policy to the most potent symbols of national life.

In any area of public policy those responsible have to strike a balance between being too insouciant about the past and being dominated by it. It is not rational either to expect a *tabula rasa* or never to admit the possibility of change. In any case, subjective conceptions of what history does or does not mean will always have a significant bearing on what decisions get taken. Decision-makers would therefore be well-advised to distinguish between three kinds of legacy, in terms of their own freedom of choice and ability to act: those so deeply engrained, in institutions, dispositions or culture as to be virtually ineradicable by acts of policy – such as the United States' current position as first power in the world; those which are still deeply rooted but which might with a considerable effort be turned around within a political generation – British attitudes to Europe might fall into this category; and those which are either relatively recent, or superficially established, and can therefore be averted, or manipulated without too much difficulty – German embarrassment over the 1991 recognition of Croatia and Slovenia is an example here.[68] If a given problem is seen as having the wrong degree of rootedness in the past – too much or too little – problems will undoubtedly follow, as Imre Nagy tragically discovered after his challenge to the Warsaw Pact's presence in Hungary in 1956. This was not simply a matter of underestimating Soviet power; Nagy got wrong Moscow's sense that history now demanded a buffer zone against Germany. Unfortunately for Hungary, it and the other central European states were the chosen instruments of this new history.

Own Goals

Foreign policy actors pursue different goals simultaneously, with varying degrees of self-consciousness and clarity. When pressed they usually take refuge in the old notion of the national interest, which these days will not stand analytical scrutiny. They prefer to hide behind a screen of presumed unity and collective responsibility rather than dissect their own real goals, which will inevitably be partisan as well as high-minded, with some rather more feasible than others.

The idea of the national interest is inadequate as a guide to foreign policy goals primarily because it is tautologous. No policy-maker is going to declare against the interests of his or her own state (since it is states we are speaking of, not nations, '*raison d'état*' is the more accurate term) and therefore all can be assumed to be pursuing in a general sense the national interest. The real question is, paraphrasing James Rosenau, 'which interests are deemed to be national, and why?'[69] The analysis of subjective and competing versions of the national interest then leads us into the important areas of ideology, values and private interests. Indeed, in this writer's view the national interest is not something that can be usefully objectified in terms of power, security, prosperity, independence and the like, all of which can be taken for granted as the high level goals of all state foreign policy, but which lead to disagreement as soon as discussion becomes more specific. Rather, it is only of use as a measuring stick. On the one hand it enables us to judge whether a given policy is genuinely a national, or public, collective concern, or instead a private, group or sub-national goal masquerading as the former. On the other, it should help us to see whether a goal or policy is really derived from an *interest,* in the sense of a stake which a given unit has in a problem, as opposed to being a value, preference or mere aspiration. Both sets of distinctions are vital, but combining the terms 'national' and 'interest' only confuses the matter.

Decision-makers are not going to give up thinking in terms of the national interest overnight. But unless they engage in more self-analysis of their objectives they risk confusion and worse. As a British newspaper observed of the US President during the phoney period of the Gulf War,

thus far Mr Bush's reasons for going to war have criss-crossed between a bewildering variety of causes from defence of oil fields, to upholding international law, to stamping on a new Hitler, to building a new regional security system and upholding American values. The latest reason, offered by an obviously frustrated Mr. Baker [Secretary of State], is 'to save American jobs'.[70]

Even allowing for a certain amount of tactical obfuscation, this multiple reasoning betrayed a degree of policy uncertainty which made it more difficult to make the eventual decision to use force seem legitimate, particularly amongst those already hostile to the United States.

It is not an argument for excessive rationality to say that decision-makers should understand the taxonomy of foreign policy goals. If they have no sense of direction or priority they will be forced back on serendipity and chance. At the very least they should be able to differentiate their objectives along four separate continuums.

First, they should have a sense of the *time-frame* they wish to deal in. A goal such as 'rolling back communism' is something that most intelligent politicians would only consider as a long-term strategy; if it were attempted even in the middle-term it involves very high risk. China understands *re* Taiwan what General Galtieri did not over the Falklands/Malvinas, namely that urgency will be counterproductive when others' conceptions of vital interest are at stake. Conversely, an overly long-term perspective can lead to missed opportunities, as some people argue is now the case with the British government's 'wait and see' policy on the European single currency. The most difficult assessments fall into the middle-range category, that is, within the maximum period of a democratic government's life. All new policies have to start somewhere, but if a government starts down a difficult road towards a destination it has little chance of reaching, it must expect problems. The classic case in recent years is Turkey, which has kept pressing for membership of the EU without any real chance of success. This has produced angry disappointment at home, and persistent conflicts with the governments seen as responsible for a veto on Turkey. Ankara might have been better advised to have accepted that the question of entry would be kept on the back burner while extracting a high price from the EU Member-States for doing so.

The second continuum is that of *explicitness.* All actors display a difference between their declaratory and their operational goals, that is between those they claim in public and those they are really pursuing. Nor is this a matter of the contrast between open, democratic regimes and deceitful autocracies. Few foreign policies have been more transparently clear in their ultimate aim than those of Hitler or Mussolini, while Britain, France and Israel each had well-disguised hidden agendas during the Suez crisis of 1956. Governments of any colour can sometimes be unaware that their actual criteria have drifted away from those they are publicly known for. It is no surprise that Joschka Fischer, as Germany's Foreign Minister, maintains the rhetoric of his Green Party origins while pursuing policies barely distinguishable from those of his FDP predecessor.

In terms of explicitness, goals fall into three main categories which in practice are often confused: those, like the United States' world role, which are taken wholly for granted, being part of the 'habits and furniture of our minds';[71] those gently floated but without any real hope of achievement, just as the idea of unification was kept alive by the FRG during the Cold War, but in the most discreet manner; and those which are consciously pushed as major priorities – like Vietnam's determination in the late 1970s to counter Chinese influence in Cambodia. Goals may move from one level to another, but if they do so it should always be with the appropriate degree of self-consciousness and consensus. A large part of the problem that Britain has encountered over the EC in recent decades is the fact that some opinion-formers have stopped assuming that national sovereignty is an inviolable value, without taking enough voters with them. Conversely, Anwar Sadat paid the ultimate price in Egypt because he shifted his country's foreign policy objectives away from the destruction of Israel towards compromise. In doing this he could not have been clearer, but he also misjudged the extent to which such a change required advance preparation of the ground at home.

This brings us to the third continuum, that of the *values at stake*. Decision-makers, but also the citizens who criticize them, often fail to distinguish between their own state's particular stakes, and those which involve all participants in the international system. This is Arnold Wolfer's distinction between 'possession' and 'milieu' goals, and it comes close to (but is not identical with) the difference between policies which for the most part can be pursued unilaterally and those which require multilateral, if not universal, action.[72] At either level the concern can be revisionist or conservative, that is, for perceived improvements or to stop things being changed. But it makes a huge difference, for example, as to whether a state's concern is principally to see the United Nations become a more effective player in international politics by, say, reforming the Security Council, or just to maintain/acquire its own seat. Naturally the preferred position is to bring the selfish and the collective interest into line, particularly in terms of public relations, but it is an illusion to suppose that this can be done for most states most of the time.

At this point the analysis can no longer be restricted to ends; means are inherently part of the equation. For few actors are indifferent to the ways in which they (and certainly others) pursue their goals, particularly when they affect others, as by definition they almost always do in a world where there is no longer any *terra nulla*. If the best way forward is seen to be the acquisition and insouciant use of power, then equal and opposite reactions will usually be forthcoming. At the opposite extreme, if considerations of power are wholly neglected, not only is it unlikely that the desired aims will be achieved but it is quite possible that the status quo will change for the worse. This was most obviously the case with Belgium and the Netherlands in the late 1930s. It will be noted that these two end points of the continuum of values, what Wolfers called 'the pole of power and the pole of indifference', correspond to power politics and the balance of power on the one hand, and isolationism and introversion on the other.[73] Neither, in these times, can be seriously counted as foreign policy strategies in its own right; they are rather tendencies which some states lean towards more than others, partial means towards more substantive ends.

Despite this qualification, it is of the highest importance for a given set of decision-makers to consider whether or not a given value is particular to their unit, shared with a like-minded group or genuinely universal. All too often policies suffer from ethnocentrism in assuming that the interests of *x* coincide with those of the whole society of states, or in the reverse circumstances when a general consensus fails to take account of the view of a particular state in a crucial position, as when Malta's acceptance of the Helsinki Accords was wrongly taken for granted in 1974–5. The most dramatic examples of this kind of category error in foreign policy come when a state decides to crusade abroad for its own set of domestic values. Attempting to export your own values according to a parochial sense of self-righteousness is always a recipe for conflict and usually for disaster, whether conducted by a great power seeking to recast the whole system (Napoleonic France, the Wilsonian United States) or a smaller state in the grip of revolutionary fury (Gaddafi's Libya in the 1970s, Taliban Afghanistan in the late 1990s).

Perhaps more mundane and more common is simply deciding on where the boundary of the like-minded, or the region, stops. The Organization of African Unity has been weakened by uncertainties over the degree of common purpose shared by its sub-Saharan and north African members, just as the Organization of American States has been by disputes over whether or not to include Cuba. The European Union is in a deep state of uncertainty as to how far it can enlarge itself to the east without changing its fundamental character. So a foreign policy has often been launched more on the basis of hoping for the best than of a clear-sighted appreciation of who, and which values, might actually be served by the action in question.

The last continuum of foreign policy goals is that of the specific *targets* of action, and the same kind of problems occur here. For any given policy it usually matters a great deal as to who or what is being targeted for influence. For example it took the EC states some years to realize the practical importance, in order to move on the Middle East peace process, not just of shaping attitudes in Washington as well as Tel Aviv, but also of congressional and public opinion within the United States. Within the EC, likewise, Mrs Thatcher showed increasing frustration as it became ever clearer that she had no real idea of whom to influence among the Twelve if she wanted to give her own views a better chance of success. Italian leaders, by contrast, understood much more clearly the importance of keeping open lines of communication to Paris and Bonn, and were accordingly able to play a much weaker hand more effectively. More dramatically, had President Truman realized in the autumn of 1950 how crucial it was to convince China that his policy was neither to reunify Korea nor to undermine the Chinese revolution, he might have been able to avoid Beijing's military intervention and the appalling waste of life on all sides which followed over the next three years.

The targets of foreign policy will vary, from individual states to elements within a state, from whole groups of governments to transnational actors. What is important is not to be blundering about in the dark as to whom or what one is trying to communicate with and/or influence. In this respect the point is the same as with the other three parts of the taxonomy of foreign policy goals. Nothing is fixed in stone; goals are in constant and necessary evolution. But serious blurring either within or across the categories mentioned will usually cause problems. If nuclear non-proliferation, or human rights, are thought to be desirable goals to be pursued in the long-term, but particular targets are then singled out according to the exigencies of the moment, a whole new raft of problems will suddenly spring up. If a short-term goal, deemed urgent, is pursued without it being made sufficiently explicit or communicated to the relevant other party, as was the case with the Soviet attempt to assist Cuba with missiles in 1962, it is not wholly surprising if a crisis results. Even retrospectively, if we want to evaluate the success of a foreign policy we need to be able to know how directly the policy was being pursued, in what time frame, and on what criteria. This should not be too much to ask even of a bounded rational actor.

Avoiding the Worst

Bearing in mind the many constraints on decision-makers deriving from their multiple environments – bureaucratic, political, psychological, external – it almost seems absurd to expect them to behave rationally.

DMs – multiple environments –

Certainly the classic picture of a group operating on the basis of clearly thought-through goals, leading to choices made on maximum information in conditions of calm, will only come near the truth on rare occasions. And yet it seems equally invalid to abandon the idea of rationality altogether, in favour of a chaotic picture of stochastic decision-making. Leaders themselves tend to believe they are acting rationally, and citizens have to trust that they are being governed on that basis. What is more, most governments set broad strategic directions within which bureaucratic and domestic politics (each with its own, subordinate logic) take place. How then, are we to make sense of the tension between the persistent aspiration to rationality and the practical impediments to its achievement?

One way forward is to accept that substantive rationality is impossible to agree on. Who can say if it is inherently rational for a developing country like Pakistan to acquire nuclear weapons, or for a rich one like Switzerland to hold on to neutrality, given the political judgements which immediately come into play? Even lowering our sights to procedural rationality does not remove all the problems, as Steiner has shown. In some circumstances we may need to trust in the intuition and emotional capabilities of our leaders, which goes against the grain of the cerebral, knowledge-based paradigm normally associated with the word 'rational'. The modernity which the West has given to the world is distrustful of chance, superstition and fate, and puts a premium on the ability to control actions and the environment. This approach has many achievements to its name, but even in natural science breakthroughs often occur by short-circuiting recommended procedures.

The study of foreign policy suggests that the best way out of this impasse may be to invert the usual process and to ask whether or not we can identify those approaches to policy-making which are positively *irrational*, and for which the risks far outweigh the occasional possible benefit. This will primarily involve matters of procedure, but there is also a certain convergence of procedure with substance, in that the extremes of irrationality are undoubtedly associated in international relations with the tendency to use the state as a private instrument, regardless of the wishes of its citizens, and with a proclivity for hostility towards foreigners. Most observers would regard these tendencies as irrational to a degree that goes far beyond the miscalculation over the ends–means relationship.

Thus, although we cannot specify, say, that 'multiple advocacy' is inherently rational and always desirable in decision-making, we should be on surer ground in arguing that the following types of behaviour would, more often than not, lead to serious problems in foreign policy:[74] acting on impulse, or whim; failing to ensure a basic level of inter-departmental coordination; disregarding the need for good quality information and analysis; neglecting consequences beyond the immediate; failing to communicate intentions and vital interests to other actors; failing to ensure domestic support. Naturally there is no one-to-one correspondence between the occurrence of one of these pathologies and policy failure. Indeed, some may at times be turned to advantage, especially in making possible rapid and counter-intuitive actions. But persistence in them is very likely to be counterproductive. The career of Adolf Hitler is the supreme case in point.

This negative approach, through clearing the ground of sloppiness in decision-making, might be thought nearer to mere reasonableness than to rationality. It is not, however, a trivial matter, as self-indulgence in official decision-making is likely to be serious in terms of outcomes, not least for the masses who bear the consequences of high-level foul-ups. In the late twentieth century an increasing proportion of foreign policy-makers recognize that they have a responsibility both to their own citizens and to the international system as a whole. They therefore should not conduct themselves in an 'irresponsible' manner, that is by taking excessive risks in the manner in which potentially explosive issues are decided. Linklater puts this in a wider context by arguing that rational-ism requires an acceptance of 'multiple communities of discourse [which] can promote new relations between universality and differ-ence'.[75] However that might be – and it is devoutly to be wished – if those responsible for official policy consciously try to put aside those approaches to making decisions which downgrade thought, empathy, consultation and clarity, they will be demonstrating a commitment towards reasonableness and responsibility in this most dangerous of arenas, international politics, without limiting themselves to the higher selfishness of concern for their own society alone. As Vertzberger has pointed out, 'to recognize that decisionmakers cannot always be opti-mally rational ... does not preclude judging their responsibility ... the price of power and authority is responsibility, no matter what'.[76]

We shall see in Part III how a sense of responsibility pulls in differ-ent ways, and how the tension between internal and external con-stituencies can to some extent only be resolved by a philosophical discussion of the ethics of foreign policy. Nonetheless, decision-makers still need some guidance on praxis, and whether they use the word or not they will usually cast around for a 'rational' approach, in terms of how best to translate values into achievements. And in this respect the now extensive foreign policy analysis literature suggests two broad conclusions: first, that since it is all too easy to confuse ends with means, or different types of goals with each other, a degree of self-consciousness is to be recommended, with basic assumptions being thought through and articulated, both by individuals and groups – decision-makers would then stand a better chance of being able to hold to a strategy without being blown off course by the multi-layered politics in which they are perpetually engaged, or entangled in their own overlapping goals. For example EU leaders really should have thought through more clearly what they wanted to achieve with the policy of eastern enlargement, and what the trade-offs with other goals would be, before committing themselves at Copenhagen in 1993 to what has turned out to be an increasingly messy and difficult process. Second, they should adopt what we might call 'flexi-planning', that is, setting broad strategies without specifying too much detail, and without being excessively committed to them where things are evidently not working out. A general openness of thought and process is desirable if obstacles are to be circumvented and new possibilities are to be exploited. A sense of direction, however, together with a broad coherence of activity, is indispensable in most human endeavours, and medium-term planning need not be a straitjacket.

Thus the notion of rationality need not be abandoned altogether, so long as it is not interpreted too narrowly or too prescriptively. In foreign policy the stakes are certainly too high to risk a conduct of affairs which dispenses with, or even just downgrades, the values associated with reason and rational process. There are many examples from the twentieth century alone of what happens when rationality is out of proportion, at one extreme scorned and at the other elevated to the status of science. It should be seen as a vital background value, not a godhead to worship or destroy.[77]

6

Implementation: Translating Decisions and Capabilities into Actions

If the problem of agency in international politics is in the first place a matter of identifying the decision-makers who make a difference, and those to whom they are responsible, the dimension of implementation must not be neglected. We must ask whether decisions once taken do get translated into the actions they imply, or whether what is actually done is the product of delay, distortion and a further round of political conflict. A great deal of literature now exists which suggests the latter picture is far nearer to the truth than the former, which is peddled by politicians and, not unreasonably, expected by the public.

Implementation has two distinct aspects: that of slippage between political decision and administrative execution, and that of the capacity to do what is intended, given the limitations of the capabilities and instruments at the disposal of foreign policy. The first is closely related to the problem of bureaucratic politics discussed in Chapter 3, and the current chapter accordingly gives more attention to the second. Yet before either can be tackled the concepts of acting and action themselves need further attention.

More than a Technicality

The first thing to say about action is that it can barely be separated conceptually from the stages of decision-formulation and decision itself in the policy process. A flow chart typically represents the process as starting with the identification of a problem, continuing with the collection of information, followed by the formulation of options, until the point of decision is reached. The implementation phase, when action occurs, is then something of a coda, consequential on the taking of decisions. Quite apart from the fact that such a picture sets up the ideal-type of rationality heavily qualified in Chapter 4, it also makes the various stages of policy-making seem rather more separated than they tend to be in practice. For example, a problem can arise out of a state's own decisions, as with Cyprus's agreement in January 1997 to buy Russian ground-to-air missiles, which then provoked a whole host of problems for the government in Nicosia, well before any implementation. Indeed, it can be surmised that Cyprus hoped not to have to go through with the purchase, and was gambling on giving itself more leverage on the USA and western Europe.[1] Similarly, a decision can itself amount to an action, especially when made public, as with that of Romano Prodi's Italy in late 1996 to throw all its energies into seeking entry into the European common currency, in the face of widespread scepticism. That simple expression of priority changed the environment for its partner states, particularly Spain and Greece. Lastly, although the term 'action' implies a physical, concrete set of activities, it often takes a purely linguistic form. A declaration can be a démarche, or a way of changing direction. It is no less a way of changing the political environment than a movement of troops or the selling of gold reserves.[2] Even decisions which are kept secret are actions in the sense that they ignite a new chain of events, they *do* something (the dictionary definition of an action), even if this is not at first noticed by others.

Thus when confronting the problem of implementation we should always be aware of the fundamental misconceptions which tend to attach to it. The first is that outlined above, namely that implementation is not merely technical, but integral to the whole policy-making cycle and very often difficult to distinguish from its other phases. At the least, implementation feeds back into the original decision and often also begets new problems. The second arises out of the discussion conducted in Chapter 3: namely, the operations of the bureaucracy are important to, but not synonymous with, implementation; it was argued, furthermore, that it is not helpful to consider bureaucrats' and politicians' roles in foreign policy-making except in relation to each other. The third is an extension of the critique of classical rationality: when it comes to deciding how to put decisions into practice, the analogies of the golf club or the surgeon's scalpel are inappropriate. It is not just a matter of choosing, precisely, the best tool for the job. In foreign policy there are a limited number of possible instruments – they can be classed as the diplomatic, the military, the economic and the cultural – but they are almost always used either in combination or with some potential held in reserve. The differential uses of these instruments will be analysed in the main part of this chapter, but except in a highly structured relationship between like-minded states (as, for instance, in trade relations between the United States and western Europe) it is rarely possible to compartmentalize, to deny oneself recourse to the full range of possible pressures. Even in transatlantic relations there have sometimes been unpleasant surprises, as action has suddenly spilled out of the accepted channels into other, more unstable ones, as with the US pressures on sterling over Britain's invasion of Suez in 1956, or European refusals to allow US overflights for the attack on Libya in 1986. In conditions of flux the choice of instruments becomes at once more uncertain and more crucial. The Soviet Union's installation of missiles in Cuba in 1962, and the United States' move to a DEFCON III alert of its forces during the Middle East war of October 1973 both precipitated major crises.

Power and Foreign Policy

Power is a foundational concept of political science and a central pillar of International Relations. Its relationship to foreign policy, however, has been neglected, partly because foreign policy has just been subsumed in general discussions about conflict and the rationale of the state. Hans Morgenthau's *Politics among Nations* gave us the classic billiard-ball realist view, while George Modelski's *A Theory of Foreign Policy* made an explicit attempt to operationalize power as the currency in which foreign policy-makers deal.[3] The huge amount of writing which has subsequently appeared on power at the international level makes it important to take stock of what power means in the sphere of foreign policy.

The practitioner seeking to act on behalf of his or her country faces three different dimensions of power, even if it is a rare individual who is willing to begin, like the analyst, from first principles. These are: power as an end; power as a currency, or means; and power as a context, or structure.[4] These themes have not always been distinguished, or connected up to the problem of agency. For the most part they have been used to generalize about the character of international politics. What follows seeks to correct this imbalance.

Power *as an end in itself* represents a popular view of politicians and their motives. Actors are seen as out to maximize their own personal power, for the psychological satisfaction involved in controlling others, and for the glory, money and opportunities that come with it. When acting on behalf of states they blur, in this view, the distinction between their own aggrandizement and that of the state and come to identify the fate of the latter with themselves.

Needless to say, this is largely a caricatured picture. But it is not always false. There are examples of Harold Laswell's 'mad Caesars', willing to subjugate whole peoples, even continents, in the pursuit of their personal lunacy. The very terminology assumes that orgies of power and cruelty were the norm in the pre-modern past and have become virtually unknown in our own era.[5] Both assumptions are inaccurate. Most mediaeval rulers exercised caution, even cooperation, in foreign relations, while the twentieth century has witnessed not just the excesses of Hitler and Stalin but also those of more mundane gangster-politicians, such as Saddam Hussein and Pol Pot. The truth is that while individual cases of power-worship can erupt unpredictably, for most of the time states are in the hands of those who, however ruthless, are essentially concerned with power for what it can do to bring them closer to objectives with a much wider reach. Even Hitler had far higher ambitions than the mere accumulation of power for its own sake. He had a view, warped and bizarre as it was, of a particular kind of civilization to be extended across the globe, not least as the best way of destroying the twin evils of communism and international finance capital.[6] The advance of the Nazi Party was identified with this vision.

Even when leaders may seem to be pursuing an improvement in their international power position (or what is known these days as 'relative gains') for its own sake, there are always implicit questions to be answered about the extent and the nature of the expansion. How much power is enough? For the relatively small numbers of the megalomaniac tendency the problem is that they are precisely incapable of such rational calculations; any gain simply whets the appetite for more. But by the same token, those who pursue revisionist ends while accepting some limits are almost certainly concerned with specific objectives and not with the drive for hegemony. Gamal Abdel Nasser, for example, leader of Egypt between 1954–70, was intermittently demonized in the West as a threat to world peace when he was in fact concerned to reassert Egyptian interests and to counter the growing strength of Israel – policies unpalatable in many quarters, but perfectly compatible with the classical, instrumental model of statecraft.[7]

There is a fine line between power as a value in itself and power as a means to an end. After all, power-worship is always to do with the desire to coerce and to dominate. What is then done with the capacity to dominate may be seen as the underlying value for which power is sought. But this is a scholastic distinction which cannot be sustained in practice when dealing with the overall careers of a Hitler or a Stalin. The most that can be said is that some dictators begin with a vision for which power is only the means, even a noble vision, but that this is all too soon subordinated, and then forgotten, in the determination not to relinquish power once gained. This – following Lord Acton's view of absolute power corrupting absolutely – is now a commonly held view of Lenin, for example. On the other hand in the context of foreign policy it must not be forgotten that many of those who seem intoxicated by power domestically are perfectly capable of acting prudently, even reasonably, in relation to other members of international society. Men like General Pinochet in Chile or Daniel Arap Moi in Kenya have had a shrewd sense of the limits of their external power. Lenin himself came to power precisely because of his ability to know that what could be done at home depended on accepting the need to surrender to Germany in the Great War.

Arnold Wolfers' analysis of the spectrum between 'the pole of power and the pole of indifference' is still the most useful way of approaching the problem.[8] Wolfers sees foreign policy actors as varying widely in their attitudes to power, with most situated between the two extremes of an obsession with an all-out struggle for power on the one hand and an apparent indifference to that same struggle (as with Switzerland) on the other. In most cases, says Wolfers, 'to treat the quest for power, positively or negatively, outside the context of ends and purposes which it is expected to serve ... robs it of any intelligible meaning and also makes it impossible to judge its appropriateness or excessiveness'.[9] One of these very ends, however, is the 'security dilemma' of which Wolfers also talks, following Rousseau and anticipating Kenneth Waltz, namely that in an uncertain world the craving for security makes most leaders seek an insurance policy against unforeseen dangers, some margin of capacity over that which is necessary in a stable environment.[10] Thus power becomes important both in its basic sense of the ability to act for oneself to achieve one's own ends, and in that of a reserve capacity to be drawn on in crises. This is the justification for standing armed forces and for the whole modern apparatus of defence policy, currency reserves and emergency powers. It is, indeed, logical and instrumental to pursue some degree of general power. Whether it follows that policies like Britain's Two Power Standard or the US desire for a perpetual lead over the USSR were rational, rather than aggressive and counterproductive, is then a matter for debate.

SO – general power;

Power as currency explicitly deals with the question of power as the means to further ends derived from other values. Modelski's economistic metaphor implies the idea of reserves discussed above and can be turned on its head to include the idea of a strong economy as the source of power in international relations.[11] If states have both interests (I) and values (V) which they wish to preserve and project, then the two can be subsumed in the idea of *core concerns* (I + V = C). These all revolve around one or other of four universal issues – *security, prosperity, identity and prestige* – although they will be interpreted very differently according to context. All will require both a measure of generalized power, ideally with a margin of surplus in reserve, and particular kinds of resources appropriate to the purpose.

What counts as generalized power may itself change over time. A currency only has value if it is recognized by others, and power thus always has a relational element.[12] If an adversary does not fear your warpaint, or your nuclear weapon, or the general system stops valuing gold, or membership of the UN Security Council, then your assets can rapidly waste before your eyes. One of the best examples of this is the Austro–Hungarian Empire in the nineteenth century, when the waning mystique of historical monarchy could no longer inspire respect among subject peoples or abroad, leading to a final spasm of self-assertion before final collapse.[13]

Just as a money supply can be fixed or inflated, and rewards can be absolute or relative (in this sense the political science use of the term 'relative gains' is inverted) so power in international relations can at times be zero-sum and others variable sum. If Ireland gains a given net sum from the European Community budget then it follows that there is so much less for everyone else (unless the budget is expanded). Conversely, the growing membership of the European Union might produce short-term costs but long-term gains even for those who have financed enlargement. Actors have to make continual judgements as to which game they might be playing. Equally, when they are required to translate their strengths into action, they should be aware that power is not exercised in a vacuum, but rather *over* some party and *for* some purpose. Moreover, it requires an understanding as much of its limits as its possibilities. That is, at some point the coerciveness and the threats will have to stop, and the dealing will have to begin. The possession of power means that one's own fate can always be determined to some degree. The question is, what is that degree, and what kinds of compromises with others can be struck? A state with many advantages on paper can misuse its power, whether through over- or under-estimation, if its leaders do not have a good sense of its scope – and its context.

By *power as context* is meant the proposition that foreign policy actors operate in an environment where they cannot sensibly *disregard* power (Wolfers' term 'indifference' does not quite hit the mark; even the most naïve and sanguine decision-maker is still a politician). The waves of theoretical attacks on realism in recent decades have led to the absurd implications not only that states are of subsidiary importance in international relations but also that the uneven distribution of strength between them is a matter of quite minor intellectual interest. It should be axiomatic, and without implying the whole baggage of realism, to accept that power is a critical element in all social relations, and, by definition, in politics. In international relations, moreover, the means of attenuating the exercise of power are still only patchy, and it is a foolhardy person who writes it out of the script.

Practitioners quite commonly, and disastrously, overlook the external 'realities', by which is meant simply those factors outside the control of the actors in question. Chamberlain in 1938–9 and Stalin in 1941 are the twentieth century's most notorious examples, but the government of Cyprus in 1974, and François Mitterrand's economic policy in his first two years in power, 1981–3, are just as relevant and probably more typical. However elevated the actor and however limited the problem, those who ignore the intractability of the external context risk ending up in deep water. President Clinton's humiliating about-face in Somalia in 1993, unable to cope with the local warlords, simply continued the long line of superpower embarrassments, from Yugoslavia and Vietnam to Afghanistan and the Lebanon. It in turn has been dwarfed by the terrorist attacks of 2001, made possible by the deep solipsism of US security culture in the 1990s. Even Henry Kissinger, the arch-priest of the rational use of power, misjudged the docility and ineffectiveness of the Europeans in 1973–4, and suffered an embarrassing set-back as a result. Smaller powers find proportionately greater problems. If Finland had behaved towards the Soviet Union with the same cavalier disregard of potential threats that the Low Countries displayed in the 1930s, it would either have been quickly absorbed into the Warsaw Pact or have provoked a world crisis.

Those who behave in the opposite way, as if foreign policy were only about power, are just as doomed to hit trouble. Mussolini, dazzled by the gains of war and by the dominance of his German ally, increasingly parted company from his more realist foreign minister, Count Ciano.[14] Ciano paid with his life for doubting the durability of these assets; Mussolini and thousands of others eventually paid with their lives through the Duce's blind faith in them. In the 1970s the Shah of Iran believed that the combination of repression and American support made his regime in Iran inviolable. In fact it simply made the violence of the revolution which overthrew him the greater. A decade later the leaders of the Soviet Union trusted too much in the formidable apparatus of conventional power they had built. The fate of their regime is the greatest single testimony to the weakness of power politics as a guide to action and adaptation.

The context of power also means understanding structures. Susan Strange argued that structural power was fundamental, and that there were four principal structures in international relations, focusing on security, money, trade and information. If, like the United States, a country is able to dominate one or more structures then it will have a decisive role in international affairs. This is a point of great relevance to the present argument, in that not only do foreign policy actors have to cope with the power of the structure(s) in which they operate, but they also have to face the issue of who has the power *to set* the structure(s). Henry Kissinger has said that 'structures are instruments that do not of themselves evoke commitments in the hearts and minds of a society'.[15] They are abstract entities. Nonetheless, both the power to act and the ability to exert power over another require an understanding of the nature of the wider context in which action has to take place.[16] The problems of system-dominance and system-change will be dealt with in the next chapter of this book. For the time being it is enough to note that states vary enormously in their ability to shape the external 'milieu'. The very language of foreign policy – 'superpowers', 'great powers', middle range powers', 'small states' and 'micro-states' – is a way of trying to express these differentials. Indeed, it might be argued that the definition of a superpower is that of a state with the capacity to act globally and the potential to change the whole system, whereas a middle power's influence is confined to a particular region and/or issue-area.

The Spectrum of Means

The problem of the means available to foreign policy-makers is not at all as straightforward as it might seem. To be sure, a taxonomy of means can easily be constructed and individual subjects, like economic sanctions, analysed. But means are rarely so easily separable in practice, and they vary in the situations and time-frames in which they can be used. What follows tries to address these two forms of variance and to provide some integrative framework, in the form first of a continuum, and second of a pyramidal model showing the interrelationships between the resources, capabilities and instruments of foreign policy.

A useful starting-point in this task is the distinction between hard and soft power.[17] Hard power is that which is targeted, coercive, often immediate and physical. Soft power is that which is indirect, long-term and works more through persuasion than force. It has been defined as 'getting others to want what you want', through co-optation.[18] Some observers take the view that hard power is becoming increasingly redundant and that soft power is the way in which foreign policy will be conducted in future. Carrots are replacing sticks. Be that as it may, there has always been a distinction between power and influence, and the hard/soft distinction is an evolution of that idea, as Figure 6.1 shows.

Canadian foreign minister Lloyd Axworthy argued – somewhat defensively – that 'soft power does not mean wimp power'.[19] The use of slow-acting, opinion-shaping instruments can still be a form of coercion, albeit barely understood by the target. They may also need to work in conjunction with traditional means. Whereas hard power focuses on the target itself, soft power seeks primarily to change the target's environment. This is the realm, at the international level, of Vance Packard's 'hidden persuaders' and of agenda-setting. Governments have come to recognize more explicitly in recent years that the capacity to shape images and values can have concrete pay-offs.[20] This is not to say that they no longer show interest in instruments at the hard end of the spectrum or reap dividends from them. But the wider range of foreign policy instruments now available, and their overlap with the values of conflict versus cooperation, makes decisions on which route to go down particularly problematical. In some societies there may be political pressures for 'civilian' means to be used, even if the risk of failure is itself likely to be high. The issues of cost and time-frame are also central: military strength can be exponentially expensive; the policy of projecting a country abroad, as with the French *rayonnement* of language and culture, can itself represent a major drain on the public purse. Diplomats are cheap by comparison. Yet the links between investment and gain are never likely to be wholly clear. Whereas the non-use of

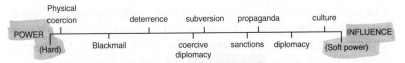

Figure 6.1   **The continuum of power in foreign policy**

costly armed services at least suggests that deterrence might be working, favourable attitudes towards a country and its products might be the result of factors wholly separate from public policy. Who needs the Voice of America when you have Hollywood and CNN?

Most actors with the luxury of choice will prefer to have a range of instruments at their disposal, from both hard and soft ends of the spectrum, and will often need to use them in combination. The measurement of costs and benefits therefore has to be taken on trust because of this very multifacetedness of foreign policy and because of the long time-lags involved. More relevant is the 'insurance policy' approach, whereby states decide how much cover they need and can afford, and which time-frame is most important to them. They then adjust their policies and outlays as circumstances change, both for better and worse. This was almost literally the view taken in relation to the post-1990 'peace dividend', although the inertia of alliance systems meant that it proved surprisingly difficult to cash in on the end of the Cold War. Still, the approach should give democratic legislatures and public opinion some way of getting to grips with the previously arcane and over-protected area of spending on external policy.

Before discussing the substance of the major instruments of foreign policy, one last theoretical issue needs clarifying. This is the pyramidal relationship between resources, capabilities and instruments. Figure 6.2 shows that the distinction between these three terms is far more than semantic.

Resources are the elements, derived from history and geography, which constitute what Renouvin and Duroselle called the 'basic forces' of foreign policy, which determine the limits of a country's impact on the world – if not of its ambition.[21] These include the minerals in the ground, the fertility of the soil and the quality of the climate. Position, size (of both territory and population) and degree of development, are all things which governments inherit and can only be changed over generations, if at all, assuming that territorial aggression is ruled out. French governments, for example, tried strenuously to increase their country's population size after 1870 but with very limited success. Resources matter immensely, but they are not in themselves operational instruments of foreign policy.

To reach the level of instruments, indeed, resources must be operationalized into *capabilities.* These are the recognizable elements of a modern government's responsibilities for which separate departments might exist and where decisions may hope to have an effect, at least in the medium term. They include the armed services, technological

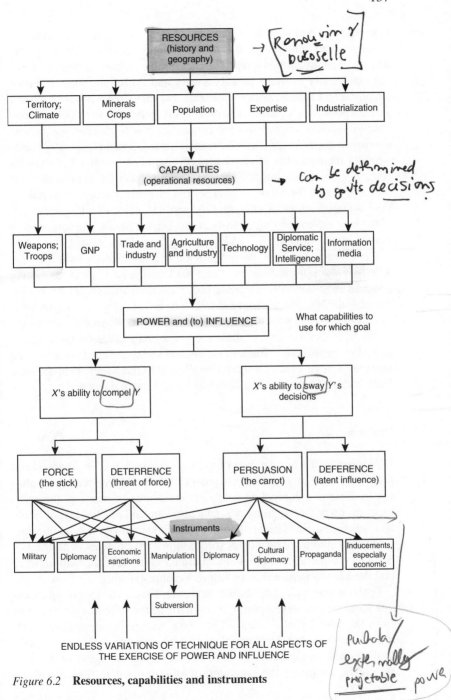

Figure 6.2 **Resources, capabilities and instruments**

capacity, levels of education, patterns of trade and diplomatic representation and the general strength of the nation's economy. Unlike power and its use, capabilities tend to be measurable, and decisions need taking continually to shape their character and evolution. Such decisions usually affect foreign policy problems, but they do not always follow a foreign policy logic. Japan rebuilt its whole economy after 1945 for reasons of survival; the unexpected consequence was the emergence of an economic superpower. British financial retrenchment after 1979 incidentally damaged the effectiveness of institutions with a key external role, such as the diplomatic service, the BBC and the universities. On the other hand, the Soviet Union set out quite deliberately to repair its post-war technological vulnerability and, by major (if ultimately self-defeating) efforts, managed to beat the United States into space, with both machine (Sputnik in 1957) and man (Yuri Gagarin in 1961).

Capabilities, however, do not provide decision-makers with manageable *instruments*, which amount to what Don Puchala called 'externally projectable power'.[22] While being both more numerous and more specific than capabilities instruments fall into four broad categories: diplomatic, military, economic and cultural. Coercive (hard) strategies draw on instruments from the first three of these categories, and persuasive (soft) strategies may use all four.[23] Endless varieties of technique exist for any given instrument, none of which should be allowed to run ahead of capabilities. Each instrument has its own distinctive problems of agency.

Diplomacy

Diplomacy is the human face of getting your own way in international politics, as well as a crucial instrument for building international stability. In these two competing roles lies the source of much of the argument over whether diplomacy is anachronistic and reactionary, or irenic and indispensable. The confusion is compounded because of the fact that most diplomatic agency is still the preserve of states, with the UN Secretary General and other international civil servants outnumbered and themselves hemmed in by intergovernmentalism.[24]

Professional diplomats do not, however, have a monopoly on diplomacy. As we saw in Chapter 4, many parts of the state machinery, apart from the ministry of foreign affairs, now engage in international relations.[25] As such, they have many openings to practise diplomacy in their dealings with foreign counterparts. In this respect all agents of the state should be aware of the considerations important to their diplomat colleagues, and the latter's advice should be taken seriously, even if it is not always followed. If Sierra Leone had had an effective diplomatic cadre, for example, its 27-year-old president would probably not have come within an ace of expelling the ambassador of its biggest aid donor (Germany) in 1993.[26] For their part, the specialists are fighting a losing battle if they seek to preserve a monopoly over diplomacy. They need to work with their 'domestic' colleagues, not against them.

As a means of implementing policy, diplomacy is particularly important to weak states. With few resources they have little choice but to play a poor hand as skilfully as possible. Yet these are also the states with the smallest and least experienced diplomatic services. As with the biblical dictum that 'to those who have, more shall be given', so it is the case that the more powerful states, with a wide range of instruments at their disposal, tend to be the most effective at the use of diplomacy. Yet all kinds of state rely on diplomacy for the bulk of their external activity, and as the crucial conduit through which other means can be funnelled. Most radical governments start with Trotsky's intention of 'issuing some revolutionary proclamations to the people and then shut up the shop', but soon turn to conventional diplomatic methods as part of coming to terms with an unignorable outside world. For diplomacy turns out to be an inherent part of any kind of action, from serious crisis ('crisis-management') through tough negotiations (the Oslo Accords on the Middle East) to routine, 'low' politics (diplomatic exemptions from parking fines). Only unsophisticated regimes conclude that they can rely on the self-executing effects of power, unmediated by diplomacy.

There are four functions which diplomacy in this broad sense performs for the international actor: communication; negotiation; participation in multilateral institutions; and the promotion of economic goods. The four are continuous, unavoidable, and to an extent, overlapping.

The key function of *communication* does not mean, as is too often assumed, miscommunication. To be sure, any independent actor has to keep some information private in order to serve its own ends the better. Key judgements on the timing of initiatives and concessions are simply not possible in conditions of publicity. But this does not mean that proactive deception makes for good diplomacy. Harold Nicolson pointed out over sixty years ago that *policy* should be in the open even if negotiation required confidentiality.[27] Indeed, if long-term intentions are not communicated clearly to both friends and adversaries the consequences can be disastrous. In his unjustly neglected first book, Robert Jervis showed how actors read each other's intentions from a combination of signals (deliberate) and indices (inherent characteristics,

JERVIS → (intentions)

not intentionally manipulated, such as monthly trade figures).[28] Unfortunately both are easy to misread even when not manipulated. Ambiguity is so quintessential to diplomacy that governments need to be highly self-conscious about the signals they wish to send on matters of importance. Did the United Kingdom, for example, intend to distance itself so significantly from the original Six when it sent only a junior official to the Messina Conference of 1955? When six years later the Macmillan government decided to apply for entry to the European Economic Community it had an uphill struggle in part because of the negative messages conveyed by such off-hand gestures. Conversely, when General de Gaulle shouted '*vive le Québec libre*' from the balcony of the Montreal City Hall in 1967 he intended to demonstrate support for French Canada but had probably not envisaged provoking the diplomatic crisis with Ottawa which ensued.[29] Even more seriously, one can narrate the onset of the two world wars quite plausibly in terms of signals wrongly calibrated and misunderstood. Certainly the nature and timing of the outbreak of both conflicts owed much to failures of diplomatic communication.[30]

As an instrument of policy, diplomacy also has the capacity to be a force for sophistication and caution, as the European Left began to realize in the 1980s after decades of berating appeasement. It is a way of breaking log-jams and avoiding the risks and costs of violence, so long as not everything is wagered on its success. Without skilful diplomacy the Federal Republic of Germany would not have been able to launch Ostpolitik in the late 1960s and thus prepare the ground for eventual reunification – itself a triumph of imaginative negotiation. Similarly, only patient, pure diplomacy by Nixon and Kissinger was able finally to put an end to the damaging rupture between the United States and China, which, lasting from 1949–71, long outlived its original rationale.[31] Many key individuals, particularly in vulnerable states, have been able to preserve their countries from potentially catastrophic consequences. The most dramatic example of this is the late King Hussein. It is easy to think what might have happened to Jordan, caught as it is between Israel, Iraq and Syria, without his subtle ability to balance relationships within the region.[32] In the wider international system, statesmen like Tito and Nehru managed to loosen the structure of the Cold War and to give a voice to many smaller states by their creation of the Non-Aligned Movement. Diplomatic communication in this sense is a political activity of the highest importance.

The second function of diplomacy is the capacity to conduct *technical negotiations*, often of extreme complexity. Where a great deal hangs on the outcome, as with the Paris Peace Talks at the end of the Vietnam War, or the build-up to the Oslo Accords of 1993, the identity of individual diplomats, and their degree of experience, may turn out to be crucial. In other negotiations, such as almost all those on arms control between the superpowers, or in those between Britain and China over Hong Kong between 1982–4, and again in the 1990s, considerable stamina is required, together with a deep understanding of the culture of the interlocutor.[33] Even on what might seem a secondary matter such as Switzerland's discussions with third parties over what to do about the gold stored in its vaults which had been stolen from victims of the Holocaust, both negotiating ability and a wide range of technical expertise were required in order to deal with the legal, political and moral dimensions of relations with Israel, the United States, the United Kingdom and many other states. Negotiation in the international environment, in other words, is now less than ever a game for the gifted amateur.

Diplomacy in multilateral institutions is an important part of any foreign policy. States, and indeed non-state actors who increasingly have access to intergovernmental organizations (IGOs), have to know how to conduct themselves in an environment which requires a balancing of national concerns with the purposes for which the IGO exists in the first place. Part of this involves coalition-building and the maintenance of diplomatic solidarity among like-minded states which are nonetheless subject to many centrifugal forces. Part involves balancing private negotiation with the posturing of a public diplomacy intended to appeal to hearts and minds, often across national boundaries. There are also many specialized multi-partner dialogues, such as the 93-member network linking the European Union and states from Africa, the Caribbean and the Pacific, or the 52-member Organization on Security and Cooperation in Europe. The challenge here from the viewpoint of the individual actor is to achieve collective goals, such as the transfer of resources to the poorest LDCs, or the stabilization of potential flashpoints, without incurring disproportionate national costs or compromising particular interests. Success is sometimes simply impossible, and it can require political as well as technical flair, as the Italian Ambassador to the United Nations, Paolo Fulci, showed in the 1990s with his effective campaign to mobilize the smaller countries in favour of a more 'democratic' reform of the Security Council than that represented by the plan to admit two new members, in Germany and Japan.[34] In 1982 the British Ambassador, Sir Anthony Parsons, had also showed the value of understanding how the UN worked, when he rushed through a Security

Council Resolution condemning the Argentine invasion of the Falkland Islands before the friends of Buenos Aires could mobilize.

Economic diplomacy is ever more important. It derives from the need to promote national prosperity and to conduct a foreign economic policy to that end. Much of it derives from the 'management of interdependence', through organizations like the OECD, G8, IMF and World Bank, and is thus subject to the same observations as those made immediately above. But here more sharply than the UN most states face the hegemony problem, or how to deal with the preponderance of the United States. In extremis this means negotiating from a position of weakness in the pursuit of loans or the rescheduling of debts, as even Britain discovered in 1976. It means trying to preserve as much of sovereign independence as possible without forgoing the desired help – a recipe for internal upheaval, as Argentina discovered in 2001. Arguably most western European states managed to do this in the discussions over the proffered Marshall aid in 1947–8, but Soviet diplomacy was not sufficiently confident or adept to be able to bind in the United States to commitments while retaining its own commitment to socialist economic planning.[35]

Most economic diplomacy is, however, more routine than Marshall aid or an IMF visitation. It consists in giving a boost to the export efforts of the country's enterprises and attracting the inward investment which will produce jobs. Japan was the most effective state in the post-war period at forging a public–private partnership in export promotion, but the German government has also succeeded in managing capitalism both at home and abroad to the direct benefit of its population. Britain under Thatcher and her successors has been able to attract a surprising flow of inward investment, helped by legislation to weaken the labour movement and a limited, but strategically important, number of interventions in such firms as Rover, Rolls Royce and British Aerospace, where there is an international dimension. Furthermore, in order to get contracts abroad various governments resort to under-the-counter promises of development or military assistance, which risks legal and political embarrassment if the news becomes public.[36] It can only work if decision-making is strongly centralized and lacking in transparency. For its part the private sector usually welcomes help from the state, so long as it is not too discriminatory. Export credit support is effectively a form of subsidy, and diplomats often have valuable local contacts. Thus British firms successfully protested against cutbacks in embassy staff in the Gulf in 1993.[37] Conversely, French commercial relations with Turkey were damaged by the bill which went through the

Assemblée Nationale recognizing the Armenian genocide of 1915.[38] Multinational enterprises may have more turnover than many states, but they still have to engage in complex and often costly diplomacy with governments in order to secure rights to build bridges, drill for oil, beam in satellite programmes and buy up parts of the economy deemed strategically important. It is no wonder that political consultancy, or risk analysis, has been one of the fastest-growing corporate sectors in the past twenty years. TNEs, like states, cannot do their business without engaging in politics and therefore in diplomacy – with each other, and with states.

The Military Arm

If the use of force is always political, as Clausewitz famously asserted, then foreign policy almost always carries with it the implicit threat of force. Not violent force, necessarily, as the 'democratic peace' between OECD states currently illustrates. But some implication of possible threats and coercion is ever-present in international politics. This is, in effect, blackmail, and it can take many forms, from the United States threatening to ban the import of cashmere sweaters from Scotland to Yeltsin's warnings of conflagration if NATO intervened in Serbia. Sometimes, therefore, diplomacy is more coercive than cooperative; just as military force is usually more implicit than actual. This overlap between diplomacy and force is what has been termed 'coercive diplomacy' by Alexander George and his colleagues.[39] As we saw with the theoretical analysis of power, threats to withdraw ambassadors, impose economic sanctions or subject a state's population to a barrage of propaganda are no less coercive in purpose than threats to invade or mount punitive air raids, even if they are designed to limit the escalation of conflict in the first instance.

Those threats which, by contrast, carry an explicit reference to possible military action if the target does not comply always risk events spinning wildly out of control. They are a gamble on big returns and big losses, which is why cautious democratic decision-makers are usually averse to them, while less restricted autocrats will at times be unable to resist the temptation. In relations between states not already entwined, whether by formal pact or sheer political proximity, the possibility of military force being used swirls darkly around the periphery of events. This in itself can be a discipline for rational policy-makers, but the mere existence of sizeable armed forces and military expertise is a standing reminder of the fact that there is always one instrument in reserve if diplomacy does not work.

'Diplomatic history is littered with conflicts that escalated far beyond the goals either party initially perceived to be in conflict as a result of needlessly severe coercive tactics employed by one or both parties'.[40] The work of many authors shows that although the threat of military force sometimes works, it is also likely to lead to its protagonists surrendering their initial control over their own actions, as they become squeezed between unforeseen reactions abroad and the expectations unleashed at home. Force can be threatened in secret, as with Prime Minister James Callaghan's successful deterrence of an Argentine invasion of the Falklands in 1977 by dispatching a small taskforce to the South Atlantic, but secrecy will rarely prove feasible for long. President Kennedy conducted the first part of the Cuban missile crisis in private, but journalists got wind of the lights burning late in the State Department, and after only a week some public announcement became inevitable. The possibility of humiliation in the eyes of the world thus became a dangerous extra pressure towards escalation.[41] In the seven cases studied by George and Simons, only two (Laos 1961–2 and Cuba 1962) are seen as examples of successful coercive diplomacy. The other five (pressure on Japan in 1941 before Pearl Harbor, on North Vietnam in 1965, on Nicaragua under Ronald Reagan, on Libya in 1986 and on Iraq in 1990–1) display more evidence of dangerous complications than of productive results. At the most, the authors conclude, coercive diplomacy 'is highly context dependent'.[42]

If this is true for the threat of military action, it is even more so for the actual use of force. One of the reasons why Saddam Hussein did not soften under the pressure of coercive diplomacy between August 1990 and 15 January 1991 was that he did not believe that the US and its allies would risk the dangers of unleashing war. In this he was mistaken, and his army was quickly driven out of Kuwait by overwhelming force once the ultimatum had expired. It remains true, however, that the use of violence is evidence of the failure of foreign policy, even where it succeeds spectacularly, and it may have long-term consequences which are both harmful and unforeseeable. Military action can cut through the Gordian knot which diplomacy has failed to unravel, but it also rarely 'solves' problems in the sense of relegating conflicts to the history books. It often simply postpones their recrudescence and exacerbates them.[43]

Armed forces are a relatively crude instrument, whether used proactively or, as is more often the case, as a deterrent. For most states most of the time success consists in their not being used. The age of military triumphalism has passed. This means the military is often regarded as just another part of the state bureaucracy. It is worth examining in a little more detail, however, the differing possibilities of revisionism and deterrence which they represent for foreign policy-makers, given the special autonomy and access to resources the military enjoy.

So far as *revisionism* is concerned, or a state's ability to improve its perceived position, it is an unfortunate truth that military force does on occasions work. Even in the post-1945 era there have been many examples: Israel in occupying and holding onto new territory from 1967; India in occupying Goa in 1961 and creating Bangladesh in 1971; Turkey in dividing Cyprus in 1974; Serbia and Croatia in gaining territory from Bosnia between 1992–5; the United States in changing the regimes in the Dominican Republic in 1965 and Grenada in 1983. These examples could be multiplied – but equally, they could be countered by those of the failed use of force. The Soviet Union's blockade of Berlin in 1948, and invasion of Afghanistan in 1979 both back-fired; the United States suffered humiliations in Cuba in 1961, Vietnam between 1964–75, and Iran in 1980; North Korea, Argentina and Iraq all launched invasions which were then reversed.

The conclusions to be drawn from this mixed record are fourfold: (i) the overwhelming, decisive and short-term use of force can work; (ii) force is only an option for the already powerful, but even then success is far from guaranteed; (iii) the use of armed force is increasingly seen as dangerous and unacceptable by the international community, because it tends to sow more dragons' teeth for the future; states are therefore ever more concerned that their actions should be legitimized, usually by the United Nations; (iv) force is more likely to work when the apple is already so ripe as to be about to fall – that is, when the target is already vulnerable. Given these factors, decision-makers should regard the use of their armed forces more as an exceptional eventuality than as one of the principal instruments of their foreign policy. Conversely, it is foolish in the extreme to rule it out *ab initio*, as NATO did with ground troops in the conflict over Kosovo in 1999. There are some actions, unfortunately, which just cannot be reversed by other means.

The same sorts of consideration, particularly those relating to the possibility of acts back-firing, apply to the variant of military force which we call *subversion*. The assumption that even a superpower can manipulate the evolution of another society by covert means is a dubious one. It is likely that in the long run subversion breeds even more antagonism and resistance than invasion and occupation, which do at least clarify the nature of the enemy. The US Cold War involvements in

Latin America (notably Guatemala, Chile and El Salvador) and in Iran left Washington with a legacy of profound hatred that will take decades to fade.[44] Revolutionary Iran, Libya and Afghanistan all over-played their hands with their encouragement of transnational terrorism.[45] This strategy simply exacerbated divisions within the Islamic world. Apartheid South Africa's ruthless interventions in the neighbouring black-ruled states probably hastened its own demise by reinforcing the solidarity of the front-line states and their links to the ANC. Subversion, in short, like most forms of violent attack, can succeed in its own terms. But the costs are no less high for being delayed.

The military arm is more conventionally deployed for reasons of *defence and deterrence*. The full range of armed services fulfils this function, but the term deterrence is particularly associated with nuclear weapons. This is an error in the sense that certainly no more than a dozen states possess deliverable nuclear weapons, declared or undeclared, out of around 190 in the world. Why do some see nuclear weapons as indispensable, and others as irrelevant to their security? The answers are largely to be found in history and in strategic position. The United States, Britain and the Soviet Union acquired nuclear weapons as a direct consequence of the need to defeat Hitler. They have found, partly through the competition of the Cold War which then immediately ensued, that it is much more difficult to relinquish nuclear weapons than to gain them. Nuclear disarmament has seemed to all three at times desirable in principle, but too likely to send signals of weakness in practice. And large vested interests have grown up around the nuclear armouries.

For its part, China acquired nuclear weapons as a consequence of its deteriorating relationship with the Soviet Union and the fear that Moscow might launch a pre-emptive strike against it. This dyadic dynamic has been repeated in the symmetrical acquisition of nuclear weapons by Israel and Egypt (both determinedly kept secret, however) and more recently by India and Pakistan. Argentina and Brazil were at one point going down the same road. Other states, like Iran, North Korea and Iraq have also made some moves towards acquiring nuclear weapons, although whether out of fear of attack or to induce fear in others is not wholly clear. The United States and its allies have taken an increasingly strong line as self-appointed enforcers of nuclear non-proliferation in recent years, which has raised the costs significantly for any state wishing to cash in on its theoretical sovereign right to acquire such weapons.

Most states, however, have given no serious consideration to the possibility, and indeed see every virtue in promoting the nuclear non-proliferation regime inaugurated by the multilateral treaty of 1968.

Why is this? The answers are straightforward. First, even with modern technology, the costs of an advanced research programme on nuclear warheads, including testing, security and delivery are prohibitively high for all but the richest or most determined. Second, developing a nuclear weapon is a most dangerous step. It will create fear in neighbours, draw the attention of the great powers and possibly lead to the kind of pre-emptive strike that the USSR is rumoured to have considered against China in 1969, and which Israel actually carried out against Iraq in 1981. Third, nuclear weapons have only marginal utility. They are only likely to be of use in deterring a *nuclear* attack, given that the outrage caused by a nuclear power even threatening to use its weapons against a state not possessing them would be enough to plunge the world into crisis. They tend to be seen as weapons of last resort by societies that can imagine themselves in desperate straits. This is why the white government in South Africa developed some limited nuclear capacity, as has Israel, but Sweden, Australia, Nigeria, Thailand and many others feel no such compulsion.

Conventional deterrence is a far more common and useful instrument of policy. When it does not work, then actual defence capabilities come into play, and states vary enormously in their ability to protect themselves against attack, depending on the size and quality of their armed forces, but also their inherent degree of vulnerability. Canada, for example, needs only a limited naval capacity for self-protection, assuming that the United States is not only no enemy but that it also provides a nuclear umbrella. For the most part foreign and defence policy are intended to work hand in hand so that a potential adversary always thinks twice before risking aggression. This is certainly Israel's strategy, which has succeeded beyond expectations. Despite its numerical inferiority with respect to its enemies, the strength of Israel's conventional forces, demonstrated four times in battle since 1948, has led Egypt and Jordan to make peace, and Syria and Iraq to behave with great caution. This is independent of the strategic support which Israel receives from the United States. A limited use of military power may also be seen as necessary for exemplary reasons, as when China briefly invaded Vietnam to remind its assertive smaller neighbour of the realities of the regional power balance in 1979.

In this way the defensive functions of military force all too easily blur into its offensive side, and the risks of any perceived military threat can be readily seen. The military instrument is qualitatively different from the other instruments of foreign policy in the threat it bears and the risks it unleashes. Even the build-up of apparently defensive arms in peacetime can be seen as an act of aggression and lead at best to unstable arms races and at worst to pre-emptive strikes. For this reason security needs to be understood in a much wider and longer-term perspective than that provided by conventional defence analysis.[46] The history of Alsace-Lorraine between 1870 and 1945, when it changed hands four times between France and Germany, shows that defence, even if elaborate, and deterrence, however formidable, do not in themselves produce more than short-term results. The problem was only finally resolved by the complete remaking of the international politics of western Europe, and by the use of other instruments altogether, primarily economic and cultural, within that new structure. Military power is therefore at once a dramatically effective, even indispensable, arm of foreign policy and one which is peculiarly limited, being vulnerable to ways of acting which are more subtle and far-reaching in their ability to shape political and social structures.

Economic Statecraft[47]

Economic statecraft goes beyond the economic diplomacy which we have already described as preoccupying public officials ever more in their conduct of external relations. It refers to the extent to which an actor can pursue its goals through the use of economic instruments, even when the content of the goal is not centrally economic. It is not about foreign economic policy in the service of economic goals, important as that is.[48] Given the starting point of linkage between politics and economics, between foreign policy and the pursuit of wealth, this means analysing the extent to which economic instruments are indeed at the disposal of the state, whether as carrots, sticks, or forms of structural power.

Most economic statecraft is a question of making some use of what is happening anyway, through trade, investment or development aid. In the economic realm, only sanctions represent a purpose-built foreign policy instrument, and even they cut across existing arrangements. For ten years before the Treaty of Maastricht the European Community could not decide whether sanctions were an economic or a political phenomenon. The other economic factors have to be nudged or exploited as and when possible without damaging too much their existing rationale. For international economic activity derives for the most part from the private sector, while foreign policy is largely the business of states. There is therefore an uneasy public–private relationship at the heart of economic statecraft. Firms are often deeply unhappy about the restrictions imposed by boycotts and embargoes; governments see private industry as engaged in subversive sanctions-busting. Public money can be used as sweeteners to obtain contracts for private enterprise where the 'national' interest may be less than clear; 'trade' can pioneer a path where the 'flag' can only follow later. Moreover, despite the ambiguities of the public–private relationship from the point of view of the actor, from that of the recipient the distinction may seem trivial and the reality that of external pressure, even neo-colonialism.

From whichever viewpoint economic instruments are viewed there can be little doubt that they are slow-moving in their impact, and more complex to operate in an era of relative laissez-faire than one of autarky, such as the 1930s, when politics and economics came together in such straightforward demonstrations of power as the Japanese Greater Co-Prosperity Sphere in East Asia, and the Nazi penetration of south-eastern Europe through tying its currencies to the Reichsmark. In the post-war era the United States provided the liquidity vital for international reconstruction but exacted the price, through the Bretton Woods system and the Marshall Plan, of a system of free trade and fixed exchange rates which in turn was used to insulate western Europe against communist influence and promote European integration.[49] In the current system, where capital moves far more freely and trade liberalization has become entrenched, it is far more difficult for governments either to act unilaterally on major aspects of political economy or to disrupt the normal workings of the market for anything less than a national emergency. That said, the use of economic sanctions has paradoxically been on the increase over the past twenty years, as states have sought alternatives to the dangers of military force and the pressures for an ethical component in foreign policy have mounted.[50]

Sanctions represent the sticks of economic diplomacy, and include the boycott of imports, embargoes on exports, restrictions on private business and travel and the imposition of price rises through punitive duties. (See Table 6.1 below, adapted from Baldwin, *Economic Statecraft*, p. 41.) Although commonly thought not to work, in the sense of not achieving their political ends, they always impose some costs on the target (as well as on the author), and may serve various ends beyond those officially declared.[51] Moreover, there have been cases where sanctions have had a dramatic impact on international politics, even if they have not always been well controlled. The US threat against sterling helped to bring the Suez expedition to an end abruptly in 1956, and the oil supply restrictions (whether directly or by price) imposed by OPEC

Table 6.1 **The range of economic sanctions (actions and threats)**

Trade	Capital
Embargo	Freezing of assets
Boycott	Controls on capital movements
Tariff increase	Controls on money-laundering
Tariff discrimination	Aid suspension
Withdrawal of 'most-favoured nation' (MFN) treatment	Expropriation
Blacklist	Taxation (unfavourable)
Quotas (import or export)	Withholding dues to international organizations
Licence denial (import or export)	
Dumping	
Preclusive buying	

Glossary

Embargo	prohibition on exports, sometimes used to refer to a ban on all trade
Boycott	prohibition on imports
Tariff discrimination	imports from the target may be treated less favourably than those from other countries
Withdrawal of MFN	ceasing to treat imports from a country as favourably as similar imports from other countries are treated
Blacklist	ban on business with firms that trade with the target country
Quotas	quantitative restrictions on particular imports or exports
Licence denial	refusing permission to import or export particular goods
Dumping	deliberate sale of exports at prices below production cost, e.g. to gain market advantage, or to disrupt the target's economy by depressing the world price of a key export
Preclusive buying	buying up a commodity in order to deny it to others
Freezing of assets	impounding financial assets
Controls on money-laundering	active investigations into the purposes of bank accounts and transfers, conventional and off-shore
Expropriation	seizing property belonging to target states or enterprises
Taxation (unfavourable)	discriminatory taxation of target's assets

Source: Adapted by kind permission from David A. Baldwin, *Economic Statecraft* (Princeton: Princeton University Press, 1985), p. 41.

in 1973 and 1979 focused world attention very clearly again on the roots of the Arab–Israel conflict and its dangers for the rest of the world. What is certainly true is that sanctions are not precise tools whose impact can be predicted with confidence. Rather, they can usually be parried, if the target is prepared (as they usually are, given the threat to their reputation for sovereign independence) to pay the inevitable price for defying states on whom they are dependent, and at times the whole international community.[52] Cuba's capacity to defy the forty-year long US blockade is a case in point.

It is the long-run use of economic power which has the most profound impact. Indeed it has proved over the past fifty years to be the most effective way of pursuing foreign policy goals – so long as you are rich, powerful and capitalist.[53] The sheer strength of the economies of north America, western Europe and Japan has given them the capacity to penetrate every part of the globe and to project their values and way of life onto other societies. This is partly through the deliberate use of carrots such as trade preferences, loans and grants on privileged terms, but mainly through the normal workings of commercial expansion.[54] Admittedly a hit-and-miss process, this has conferred significant advantages which the leaders of these countries show no sign of relinquishing. Indeed, they have gained confidence in the historical rightness of their policies since the end of the Cold War, and it is now standard practice to insist on political 'conditionality' for all kinds of development assistance.[55] Refusals, 'delinking' and ideological hostility are still all possible for those states facing this kind of friendly blackmail, and apart from the general goals of democratization and economic liberalization it is difficult to tie particular outcomes to the exercise of economic dominance. But there can be little doubt that spheres of influence have been constructed on the basis of the projection of wealth abroad, notably in Latin America, where the United States has managed to maintain a congenial order without significant military effort, and in the Gulf, where Saudi Arabia's preponderant position among the oil producers makes it also politically dominant (although not, it should be noted, to the point where it could persuade Jordan to join the anti-Iraq coalition in 1990–1, always assuming that was its aim). In east and central Europe, the European Union's use of economic instruments is making it the key player in the region.

Not every wealthy state wants to use its potential for political impact. Germany and Japan have moved only imperceptibly towards becoming 'normal' states in recent years despite their position as the third and second largest economies in the world. They have their own regional zones of influence, but prefer their economic leverage to be used in a multi-lateral context.[56] Perhaps this is wise, for foreign policy can lose wealth (through over-stretch, war, or simply an excessive sense of international responsibility) but it can rarely create solidly based prosperity.[57] Once again, the Soviet Union is the exemplar of a state which felt its survival required priority being given to foreign and defence policies, which proved in the end, by their very unsustainability, to be the problem rather than the solution. Here the priority of politics over economics ultimately caused collapse, albeit a very particular kind of politics.

Nazism, by contrast, used foreign and domestic policies in harness to revive both the economy and national self-respect, until its inherent hubris brought Europe as well as Germany down in ruins. Arguably this excess was not inevitable, but the experience has led to the relative separation of economics and politics in the post-war system, which creates opportunities but also confusions for foreign policy-makers seeking the right instrument with which to act. As with the European Community, the preferred way forward has usually been to use economic and political tools in parallel rather than tightly linked. This has the consequence – an advantage or disadvantage depending on the point of view – of making it difficult to assign responsibility for policy among the various bureaucratic actors, national and intergovernmental.

Culture

Culture is entwined with propaganda as an instrument of foreign policy, but the two are not identical. Little propaganda has any cultural value, and most culture is a wholly spontaneous affair, independent of political exploitation. Moreover, whereas culture is right at the soft power or influence end of the continuum, propaganda is often coercive in its attempt to impact forcefully on the attitudes of its targets.[58] There is an arrogance about the most self-conscious propagandists which reveals the attempt to control quite clearly. Hitler said that 'by clever propaganda even heaven can be represented to the people as hell, and the most wretched life as paradise', while for Goering rallying mass support meant that 'all you have to do is tell [the people] they are being attacked, and denounce the pacifists for lack of patriotism'.[59] Soft, cultural power is less at the behest of governments and operates over a much longer term.

What culture and propaganda have in common is that they both seek to influence peoples more than governments. By changing the domestic environment of other states they are intended to undermine a hostile regime and/or to spread the values of those seeking to act. Success requires some evidence of internal changes in the target as the result of exogenous influence – what James Rosenau calls reactive or emulative linkages, whereby groups respond directly to social forces in other states, either adversely or by imitation.[60] In this case, they would not always be aware that the linkage was being manipulated deliberately; that is, that it was the product of agency.

Crude, didactic propaganda of the kind we associate with totalitarianism of various kinds is still practised by regimes which feel the world

is against them. North Korea, Libya and Milosevic's Serbia all intermittently abused their enemies and extolled naïvely the virtues of their
own society. The Ayatollah Khomeini went so far as to send a letter to
Mikhail Gorbachev in 1988 advising him (presciently) that communism
was about to collapse and that the only hope for the Soviet Union lay in
a mass conversion to Islam. For the most part no one listens to this kind
of thing, and if it serves any purpose at all it is for domestic consumption. Much more effective, and a strategy the West became more adept
at as the Cold War wore on, is the soft-sell approach, usually based on
promoting desirable activities indirectly, rather than preaching at high
volume.[61] Thus, while no measurement of effects is possible, it seems
very likely, for example, that the reputation of the BBC's World Service
for impartiality, including on occasion criticisms of Britain, does more
to promote a sympathetic understanding of British positions, official
and unofficial, than any amount of government handouts. Openness
towards foreign journalists, encouraging educational exchanges, and
the glad-handing of elites through such events as the Königswinter
or Davos meetings are other examples of the shrewd use of culture for
broadly political purposes.[62]

Politicians must tread carefully, however, in their instinct to control.
If they attempt to direct what professional people do and say in a free
society, they invite immediate reactions and bad publicity. They have
little option but to encourage, to herd and to hope for the best. The confidence to do this brings results. The CIA was eventually damaged by
the disclosure of the way in which it had secretly bank-rolled publish-
ing houses and serious magazines like *Encounter*.[63] The United States
is better served simply by making its efficient library and information
facilities available to journalists and academics, who may then be drawn
barely consciously into the paradigms of US debate.

Control is also counterproductive in relation to the arts. The British
Council or the Institut Français can facilitate tours by the Royal Ballet
or the Comédie Française, but they cannot create art. Indeed, official
attempts to get too close to popular and avant-garde culture simply
produce embarrassment. At least Anglo-Saxon societies can rely on the
power of the English language and the hugely popular film and music
industries associated with it, disseminating themselves world-wide. The
dilemma is more acute for societies like France, where there is the perception of an excessive cultural onslaught from English. Even here,
however, Paris may be best advised not to fight an unwinnable global
war, and to concentrate on reinforcing existing historical and economic
links. This is what the German government is doing quietly in eastern

and central Europe, where there is already a disposition to speak German as a second language. In general, people are more receptive to foreign cultural influence when the achievements of the source already exist and simply need to be drawn to wider attention – and when they do not perceive the foreigner as acting hegemonically. Thus in less than two decades Japan was able to turn around the international image of itself as a defeated, devastated aggressor because foreign consumers recognized the quality and availability of its products.

From this point of view, namely allowing the strength of an economy and civil society to speak for itself, with only sophisticated and understated mediation by the state, cultural diplomacy is an instrument of the West. More dirigiste regimes may be able to enjoy a short-term coup by playing host to the Olympic Games or to the World Cup, but they will always have less attractive material at their disposal. That said, it depends on what the desired target of influence is. Iran and Saudi Arabia are largely concerned to use their resources to mobilize believers within the Islamic world, and do not waste them elsewhere – although the Gulf regimes use airlines as badges of their wealth and modernity across the globe. In the same way, Egypt under Nasser engaged in an extraordinary campaign of radio broadcasting and cultural sponsorship across the Arab world in a largely successful attempt to establish its leadership role in the Middle East.[64] Whether dealing with liberal or closed societies, however, much the same rule applies as with military force: major change is unlikely to take place unless the target is already ripe for change. The Soviet Union may have been undermined by the yearning of its people for a better standard of living, but the lure of designer jeans and BMWs would not have been so seductive if its own economy had not been defence-geared and demonstrably unable to deliver the goods over seventy years.[65]

Seeking Balance

In the final analysis there are no rules for choosing and using foreign policy instruments. None should be excluded on *a priori* grounds, unfortunately even military force, unless the discourse is switched from policy analysis to ethics. If states and some other international actors wish to protect core concerns, from time to time they will need to consider using violence, or by preference merely the threat of it. To that end they will need to have considered well in advance the nature of the armed forces they might conceivably need, and to have kept them in good order. There is no point in deciding on an action only to find that the means do not exist, as Britain and France discovered when declaring war on behalf of Poland on 3 September 1939. Equally, no foreign policy instrument is a panacea. Economic sanctions have been a popular form of coercion from the 1980s on, but have only a limited record of success. Other economic means, notably the exercise of structural power in such policies as the Marshall Plan and EU enlargement, are difficult to manipulate in terms of specific consequences. They have important impacts, but of a long-term and architectonic nature. Soft power, in the form of cultural diplomacy, is growing in importance but raises the same public–private dilemma so evident in the economic realm: when official policy-makers attempt to use it they risk embarrassing blow-backs. By contrast, diplomacy is ubiquitous and unavoidable. It exists in every political action taken by one actor towards another, and is not the monopoly of diplomats. It is capable of achieving far more than is generally thought, and is relatively inexpensive. It is, in fact, the paradigm of routine international *politics*.

Still, diplomacy cannot be relied upon to implement all kinds of goals in the face of intractable outsiders and circumstances. Indeed all instruments can backfire, especially if the elements of intervention and control are overemphasized, with the sole exception of targets which are so vulnerable as to be unable to resist decisive action. Policy-makers should take on board David Baldwin's insistence that means, being inherently relational, require an understanding of the pattern of interaction between actor and target. They should also take it as given that action in international relations requires a mix of instruments, both in reserve and working in parallel. The challenge of foreign policy action from the technical point of view is how to manage relations along a number of dimensions simultaneously. From a wider, ethical viewpoint, it is how to pursue one's own concerns without damaging the shared structures of international life and without treating outsiders simply as 'others'. That is less likely to happen if implementation is not disconnected from the dilemmas of decision-making, and if instruments are not permitted to take on too much of a life of their own.

Part II
The International

7

Living in the Anarchical Society

Every effort has been made thus far to relate the discussion of the inherent problems of agency and political decision-making to the particular contexts of foreign policy. Yet the focus on actors has meant that the nature of the environment in which they operate has not been delineated. It is time to rectify the omission, without changing the perspective completely. The next two chapters deal with 'the international', that milieu in which every state is located and which indeed is in part made up of states, but also of the economic, political and cultural forces which transcend frontiers. This chapter deals with how states experience their external environment, characterized by Hedley Bull as an 'anarchical society' with elements of both cooperation and conflict in uneasy coexistence.[1] It looks at the interplay between material and human factors in making up the outside world, and at the extent to which states are caught in a web of institutions, rules and expectations which shapes their foreign policy orientations. Chapter 8, by contrast, moves away from the state system to analyse the less visible, but perhaps even more determining, set of pressures deriving from globalization in its various aspects, and from the other sites of agency which have arisen in international relations. The role of foreign policy in this evolving and multilayered international environment is an intriguing question.

The Outside World

Nearly forty years ago Joseph Frankel wrote that 'relations among single states are ... intimately related to the matrix of international society as a whole but the study of the latter is hampered by many difficulties

(margin notes: English School Sociology State)

and has scarcely made a start'.[2] The situation has been almost wholly reversed since then. International society was launched as a subject in the 1960s by the 'English School' of International Relations scholars, among whom Charles Manning, Martin Wight, Hedley Bull, Alan James, Adam Watson and John Vincent were particularly influential.[3] Bull's book of 1977 soon became a key point of reference in the burgeoning subject of International Relations. It was therefore perhaps not surprising that a whole generation of scholars became preoccupied with the extent to which there was such a thing as a society of states, and if not, how they might best characterize the *tout ensemble* of international relations. How the component parts of that society experienced its constraints, and how they behaved in it, was only of interest to this school insofar as they threw light on the central issues of realism and rationalism, namely the tendency of states to go to war, and the conditions in which they discover common interests. The normative dilemmas lurking just beneath the surface were also beginning to be debated, principally in terms of what justice at the international level might look like. The more empirical or analytical questions, however, of what foreign policy patterns could actually be discerned, and how the dilemmas of choice played out in political decision-making, were generally passed over and left to the historians.

Things were not quite the same in the United States. While the British were understandably preoccupied with coming to terms with the pressures of the wider system, it was hardly possible for a country rising to the position of superpower to neglect the dilemmas of action. The emergence of classical realism after 1945, articulated by Hans Morgenthau, Reinhold Niebuhr and Arnold Wolfers went hand in hand with an interest in statecraft and even issues of moral responsibility. Soon, however, the evident power of scientific rationality had spawned the behaviouralist movement, which focused among other things on foreign policy decision-making and hoped to extend the logic of micro-economics to the study of politics. This created what we now know as foreign policy analysis, but also increasingly distanced academic work from the substance of political argument.

The other main trend in the American study of International Relations, from the 1950s on, was the increasing sense of a bipolar strategic system, geared to the emerging logic of nuclear deterrence. This also had the effect of distracting attention from the pecularities of states and their ideologies, even if the insistence in FPA on the connection to domestic society, and on bureaucratic politics, helped to redress the balance – and was given a boost by some of the fiascoes of the 1960s.

Eventually, however, systemic perspectives won out. Once Kenneth Waltz had invented neo-realism in 1979, American International Relations focused on the dynamics of bi- and multi-polarity and the strategies, derived from game theory, which seemed necessary to survive in a condition of self-help anarchy.[4] Just as with the English School, but for very different reasons, foreign policy had become theoretically disconnected from international politics.

Waltz advocated this very disconnection. He did not shrink from criticizing Morgenthau, Allison and Herbert Simon for their 'confusion' of the explanation of 'the results produced by the uncoordinated actions of states' (that is, the international system) with 'the tendencies and styles of different countries' policies' (that is, foreign policies). He accepted that the two levels were linked and that each therefore tells us something about the other – but different things.[5] As a result, neo-realists abhor 'reductionist' approaches which try to explain the pattern of international politics by looking inside states, and they use very parsimonious assumptions about state motivations.[6] Their approach is really a variant of structuralism, which has dominated thinking about international relations for two decades, and by definition tends to play down the role of actors, states or otherwise. They tend to assume that states 'weigh options and make decisions based *primarily* on their strategic situation and an assessment of the external environment'.[7] If they do not, they will 'fall by the wayside'.[8] Even those who sympathize with this external–determinist perspective are likely to view it as an overly Procrustean approach to the kinds of complex pressures experienced by, say, Egypt as it operates simultaneously in the Arab League, the regional balance and the international capitalist system, to say nothing of coping with a rich and complex internal situation.

World systems theorists, and those who see social movements as the motor forces of world politics (sic) are also structuralists, in that they identify an overall framework, or set of forces, to which the component parts are ultimately subordinate. The same is largely true of those working with interdependence or globalization assumptions. As with the neo-realists, foreign policy gets strangely bracketed out. The strong growth of interest in normative issues has returned some of the focus to actors, but for many of those working in the field the key actor is now the individual, and the framework that of 'cosmopolitan democracy'.[9] Foreign policy, or the collective political attempt to find a strategy for managing in the world, qua state or qua NGO, has seemed either contingent or simply irrelevant to too many general theorists of International Relations.

For their part, regional or country specialists have continued to interest themselves in foreign policy, but they rarely do more than sketch the international environment in which their subjects are located. They usually assume that states and other actors are part of a system, based on regular patterns of interaction, feedback and homeostasis.[10] They may well also operate on the basis of the distinction between the psychological environment (in which decisions are made) and the operational environment (in which they have to be carried out). But neither assumption is likely to be very explicit.

The situation of the empiricist who wishes to relate his or her work to a general understanding of international relations is complicated by the fact that even these two assumptions have become problematical. The constructivist movement means that the idea of a clear structure to the world, let alone a discernible separation between it and what goes on in our minds, is often now seen as unsophisticated. Many view international reality as being made up of the norms and beliefs held by actors (sic), and constantly renegotiated according to events. These beliefs themselves result from the dialogistical processes of participation in the multiple levels at which international politics takes place. This is why the English School is once again attracting so much interest.

It is noteworthy that the various forms of constructivism (for there are both strong and diluted versions to be found) require us in principle to place actors centre-stage, even while debates rage as how best to characterize their environment – as society of states, capitalist core–periphery system, or global governance. It is thus difficult to escape from the idea that there is something outside ourselves which we may or may not perceive accurately, being rewarded or punished according to the accuracy of our understandings. This means both that there is a vacuum to be filled about the processes connecting actors and the system, and that the concepts of perception and misperception can hardly be avoided (for reasons expanded on in Chapter 5). It is around these two points that this chapter revolves. Before proceeding with them, however, it is important to clarify the conception of the external environment being used.

The idea of an international society sees states as developing common understandings and practices to the point where it can be argued that governments are constrained in their actions not just by considerations of prudence but also by a certain sense of common cause. This notion has been both attacked and extended, to the point where we now face a bewildering litany of alternative terms and interpretations.[11] It has been attacked both for privileging the power of governments and for peddling liberal illusions over the extent to which a real 'international community' exists, over and above the annexation of the term by the major Western powers.[12] Yet it has still been extended in two ways: into the normative sphere, by talk about the obligations of states to promote certain universal values, in particular those of human rights;[13] and epistemologically, in the sense that, in Alexander Wendt's words, even anarchy (and society) is what states make of it. The outside world ceases to be a dismal iron cage and becomes instead a realm which can be remade according to the will of actors – assuming their separate wills do not cancel each other out.[14]

So far as this book is concerned the main need is to do justice to the greater sophistication of contemporary thinking on the nature of the international system, and to indicate its implications for decision-makers, whose external environment can no longer be taken as given. The neo-realists have sacrificed far too much in the pursuit of parsimony. If we return to Bull's 'anarchical society' we see that behind the elegant paradox lies the basic truth that elements of society coexist with elements of anarchy. By 'society' is meant the habit of cooperation, the condition of being rule-governed. By 'anarchy' is meant the unpredictability and untrustworthiness of the behaviour of some actors, some of the time. We cannot and should not choose between these two tendencies. Clearly their coexistence makes for tension, uncertainty and dilemmas of policy which could require some degree of self-reliance, and to some degree reinforce a fear of anarchy. Yet uncertainty and patchiness do not lead to a universal falling-back on worst-case assumptions. Variation is partly geographical, where western Europe is close to being a *gemeinschaft* and other regions are not even *gesellschaften*, and partly chronological, in that zones like West Africa can go from stability to literal anarchy in a few years, while South East Asia shows signs of being able to reverse the process. In this sense the international system resembles Cimabue's flood-damaged 'Crucifixion' in Santa Croce, Florence, with some areas sharp and detailed, others empty and imprecise. What there has not been, is a going into reverse. The achievements of international law and organization in the past century were limited, but they have gradually been consolidated. The failings of the League of Nations, to which many attributed the outbreak of the Second World War, led not to the abandonment of universal organizations, but to the development at San Francisco in 1945 of a more robust and extensive model.[15] International law has steadily expanded its scope and transcended its image of hope triumphing over experience.

Anarchy still has an alarming capacity to break through, often in the most unexpected ways. We cannot assume that we are advancing steadily and inexorably towards a perpetual peace. The descent of Yugoslavia into savagery was an existential shock to the post-modern societies of western Europe.[16] The acquisition of nuclear arms by India and Pakistan and the deterioration of their already fragile relationship has exposed the thinness of the constitutional provisions of international society. The attacks of 11 September 2001 ended the fear-free lives of prosperous westerners. On the other hand, elements of solidarism now extend well beyond inter-state relations, and indeed are to some degree independent of them. 'Cosmopolitan' networks between individuals or private associations may not live up to the expectations of fostering the unity of humankind often placed upon them, but they do cut across the pretensions of states to speak always for their peoples, and they fill in some of the gaps left by the sparse achievements of intergovernmentalism.[17] In short, they represent elements of 'world' society. By the same token they can complicate life for official foreign policies through creating other levels of agency.

Understanding agency requires bringing together the notions of inter-national society and world society. In reality, as Henry Kissinger liked to say, everything is connected. Decision-makers have to work in an environment which is not neatly divided along the lines of competing academic paradigms. On the other hand they have their own conven-tional divisions, enabling them to make sense of what would otherwise be a teeming, incomprehensible mass of sense-data. What then, from the viewpoint of the actors (and our understanding of them, which is not the same thing), is the 'international' like? What are the predominant features of their external environment?

The most accurate response is that decision-makers have a sense of international relations more than anything else as a system. That is, there is a regular pattern of interactions, across many if not most of the issue-areas affecting human life, between separate societies still ultimately 'foreign' to each other. Some of these interactions operate in more established channels and on a more intensive basis than others. Yet the globe is now more united than fragmented, in the sense that virtually all its territory is now politically accounted for, and all regions are exposed to myriad contacts from the outside. The units of the system are states but also other actors and communities which cut across states. Its boundaries are twofold: those where human activity encounters the physical world, of climate, topography and so on, and those (more blurred) where international transactions stop and the life which is pri-marily domestic begins.

This system has various different levels, mysteriously but definitely interconnected. It would be wrong to call them 'sub-systems' because

epistemological

that would imply that we can confidently identify the nature of the primary system from which others flow. Despite the arguments which rage over this very question, over whether to privilege security and states, capital and firms, knowledge and technocrats, the fact is that we are in an epistemological blind spot. We have no way of *knowing* the origins and direction of the causal flow. Without that knowledge we have no option but to conceive of a model – like the globe itself – with no top, bottom, sides or centre, girdled by different bands of activity, distinct but often overlapping. Each band-width may be shaped or animated by different forces, perhaps states, perhaps social movements or historical trends. They may gradually be coming together, with a hierarchy of power emerging – as Susan Strange thought the United States tended to dominate her four power-authority nexuses.[18] Or they may come and go, with unforeseen dimensions yet to come, like a kaleidoscope. All we can usefully assume is that there are different dimensions of the international system, and debate first how to identify them, and then how they relate to each other.

The assumption here is that the world has three distinctive logics: the logic of economics (including structures of trade, production and investment); the logic of politics (which is the competition over how the world is to be organized and resources to be allocated); and the logic of knowledge, which deserves to be seen as an equally autonomous realm because of the impossibility of confining ideas, which flow like water through every crack. Naturally economics is a preoccupation of politicians, and economic actors sometimes play politics. Scientists and thinkers deal in everything. The point is not that subject matter can be sealed into separate compartments, which it obviously cannot. Rather, that the processes of behaving economically, politically or intellectually have each their distinctive priorities and dynamics, which can be influenced and interfered with from outside but not substituted. It might be possible temporarily to extinguish one logic, but if one is run according to the precepts of another, the desired results will not be forthcoming. This has been historically the case for scientific life under theocracies, as the persecution of Galileo reminds us, just as it was for the economies of the Soviet bloc. Conversely, where political life is monetized and reduced to a pale imitation of the market, as is virtually the case in the United States today, democracy will be compromised.

This non-hierarchical, multi-banded system is far from the limited anarchical society of states with which we began. It encompasses the whole range of competing actors on the world scene, together with elements of both conflict and cooperation, fragmentation and solidarity.

Different dimensions, and issue-areas within them, will exhibit different patterns of authority and/or dominance. Some will be chaotic, some well enough organized to be denoted 'regimes'.[19] The only thing certain is that from each will come bubbling up an endless supply of new events, initiatives, problems and ideas, all of them affecting the actors and logics of the other dimensions in a fascinating array of unpredictable chemical reactions. This is the tumult of change which many see as defining the modern world, and which James Rosenau has captured in terms like 'turbulence' and 'cascade'.[20] It makes understanding, let alone acting, whether on behalf of Nestlé, the Moslem Brotherhood or the People's Republic of China, a challenging and often costly affair.

This has been little more than a sketch of what the modern world system means. From our perspective of agency and responsibility in foreign policy, it is important to look more closely at how things work. What follows does this on the basis of the diluted structurationist assumptions laid out in Chapter 1, namely that actors constitute some structures in themselves and that they interact all the time with the structures in which they are embedded. Thus they both live in the international system and its various bands, or dimensions, and are shaped by it; they help to constitute the system, giving it life, and are constrained by it. Hierarchies exist, but are multiple and always subject to movement. On this basis, the analysis will cover: the material, or physical aspects of actors' environment; the semi-material aspects, including political geography and political economy; and the political aspects, which actors largely make for themselves.

I. Material Conditions

The international system may consist of the various dimensions of human action, but the actions themselves are also played out in a physical world which is as external, independent and slow-changing as anything can be in history. This is why geography is often included in the category of the external environment in foreign policy analysis, when it is perfectly evident that territory, resources and topography are all divided up by states and constitute part of their internal configuration, together indeed with airspace and territorial waters.[21] The *pattern* of geography, with its distribution of features, is largely independent of political action, even if competition for its advantages is perennial. A contoured map of the world, naked of political divisions, looks much as it would have done, had cartography been up to the task, in 1492, in

500, or even in the 5th century BC, the age of Thucydides. Physical features are difficult to change by human action even where sovereign control is undisputed. All decision-makers have to cope with this fact, but also with the changing relationship between the physical, the political and the technological in every age.

Some major changes have been made to nature by deliberate political action, and for a variety of strategic, economic and cultural reasons. Of these the most dramatic have been the Suez Canal, the Panama Canal and now the Channel Tunnel, but of equal importance in terms of opening up connections between different regions have been the Alpine railway and road tunnels between Italy and its neighbours France, Switzerland and Austria. The great motorway networks which link Germany, the Low Countries and France, as well as the above-mentioned countries, have also facilitated trade and population movements. All of these achievements, it is true, are highly susceptible to interruption by determined subversion, just as that even greater challenge to nature, air travel, is vulnerable. But the fact remains that they are very rarely blocked, and then usually when war has already broken out. The Suez Canal has twice been put out of action, but only once for any length of time, between 1967–75, and the Panama Canal has never been seriously threatened. These human constructs soon become perceived as part of the geographical givens themselves, not least because the great powers usually have a powerful interest in keeping them open.[22]

It is also the case that we have changed our physical environment without intending to. The advance of science means that the airwaves and space have become a crucial dimension of life and politics while mountains and rivers are less important. The industrialization of much of the globe, meanwhile, has placed a premium on resources such as oil, uranium, water, fish and manganese, with the result that the seabed, over-flying rights and access to secure energy supplies have moved to the top of states' concerns. By contrast, grain, coal, iron ore and now gold have become relatively less important. The ecosphere has also dramatically come into play as an issue in both domestic and international politics. Burning forests no less than drilling for oil invites instant foreign interest. Not only has the quality of our air and food been placed in question through a combination of increased dependence on external supplies and pathologies which are no respecters of frontiers, but our very climate and sea-levels may be at risk. It would take rather less than the catastrophic changes imagined by the doomsayers to have a very disruptive effect on international politics, particularly in regions like South East Asia or Oceania.

The physical world, therefore, consists in much which we inherit and must find a way to live with, plus other phenomena which we may have collectively created but are no less difficult to manage. Together these things shape security concerns, in that they present states with particular problems according to position, size – and period of history. The military balance and the economic league tables are intimately connected to a society's physical patrimony. In the first half of the twentieth century some influential academic work on geopolitics, which we may recognize as a primitive form of International Relations theory, produced largely by geographers, suggested that this matrix had a decisive effect on a state's foreign policy, and indeed on the global balance of power. Various factors were identified at different phases of this intellectual fashion; when taken up by policy-makers they became semi-fulfilling prophecies, ultimately with disastrous results. All revealed the obsession of the times with a neo-Darwinian view of international relations as struggle and survival, which reached its nadir in fascism.[23]

Of the main variants of geopolitical theory, Alfred Mahan was the first to influence policy, through his stress on the importance of seapower and President Theodore Roosevelt's subsequent decisions to build up the Navy and to ensure US control of the new Panama Canal (in the Hay-Bunau-Varilla Treaty of 1903).[24] The most malign, if scarcely intentional influence, was exerted in combination by the Englishman Halford Mackinder and the German Klaus Haushofer, whose contrary belief that power had now shifted to those controlling great land masses, and in particular the 'heartland' of the 'world-island' of Eurasia, provided Hitler with some of the conceptual architecture he needed for the policies of *lebensraum* and world domination.[25] The madness of 1939–45 then discredited overtly geopolitical theories but it did not prevent ideas like the 'iron curtain', 'containment' and 'the domino theory' perpetuating the belief that foreign policy had to follow strategic imperatives deriving from the territorial distribution of power across the earth's surface.

This kind of grand strategy seems no longer relevant after the end of the Cold War. Even before 1989 it was not the central reality for the majority of states. The twin developments of intercontinental ballistic missiles and a widely disseminated sense of the futility of territorial expansionism had meant that the increasing numbers of new states had little stake in the 'great game'. It would be idle to deny that local and regional balances of power exist, or that geography is still important. It is just that, for once, some lessons have presented themselves, and been learnt. Single-factor explanations like globalization or 'the clash of civilizations' have their lure, but they will soon be like geopolitics in the old sense, a mere curiosity.[26] Decision-makers are generally more aware of the complexity of their environment.

Geography is now important in terms of the location and renewability of resources, and the ecological consequences of pollution. It still affects political action through the position, size and boundaries of states, but in much more subtle ways than was previously allowed. In place of the classical notion of 'natural frontiers', which only ever applied to a few locations, we now discuss 'border regions' which overlap legal frontiers, and where economic and cultural life, if not political arrangements, changes only gradually over hundreds of kilometres. This approach is important in relation to societies' sense of identity, which is inevitably complex: feared neighbours often have an uncomfortably large number of shared characteristics, and differences may seem less sharp in the context of a common regional identity, or climate and topography held in common.

The random way in which frontiers are superimposed on the world means that states vary enormously in size, mineral wealth, access to the sea, vulnerability and cohesiveness. This is the real meaning of geopolitics. Some come under great pressure through being in difficult physical circumstances, such as Bangladesh. Others, like the United States, seem to possess every card in the pack. But this is the product of geography in conjunction with history, and political action. The United States was created by immigration, war, political creativity and economic vitality. Bangladesh is in the situation it is, in the first instance at least, because of the artificiality of the divided Pakistan created on independence in 1947, and because of the dangerous international consequences which would have followed any attempt to absorb East Pakistan into India in 1971. States therefore have to work with the political geography they have, however unjust. They cannot be indifferent to it, and they can only change it at the margin. Their physical characteristics have important implications for all areas of public policy, not least foreign policy. Even distance, which many thought had been rendered insignificant by technology, must still be factored in, as Russia knows only too well through the high costs of sustaining its remote eastern provinces.

Size, location and the rest always denote costs and benefits for any given state. These are not straightforward to calculate. Bigness does not necessarily mean great resources. It depends on terrain and population, as the histories of Russia, China and India show. Conversely smallness can work to a state's advantage, as in Switzerland and Singapore. States,

"political geography" re.US.

through their decision-makers and ultimately their peoples, always have choices about how to interpret their physical situation, although these choices can only be implemented over a long term, through intergenerational consensus. Perceptions, abilities and determination are all important. In response to R.G. Collingwood's argument that it is how the people living on an island respond to their situation that determines their degree of insularity, O.K. Pate drily responded that 'people cannot conceive of their insular position in any way unless they live on an island'.[27]

Because the physical environment in which political actions take place is in one sense more genuinely 'external' than the social world of 'foreigners', it has a particular impact on choice. On the one hand it imposes costs, limits and difficulties. If a government tries to ignore the vulnerability of its borders, or gambles on good harvests it cannot be sure of, it may well be severely punished by events. On the other hand, it shapes attitudes and decisions by providing, in interaction with politics and technology, differentiated opportunities. This is not the anthropomorphic 'beckoning' of what the Sprouts called 'environmental possibilism', but the simple recognition of the fact that territorial states are bound to operate on notions of proximity, region and potential threat – which might come from floods or depleted fishing stocks as much as aggressive neighbours.[28] The territorial state is a material, not a virtual entity. Thus Turkey finds itself inherently torn between European, Transcaucasian and Middle Eastern patterns of friendship, while communist Cuba, at odds with its giant neighbour, had little choice but to seek support from outside the western hemisphere.

These choices are in no way inevitable. What matters is the long-run pattern of reactions to the matrix of constraints and opportunities which the material situation provides. Through successive governments and phases of domestic politics, states take responsibility for their own orientations, as the number of apparent geopolitical anomalies testifies. Yugoslavia, for example, might be considered the paradigm case of an artificial state, created by treaty in the face of geographical and ethnic obstacles, and ultimately foundering. But one should also ask how was it that such a state managed to survive between 1919 and 1992. To which the answer, crudely, is: through a combination of international political necessity and domestic leadership. Other examples of politics flying in the face of geography are the European seaborne empires, and the fact that Italy remained fragmented rather than united between c. 455 and 1861. But all such cases suggest both the complexity of causation, with internal and external factors interacting, and the tendency of geographical chickens to come home to roost when states can no longer bear the costs of pursuing inherently difficult enterprises. A contemporary case might be thought to be the Gulf sheikhdoms. So long as the price and supply of oil is sufficient, these statelets will be wealthy enough to make gardens in the desert, and to build up sophisticated armed forces. If that circumstance should change, their basic vulnerability will lead to an upheaval in the politics of the region. In short, while the material environment in itself does nothing, it must always be factored into decision-making. If ignored it may eventually be cruelly felt.

Semi-material Conditions – or the Politics of Human Geography

The international system operates inside a physical context which is itself, as we have seen, in constant interaction with human thought and agency. The grand theories of geopolitics have been exposed as incapable of doing justice to the complexity of this interaction. This has produced a more truthful 'political geography' which interlocks with sociology or International Relations.[29] It has also begun to link up with another important channel through which the physical world is mediated, that of international political economy (IPE).

Although IPE covers a great range of subjects, in this context it refers only to the set of factors which foreign policy actors encounter when engaged in the pursuit of wealth – external but man-made. Features such as ports or international airports can be built and structures improved. Yet in practice it takes a long time to acquire new assets, since patterns have to be shifted which are systemic in nature. The Dutch ports, with their big hinterland, are still as important to Europe's trade as they were three hundred years ago. The London docks, by contrast, gradually declined with the loss of empire, and instead Britain had to develop the world's biggest international airport, at Heathrow. This reinforced the century-old 'fact' of London being an international crossroads, which would take decades for Amsterdam or Frankfurt to supplant. This fact is 'external' to the Netherlands and Germany, but not permanent, at least not in the sense that the Atlantic Ocean is permanent.

Technology, however, has changed the significance even of oceans and mountain ranges. They hardly represent the same obstacles as even 100 years ago. Some observers hold that the creation of virtual networks through high-speed computers has neutralized most of the geographical features of the earth.[30] This is too extreme. What has happened is simply a change in relative costs; if a society can afford to pay the costs of air freight it can import exotic foods to eat with the same freshness as local producers. If not, that and other options, such as the projection of military force or even the participation of officials in international meetings, will prove impossible. Computers can only make up some part of this kind of capacity, not least because they too consume expensive resources, including highly educated labour. Not all of this is true dependence, since the year-round supply of fresh avocados, or even the tenure of a far-flung base, is not a vital interest.

In the same way, the possession of key physical resources such as minerals, water and fish stocks only takes on significance in relation both to the ability to exploit them, and to the premium put on them by the global system at any given point of history. Mines and oil rigs can be opened or shut down with considerable flexibility and deals done with multinational companies if the indigenous capacity does not exist. What is less amenable to change is the possession of facilities which require not just market advantage but also *recognition* (and persistent use) by a substantial proportion of other members of the system. These facilities, which equate to the factors of modern production, are principally labour, plus various kinds of services, particularly education, finance, commerce and transport. It may seem paradoxical that these elements, so much more abstract than mines and factories, should be considered part of the semi-material world, but in practice the cultural attributes needed to make stock markets, banking centres and transport networks can only be acquired slowly, and they soon take on a material solidity which cannot easily be substituted. Indeed, it is difficult to create them by design. Thus the People's Republic of China recognized the valuable international asset that was Hong Kong, and conducted negotiations with Britain so as to preserve and incorporate it. Similarly the states (or rather, the elites) of the Third World have continued to look to the old metropoles such as Paris and London for investment services, freight forwarding, medicine, secondary and tertiary education, sport and entertainment, consultancies, and technical standards. The City of London, the Dow Jones Index, Volkswagen, the Nobel Prize Committee, the Italian Serie A and the Académie Française are all examples of institutions which set the highest standards and provide services which are difficult to replicate. They therefore form an important part of the semi-material, external environment in which states and other international actors have to work.

What is more, these services tend to have fixed physical locations, in countries with particular historical or geographical advantages. It does still matter where on the earth's surface an actor is located, from the

•IPE•

point of view of international political economy as much as classical security. Despite their many advantages, for example, the cities of Latin America do not figure prominently in the provision of key services in the international political economy. Indeed, it is difficult to resist the conclusion that the centre–periphery model introduced by critics such as Raúl Prebisch and André Gunder Frank from the 1950s on has some descriptive power. It is revealing that skilled labour continues to drain from those places where it is sorely needed to those in which it already exists.

There is one special case where position and physical conditions still directly affect the quality of human enterprise, namely agriculture. The examples of the Soviet Union and India show that where the climate is adverse and social organization inappropriate, it is immensely difficult to produce food surpluses at affordable prices. States which then get locked into the cycle of expensive imports and weak currencies are always on the defensive in their foreign relations, and fall into various forms of dependency, such as that of Iceland, rich but over-reliant on fish, on the United States.[31] Those, by contrast, which enjoy the temperate conditions supposedly ideal for human life to prosper, not only incur fewer costs but also generate surpluses to exchange for other resources.[32] It is certainly easy to see how Poland's harsh environment, in comparison, say, to California, makes its situation particularly difficult. On the other hand the limits of this single-factor explanation are exposed by the evidence of the Scandinavian countries' ability to prosper despite their cold climate. It will be interesting to see how Poland progresses now that it finally seems to have been released from the political domination of its two great neighbours. The signs are promising but it will probably take decades before we are able to judge.

In general a state needs a combination of features if it is to be in a position to create a favourable human geography. Certainly the lack of one crucial element such as population (in particular a large skilled workforce) will restrict a state's international influence. Canada and Saudi Arabia are cases in point, despite their wealth. India, Nigeria and Brazil, which suffer from poverty and problems of infrastructure, all have more long-term potential to become power-centres. That said, such predictions have been made for many years, and the two first-mentioned states demonstrate the importance of intervening social and political variables in determining influence in both the international political economy and the international political system. What is more, how long is the 'long term' in international relations?

The external environment, therefore, is both vital to any foreign policy actor and made up of matter which is far from inert. 'External' does not mean just those things outside the territorial boundaries and sovereign jurisdiction of an actor; it means all those things which are outside the social and political processes by which the actor comes to its choices. Some of these things are purely physical, and may occur inside territorial limits, as with topography, climate and mineral resources. Even more of them are semi-material, created by human beings acting on the physical world, but slow-changing and relatively immune to political intervention for all that. In this context the scope for agency is limited.

Political Interdependence

The political band, or logic, of the international system is wholly a human product, and it exists mostly in the minds of decision-makers. In material terms the international political system can only be glimpsed, in the form of the various institutions which enable states to come together, and judgements to be made on their behaviour. Of these the most important are the buildings of the United Nations in New York and Geneva, and the International Court of Justice, plus the new International Criminal Court, in The Hague. The regional institutions, notably those of the European Union in Brussels, are also manifestations of the international political system.

An observer who expected the outputs of these institutions to reveal the workings of the system as a whole, however, would be sadly misled. Although they now total around 400, in comparison to only 37 in 1909, intergovernmental organizations constitute only one of the five main sources of political constraint and interdependence at the global level.[33] The others are: international law; informal norms; other states' foreign policies, and in particular the hierarchy of states; transnational processes, including international non-governmental organizations (INGOs). Before each is discussed briefly in turn, the notional character of the international political system needs further explanation.

A set of relationships with a regular pattern and a character that goes beyond the sum of its parts constitutes a significant structure for any of its constituent units, even if the relationships are only lightly institutionalized.[34] Thus the international political system, which is undoubtedly only partial, intermittent and contested, and which consists mostly in the expectations and assumptions of its participants, is nonetheless an important structure for those responsible for foreign policy. It both constrains them and shapes their opportunities. Despite its notional quality it is not random or evanescent. On the contrary, there is a generational accumulation of beliefs, procedures and expectations, much of it written down and some of it taking an institutional form. This makes it not so susceptible to change by any given actor, although the converse is also true, that there are few formal enforcement mechanisms. In the context of foreign policy-making, the important thing to note is that the international political system cannot be discounted. Most actors therefore factor it prominently into their decision-making, sometimes indeed to the intense irritation of domestic critics who think too much notice is being taken of external considerations and that not enough political will is being displayed. What is more, states' own identity is increasingly shaped by their political context.

Actors tend to expect both elements of anarchy and elements of order in their external political environment, although the balance may vary over time. Most are thus plagued by a constant sense of the difficulty of managing the affairs of the state or organization for which they are responsible while trying at one and the same time to: (i) accrue benefits; (ii) achieve protection from actual and potential threats; (iii) avoid incurring too many costs and constraints imposed from the outside; (iv) uphold what are perceived as important rules of order; (v) build a degree of international solidarity, both for its inherent value and for the technical advantages in specific fields (such as non-proliferation). In facing this perpetual balancing-act, decision-makers find themselves caught in the condition of interdependence.

Interdependence is mostly associated with international economic life, but it is a concept which is at the heart of the very idea of an international political system.[35] Its key attributes, sensitivity and vulnerability, describe very well the conditions which even powerful actors encounter as part of their involvement in international politics.[36] That is, when change occurs in one actor others also experience some disturbance, because their internal system is in part plugged into that of the outsider. This will show itself either through the 'sensitivity' of immediate but ultimately manageable reactions (such as the transfer of price inflation) or in a more serious 'vulnerability' to actual dislocations (such as reduced oil supplies during war in the Gulf). Both the examples given are from political economy, and many more could be cited, particularly in relation to the environment and debt rescheduling (no-one wants to risk the ripple effects of a country like Mexico going bankrupt).

Classical politics often operates in the same way. One state's domestic 'solutions' can easily be another's problems, as the history of almost any revolution demonstrates.[37] The French and Russian revolutions spread alarm far and wide beyond their frontiers (partly through hysteria, but that is another story), precipitating two decades of war. The mechanism of interdependence works in the first instance through direct knock-on effects inside domestic society. These cannot easily be insulated from foreign policy, and soon complicate relations between governments. This is particularly so where states are intensively connected, whether through some regional community, or conversely through an adversary partnership. An example of the former is ASEAN, where despite the importance of sovereignty as a founding principle, any upheaval in one member state closely affects the others – even if the smaller members are more at risk than the bigger, interdependence usually being asymmetrical.[38] An example of the latter is the Indo-Pakistan relationship. When the Bharatiya Janata Party (the BJP) came to power in New Delhi in 1996, with its militant Hindu rhetoric, it caused alarm in Karachi and exacerbated the problems over Kashmir, which ultimately led to nuclear testing on both sides. In this sense, as we shall see in Chapter 9, domestic and foreign policy developments are often intimately connected.

This is, however, only one side of 'political interdependence'. The other derives from the common membership of the anarchical society. The effects of the latter in shaping the attitudes and behaviour of foreign policy actors should not be underestimated. They derive from, and are evident in, the five sources of interdependence mentioned earlier, and it is to these that we now return.

The first is the *institutional web of international organizations*. Whatever the variable performance of these organizations, the norm for states is now participation. All states are members of some, and most take part in many, whether they are universal or regional, technical or security-related.[39] This shows both that such institutions serve functional purposes and that states are concerned not to be left out of a common system. Together they certainly represent a complex and growing network which generates a vast range of bilateral and multilateral diplomatic exchanges. Various socializing and constraining effects cannot be avoided, which is why some states still exert their right not to join, as with the refusal of the Swiss people in 1985 to join the UN (finally reversed in the referendum of 2002), and Norway's referenda decisions in 1972 and 1994 to stay out of the European Community. The weak feel these more than the strong, as with the imposition by the US-dominated World Bank of structural adjustment policies on the Third World, but even the strong have to accept the process of negotiation and compromise which IGOs epitomize. The very presence of the UN General Assembly in New York, perceived by

US opinion as a platform for criticisms of the host country, is a standing reminder to the government in Washington that participation in an international organization is not a one-way street, even for a superpower. Security Council Resolutions may be relatively easy to manipulate, but reform of the UN institutions requires a wide consensus in the form of a two-thirds majority of the General Assembly.

International organizations also provide a platform for ideas that the bigger powers do not always find acceptable, such as the critiques of neo-colonialism which grew up in the Group of 77 (soon 120 plus) in the 1970s, accompanied by the setting up of UNCTAD (the United Nations Conference on Trade and Development). The demands for a 'new international economic order' changed the agenda of international politics, and if they did not succeed in their own terms, may well have contributed to the growing confidence of various new states and transnational political groups in challenging what they perceived as the hegemony of the rich western grouping. This could not be ignored, as the subsequent challenge emanating (albeit in different ways) from states like Libya and Iran on the one hand, and Malaysia and Singapore on the other, demonstrated. This access to agenda-setting has also been evident in the ability of the smaller and more progressive western countries to push environmental and human rights concerns through special conferences like that on the Environment in Stockholm in 1972 and on Women in Beijing in 1995. Such states have also found regional groupings of great usefulness in raising their individual profiles and projecting their own concerns, as Ireland did with the European Political Cooperation/Common Foreign and Security Policy of the EC/EU, and as the Irish government did with its realignment of neutrality in the 1990s.[40] Canada, likewise, has managed to emerge from the shadow of its neighbour and ally through its distinctive commitment to UN peacekeeping.

International law is much better understood as a source of political interdependence than as a framework of governance. Whereas international law is too basic and patchy to be 'obeyed' by states its gradual evolution has produced a set of agreements and principles that operate as points of reference across the variety of ideological viewpoints in the international system. After all, international law largely derives from states themselves and serves the vital, formal function of both establishing and delimiting their sovereignty. Beyond this, it draws them into a process of common dialogue and shared procedures which makes them, in Stanley Hoffmann's words 'system-conscious'.[41] More particularly, as Louis Henkin pointed out, foreign ministries become 'treaty-geared' because they cannot afford to risk a possible disadvantage if new law is left to be made by others.[42] This kind of 'prisoners' dilemma' stimulus means that governments are appointing ever more international lawyers, and often need to hire freelance top-guns for important disputes – as both sides have done over the issue of a divided Cyprus at the International Court of Justice.

On the other side of the coin, states always feel the need to justify any breach of international law, and usually to find some legal justification.[43] A country can always choose to ignore the ICJ and its judgements, but it thereby gives its critics a potent argument which may take decades to recede, as the United States did in its high-handed treatment of the Court over Nicaragua. The Soviet Union's gradual isolation in international politics after its invasions of Hungary in 1956 and Czechoslovakia in 1968 came about partly through its inability to convince most states that the 'Brezhnev Doctrine' of limited sovereignty was a desirable innovation in international law, let alone a retrospective justification.[44] Ultimately, all states need international law so as to conduct transactions, to regulate specialist areas like atomic energy or civil aviation, for protection against illicit interference and to establish the principle of reciprocity. The fact that they exploit the law as well as observing it, and do so differentially, just means that decision-makers have to be even more attentive to this dimension of their external environment.

Closely related to international law, but not synonymous with it, is the third source of political interdependence, namely *informal norms*. These can run ahead of formal rules, or lag behind them. They have none the less force for being even more diffuse than international law. By 'norms' is meant the general principles and working assumptions that states acknowledge in their daily participation in international relations. They are many and various, and tend to be general, imprecise and often observed in the breach. What is more, they are in a condition of evolution, and in a number of different directions simultaneously. Among the most prominent are: *pacta sunt servanda*; the illegitimacy of aggressive war, the value of peaceful coexistence and the rights of non-intervention and self-determination; the illegitimacy of terrorism; the right of interested parties to an action to be consulted; the responsibility of states and individuals for 'crimes against humanity', that is, genocide and the wanton murder of civilians; the right to sell goods abroad. Most if not all of these principles are articulated either in the UN Charter or in some particular international convention. They represent to some extent the *ius cogens*. Yet law is only part of their legitimacy, given their generality and the impossibility of enforcement.

The rest derives from their existence as common discourses between states, extending perforce to other actors. The nature of a discourse is to include and highlight certain values, while excluding or ignoring others.

Such discourses are generated by intergovernmental relations on the one hand and the cosmopolitan processes which eat away at state monopolies on the other. Yet these two things cannot be kept in separate compartments. Much of the thinking about human rights which has become increasingly prominent in the past fifty years derives from what the victorious states did at Nuremberg, at San Francisco in 1945 and in the Universal Declaration of Human Rights in 1948. To be sure, commitments made then have taken a long time to ferment, but that is precisely the point about discourse and norms. In the international political system it is not enough to announce a new principle; it has to become internalized and achieve a consensus before it will appear in actions. That happens dialectically, through the slow process of interaction between governments, some keener than others, and private groups. The same was true of civil rights in eastern Europe, where spontaneous resistance to Soviet authoritarianism was given a considerable boost by Moscow's agreement to the final principles of the Helsinki Accord of the Conference on Security and Cooperation in Europe in 1975. Almost without noticing, the Soviet government had acknowledged the legitimacy of human rights concerns and given its dissidents crucial international footholds in their ascent towards liberty.

In this process of establishing norms, publicity and transparency are of crucial importance, as Kant foresaw two hundred years ago: 'all actions affecting the rights of other human beings are wrong if their maxim is not compatible with their being made public'.[45] In the modern world international actors have no choice but to have their deeds, if not their manoeuvres, appear in public on a daily basis. This means that what is usually termed – with more than a touch of reification – 'world opinion', casts perpetual judgement on decision-makers, some of whom are unused to any kind of exposure to democratic comment. World opinion is a difficult idea to pin down, but it is clear that it means something to those who participate professionally in international affairs, as the term is in constant use.[46] It is the expression of a myriad official and unofficial voices, and may be linked to the idea of *confidence*, which we know is crucial in currency markets and may also affect the operation of the fragile international political system. To the extent that actors show concern for world opinion, or general confidence, they reveal themselves to have internalized certain common values, to do with not wishing to alienate or outrage foreigners, or to be unduly isolated.

They do not wish to give outside critics the capacity to link up with domestic opposition, and they do not wish to destabilize their diplomatic relationships.[47] If confidence breaks down, long-established patterns of alliance or stability may be called into question.

This concern, as Woodrow Wilson also hoped, is connected with the notion of civilized behaviour, which no decent government would wish to transgress. The practice may be far from being implemented, but the notion, or norm, is in circulation. The international community cannot prevent genocide, but states no longer feel able to walk by on the other side on the grounds of non-intervention and cultural relativism. The NATO action against Serbia in Kosovo was an indication that international standards are beginning to be acknowledged even for internal affairs, and indeed that domestic and foreign policy are once again being seen, as they were finally in relation to Hitler, as two sides of the same coin.[48]

Concern over genocide, or enforced population movements, is at once the most dramatic and the most difficult example of how international norms shape behaviour. Most foreign policy, by contrast, is routine, dull and rule-bound – with the rules generated as the result of incessant international dialogue. Certainly most have more to do with gradually internalizing shared norms than with any fear of incurring sanctions. The United States sometimes behaved with appalling ferocity in the Vietnam War. The fact remains that it did not use all its overwhelming force, including battlefield nuclear weapons, and eventually had to accept defeat. In the last analysis there was no question of trying to annihilate North Vietnam, knowing as the administration did that it would be opposed by critics at home and abroad, and having, as Johnson and even Nixon did, some moral sensibility.[49] Similarly, although the United Kingdom fought four 'Cod Wars' against Iceland between 1958–73, it did not employ its superior naval strength and thus had to accept Reykjavik's extension of its coastal waters to a twelve-mile limit. No doubt NATO unity and US concern had something to do with this, but a modern British government could not be seen to be imposing violence on a small country if there was any risk of appearing to be in the wrong.[50] Less dramatic than either of these wars are the many instances of states conforming with diplomatic practice, for instance in granting immunity to embassy personnel accused of crimes, over and above domestic protests. The sending of emergency aid in natural disasters, even when there is no likelihood of reciprocity, is another sign that there are certain values which are diffused among states even where they are not codified or enforceable.

The fourth source of political interdependence is the *hierarchy of states*. This is not a mere synonym for the balance of power, which is far too crude a notion to cover the richness of what occurs in the modern international system. In any social environment the actors, or units, have to have some way of understanding their relative positions in the system, and this usually involves some kind of pecking order, or league table. In international relations this seems straightforward, given the disparities in size and power between states, but it is not, and not just for the familiar reason that some multinational enterprises dispose of more wealth than many states. It also derives from the fact that the majority of the members of the United Nations exist between the two extremes of superpower and micro-state. The international middle class is by far the most numerous and growing level of the social stratification.

In day-to-day diplomacy states know their place quite well, in the sense that they understand where they can exert influence and where they cannot. They do not follow any formal classification of wealth or power, along the lines of the OECD indicators, but they have to have some way of understanding the international system, even of visualizing it. Decision-makers therefore tend to think of their state as operating in a particular region or issue-area, according to its circumstances, and do not pretend to the global range that the United States takes for granted. Needing a simple model to provide guidance they tend to fall back on geographical proximity or the law of comparative advantage as rules of thumb.

No doubt conservative by disposition, foreign policy-makers rarely display signs of radical revisionism, and when they do they find the whole weight of the existing order of things (Schattschneider's 'mobilization of bias') against them. The hierarchy of states presses strongly down from the top, and rebellion against its ordering is difficult. Only the most determined and reckless leaders rise to the challenge, of whom Napoleon and Hitler are the archetypes, and ultimately they both managed to unite a winning coalition against them. This is not to revert to the traditional argument that the balance of power determines states' choices – although at times the strategic situation is compelling. Rather, it is to say that any state which wishes to alter some or other element of the informal hierarchy which exists throughout international relations, whether in the workings of international institutions or decisions on selective interventions, has to expect powerful opposition from those who benefit from the existing order of things.

The current beneficiaries of the status quo are, for the most part, the states of what is loosely called the West, but we simply do not have enough experience with a global system of 190 states to know whether their advantages are primarily those of historical positioning, or those of more effective socio-economic systems. The answer is probably both. Certainly after the collapse of the Soviet Union it has become even more difficult for any smaller state which wants to defy western-generated orthodoxies, especially in foreign policy. The price of sovereign independence, which seems such an anomaly for many small and/or weak states, is avoiding pretensions in international relations. Seeking to preserve and protect one's existing position, which often means the simple fact of statehood, is the most that the majority of states can aspire to in terms of their contribution to how the international system is run (if 'run' it is). In times of flux, or when a major power is in difficulties, some states may see tempting possibilities, but the onset of a major crisis usually shows all too starkly the limits of such aspirations. The hopes of the new Armenian state in 1920 were soon crushed by Turkey and Russia. Hungary's weaknesses were badly exposed in 1956, just as Egypt's were to be by the war of June 1967.

If all foreign policy is constricted by other states, the actions of *international nongovernmental organizations* (INGOs) and other transnational processes also create points of political sensitivity and vulnerability. This issue will be dealt with more fully in Chapter 8, and for the moment it is simply worth observing that INGOs both interact with governments and have their own, more autonomous realm of interaction. They have developed close lobbying relations across the range of national administrations, and with intergovernmental organizations. Equally, they by-pass governments and can have direct effects on public opinion inside states. This complicates official policy-making considerably, as the two-level game becomes triangular. It also has the capacity to generate new phenomena altogether, known as 'private' or 'municipal' foreign policies because they flow from elements of civil society and local government.

Thus state decision-makers encounter INGOs as an inherent part of the environment to which they must respond, intermittently capable of exerting a leverage which can be costly to resist. In this respect the international political system bears some resemblance to the cobweb model of a 'world society' associated with John Burton, but subsequently developed in varying directions. It departs from Burton, however, in that it incorporates both the network of inter-state contacts, and institutions, and that of non-governmental activities.[51] It is, for instance, constituted in part by what we called earlier in this chapter the 'knowledge band' of the international system. Much of this is not relevant to the political environment of foreign policy, but some certainly is. The medical community's transmission of knowledge across frontiers about hip replacement surgery is technical and low profile; yet what it does about AIDS (in conjunction with the World Health Organization) is highly political. The Spice Girls' world tour was of only commercial and cultural significance; by contrast the world-wide emotional appeal of John Lennon's pacifism arguably made a contribution to undermining the values of the Cold War through generational change. These examples suggest that world society can influence foreign policies, just as foreign policies can shape world society. The influences are felt, however, in very different ways and time-frames.

Opting Out and Other Forms of Resistance

Although the international system displays considerable elements of interdependence, both political and economic, this does not mean that there is no way for particular actors to retain or to create space for themselves. There have always been examples of states managing to defy the great powers, if only for a period, not least because the system is too big, geographically, and too complicated to be policed by a few states. Thus there are always differing general strategies available and a wide range of possible responses to the same conditions. The external environment looms large, and it may not be foolish at times to talk of 'system-dominance', but it is not *determining*. Apparent anomalies like the survival of Castro's Cuban regime may be explained by reference to the balance of power (although it is now ten years since support from Moscow ended) but cases like Ceauçescu's Romania, which balanced internal conformism with a foreign policy defiance of the Soviet Union, do not fit into that mould. The same was true, for a time, of Nyerere's Tanzania, which pursued its own model of development independent of pressures from East and West, led by a distinctive figure who simultaneously coruscated capitalism and translated Shakespeare into Swahili.

Many states choose to cope with the pressures of the system by conformity, to the wishes of a powerful neighbour, to an alliance or other form of diplomatic coalition, or to the general rules set by by a combination of consensus and hegemonic leadership. Those who do not fit into these categories – and many states change their positions over time – still have a number of different ways of manifesting their independent capacity for agency. They may be summarized as neutrality, self-assertion, isolationism and eccentricity.

Neutrality takes a wide variety of forms and goes well beyond the technical meaning of staying out of armed conflicts. It may be used to cover the wide range of means used to avoid commitments to the major groupings in international politics. Under this heading we may group the many states who associated themselves with the Non-Aligned Movement as a way of achieving solidarity among those who resisted the gravitational pulls of the two Cold War camps. The neutral and non-aligned (the former name of groupings at the UN and the OSCE) include states like Switzerland, and Sweden, with the resolute and historical determination not to get dragged into great power conflict, and well-prepared to defend themselves, as well as Finland and Yugoslavia, engaged between 1948 and 1989 in a desperate and skilful balancing act between East and West. The category also contains Ireland, a thoroughly western state which has used neutrality as a way of differentiating itself from the UK, and Laos, which as a land-locked state has tried traditionally to avoid throwing in its lot with any of its neighbours – Cambodia, Thailand and Vietnam.

If far more states pursue neutralist strategies than at first appears then the reverse is true of *self-assertion*. Great power rhetoric makes it appear that maverick states are regularly endangering international order. In practice, very few countries risk drawing hostile attention to themselves by challenging the status quo, certainly in general terms but even on issues of importance to themselves. When a state does behave in a self-assertive and unmanageable way, it soon finds itself a pariah, which tells us something about the conformist nature of the international system. At least in the Cold War a state which was anathema to one side usually found support on the other, although geopolitics also played its part, as Dubcek discovered in Czechoslovakia in 1968 and Allende in Chile in 1973. Some pariahs, like Libya and post-revolutionary Iran, avoided this Procrustean bed. They partly chose their status and partly had it thrust upon them. In the post Cold War period, having an unpleasant internal regime brings a state to the verge of pariah status, as South Africa became under apartheid.[52] As before, however, it is the perception (on the part of the dominant powers) that a state represents a threat to the existing order, as with the prospect of North Korea acquiring nuclear weapons, or Serbia apparently seeking hegemony in the Balkans, that confirms the image. Libya may gradually be coming in from the cold, but it will be far more difficult for Iran.

Isolation can go with being a pariah, or it can be deliberately sought.[53] Albania in the Cold War, and Burma/Myanmar now, are the best examples of states pursuing a strategy that seems to most observers anachronistic and self-defeating. Isolation is, however, the natural reaction of some governments (their peoples usually have no choice, since isolation requires authoritarianism to enforce it) to what they see as illegitimate external interference or cultural contamination – at the time of writing, Robert Mugabe is taking Zimbabwe down the same road. In its way this is an assertion of independent agency in an ever more confining international environment, although perhaps the exception that proves the rule, since few wish to emulate Burma. Isolation may be valued for its own sake, as a form of self-reliance and sovereign independence, but it may simply be seen as preferable to the alternatives. This 'ourselves alone' image is a very powerful one, as embattled Serbia demonstrated in 1999. On the other hand, isolation, like neutrality, is never absolute. There will always be some contact, some trade deal which will be quietly welcome.[54] Finally there is the small group of relatively isolated countries which desperately wish to escape the condition, usually through diplomatic recognition. The Turkish Republic of Northern Cyprus is the best current case in point, although as with Taiwan, the practical problems of isolation are alleviated by having a powerful patron.

Eccentricity is a less durable strategy for resisting the weight of the international system than the other three. It is mostly associated with particular leaders, and can be seen as a residual category for the various foreign policy stances which are *sui generis*. New Zealand under David Lange rather startlingly departed from its normal pro-western quietism to criticize strongly French and American nuclear tests in the Pacific. The consequence was a raising of the profile of both New Zealand and the issue, but at a political price relentlessly imposed at home and abroad. New Zealand exerted its sovereign right to ban visits from nuclear weapon carrying ships, but thereby lost its US security guarantee, and domestic opposition to the government was stirred up from outside.[55] By contrast, Malawi drifted further and further into unnecessary isolation as the result of the idiosyncrasies of Hastings Banda's personal rule, from which it has only just emerged, and Slovakia made one of the biggest blunders in contemporary history when it voluntarily separated from the richer Czech Republic in 1993. National independence might have been served, and the beliefs of Vladimir Meciar and his party, but the standard of living of the Slovakian people, and their chances of entering the European Union, were clearly damaged.

Only the peoples of these states, and history, can judge whether the various strategies employed to resist, opt out or merely diverge from the orthodox paths in foreign policy have been worthwhile. What is certain, however, is that there remains plenty of scope for divergence among the actors of the international system despite the pressures for conformity and conservatism which it contains. It largely depends on which set of costs a community prefers to incur – assuming the political choice is so clearly and rationally set before them.

System Change

This chapter has tried to show that the external environment remains central to any foreign policy, even if it is not its only rationale, as might have been thought in previous generations. This 'outside world' has various dimensions, according to separate functional logics, involving the co-existence of the society of states with transnational relations. Nonetheless it remains external in the sense that it is not easily susceptible to change and it is not part of the political *process* which generates decisions. It also consists to a large degree of material or semi-material conditions, which may be misperceived but which make their presence felt at some stage or other of the decision cycle.

The question then remains of how the international system changes. It is not static and it is not equally 'external', that is outside the control of an actor, to all. Is the system driven by impersonal historical forces at work, or by a small group of privileged actors? Or is it pluralist, in perpetual motion and the sum of all its parts interacting? The three possibilities are hardly incompatible, and all have their element of truth. What is difficult to deny is that the world is not only in flux but that it can move a very long way in a mere half century, at no-one's particular behest. The Europe of the iron curtain was not envisaged by any of the victors of World War, yet it determined much of their politics from 1947 to 1989. Imperialism was opposed by many, states and peoples, but no-one imagined that almost all the European colonies would disappear between 1947 and 1964. History is always on the move, and it manifests itself to us largely in the form of the changing world of which our individual agency, even at the level of powerful states, constitutes only a small part. Philosophers and commentators, whether Hegel and Marx, Fukuyama and Paul Kennedy, seek to unlock its secrets for us and to identify the reason of change. But there are no short cuts to understanding this massive system in which foreign policies provide points of reference for action and responsibility. Policy-makers have little choice but to take a series of bets on the international trends which will provide new challenges, and those which will consign some of their policies to the rubbish heap. It is no wonder they are generally cautious.

8
Transnational Reformulations

The international has always consisted in part of the transnational. Not only has there never been an era of purely inter-state relations, but it is perfectly arguable that the proportion of transactions controlled by governments has been lower in the past – for example during the Reformation and the Counter-Reformation – than it is now.[1] The world of governments and the world of peoples have always co-existed, over-lapped and interfered with each other. Adding the distinction between the internal and the external we get a four-box quadrant with meaning to both the scholar and the practitioner (Figure 8.1).

Where governments dominate internally, the state is powerful; where they dominate externally, they produce official diplomacy, inter-governmental institutions and war. Where peoples have more scope, they produce a strong civil society inside the state and transnational relations internationally. Since no quadrant is sealed off from the others, and positions vary on both axes, all the phenomena noted are

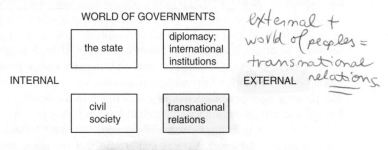

WORLD OF GOVERNMENTS

the state	diplomacy; international institutions

INTERNAL   EXTERNAL

civil society	transnational relations

WORLD OF PEOPLES

external + world of peoples = transnational relations

Figure 8.1   **Governments, peoples and international relations**

187

subject to influence from the others, and indeed tend to blur into them. Politics both within the state and outside it will therefore need to be conducted with some sensitivity to the proximity of other forces and kinds of activity.

All this is fairly well-known. While Thomas Risse-Kappen wanted to 'bring transnational relations back in', they never in fact went away after first being noticed in the pioneering work of Rosenau, Keohane and Nye at the start of the 1970s. They had become part of the orthodox analysis of international relations for all but that rather naïve tendency which assumed that neo-realist theory was co-terminous with thought about international politics in the global epistemic community. There has been a lot of general writing about transnational relations and the state, and about the state's impact on transnational relations. Indeed, a genealogical approach to the current preoccupation with globalization would discover close connections with this well-established debate.

Far less developed, however, whether in the transnational or in the globalization literature, have been the implications for foreign policy. This is surprising given the fact that the concept of transnational relations first arose in the context of foreign policy analysis, as a refinement of the government-to-government model of interactions.[2] We have learned a good deal about the state, and about world politics, but not about the specific category of state actions which is foreign policy. As we saw in Chapter 1, this is probably because many have come to regard foreign policy as almost a residual category, but the effect is to elide the distinction between structure and agency and that between world politics and the actors it contains. There is a real lacuna in terms of focusing on the actions of both states and transnational actors (TNAs) *at the international level*, and not just in terms of 'sovereignty at bay'.[3] This is the gap tackled in the present chapter, with due regard to the conceptual problem of distinguishing between foreign policy and foreign economic policy. Just as not every action of a TNA is automatically political, so not every aspect of state activity abroad need be counted as foreign policy (as opposed to 'external relations'). Foreign economic policy will be foreign policy when it seeks to shape the international environment and/or projects the fundamental concerns of the society from which it derives. Otherwise it will be mere economic diplomacy, just as much of the activity even of a foreign ministry is diplomacy rather than foreign policy proper.

It follows that relations between TNAs and states vary in their nature. Sometimes they take place largely inside the state, and relate to the economic structure of the country, through such matters as the siting of factories or the criticism of a human rights record. At other times they will

TNA's

take place in the international sphere, relating to mutual involvement in such matters as the international whaling regime, arms control or the negotiation of a Multilateral Investment Agreement. Finally, they may involve a direct clash between a state's foreign policy and the TNA. These categories are based on the assumption that it is by no means so difficult to distinguish between the domestic and the international as many contend, inherently connected as they are.[4] It is the last two categories which provide the focus of this chapter.

A Transnational Environment

Although it makes sense to start with the inter-state environment when analysing foreign policy, for any decision-maker the outside world is holistic, including at once material conditions, interactions between states ('the state system') and the inchoate mass of links between peoples and private associations that we call transnationalism. It is possible that in the course of time the importance of states will shrink, and the state system with it, to become a merely ceremonial part of this transnational environment, or world society; for now the balance is much more evenly struck. Still, the nature of the wider environment in which states and other actors have to operate needs clarifying precisely because of the uncertainty about its extent and evolution.

The definition of transnational relations is relatively straightforward, given the work that has gone before. Nye and Keohane said that *transnational relations* consisted in 'contacts, coalitions and interactions across state boundaries that are not controlled by the central foreign policy organs of government'.[5] *Transnational actors* are those private groups or even individuals who, while they require physical facilities inside states, do not need governments in order to conduct international relations. They act directly either upon other TNAs or on other governments. These definitions exclude the transgovernmental contacts discussed in Chapter 4, but otherwise include the whole range of activities of 'world society'. Only a small part of them will be relevant to foreign policy at any one point and time.

The quality of the transnational environment in which actors move is highly variable. It includes elements from all three of the 'bands' or logics in the international system identified in Chapter 7, to do with economics, politics and knowledge. These distinctions cut across those between the state system and transnationalism, as all three logics involve official and unofficial actors. Equally, states and TNAs operate in an environment which is both physical and of their own making in relation to all three logics. This is true even in the area of knowledge, for example, where the splitting of the atom cannot be forgotten and therefore constitutes a material circumstance to be taken into account.

This analysis is required so as to demonstrate not only that agency at the international level involves different kinds of actors, but also that the actors operate in a multi-layer environment not easy to reshape, and in time-frames which are longer than the career of the average politician. This is as true of the transnational environment as of the state system.

The transnational environment could be equated with *globalization*, the dominant way of understanding the world for both politicians and informed citizens during the 1990s. This has its advantages, but in relation to foreign policy it is something of a red herring. The advantages lie in the fact that the term is instantly recognizable, and that it connects up to the everyday experience of those who lose their jobs because of an economic down-turn on the other side of the world, or who watch the Kosovan crisis unfold on real-time television and then find refugees from that conflict housed within days in the next street. It is also true that the term is comprehensive in scope, indeed holistic, that it has been taken up by politicians like Tony Blair and that it is the daily intellectual currency of opinion-forming reviews like the *Economist*. The media, and university courses, help to reproduce the idea and to make it self-fulfilling among the mobile, international classes. It is truly an idea of its time, in that it provides us with a way of understanding the post-Cold War world, no longer artificially divided, and in its post-modern challenge to all understanding based on fixed points. Given the way we live now, it is both a necessary simplification and a dominant elite construct.

The globalization literature is so immense that any generalization about it is risky. David Held has suggested that its protagonists fall either into the 'hyperglobalist' or into the 'transformationalist' school. The hyperglobalists believe that the emerging world market dominates most aspects of our life on the planet and renders nugatory attempts to pursue distinctive, let alone reactionary, paths of development. The transformationalists are more cautious, arguing only that the present is an epoch of rapid and wide-ranging change, driven by global socio-economic processes which are loosening, if not destroying, the bonds of traditional political communities.[6]

The implications of both schools for foreign policy are clear enough – although barely addressed in the globalization literature. Most political action by governments which does not try to harness globalization is doomed to failure, and traditional foreign policy, with its tendency to

assume the primacy of the political, may already be barely relevant. This is because both hyperglobalists and transformationalists adhere to two basic propositions: first, that a single world market is coming rapidly into being; second, following Marshall McLuhan's arguments of the 1960s, that a global village is being created, where we share the same news, concerns, gossip and consequences, across the full range of human activity. In this second sense globalization goes far beyond the economic indicators with which it is often associated.[7] We are members of an immanent world community, which limits the nature of the politics which can be conducted within it. States, indeed, increasingly have to give ground to other actors more adapted to the new realities.

What value do these two central propositions have, and how far should our understanding of international politics be based on them? The first certainly has a good deal of force. It would be foolish to discount the experience of those working in finance, trade and labour markets who feel their environment to have changed radically and need to look increasingly beyond their traditional protectors (governments, trades unions) when they want *action* on their concerns. The disciplines of the global market are now felt inside every producing country. Yet even here it is easy to oversimplify, given that many states have powerful instruments at their disposal for economic management, and that global trends are far from uniform. The market, indeed, is hardly a level playing field in any area of economic life. The globalization thesis also suggests little – beyond the logic of commerce and profit-seeking – about where agency should be expected, if not at the old sites, and it is therefore fatalistic in its import about the political management of globalization and its consequences. It certainly has few connections with foreign policy, even via foreign economic policy, as the assumption is that gradually the state will have to surrender ever more to the private sector and will come to see the futility of attempting to intervene, whether at home or on the world markets. The problem of resolving the differences between existing territorial communities is left to one side.[8] As a hypothesis, globalization points to an ever smaller area for public policy, with the defeat of sterling by currency speculators in September 1992 the classic case in point. The best that can be hoped for is extended intergovernmental coordination, partly through institutions like the IMF and G8, but particularly through powerful regional groupings.

The second proposition remains the same interesting general insight it was 35 years ago, with no particular build-up of evidence to justify a step-change to the status of accepted truth. Most observers would regard the idea of a global community as inherently less convincing than the economic proposition, and even if taken as a point of reference it has to be so hedged about with qualifications as to lose most of its meaning. This is particularly so in relation to politics, in the implication that we are all increasingly involved in the same events, and *share their consequences*. For while we may well be more aware of events in places like Kosovo or East Timor (and does this 'we' include the hundreds of millions who still live peasant lives, whether in rural China or Poland?) awareness is a very different thing from the politically crucial attributes of caring, acting and effecting. What is more, the state exists partly to mediate the tide of happenings in the world, and we expect it to act as a filter, according to whether we need, or are able, to do anything about them. We want the state to set an agenda, and to help us make sense of a challenging world. It should enable us to *choose* whether or not we share the same consequences as others in other parts of the world – whether unfortunates, involved in war, or fortunates, taking part in prosperous joint ventures like the EU. To say, as is often said by those disposed to interpret the world through the lens of globalization, that 'we have no choice but to be involved' in *x* or *y* is to engage in a sleight of hand. There may well be new pressures on an American government to take a hand in the Northern Ireland peace process, or on us all to be concerned about the slaughter in Algeria, but this does not mean that our acting, so as 'to do something', is inevitable.[9] Furthermore, our engagement is of a wholly different kind from that of those directly involved, who either have participation forced upon them or whose values are so intimately affected as to make responding a matter of instinct and identity. Choices, complexity and differential political processes make for a wide range of barriers to isomorphism in the case of globalization as a cultural and social mechanism.

Thus the transnational milieu is not best discussed in terms of globalization, which both misleads and claims too much, especially in the domain of international politics. It is ironic that this is particularly the case where analysts of globalization have been imaginative enough to see that more is at stake than market integration and a crude form of material determinism. The wider the scope, and the bigger the generalizations, the more the issue of agency is left behind, and foreign policy gets treated as a specialist side-channel. Even those who believe enough in globalization to take to the streets against it display a baffled anger as to whom they expect to do what. Those for whom international agency is not only vital but connected significantly to foreign policy undoubtedly need to cast their understanding of the transnational environment in less general terms.

Behind the slogan of globalization is a more interesting, subtle reality. The co-existence of states and TNAs produces a swirling interplay of forces heading in no clear direction. The most important characteristics of this interaction are constant change, mixed actorness and lack of structure. Both states and TNAs have to come to terms with these features in virtually all issue-areas. To this extent the prophets of holism are correct.

Constant change is the human condition, but one of the key issues in understanding ourselves is to be able to distinguish between change which is superficial and that which confronts us with significantly new conditions of life. In international relations the evolution of the state system over 400 years has involved managing change and providing a structure for an otherwise anarchic set of relationships.[10] The society of states has therefore been both progressive and conservative, in that it has provided meliorist possibilities but has also often legitimized a particular order against demands for change which have seemed too radical or disruptive. International society does change, and not only through war, as we have seen with the major expansion in the number of states since the end of colonialism, and with the astonishingly peaceful end to the Cold War. Nonetheless, given that most states have a vested interest in preventing the system's complete breakdown, it is fundamentally slow-moving in the way it confronts new possibilities.[11]

By contrast, the transnational environment is in constant flux because it has no structure, and no institutions of its own. It is entirely actor-generated – a new Kenneth Waltz has yet to emerge to identify its structural features. This means that at one level all of its outputs are changes, but equally that it is difficult to sift the ephemeral from the structural, and the intentional from the incidental. Even those running TNAs will not know whether what they are doing is making a difference, let alone having a long-term effect. State actors are in the same position. Both also have to cope with the mixed actor environment.[12] TNAs can hardly ignore states; indeed their rationale is often to change state policies, and in certain cases, like that of the environment, if they cannot affect state decision-making and/or get Green parties elected to power, they face immense frustration. For their part, governments will be punished by events if they assume that international politics consists simply in negotiations with other states. In each policy area they now have to calculate the mix of different *kinds* of actor they need to deal with, and what kind of rainbow coalition it might be necessary to assemble to influence the various forces in civil societies and private enterprise, as well as intergovernmental institutions. As Hocking and Smith say, much policy has to be conducted 'through a variety of bilateral, multilateral and plurilateral channels'.[13]

The transnational environment is the result of a quantitative shift which may now have become a qualitative one. That is, there have always been non-state actors and transnational political forces. It is just that now the number and degree of organization of TNAs has put them on a more equal (but still not a substantively equal) footing with states. Whereas anyone running a church, pressure group or corporation assumes that governments will be their interlocutors on many of the issues of concern to them, the truth of the converse has dawned more slowly in national capitals. While politicians and public officials still look first to their peers when engaging in international deal-making, the growth of conferences like that at Davos is an acknowledgement that their environment is changing.[14] The greater willingness of publics to criticize authority means that governments can hardly afford to ignore organized opinion, even that which is transnational. The apparent importance of Papal visits to diverse regimes, even in countries where Catholics are in a minority, is another indication of the mixed nature of modern diplomacy. However, this very fact means that decision-makers are often confused as to the nature of the system they are working in, and anxious about its seemingly constant quality of change. This explains the attraction of one-stop ideas like globalization, whatever their scientific deficiencies.

A Taxonomy of Actors

The range of transnational actors is surprisingly wide. All kinds of different entities of varying sizes now 'act' in international relations and complicate the environment of states. A first step in the process of trying to make sense of this variety and the activities being pursued is to construct a taxonomy of the TNAs.

The most straightforward way to do this is to categorize according to type of organization. Thus we can distinguish churches, multinational corporations, trades unions, political parties and terrorist groups from each other. This is helpful in terms of giving us a sense of the breadth of the category – just as states themselves vary greatly.[15] What it cannot do is give guidance on the roles or importance of these actors. Another approach would be simply to rank TNAs in terms of size and/or power, so that one would have some equivalent of the hierarchy of states to work with, and indeed a sense of the major rivals to states. Yet this also soon becomes unsatisfactory, since the comparison is rarely of like with like. How, for instance, can the size, let alone the power, of the Catholic Church be compared to that of the Ford Motor Company, or to Amnesty International? Simply to pose the question is to establish its futility.

A more useful basis for categorization is to distinguish between those TNAs which are (i) *territorial*, that is, they either use or seek some territorial base, like states; (ii) *ideological/cultural*, since they seek to promote ideas or ways of thinking across national frontiers; (iii) *economic*, because their primary focus is wealth-creation. This tripartite division has the advantage that virtually every TNA fits into it, that the powerful but rather particular group of transnational corporations gets its own category, and that those actors which do not fundamentally challenge the state and the state system, but rather wish to get on board, are not confused with those for whom states are either the problem or an irrelevancy.

Let us expand on the contents of the three categories. The *territorial* group contains the best known and perhaps the most formidable antagonists of individual states, if not states as such. The Palestine Liberation Organization (PLO), the African National Congress (ANC) and the Workers Party of Kurdistan (PKK) are only the best known of many well-organized politico-military organizations which have pursued *de facto* foreign policies in pursuit of clear goals.[16] They have often commanded the maximum attention of even the most powerful states. In consequence they have sometimes been labelled mere terrorist groups, but this is not helpful. Very few acts of terrorism have arisen from an anarchistic attachment of value to the act of creating terror in itself. Most, however cruel and unjustifiable, have been committed in the pursuit of a political cause. What is more, they have sometimes produced results, although whether the end can ever justify these means is another matter, and one for political philosophy. It is ironic that actors in this category so often put themselves beyond the pale, for by definition they want to join the club, not to destroy it.

Success in their endeavour would mean that a territorial TNA would disappear from the category, as the ANC has done. On the other hand those who do not manage to replace a regime or create a new state then find it difficult to continue an international campaign indefinitely. The Kurds are having to face the fact that a state of their own is unlikely to be achieved, just as for long years both the Jews and the Armenians had to accept the fruitlessness of their struggles for statehood. Actors of this kind sometimes form coalitions of pure pragmatism in the struggle with states. This was the case with the gun-running activities of the Irish

Republican Army (IRA) and its contacts with radical Arab groups in the 1980s. They can also be adept at making alliances with sympathetic states, as the IRA did with Libya, or with particular groups inside other states, as Sinn Féin, the IRA's political wing, did in the United States.

The other kind of territorial actor to be found is the sub-national unit. Cities, regions, states inside federations have all produced 'local' or 'municipal' foreign policies.[17] They have done this for diverse reasons, even if all share a dissatisfaction with the monopoly of central government over foreign policy (defence policy being usually a step too far). The mayors of cities like Paris, Moscow and New York are inherently well-known international figures who exploit their profile for domestic political advantage, and conversely use their strong constituency base to act directly in international affairs, as with Mayor of New York Dinkins' visit to South Africa or Ken Livingstone in London advocating British membership of the Euro. Less instrumentally, the German Länder have a constitutional role in foreign policy, while individual Canadian and US states, notably Quebec, Florida and California have been quick to take their own positions on international issues close to their own interests – in this case *la francophonie*, Cuba and immigration from Mexico respectively.[18] Regions tend to be particularly active in commercial self-promotion and other aspects of political economy, but towns and cities have been notable for their involvement in peace-building exercises, whether through twin-towning or the declaration of nuclear-free zones. These naturally have zero impact in the short run but may well influence civil society over time.[19] They can be influenced and coopted by governments but depend on genuinely local common interests to sustain them, as with the post-war ties between the two steel cities of Sheffield (UK) and Donetz (USSR). Municipal foreign policy may be too grand a term for this kind of thing, but because they are literally grounded in territory as well as in legitimate political institutions, the activities of cities and regions can represent very concrete outputs, backed by resources. They therefore have the capacity both to embarrass governments and to create new international networks of their own.

The second category into which we may group TNAs is the *ideological/cultural*. This in turn contains different kinds of actor, but they share a commitment to spreading ideas and a relative disinterest in territory, and in the conventional bases of power. They are therefore at once competitive with states in the transnational environment and focused on influencing them, since they lack the means to achieve their desired ends by themselves. An obvious sub-group here is the single-issue cause organization, promoting one particular end internationally and possibly losing prominence thereafter. The European Nuclear Disarmament movement in the 1980s was a noticeable case in point, growing as it had done out of the purely British Campaign for Nuclear Disarmament (CND) and exerting considerable pressure in favour of a theatre nuclear arms negotiation. Another notable example is the Anti-Apartheid Movement, which mobilized opposition to the white regime in South Africa most effectively for three decades. Less political, but still a considerable factor with its five million members and offices in forty countries, is the World Wildlife Fund, which attempts to shame (and help) countries which do not protect their endangered species.

Much more durable ideological actors are those which might be described as the proselytizers, those who seek to promote a vision of the good life despite, or indeed because of, the resistance to be found in many states to their message. Here we find churches and religious sects, the Socialist and Communist Internationals, and their modern imitators in the form of the Liberal and Christian Democratic international networks, idealist groups of various persuasions, including the United Nations Association, together with Amnesty International and Greenpeace, which have moved beyond their pressure group origins to promote a whole way of life. These actors are helping to construct a common global discourse on politics, although discourse, of course, is very far from being the same as consensus. The politically inclined may wish to win over governments, but their basic aim is convergence between the units of the international system around their preferred values.

The churches, and in particular the Roman Catholic Church, are not only the transnational actors with the longest historical roots, they are older than states, older indeed than the idea of the state. They have had to come to terms with the power of states, as with Anglicanism or the Gallican compromise in France, but they retain extensive transnational networks, and a claim on the ultimate loyalty of the believer. Nor is this a matter solely of private faith. The Papacy still has the capacity to influence the birth control patterns of millions in poorer countries such as Mexico and the Philippines, and has acted as a form of political opposition in communist Poland and El Salvador. No other Christian church has had such potential, but the importance of Archbishop Desmond Tutu to black South Africans and to the international campaign for sanctions against South Africa should remind us of the legacy of protestant missionaries in Africa, where a 'black theology' has grown up which cuts across already artificial state boundaries, and where evangelicanism has taken hold. On the other hand, Christianity is not always a subversive force in such situations. The biggest church in southern Africa is the

Zionist Christian Church of Moria, which, while wholly black, preached the value of accepting law and order even under apartheid.[20]

The transnational qualities of religion have been underestimated by secular-minded state decision-makers, in particular in the West.[21] Where the historical pattern of communities of faith does not coincide with state boundaries (as it rarely does, in fact) there is potential for serious conflict, as we have seen in Nigeria, in Bosnia and in parts of South East Asia. This is less a matter of fundamentalist crusading (although a trend in that direction can be discerned in a number of the world's religions) than of political identity becoming expressed through religion, which almost always has a transnational reach and structure rather than being coterminous with the state.

Transnationalism does not, any more than statehood, imply uniformity or homogeneity. Jews world-wide have suffered the consequences of being stereotyped as a people without loyalty to the states in which they live. The culmination of this persecution is that probably the only thing which unites Jews everywhere is a determination not to see the *state* of Israel destroyed. Some fundamentalist Jews have, nonetheless, operated transnationally in attempts to push Israel in their favoured, theocratic direction, and US foreign policy into a commitment to 'eretz Israel'. In doing so they have demonstrated the divisions within the world of Jewry, like any other religion.

Islam is also too readily seen by non-believers as a single entity, rather like the Vatican with a guerrilla army at its disposal. In practice, the world of Islam is as variegated as that of Christianity, with a wide range of different positions held on politics and international affairs.[22] Furthermore, the institutions of the Islamic world, such as the Organization of the Islamic Conference, created in 1972, are resolutely intergovernmental and powerfully influenced by the patronage of Saudi Arabia. Yet the fact that Islamic theology sees church, state and civil society as integrally connected means that there is much potential for political activism, and long before Al Qaeda the activities of organizations like the Muslim Brothers and Hamas have made governments tremble, notably in Egypt (with the assassination of Anwar Sadat) and during the current civil war in Algeria. There is a transnational element to this activism, although not as much as is commonly supposed. It is in fact important to distinguish between Islam as an important (and highly differentiated) factor in the interaction between domestic and foreign policies, and Islam as a transnational actor, in which capacity it largely exists in the form of specific groups. To the extent, indeed, that there has been any kind of movement to create an Islamic 'world society' it has arisen out of the foreign policies of particular states, namely Iran and Taliban Afghanistan – representing a Shia and a (very particular) Sunni version of Islam respectively.

Political proselytizers come and go, transnationally as nationally. The links between political parties are in any case always stronger when the parties in question are in government, as is currently the case with the European centre–left. When not, transnational solidarity is usually brittle, as in the famous case of the re-nationalization of international socialism in the run-up to the First World War. The workers of the world could not unite, even where they were free from chains. In more recent times activities of this kind have been less ambitious and arguably more influential. The German party foundations in particular have made all kinds of links with their equivalents abroad, at both ends of the political spectrum.[23] The political groups of the European Parliament have made slow but steady progress towards becoming transnational parties.[24]

Party operations may be transnational but they are also para-statal. This is not true of organizations like Amnesty and Greenpeace, which began with limited, functional goals and have grown almost despite themselves into *de facto* international parties, far in advance of single-issue politics and able to influence political agendas and affect policy-making in states of many different types. Oxfam is another pressure group that has become a brand name, with the capacity to raise voluntary taxes world-wide and link both technical expertise and political activists on the ground in the pursuit of developmental goals. The changes in western policies in recent years in the areas of both development and human rights certainly owe a good deal to the persistent campaigning and ability to harness resources transnationally of these major organizations. They have spawned many imitators, but remain in a separate category from the specialized pressure groups discussed earlier.

More at the cultural than the ideological end of the spectrum are those in the knowledge business, who have an interest in spreading information and ideas independent of the needs of the state they are based in. They include the media (but the media empires of Rupert Murdoch and others belong more in the business category), plus scientists and educators. In essence they are the functional networks of experts – meaning those whose first concern is to understand the world – who have come to be known as 'epistemic communities'.[25] This 'knowledge band' of the international system has the capacity to generate structural changes, as we have seen to dramatic effect with information technology in the past twenty years, simply as the result of professional activity. States thus find that while they can intervene and even control some areas of knowledge-development – nuclear weapons and outer space are prime examples – much of the rapidly changing scientific environment leaves them with little choice but to adapt. The same is true of news. Once a story breaks it is impossible to confine it, given the speed of communications and the way the world's media now feed off each other. The international news agencies in particular have a key role in deciding on news priorities and shaping debate. The 'CNN effect' (meaning that governments now have to be sensitive to opinion at home and abroad because their actions are exposed in real-time, world-wide) is grossly exaggerated, but it remains true that a regime can no longer avoid opposition or embarrassment just by closing down its own press and TV. There exists what has been called in the European Union context the '*communauté de vues*', which soon filters through into intergovernmental relations and which through linkage politics (see below) can strengthen domestic opposition.[26]

On occasions epistemic communities are capable of mobilizing themselves to become temporary international actors, with the aim of changing public policy. International media campaigns are not unknown on relatively 'soft' subjects such as famine relief, but on anything more controversial they tend to be forestalled by editorial diversity. Effective humanitarian action is more likely to be mobilized by ad hoc coalitions of specialists, preferably with wide reputations and operating out of universities. *Médecins sans frontières* is an example of an actual organization produced by doctors concerned with the relief of suffering in the Third World, founded in 1971 by the French humanitarian activist Bernard Kouchner, who eventually rode into ministerial office on the back of its success. Less structured but equally effective have been the groupings of environmental scientists which have kept up the pressure on governments to acknowledge such problems as the polar holes in the ozone layer, not least by suggesting constructive responses. They have worked hand in hand with pressure groups, and have determined the agendas of intergovernmental conferences, if not the outcomes.[27]

Even more striking is the impact of senior US and Soviet scientists on arms control negotiations between the superpowers. Fear of nuclear war led to the starting of the transnational Pugwash conferences in 1957 and, despite the security problems, figures from both sides managed to stay in touch through the Cold War – partly because they represented potentially useful back-channels for Moscow and Washington. Given the nature of this issue-area it is impossible to know the full truth of the matter, but it has been argued quite convincingly by Matthew Evangelista that these transnational networks were crucial in making possible some of the breakthroughs in nuclear arms control of the 1980s. The Soviet Union confirmed the hypothesis that a state which is difficult for transnational actors to penetrate initially can change quite quickly under their impact once access has been gained. Once influenced at the top, an authoritarian system can ensure relatively quick responses further down the ladder.[28]

A final, but significant, example of an epistemic community achieving policy impact is that of the economics profession. As economists became sceptical about the benefits of Keynesian, demand-led economic policies, particularly in the United States, so they turned to supply-side analysis and followed through the logic of liberalism by recommending monetary discipline, privatization and free trade. These ideas have been taken up by governments which ten years earlier would have been their mortal enemy. The profession naturally covers a wide range of views but it is striking how quickly the Keynesian orthodoxy has been replaced, first at the intellectual, and then at the political, level. This can be interpreted as reason working its way through, but few social scientists would be willing to accept such a naïve view of the role of ideas in politics. There are many causes of the revolution in economic policies which occurred after 1980, but one of them was the power of the top university departments in the United States to engineer a new consensus among academic economists. In Thomas Risse-Kappen's phrase, ideas are not 'free-floating'.[29] This is true, indeed, of transnational phenomena in general.

The third and last category of TNAs is the *economic.* In part this includes the familiar multinational producers such as General Motors, Philips and IBM, but it now extends to the corporations in the service industries such as McDonald's or Lufthansa, and media giants such as Mediaset. Sport and crime now also generate big transnational businesses. The activities of these enterprises is undoubtedly one of the most important facts of the early twenty-first century. They impact directly on the lives of millions, and they are a central factor in the making of state economic policy. The whole issue of the evolution, and possible decline, of the state is closely related to the nature of their power. The very importance of these questions, however, leads to a certain repetition and lack of discrimination in the debate. The issue here is distinctive and more specific: in what respect are transnational businesses independent actors in international politics?

At one level the answer to this question is disarmingly straightforward. Within the international economy, and collectively, the Transnational Enterprises (TNEs) are big players. Given that they have

TNE's .

certain values and interests in common they are able to exert powerful pressures in favour of trade liberalization, tax incentives and havens, favourable regimes for the free movement of labour and the exploitation of minerals. They did, for instance, manage to undermine the project for the mining of the seabed in the common interests of mankind.[30] Equally, either individually or in groups, they may occasionally be able to precipitate change in particular states, as famously happened in Guatemala in 1954 with the United Fruit Company and Chile in 1973 with ITT. TNEs represent a heavy weight in favour of a particular order of things, particularly in the international economic 'band' of the international system. In relation to their interests they play politics persistently.

The other side of this coin is that the TNEs are inherently competitive amongst themselves and rarely have the will or the capacity to act collectively, as states to some extent can do. What is more, they need to work with states, and not for their destruction. TNEs' objectives occupy a relatively narrow spectrum, relating to profit, expansion, stability and modernization. They rarely show interest in becoming quasi-polities by taking responsibilities for communities and striking positions in political debates. Even Cadbury and Walt Disney, which have gone some way down the road of social action, quickly discovered the limits of their impact on wider society. Indeed corporations are often accused of being only interested in profit, with an amoral attitude towards the values of the regimes they deal with. In consequence they have become concerned with the public relations value of achieving an image of 'corporate responsibility', but the nature of their agency in international politics is very restricted. *Qua* international actors they generate inputs, beyond the logic of their daily business activities, to inter-state discussions on the relevant regimes of the international political economy, such as trade, the environment and intellectual property. Yet their most notorious political interventions are in the internal affairs of particular states, if not at the actual behest of their own parent government then at least in line with its policies. On the other issues of international relations, such as war, security, international institutions, border disputes or human rights they have little distinctive to say.

This generalization must be qualified, in that it covers the criminal entities capable of actually creating some security problems, as with drug-running in the Caribbean or small arms sales in the Third World. More positively, organizations like Eurovision or UEFA have probably done more to create a sense of shared experience among the peoples of Europe than the rhetoric of a thousand politicians. Still, even these things are by-products of their normal activity, examples of functionalism in action.[31] It is not in the nature of TNEs to *set out* to achieve such ends; consequences and intentions must always be distinguished. Nonetheless, some TNE activity has a considerable impact on the general environment in which state foreign policies are implemented. This can be negative, as with the sanctions-busting operation run by Shell into South Africa in the 1970s and 1980s, or the ability of European firms in 1981–2 to invoke trade rules against Ronald Reagan's attempt to stop the new gas pipeline being constructed from the Soviet Union towards western Europe. In these cases the business-as-usual instinct cut across political strategy. It can also be more positive, especially in the case of the media, which are capable of articulating and amplifying concerns like human rights independent of the wishes of host or parent governments. That said, they thereby risk effective counteractions. When Rupert Murdoch decided to remove BBC World from his Star satellite he was anticipating the damage that could be done by the government in Beijing to his chances of penetrating the valuable Chinese market.

Economic actors in the transnational environment thus enjoy considerable autonomy in their own business, the conduct of which will have a big effect on the international economy and on what states try to do in it. They intermittently impact on international politics, not always by design. In this context, but also in that of the international political economy, they should always be analysed in terms of their interaction with states. In particular, although multinational businesses are broadly independent of control by governments, they are not immune from the culture and values of the relatively small number of rich, capitalist societies from which they spring. Indeed, they are a powerful influence on that culture. This means that TNEs and states will often be pressing in the same general direction – as with the opening up of markets in the ex-Warsaw Pact countries – and against the preferences of others. Yet there are many points of divergence. While TNEs' political agency is of a general, contextual kind, states have varying, peculiar interests and a wider range of instruments to boot. Since politics is their business and their priority, they are the agents likely to have a more direct influence on international political life.

Foreign Policy and Transnational Actors: a Model

Distinguishing the different types of transnational actors helps us to appreciate the range of activity which goes under the heading of international politics, and the nature of the challenges they pose to states. It is now time to focus more directly on the nature of the relationship which exists between these incommensurable actors, with their contrasting aims and responsibilities.

Three forms of this relationship may be observed. They are derived from the problems which arise for state foreign policies, and the attempts of TNAs to conduct equivalent strategies, but they may also be applied, with the proviso that weak, poor states are significantly disadvantaged in their relations with corporations over *internal* issues, to state–TNA relations in general. The three are: normal, bargaining relations; competitive, power relations; and what can be called, following Samuel Huntington, transcending relations.[32] Their structures and implications are set out in Table 8.1.

The first of these relationships is termed '*normal*' more because it represents a functioning relationship, unlike the other two, than on any assumption that it represents the norm. The number of actors and issue-areas involved is too large for us to be able to generalize safely about what sort of relations are prevalent. What occurs here is that the TNA envisages being able to co-exist with a state's foreign policy, but wishes to negotiate about those elements it has problems with. It thus lobbies a government directly. The state in turn is relatively relaxed about dealing with the TNA (which by definition will not be 'foreign' but will have a foothold in the state's own society) and thus engages in dialogue. It may even seek to incorporate the TNA in some way, and exploit its channels for its own advantage. In consequence, deals are struck, and even when they are not, relations proceed on a routinized, trauma-free basis. In this way the two kinds of actor have managed to co-exist productively enough in the complex build-ups to the Lomé Conventions signed between the European Community and the 78 African, Caribbean and Pacific states, and in various attempts at assisting political transitions, as in South Africa and Bosnia.

The second kind of relationship is *competitive*. It involves a more overt use of power in a struggle for advantage that may involve one or both sides contesting the legitimacy of the other. TNAs tend to see little advantage in dealings with particular governments and therefore go behind their backs directly to domestic society. At its most provocative this may be deemed subversion, but more usually it simply involves the strengthening of local organizations, appeals to public opinion and attempts to weaken the hold of governments by opening up the discussion of policy options. The more sophisticated may also try to play states off against each other. In response, governments have a range of

Table 8.1 **TNA–state relationships in international politics**

	What TNAs may do	What states may do	Nature of interaction	Examples	Advantage with?
(1) Normal, bargaining relationship	request policy change; lobby.	accept legitimacy of input; engage in dialogue; coopt/incorporate in policy-making; exploit TNA access for own purposes.	compromise; deals; cooperative ventures; continuing relations.	Montreal and Kyoto Conventions; Lomé Conventions; electoral monitoring.	balanced.
(2) Competitive, power relationship	act directly on domestic environment, using public opinion as a means of pressure; form local cells; try to dislocate state power and reduce its monopoly; divide states against each other; outflank single governments by transnational opinion coalitions.	ignore; use powers over borders and legislation to deny access or weaken position of TNA; suppress; military action; inter-governmental cooperation.	hostility; may be zero-sum; polarized; unstable – states possibly divided *inter se*, TNAs possibly out of their depth politically; relates to specific issues.	Human rights clashes; *Rainbow Warrior* intrusion into nuclear test zones; disputes over technology transfer; Lockheed scandal; would-be states.	usually with states.
(3) Transcending relationship	get on with their own business; ignore frontiers as much as possible; states not main interlocutors.	try to move issue to (1) or (2); ignore; exhibit confusion; try to recruit 'own' TNAs and other private counter-weights.	uneasy; intermittent; absent; diverging assumptions and *modus operandi*; relates mostly to structural issues.	churches; TNEs; epistemic communities.	usually with TNAs.

Handwritten annotations:

- *functioning relationships – dialogue / deals.*
- *TNA's co-exist w/ state FP, to just negotiate.*
- *power struggle / or legiti-macy etc.*
- *US congress – Toshiba lobby 1987 sell equip to USSR.*
- *greenpeace nuke*
- *transcend interstate relations ↓ operate in other dimensions*

options at their disposal. They may call the TNA's bluff by ignoring their activity, reinforcing the strength of their position by coordinating with other states. More seriously, they may use their powers pre-emptively to control frontiers or to enact legislation, as ways of denying TNAs freedom of movement. At the extreme end of the continuum autocratic regimes may use security forces to suppress the interfering 'foreigners', while democratic governments may turn to military force against terrorism, striking bases abroad or adopting draconian controls over the movements of people and money.

The consequence of this mutual suspicion is escalating hostility, with conflicts increasingly seen as polarized and zero-sum. The relationship is at best unstable, with states likely to overreact as a result of the pressures of having to play a two-level game, and TNAs beginning to get out of their depth through the head-on conflict with states, sometimes becoming involved in issues – such as political authority structures – which they are not equipped to handle, and which touch on the most sensitive spots of state sovereignty. The classic case was the determination of Greenpeace's *Rainbow Warrior* crew to intrude on French nuclear testing areas in the Pacific, which produced a state terrorist response.[33] Equally dramatic were the hostile reactions of the Indonesian and Chinese governments in the 1990s to foreign human rights activity over East Timor and the incarceration of dissidents. Any TNA with a territorial or explicitly political claim is by definition on a collision course with the states affected by the claim. In political economy, international businesses have at times intervened in election campaigns, by illicit funding to their preferred candidates. Above board, but no less of a challenge, was Toshiba's lobbying of Congress in 1987 which undercut the political momentum for an embargo after its subsidiaries had sold sensitive equipment to the USSR against US policy.[34] Notwithstanding this example, governments generally hold more cards in a competitive relationship. In overt conflict their powers are more concrete and extensive, although much depends on the particular state involved.

The third kind of relationship, termed '*transcending*', is more subtle. Samuel Huntington argued that the real strength of transnational actors was that they 'transcended' inter-state relations – they operated in another dimension.[35] From this viewpoint TNAs are simply uninterested in much state activity. In pursuing their own goals – whether profit, the dissemination of an ideology, or the protection of fauna and flora – they act as if a world society were already in existence. Frontiers then become a marginal irritation, to be circumvented without difficulty by technology and the free movement of people, goods and ideas. Governments are not the principal interlocutors.

When faced by TNAs in 'transcending' mode governments may well feel unmoved and opt to do nothing. Equally, if they feel threatened by the actions they will probably try in effect to move the issue into category *one* or *two*. That is, they will either try to engage the TNA in straightforward negotiation, or to take countermeasures. Unfortunately, however, the very nature of the problem means that they may not succeed in the endeavour, either because there is no obvious point of responsibility to engage with or because the TNA is interested in neither deals nor confrontation. In this case a government will probably exhibit signs of confusion. The more astute will learn how to play the TNA game by using private groups or individuals based in their own society to counter transnationalism in its own terms, or taking its ground by adopting certain policy stances as their own.

In general, the nature of the interaction in a transcending relationship will be uneasy and intermittent, like the sound of one hand clapping. The relationship may simply be absent, as diverging assumptions and forms of agency make engagement inherently difficult. A good example of this form of relationship is the West's baffled reaction to the international resurgence of the Islamic faith. The constant tendency to place responsibility for certain developments on a small number of governments, and to identify a few groups or individuals as bogeymen, reveals a misunderstanding of the religion and its political role. Islam is too varied, too transnational and too diffused in society for western states to be able to confront it as such.[36] An intelligent foreign policy needs to discriminate between the faith and particular adherents, and in particular between beliefs and actions, but the temptation to treat Islam as an accountable political entity is often too great. It was a mark of statesmanship that in the serious crisis after 11 September 2001, the United States resisted it.

The relationship which governments have with transnational business is often of the same order. Although the two sets of actors cannot afford to ignore each other, it would be a mistake to assume that they are continually locked in a struggle over sovereignty and control of the international economy. Most corporations are, as the French say laconically about dogs, '*méchants…ils se défendent quand on les attaque*', but otherwise they are happy for governments to get on with running society.[37] For their part governments vary in their degree of interest in trying to control TNEs, but in this age of privatization they generally accept that their role in business is limited. They need, as Stopford and

Strange pointed out, to engage in negotiations with firms over investment sites, tax breaks and regulation, which is important, complex
and time-consuming.[38] But this is hardly the sum total of international
relations, and whether it is even crucial involves a value judgement
about the relative importance of political economy, security and identity
questions. On many key questions, such as the collapse of order in the
Balkans, the emergence of Palestine, or even North–South relations,
governments and TNEs simply do not have much to say to each other.

Epistemic communities are perhaps the best example of actors which
transcend conventional international politics, for good or ill. Although as
we have seen they are at times capable of pressuring governments to good
effect, their rationale is quite otherwise – the sharing and extension of
knowledge with other experts regardless of nationality. Scientists, for
example, tend to pursue links with colleagues all over the world, regardless of government-to-government problems. They may decide to follow
their own conscience in breaking off links with a given country, but in
general professional ties survive. Unless, that is, governments actually
prevent travel, as happened during the Cold War, with both sides denying
visas to academics, or suspending the exchange clauses of cultural agreements during times of tension. Democratic governments are faced in these
circumstances with the very embarrassing prospect of restricting the freedom of their own citizens in the pursuit of a foreign policy goal. They do
not wish, or know how, to intervene much in the worlds of culture and
sport. In Iran, by contrast, young people are currently exhibiting a strong
interest in western dance music, much to the consternation of the clergy.
Short of a return to the most puritan and authoritarian phase of the revolutionary regime, there is little to be done about it. The French government has discovered much the same thing in its attempts to protect the
French language. The spread of computer technology and its associated
English language terms is on a plane of international activity where governments do not belong. It is for this reason that in the 'transcending'
aspect of the relationship between states and TNAs, the latter have the
advantage. They are playing on home ground.

soft issue.

Linkage Politics

Up to this point we have shown how the international environment,
never wholly dominated by states, is now significantly transnational.
Governments have no choice but to co-exist with a wide range of different actors, and the state system operates alongside, is indeed tangled

up with, a net of transnational connections. We have catalogued the different types of transnational actor engaged in this process, and presented a model of the kinds of relationship they may have with states, through their governments. The next step is to examine the ways in which TNAs penetrate into states, impacting upon civil society and therefore at times both by-passing and embarrassing governments. This is what James Rosenau called 'linkage politics'.[39] It is to be distinguished from the advocacy of linkages associated with Henry Kissinger; that is, the attempt by a government to pressurize another by bringing an unrelated matter to the negotiating table.[40] This kind of linkage happens all the time in conventional diplomacy, more or less subtly, as with US hints of a weakening commitment to NATO if, say, the EU were to become too protectionist in trade. Most of the time the potential linkages barely need spelling out. When they do, it is usually a sign that diplomacy is failing.

Linkage politics in Rosenau's sense is a way of understanding: that is, the nature of agency at the transnational level; the kinds of difficulty that governments face when their foreign policy is being circumvented; and the sets of links which exist between the international system and the domestic environment. The latter is crucial to foreign policy-making and will be the subject of the two chapters which follow, but it is hardly insulated from the outside world. Linkage politics shows how, furthermore, any aspirations that governments might have to be gatekeepers, that is to have the exclusive capacity to mediate between the world and their own society, are doomed to failure.

The original definition of linkage politics still holds, namely that a linkage is 'a recurrent sequence of behaviour that originates in one state and is reacted to in another', with the caveat that given the ambiguity of the word 'state' it might be best to replace it here with 'society'.[41] Rosenau originally wished to escape from the 'conceptual gaols' of state-centrism, and was en route to a paradigm shift into 'cascading interdependence'. For this reason *Linkage Politics* is usually regarded as a mere curiosity or way-station in his intellectual journey. It is also disregarded because the complex matrix which it proposes as the way to study linkages is inherently unworkable.[42] Yet the scheme is worth retrieving for its central set of distinctions, grafted onto the basic definition of linkage. Rosenau distinguished between three kinds of linkage: reactive, emulative, and penetrative. The simplicity and accuracy of this insight make it curious that it has been so neglected.

Reactive linkages occur when an event in one society leads to spontaneous reactions in another, unprompted by governments. An early example was the demonstrations in London in 1851 in favour of the visiting Hungarian liberal exile Lajos Kossuth, which contributed to the dismissal of Palmerston as Foreign Secretary.[43] With modern communications hostile, popular reactions are almost guaranteed if co-nationals are maltreated abroad. Thus the taking of US hostages in the Lebanon led to various manifestations of anti-Arab and anti-Islamic feeling inside the United States. The expressions of mass concern in the Federal Republic for the citizens of the DDR in 1989 were of the same type. Even when fellow citizens are not involved, a reactive linkage can take place, as when New York dockers voted to boycott Soviet goods after the declaration of martial law in Poland in December 1981. Not infrequently these actions, while genuinely independent of governments, are not unwelcome to them, as they send signals to another state without the need for official responsibility. But they can also be embarrassing, even damaging, to the coherent conduct of foreign policy. Thus when the State of Massachusetts passed a Selective Purchasing Law barring the State from purchasing from firms doing business with the repressive regime in Burma, it was seen by the Federal government as a challenge to its and Congress's powers to conduct foreign policy and regulate foreign trade. This could not be allowed to pass, and the law was challenged successfully in the US Court of Appeals.[44]

An *emulative* linkage is essentially what the economists call a demonstration effect. An event takes place in one society and is soon imitated by the citizens of others, like the 'Mexican wave' in a crowd. Once again the demonstrations in eastern Europe in 1989 are the best example. After decades of repression, the coming of crowds onto the streets in the German Democratic Republic, and the movement of refugees to the West through Hungary, detonated similar events in Czechoslovakia. The subsequent peaceful demolition of the Berlin Wall on 7 November was an event of the greatest symbolic significance, and made impossible the position of all the repressive regimes of the Warsaw Pact. Crucial here was the loss of nerve of the Communist authorities, and the unwillingness of the Gorbachev government in Moscow to sanction bloodshed like that of 1956 in Hungary. But it was also clear that the societies of eastern Europe felt themselves linked by common experience, and were reacting spontaneously to each other regardless of particular governments. Thus even the Ceauşescu regime in Romania suddenly collapsed in the December, despite the fact that it had always advertised its independence from Moscow.

1989 was a 'world historical event' in Hegel's terms, and revolutions have almost always spawned some emulative, bandwagoning behaviour of this kind, even before the age of telecommunications. The sixteenth-century Reformation spread rapidly across societies, as did the abortive revolutions of 1848. The potential for emulation is the very reason why foreign governments are often hostile towards the prospect of revolution, as with the Holy Alliance of 1815 or the intervention in Russia in 1918. There tends to be an exaggerated fear of political contagion. Nonetheless, spillovers of this kind take place often enough, *when the underlying conditions are favourable,* and in all political directions. This happened with the spread of both fascism and communism, and in more recent times with the spread of the peace movement across western Europe during the early 1980s.

The third kind of linkage is *penetrative*, by which is meant the deliberate attempt on the part of elements of one society to enter, influence and, on occasions, manipulate another. This may be aimed ultimately at a government, and indeed may sometimes be difficult to distinguish from the operations of government agents. But there is an undoubted transnational dimension. Historically various forms of imperialism and neo-colonialism have occurred through the direct operations of missionaries, traders and soldiers of fortune. Allowing for changes of context, they continue to do so. Many French officials and intellectuals, for example, continue to regard the efflux of American cultural products, in particular those in the areas of film and popular music, as acts of informal empire. Yet there can be no doubt that these products are welcomed by many ordinary French people – indeed part of the fear of the French elite is precisely the prospect of popular emulation. The consequence is a continuing underlying tension in Franco–American relations, for all the progress in high politics. Australia has suffered something similar with the penetration of its coastal areas by Japanese capital and tourism, The result has been a degree of popular backlash (although penetration creates its own local vested interests) and intermittent diplomatic tensions. The United States has suffered the same in reverse, with the appeal of Japanese cars and electronics to the American consumer. The result is that US–Japanese relations have become steadily more delicate than security considerations alone would dictate. If Japanese firms had not very skilfully built up a base in the US, and if consumers had not proved deaf to appeals to prefer inferior home-made products, relations between Tokyo and Washington might have remained consensual and largely unruffled.

The result of accumulation of these three different kinds of linkage is that the nature of both domestic and international politics has changed, with concomitant complications for policy-makers at home and abroad.

With due acknowledgement to the existence of transnational relations right from the start of the history of the state system, the modern system is far more extensive and intensive, and the prevalence of transnationalism demonstrates that the state system itself exists in a wider context, with agency therefore occurring at different levels. Figure 8.2 shows how the funnel model, which was never wholly accurate but does represent what many governments would like to believe is foreign relations, is a gross simplification compared to the linkage politics model, let alone to that of the overlapping jurisdictions which are to be found in a diplomatic alliance between like-minded states, as in the European Union. The arrows provide examples of the kind of political transactions which can exist between societies, and between groups and foreign governments, without going through the parent government.

Linkage politics is prevalent because transnational actors are proactive, reactive and imitative. They follow their own agendas, react to states and imitate each other's successful tactics. Yet their actions are far from always being designed to cause problems for governments – indeed, the

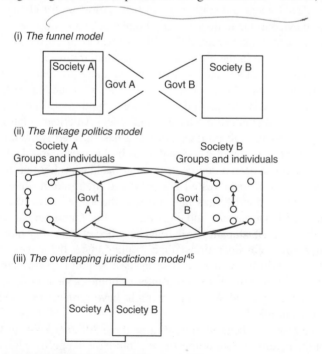

Figure 8.2   **Intersocietal connections: three models**

two sides increasingly engage. While achieving their objectives tends to be more a dream than a practical prospect, they act in many different issue-areas in international politics, including those of high politics, and cannot be lightly disregarded. As a result of their varied activity most societies in the world are directly linked into others; intermittently, and incoherently to be sure, but with sufficient continuity to ensure that governments not only look over their shoulders into the domestic environment (as we shall see in Chapters 9 and 10) but also have to assume an autonomous interaction between that environment and those of other states. The information technology aspects of globalization have made this even more routine and extensive.

It is at this point that the *politics* of linkage come in. There are countless linkages across societies – connecting art historians, steam train enthusiasts and retired politicians. Only some of them produce political difficulties, whether in the transnational realm itself or between TNAs and governments. When these issues arise it is because of competing views about how society should be organized or resources distributed, either domestically or internationally. The transnational dimension then adds a particular tension over the legitimacy of participation and an uncertainty over the location of the authority to act.

On the face of things most of the channels of action – such as pressure group coalitions, press campaigns, scientific conferences – are legitimate and innocuous, especially in open societies.[46] In practice they will not always be seen, or even intended, as such. Moreover, what the law allows is one thing; what is regarded as politically acceptable quite another. There is a fine line, for example, between fraternal assistance to a like-minded party in an election campaign, and unacceptable interference in another society's internal affairs. This will be even more true where the TNA is prepared to break laws, and in societies where it seeks to behave in a way not permitted to local citizens. Hence the mutual hostility between western TV crews and state authorities during events such as the repression in East Timor. The very act of seeking to interview a local citizen (probably themselves too frightened to speak) is often perceived as a political intervention, although it will be seen by the journalist and the society from which he or she comes as performing a service both to themselves and the community of mankind.

The web of linkage politics is the outcome of the mass of transnational activity produced by the various categories of transational actor. It feeds back constantly into all the 'bands' of the international system, affecting both TNAs themselves and states. It constitutes a distinctive form of agency in itself and thus exerts distinctive pressures on the agency of states. As a result, it is becoming increasingly difficult to know what decisions are being made, where and by whom. This has implications both for our understanding and for democratic accountability.

Confusing Responsibilities

Actors no less than citizens tend to be confused as to where power and authority lie when considering international and transnational politics. Accordingly states tend to overstate and TNAs to understate their respective roles; the one not to have their responsibilities diminished, the other not to attract unnecessary attention. If analytically one can talk about a continuum between the domain of the state and the domain of intergovernmental relations, at the mid-point of which exists the grey, 'intermestic' zone, this is of no help in terms of specifying the different functions of governments and transnational actors.

Let us take a specific example to make the point more clearly. In 1995 the tragic civil war in Algeria was beginning to take tens of thousands of lives, with western governments apparently either powerless to intervene or uninterested. At this point the Rome-based Catholic pressure group San Egidio began an attempt at mediation between the Algerian government and its fundamentalist opponents which soon made the headlines. After prolonged efforts, including a preliminary meeting, the effort was rebuffed by the military government, but it remains the single most constructive external intervention.[47]

How are we to interpret the actions of San Egidio, of whom few non-Italians had heard before these events? A realist might waste little time in concluding that the TNA was probably a convenient front for the Italian government, and possibly behind them other western governments which could not afford to be seen as publicly active. From here it is a short distance to the conspiracy theories which have always been common about those who cross borders, whether freemasons, arms dealers or peace-makers. A believer in international civil society, by contrast, would stress the autonomous will and capacity of San Egidio in the vacuum created by the cynicism and 'prudence' of the neighbouring states. More likely than either of these competing interpretations, however, is one which combines the two and accepts the messy character of events like these. Thus it is highly unlikely that the Italian government was either unaware of or opposed to the actions of San Egidio. The same can probably be said of its major allies such as

France, the United Kingdom and the United States. A strong degree of official encouragement was probably forthcoming. On the other hand the government was almost certainly not in a position to manage the intervention once begun, and was vulnerable to the political damage which ensues from failure, or even success, on the wrong terms. In this delicate and dangerous environment, where religion and human rights were as prominent as oil and patronage, all actors, whether external or Algerian, were groping in the dark and were, to some extent, interdependent.

Transnational actors are responsible only for themselves, whereas governments are responsible for the welfare of their people and often make even wider claims. Yet many of them exist precisely to pursue common interests, and their increasing prevalence among the more educated parts of the citizenry bestows a legitimacy that even states are coming to acknowledge. Some TNAs are being coopted into the processes of policy implementation, particularly in the Third World or in the aftermath of conflict, while others are coming to have an important role in standard-setting. The more this happens the more they will come to take on the bureaucratic character of states themselves, and the more necessary it will become to find ways of holding them to account. External policy traditionally gives more scope for evading such problems, but as we shall see in Part III, civil society is increasingly reluctant to leave world politics to governments. States thus face a double bind in trying to relate both foreign policy and the complex of transnational relations to recognizable democratic processes.

Part III
Responsibility

9

The Domestic Sources of Foreign Policy

Those responsible for foreign policy have to face many different directions at once: towards the states of the international political system, but also towards transnational actors; towards the close and the distant, geographically and politically; most tangibly, they must address their own constituents – the 'inside' of their own community, as opposed to the 'outside' for which they have no formal responsibility. They must face the fact that policy outcomes are vulnerable to events which are primarily 'domestic' and, conversely, that foreign policy impacts upon domestic politics. This chapter and the next deal with these two dimensions. The current chapter discusses the general relationship between the domestic and the foreign, with special reference both to the generalizations often made about the domestic 'sources' of foreign policy, and to the impact of domestic events, constitutional structures and types of regime. Chapter 10 moves the argument in a more normative direction, by considering how far foreign policy is meaningful to modern citizens and how far they are able to participate through it in the central political dilemmas which international relations raise. If most political action now has an international dimension, then the problems of choice between responsibilities inside and out, or over where to use scarce resources, become even sharper than in the days of the autarkic or the Keynesian state. If globalization also throws up a challenge to our identity, and to our ethics, then we shall also need to respond precisely through 'foreign' policy, albeit much altered from that conducted by Bismarck or even Adenauer. The domestic and the foreign, in other words, literally make no sense except in relation to each other. But this is not the same as saying that they are identical.

Sources, Constraints and Actors

No-one now believes that foreign policy is unaffected by what occurs within states. The billiard ball metaphor has been discarded, together with the notion that foreign policy is essentially a problem of strategy like chess.[1] Even neo-realists concede that there are important things which cannot be explained by international dynamics. Some analysts have gone to the other extreme, taking the view that 'for us only internal politics counts' as Richard Pipes remarked of US policy towards the war in Chechnya, or that 'foreign policy behaviour is often determined primarily by domestic politics', as Alexander Wendt observed in the context of discussing the limits of international socialization.[2] Be that as it may, careful observers have been pointing out since the 1920s that the nature of the modern state could not help but impinge on foreign policy, with its elements of mass mobilization, populism and economism. Eckart Kehr anticipated the arguments of Fritz Fischer about the distinctively 'Prussian' nature of German foreign policy, and most critics of fascism or Soviet communism made connections between domestic authoritarianism and external aggression.[3] For its part, US foreign policy was often seen as being at the mercy of isolationist domestic opinion – understandably, if not wholly accurately, after the disavowal by Congress of the Treaty of Versailles and the passing of the neutrality legislation in the 1930s. It was logical, therefore, that the phrase 'the *domestic sources* of foreign policy' should have become part of standard academic vocabulary by the mid-1960s.[4]

What does this notion refer to? It is important to distinguish between the different ways in which the domestic environment impinges on foreign policy. 'Sources' is an umbrella term, but it suggests more proactive inputs into foreign policy than the more concrete term of 'constraints', or limits. Neither tells us much about the identity of the various actors which operate at the domestic level and provide both inputs and constraints. These need to be specified separately.

The most sweeping interpretation of the idea of domestic sources is that which sees foreign policy as primarily generated from within – *das primat den innenpolitik*, referred to by Kehr. In powerful, quite self-sufficient countries like the United States, it may certainly seem to be the case that the complex politics of Capitol Hill are more crucial for international relations than any amount of speeches in the United Nations, or even bilateral negotiations with other major powers. It has often been assumed that if only the power of the Jewish lobby to determine the outcome of certain swing states in US elections could be diminished, American

policy would change and new possibilities for peace would open up in the Middle East. This is a gross oversimplification. The United States has strategic and moral interests in the survival of Israel independent of lobby pressures – which certainly exist and have their impact. It is also remarkable how much continuity there has been over decades in American foreign policy despite the vicissitudes of electoral politics.

Continuity itself can also be explained through the concept of the primacy of domestic sources, through linking regime type or the hegemony of a particular class to a certain kind of foreign policy orientation. We shall return to this approach below. For the moment two points will suffice. First, any such view renders too one-dimensional the nature of domestic influence on foreign policy. Single-factor explanations rarely convince where multiple actors and levels of activity are involved, let alone where problems are revisited over long, evolving historical periods. Most political systems, or for that matter, the internal affairs of most transnational actors, are too robust to be dominated by one pressure group or set of stake-holders. Second, the United States is untypical. Its constitution contains unparalleled opportunities for the legislature to check the foreign policy powers of the executive, and its political culture is coloured by both parochialism and anti-government attitudes – neither of which necessarily wins out, but which make presidents nervous about international commitments.

A more realistic approach to the domestic sources of foreign policy is to build on Robert Putnam's concept of the 'two-level game', in which 'chiefs of governments' are seen as playing politics simultaneously on two boards, the domestic and international.[5] There are strict limits to the uses of this game-theoretic, negotiation-centred paradigm – adding a second, domestic arena hardly transcends the failings of the familiar rational actor model – but it does capture the inextricability of foreign and domestic concerns from the viewpoint of the policy-maker. By starting from the position that foreign policy decision-makers are always 'Janus-faced', and that the two sets of concerns continually interact, we can both avoid the errors of single-factor explanation and observe what space might be available for leadership to 'make a difference'. The very fact that the two environments have different logics means that choices have to be made about both priorities and the management of complexity. This imposes considerable responsibility – and some freedom – on those conducting public policy. Even in the relatively narrow conception of Putnam and colleagues, a leader can manipulate the 'win-set', that is, 'the set of potential agreements that would be ratified by domestic constituencies in a straight up-or-down vote against the status quo of "no agreement" '.[6] The set is not self-executing, but requires considerable political effort, skill and creativity. Equally, foreign policy must be understood as subject to a continuous stream of domestic inputs, no less than international. Its 'sources' are multiple.

This notion of a stream of influences deriving from domestic politics goes well beyond the image of a decision-maker playing chess on two boards. It allows us to see that many of the domestic sources of foreign policy are unexpected, and do not conform to pre-set expectations or rules of strategy. Foreign policy is not immune from the impact of values, ideas, initiatives and upheavals, transnational in many respects but often also internally-generated. In the most dramatic instances, or in important states, these forces can even wash over the wider international system, channelled to begin with through the foreign policy of the state in question.[7] This happened with both the French Revolution and the Third Reich. Less dramatically, pressure group activity and internal party politics produced Britain's more ethically-oriented foreign policy after New Labour's victory in the election of May 1997, just as the pressure for land reform from disgruntled war veterans in Zimbabwe, combined with President Mugabe's need of an election-winning gambit, led to the occupation of white farms and an eventual crisis with Britain during 1999–2000.

Domestic society also imposes *constraints* on foreign policy-makers, in the sense of fairly stable and known limits to their freedom of manoeuvre by virtue of the particular society they represent in international relations. The interests of French farmers, inhibiting any wish a Paris government might have to reform the Common Agricultural Policy of the European Union, are a well-known example. However much leaders get seduced into making international affairs their priority, they are always pulled back by the elastic which connects them to their domestic base, often with rudely shocking results. This is partly a matter of intra-elite disputes, or the lack of resources with which to pursue ambitious plans, but it can also be the result of running ahead of domestic opinion. Although it varies with the nature of the state, certain groups will have a veto power in the sense that an initiative will require their 'ratification' (to use Moravcsik's term) if it is to have credibility abroad. The military are the traditional case in point, but in foreign economic policy banking and investment opinion (both home and abroad) will be crucial for the confidence which sustains a national currency. Even mass opinion can have this braking effect through referenda, as the French and Danish governments discovered in 1992–3 with their attempts to ratify the Treaty of Maastricht. The Russian Revolution of 1917 was an even more clear demonstration of the fact that no foreign or war policy can take for granted the support of the population who ultimately must sustain it.

An intelligent government will thus anticipate likely opposition at home and build into its foreign policy a sense of what the country will stand – something that the Soviet leaders, too used to assuming the obedience of their people, failed to take into account in December 1979 when launching the war in Afghanistan, which all too soon turned into their own Vietnam. It is possible for leaders, indeed, to exploit the constraints which domestic politics imposes on them in negotiations with other states. This is the 'my hands are tied' strategy, which, however, is likely to work only when the third party is disproportionately keen to reach an agreement. In the end it only encourages direct intervention in one's own domestic politics, to 'untie the hands', or produces a waiting game in the knowledge that domestic political constellations always change in the end.[8] Conversely, the prospect of changes of government, democratic or otherwise, makes any foreign policy-maker cautious about what he or she can promise to outsiders. Ultimately no government can tie the hands of its successors on the major issues of foreign policy, whatever the particular constitutional provisions.

The domestic environment is hardly monochrome. It consists of different *actors* and kinds of activity, which may best be conceptualized here in terms of concentric circles.[9] Since Snyder, Bruck and Sapin first conceived of the notion of a foreign policy decision-making system in which official leaders are the central but not exclusive site of actorness we have steadily added further circles of activity. Part I of this book dealt with intra-governmental politics, involving competing elites and bureaucratic interests. Moving outwards into domestic society, we encounter what may be apophthegmized as the four Ps: parliaments, public opinion, pressure groups and the press (including other media). These will mainly be covered in Chapter 10 in relation to the problem of the 'constituencies' of foreign policy – those to whom leaders feel practically and morally responsible. But there are other forces (if not quite actors) which the pluralism of the four Ps tends to conceal, namely social classes and regime-type. Both are dealt with in this chapter as instances of determining domestic factors, whose importance can be assessed on an empirical basis. There is a grey area between the individuals or groups which all too evidently possess some degree of conscious actorness and who therefore participate in the policy process, and those elements of society which may well shape policy but have no clear voice or mechanism for mobilizing interests. Thus 'the peasants', the 'working class', an ethnic minority such as 'the Hispanics' (in the US) or even the *gastarbeiter* (in Germany) may all have the potential to affect foreign policy, but they will have great difficulty in producing collective positions and are consequently difficult to observe 'in action'. All that can be done is to hazard limited generalizations on the kind of connections which might exist between foreign policy and particular configurations of class, regime or development.

More evanescent are the individual actors who can emerge from almost anywhere, with an impact of unpredictable nature and duration. Who would have said that Princess Diana would have become a crusader against land-mines, causing controversy inside her own state on a matter of defence policy? Or that an Orthodox Rabbi in Jerusalem would have not only described the Palestinians as 'snakes' at a sensitive time in the peace negotiations but also dismissed six million Holocaust victims as deserving their fate since they represented the souls of past sinners?[10] These may be extreme examples, but the emergence of more durable political forces such as the Greens in western Europe, or nuclear nationalism in India can also surprise conventional politicians and analysts. Every domestic environment is unique and is in a condition of perpetual movement.

This means that generalizations are always contingent – in particular with respect to the extent to which states function normally, at home before they even think of abroad. We have touched on this issue in Chapter 2, but it bears repeating here that some – perhaps even a sizeable minority – of the world's nearly 200 states so lack stable administrative, political and social systems, that it is difficult to conceptualize the relationship between foreign policy and their domestic environment. Where we find weak, 'failed', 'quasi' or 'prebendal' states we shall probably find weak, erratic and dependent foreign policies.[11] It is notable how little impact the Lebanon makes on its regional environment, compared to its equally small but not fractured neighbours, Syria and Jordan. The same is true of all too many African states. The penetration of the Taliban Afghan state by the private interests of Al Qaeda before long exposed that country to devastating foreign intervention. By contrast, where the military take power it is usually a sign that the state has already failed (and may be subject to more looting by the soldiery) and however undesirable for human rights reasons, this can have the effect of restoring statehood at the international level, and even a predictable foreign policy.

Complications from Domestic Events

In general, foreign and domestic politics are separate but not separable, as has been said since 1996 of European forces within NATO.[12] There are many actors who busy themselves simultaneously in both arenas, impacting on policy without much regard for formal boundaries. Equally, while issues sometimes present zero-sum choices between domestic and external goals, they usually reverberate both inside and outside the state, or transnational actor. This interconnection is most obvious in resource questions, but it also appears in relation to political culture and to the consequences of domestic change. Each of these three dimensions deserves further discussion.

On the *resources* front the issue involves the detail of public expenditure decisions as well as the long-term allocation of resources. Foreign policy is not, as we saw in Chapter 6, the most expensive area of state activity, at least in the narrow terms of diplomacy. But its associated instruments, of defence, trade promotion, and overseas development assistance, are far more costly. They provoke regular controversies over value-for-money, which all too easily degenerate into 'us' versus 'them' polarities. Do we need: another aircraft carrier, far-flung bases, embassies in Kiev or Mogadishu, membership of UNESCO, a national airline or consulates to help our more feckless compatriots around the world? Especially when the alternatives seem to be more hospitals, schools and roads, or simply mouths fed and children vaccinated against killer diseases. The issues are always more complicated than these stark choices. But there is no avoiding the facts that big commitments in international relations do imply fewer resources available for state expenditure at home, and that public debate often sets up the problem in this kind of way – charity begins at home, elections are won on the tax issue, and other commonplaces of domestic political life.

The more debate proceeds the more evident it becomes that domestic society is itself divided on the need for what might be termed 'spending beyond borders'. There are divisions between consumers, who generally favour tax cuts, and producers, some of whose jobs will depend on the arms industry, the military or the various other forms of government-subsidized international activity. Producers may also have privileged access to the bureaucracy which is so important in the policy-making process, and defence expenditure in particular has been traditionally ring-fenced because national security has been seen as the *sine qua non* of achieving other social goals. A point will sometimes be reached, nonetheless, where high expenditure on external goals imposes a crippling burden on a state, often leading to foreign policy decisions being taken for financial, domestic reasons.[13] Even the United States had to reverse its whole foreign economic policy in 1971 as the result of domestic stagnation brought on by the huge costs of the Vietnam War.[14]

An effective foreign policy should avoid getting to this point of high drama where major decisions have to be taken in one realm for reasons more to do with the other.

Essentially the pressures coming from the domestic and international environments are of contrasting types. The former can be insistent, practical, but also the product of relatively ephemeral political rows. Misjudgements, however, can lead to the fall of a government, which is why even trivial domestic problems loom large on the horizons of democratic decision-makers and why autocrats overreact to the hint of a challenge to their position. International pressures, by contrast, will be ignored *in extremis* because of supervening domestic concerns, but may ultimately have greater long-term significance, because they are seen as central to the state's very survival, through the need for either defence and/or alliance or the creation of a favourable international milieu. Bearing in mind that foreign policy-makers are often bound together internationally by common concerns and personal contacts, it can be seen why heavy domestic costs, both financial and political, are sometimes accepted for external reasons – as with the German willingness to finance the war against Iraq in 1991, or Australia's dispatch of troops to help the United States in Vietnam. In both cases the international situation was perceived to be so serious, and the need not to alienate Washington so strong, that governments accepted the inevitability of damage to other policies and to their own popularity.

If some can act as a free-rider, and therefore have it both ways – as when the US does not pay its dues to the UN or Sweden does not join NATO – for most there is a perpetual balancing-act to be conducted between the external and internal aspects of resource-allocation, with external commitments, once made, relatively inelastic. This is easiest to see in relation to the environment, where commitments to reduce CFC emissions or to preserve rainforests have practical consequences in terms of lost revenue or higher production costs. Despite the powerful lead it could give in terms of reduced oil consumption the United States will not consider serious taxes on petrol, because of the huge domestic protests which even a rise in price of a few cents provokes. The need for balance usually asserts itself in the end, however, as when two decades of taking cheap oil for granted came to an abrupt end in late 1973, or when France's neglect of its deteriorating competitive position vis-à-vis the newly unified Germany led to devastating defeat in 1870. Britain's painfully slow coming to terms with the changed nature of continental Europe after 1950 can be interpreted in the same light, while Israel's Arab neighbours will only be in a position to rectify their regional vulnerability when they are prepared, paradoxically, to commit resources to internal reform. Finally, the current members of the European Union will soon have to face the painful need to spend rather more on defence if they are serious about creating a military identity independent of NATO. A European army would have significant consequences domestically no less than internationally.

That foreign policy is subject to the swirls and eddies of domestic politics while remaining a distinctive arena can also be seen in relation to *domestic culture*. The latter is partly formed by traumas encountered in world politics, but once certain social attitudes and political forces are established they feed back to affect future foreign policy choices, often with serious consequences. The most prominent case of modern times was that of white-ruled South Africa. The regime in Pretoria tried to separate domestic and foreign politics, by denying the legitimacy of foreign criticisms of apartheid and seeking to engage in diplomatic business as usual. It also sought to use classic realist tactics by dividing its opponents abroad. In particular, this meant wooing those leaders of black African states willing to deal with them, notably Felix Houphouët-Boigny of the Ivory Coast and Hastings Banda of Malawi. This approach had some temporary success but in the long run was brought down by the impossibility of keeping apartheid in a sealed political compartment. The oppression of the black majority in South Africa ultimately conditioned South Africa's external relations, not just because of the success of private, transnational groups (as we saw in Chapter 8) but also because few governments wished ultimately to associate with a system which was historically doomed and which they and their peoples found repugnant. If it took time for this view to become established that was because domestic and foreign politics tend to run at different paces.

Other examples are not difficult to find. The anti-Americanism which is never far from the surface in Greek politics has its roots in the events of the civil war of 1946–9, the military coup of 1967 and the Turkish invasion of Cyprus in 1974 (which Washington, to say the least, allowed to happen).[15] It continues to cause difficulties for those Greek politicians and technocrats who feel they have no choice but to seek better relations with their biggest NATO ally. Events in the Balkans in the 1990s have reinforced both the domestic antagonism and the external tensions, because Greek opinion saw Serbia as having been unjustly scapegoated and its own concerns over Macedonia and Albania as having been largely ignored. This vicious circle of mutually reinforcing internal and external suspicions might be breakable by decisive action in one realm or another but it cannot be treated either as only a domestic or as only an international problem.[16]

An even clearer case of a government being at odds with its domestic political culture is Switzerland, where the whole set of indigenous institutions and political forces combines to make internationalism of the kind represented by membership of the UN and the EU, which most serving politicians and decision-makers would probably welcome, an unrealistic proposition. Norway is in a similar situation relative to the EU, while the United States, it is sometimes argued, has its own cycles of introversion and extroversion independent of the rhythms of international politics.[17] A less orthodox, but no less striking, case is Afghanistan, where the persistence of internal tribal and warrior traditions make the country both extremely difficult to subjugate and an uncomfortable ally, as the Soviet Union, the United States and Iran have all discovered over the past twenty years. Here the Afghans' long experience of external interference has produced a fierce culture of independence – and internal divisions – which then produce foreign relations far removed from those of more conventional members of international society.[18] From our analytical perspective, the important point is that the deep interrelationship of the foreign and domestic dimensions can only be properly understood by ensuring that they are not blurred into one.

The impact of *domestic change* on foreign policy has spawned a great deal of literature, particularly within the positivist tradition of Comparative Foreign Policy. Rummel, for example, confirming Sorokin, argued that conflicts inside and outside the state are unrelated.[19] That is, foreign policy is not affected by internal upheaval, and vice versa. This counter-intuitive finding is contestable, given the difficulties of coding conflict events and of interpreting statistics. The more traditional scholar, Geoffrey Blainey, once pointed out that half of the wars between 1815–1939 were preceded by major internal turmoil in at least one participant.[20] It hardly needs stressing that this meant that the other fifty per cent were not so preceded.

A more subjective, but still historically sensitive, generalization is that 'if a near-revolutionary situation exists internally, foreign policy paralysis and quiescence are more likely than belligerence'.[21] The corollary is that once a revolution has settled down, the twin consequences of its own fervour and the hostility of external conservatism can spark, for a time, a powerfully assertive, even expansionist foreign policy.[22] Civil war, by contrast, will simply paralyse foreign policy while making it at the same time more vital, as a way to cope with meddling outsiders. This was the case in Nigeria between 1964–7 when a full-scale diplomatic

civil wars

effort had to be mounted to prevent the building up of international support for the breakaway province of Biafra. Civil wars create situations of great danger both for the state concerned and for the international system, as shown by the way the North nearly found itself at war with Britain in 1861–2 during the American civil war, and by the costly intervention of the western powers in Russia between 1918–20, which arguably contributed to the subsequent siege mentality of the Soviet regime.[23]

Short of revolution or civil war, there are other ways in which domestic instability can shake up foreign policy arrangements. Even common or garden political turmoil can undermine the credibility of external policy, as was the case with the many short-lived Italian governments in the second half of the twentieth century. The similarly hamstrung French Fourth Republic managed to sound the death-knell in 1954 of the European Defence Community France itself had initiated in 1950. Yet it was to provide the further leadership necessary for the setting up of the European Economic Community. The severe crisis occasioned by the Algerian war of independence eventually brought down the fragile political system, to be replaced by the very different model of the Fifth Republic, with an assertive, independent foreign policy as one of its prime objectives.[24]

There can be little doubt that whereas for a small country a period of internal instability will only matter if it provokes intervention from the outside, for a major power it can reverberate through a range of key foreign policy problems. The United States found that the weakness of the second Nixon administration resulting from the Watergate scandal made even more problematical its contemporary difficulties with the Soviet Union, the Middle East and even its European allies. It was no coincidence that this was the era in which Henry Kissinger talked a great deal about 'linkage politics'. By linkage Kissinger meant the trading off of different diplomatic issues, and never far from his mind was the weakness of his own position in international negotiations (not least in the end-game of the Vietnam war) occasioned by the chaos in Washington. On the other side of the Cold War conflict, foreign policy often had to be put on hold for the quite long periods when ageing leaders were incapable either of action or of stepping down. The same painful saga was played out by Boris Yeltsin in the second half of the 1990s. Immobilism meant that the Russian political system cut a poor figure abroad, with Moscow virtually powerless to oppose NATO enlargement.

Internal events, therefore, like domestic culture and debates over resources, are perpetually connected to foreign policy in a two-way flow of influence which by definition implies some separation of the two realms. The scopes, issues and actors of the two arenas do overlap, which makes it sensible to talk at times of 'intermestic' politics, or of cross-cutting 'policy modes'. Yet they can still be distinguished. The contrasting rhythms and legal–normative structures of the foreign and domestic mean that they each always retain the capacity to surprise, upset and divert the best laid plans of the other.[25]

Constitutional Structures

The domestic environment is framed by a number of different forces, social, political and economic. But few things are more important for any entity than its basic constitutional structure, often outlined in a foundational document. This is even true for states which do not pretend to be 'constitutional' in the sense of subscribing to the principle of the supremacy of the law, and of liberal notions about the rights of the people.[26] No formal constitution is ever fully lived-up to, but even under autocracy there will be some form of basic pattern of government, while theory always conditions practice in the sense of creating expectations inside and outside the state as to what proper conduct should be.

In the area of foreign policy the elements of the constitutional structure which most affect outcomes are those dealing with executive–legislative relations. In federal systems the relations between central government and the constituent states are also of increasing importance. There are at least five different broad models of constitutional structure which are relevant here, and the differences between and within them can affect the style and the substance of a country's foreign policy.

These models are: federalism; the executive inside a multi-party legislative chamber; a unitary state but with powers divided between the legislature and a presidency; *de facto* dominance by a single party within a democratic structure; one-party systems. Although there is not the space to recite in detail the characteristics of the five, certain differences do need highlighting, with reference to key states like the United States, France, Britain, Japan and the Soviet Union.

Foreign policy is one of the areas which in federalist states is most clearly reserved for central government – indeed, it is the key rationale for an otherwise decentralized body. This means that in principle the non-central government (NCG) parts of the constitution are not permitted to conduct their own international relations. This varies, however, according to the nature and maturity of the system. The new German

Reich after 1871, for example, allowed the *bundesstaten* as well as the federal government to have foreign relations. Thus, following Bismarck's view that the centre should not have more power 'than is absolutely necessary for the cohesion of the whole and for the effect presented to the outside', large *staten* like Bavaria and Württemberg retained some of their diplomatic legations.[27] The German state subsequently turned through a full historical circle, with federalism suspended by the Third Reich and its unrestrained *machtpolitik*, only to be reintroduced by the Basic Law of the Federal Republic in 1949. The *Länder* were then restrained by circumstances from asserting themselves in international relations, but over the past few decades it has become clear that the widening agenda of foreign affairs has brought them into more direct international involvement. Certainly the Bonn government has had to accept that the consent of the *Länder* must be obtained for the conclusion of treaties which touch on matters normally under their competence – as do, for example, the treaties establishing the European Communities.[28] Conversely, the *Länder* have been increasingly active in direct relations with other sub-national units, following a general trend which while mostly limited to commercial and cultural activity does have the effect of squeezing national foreign policy in certain areas into a smaller space between global, regional and local pressures. On environmental issues, for example, where agreeing globally and acting locally are both vital, the regions will be indispensable partners.[29]

A federal structure both controls potential actors (units like Quebec or California evidently could be effective nation-states if given the chance) and privileges them, in the sense that they have a pre-formed identity, visibility and an infrastructure which makes some kind of international actorness feasible. Thus a number of US states have been able either to frustrate central government's external relations (as with Washington's inability to compel full domestic compliance with the provisions of the US–UK Tax Treaty) or to build up pressure for a change in official foreign policy by engaging in human rights motivated embargoes of countries like apartheid South Africa, or Burma, often against world trade rules as well as official national policy.[30] The constant struggle between federal government and the states over aspects of foreign policy swings back and forth according to wider circumstances. The human rights concerns of the 1990s advantaged the states, but after 11 September 2001 the pendulum swung back with a vengeance.

The other important dimension of the relationship between federalism and foreign policy is the check on executive freedom of action constituted by the division of responsibilities and the sharing of powers.

There is a tendency to assume that federalism implies a foreign policy which is constantly subject to restrictions and interference from within. This view is much influenced by the example of the United States, whose constitution provides for an unparalleled degree of participation in central foreign policy-making on the part of the Congress. The latter's assent is required for the ratification of treaties, for declarations of war (since 1973) and even for the appointments of ambassadors. The judiciary also has a role to play in settling disputes over decision-making, and the power of the purse is attenuated in federal systems. Such characteristics are also to be seen in some measure in other federations, notably the Federal Republic of Germany and Switzerland, in both of which the conduct of foreign policy is to a degree constitutionally decentralized.

Against this picture of a distinctively strong domestic environment in federal states must be placed the fact that the US Presidency has not found it so difficult in practice to assert its authority over foreign policy by the use of devices such as executive agreements instead of treaties or 'military advisers' sent to conduct undeclared wars. Moreover, the United States is exceptional in the degree of authority which has to be shared with the legislature in foreign affairs. The Presidency may talk up the restraints imposed by Congress, and they may be intermittent, but where else has foreign policy debate produced such actions as withdrawal from the League of Nations (1919), the televised Senate Foreign Relations Committee hearings into the Vietnam War, the War Powers Act of 1973, or the Freedom of Information Act of 1967? Other federations, like Australia, Canada, Nigeria or Brazil, display a more conventional pattern of executive dominance over foreign policy. Even where the constituent states have tried to take the opportunities which modern conditions offer them of a direct international participation, the executive has usually managed to limit their incursions, generally backed up by the courts' interpretation of the constitution.[31]

Beyond the variations of circumstance it is clear that the specific legal provisions of a constitution do make a difference. Australian federalism gives the foreign policy executive advantages compared to that of the United States and this is borne out in practice, where the government in Canberra sometimes seems to enjoy freedoms more akin to the Westminster model than to those associated with federalism.[32] The same is true in unitary states. While, as we showed above, the differences between the French Fourth and Fifth Republics did not prevent continuity in foreign policy, they certainly did affect the relationship between domestic politics and foreign policy-making. General de

Gaulle precisely cast the constitution of the Fifth Republic so as to free the hand of the executive from parliamentary interference, in part with the aim of ending the view of France as 'the sick man of Europe', so that 'today [1962] its influences and prestige are recognized throughout the world'.[33] This put France on a par with the United Kingdom for the first time, arguably, since before the Third Republic, in terms of not having a foreign policy regarded by all as perpetually undermined by domestic political weakness and introspection. Italy is currently making efforts to break out of the same trap. The endless governments of the 'First Republic' set up after the Second World War have not yet been replaced by a 'Second Republic' of alternating majorities based on clear electoral victories, which many want, but reforms have begun in the electoral system designed to achieve that goal. Part of the motivation for change has come from foreign policy, with a growing realization that Italian foreign policy was paralysed for years in part because of a parochial obsession with the politics of coalition-making in Rome, and the consequent tendency abroad not to regard Italy as 'a serious country' – that is, one with strong, stable leadership in which foreign policy is not perpetually hostage to the manoeuvres of domestic politicking.[34]

A constitution which produces endless coalition governments need not always be subject to rapid change. The Federal Republic of Germany has managed for years with a stable government consisting of the majority party, whether Christian Democrats or Social Democrats, supported in government by the minority Free Democrats (FDP) – who usually held the office of foreign minister. The model currently operates with the Greens in the place of the FDP. Even the transition to a Green Minister of Foreign Affairs, Joschka Fischer, has taken place smoothly. In Israel, by contrast, whose system combines elements of the British model with some characteristics of the French Fourth Republic, we can see that the constant difficulty of putting together a majority government in a multi-party system, combined with the unusual salience of foreign policy in the day-to-day politics of the country, makes for a high degree of unpredictability. That this would become ever more problematic for Israel (and by extension for those trying to negotiate with it) was predicted twenty years ago by Avi Shlaim and Avner Yaniv, who pointed out that 'the extraordinary publicity given to cabinet discussions and the complete absence of secrecy facilitate pressures, since parties can observe their representatives hewing to the party line'. They concluded that the compounding of intra-party divisions by inter-party ones produced 'a complex multiple fragmentation of all mainstream political forces' which would continue to damage Israeli *domose* foreign policy.[35] This analysis has certainly been borne out by the tortuous history of the peace process since Camp David.

The last example worth noting of how constitutional structure can affect foreign policy relates to one-party systems. There are two modes in which single parties can dominate domestic politics. The first is through a socialist or communist approach in which the popular will is supposed to be served not by parties competing for votes, but by a dominant, monolithic party, which embodies that will and operates on the basis of delegation instead of representation. The major historical examples here are the Soviet Union and the People's Republic of China. Although some realists might take the view that the foreign policies of these states is primarily determined by the logic of the international system, most observers believe that the dominance of the Communist Party has been at least of equal importance – which is not at all to repeat the Cold War cliché that totalitarianism is inherently aggressive. The change from the Soviet Union to Russia provides a unique test-case in this respect. Problems in relations between Moscow and the West have not gone away, and new tensions have arisen. Nonetheless, much of the adversary relationship has been dissipated, making possible disarmament, a Russia–NATO cooperation agreement, and an end to proxy wars in the Third World.[36] Some of the change is naturally due to the collapse of one side and the victory of the other, but had the Soviet Union remained communist and simply suffered an economic crisis and/or the collapse of the Warsaw Pact, it is unimaginable that the degree of cooperation which has occurred could have taken place. China's foreign policy, for example, while not generally threatening to outsiders, remains locked in the posture of suspicion and secrecy long associated with the rule of the Communist Party. Indeed, that very rule has ensured a continuity in policy which might not have been so sustainable (for example, over Taiwan) under an alternative regime.

The other mode of single-party dominance, however, suggests that constitutional structure needs understanding in conjunction with political culture. This is the kind of system which is democratic in every respect, and in which governments may actually fall with some regularity, but where the same party dominates the government for decades on end. This was the case in Italy between 1947–92, when the Christian Democrats were always the principal coalition partner, and usually occupied the key posts of prime minister and foreign minister, despite (or perhaps because of) the regular collapse and reformation of cabinets. Key individuals like Giulio Andreotti or Francesco Cossiga continued to bob to the surface whatever the particular political storm. An even more revealing example is that of Japan. Here the post bellum created a fairly stable democratic system with none of the apparent weaknesses of the Italian state. Yet the Japanese Liberal Democratic Party (LDP) remained the governing party right up to the economic and corruption crisis of 1993. The constitution allowed for change, but the people, embedded in a corporatist political culture which valued continuity, consensus and discipline, returned the same party to power persistently. The effect was to make the politics within the LDP more important than that between the parties, and in the case of foreign policy to reinforce the pro-Americanism and caution which had been the watchwords since the Peace Treaty of 1951.[37] In its turn, this foreign policy reinforced the domestic order associated with it, which was hardly surprising given that both were the products of the victors' peace imposed on Japan, and that the combination seemed responsible for an era of unparalleled prosperity.[38] Despite the worsening economic outlook, the LDP returned to power in 1996, and foreign policy continues to display continuity.

Constitutional structure, therefore, is an important factor in shaping foreign policy conduct. It can bestow strengths and weaknesses on a state vis-à-vis others, but it does not alone determine behaviour, let alone outcomes. An effective foreign policy may be achieved despite constitutional problems, but only by the expenditure of considerable effort to overcome the costs the latter impose. This will apply whether the problems are those of an over-weak or an over-strong executive. Although at first sight it may seem that compared to the role of pressure groups or the media, constitutions are a relatively arcane and marginal influence on foreign policy, the examination of particular countries shows that, in interaction with other domestic factors, the legal basis of a polity matters greatly. As realism and the tradition of bipartisanism steadily weaken, this will be ever more true. Where effective constitutions (and constitutionalism) are lacking altogether, as is still sadly the case in some parts of Africa, the chances of any kind of identifiable, accountable foreign policy are reduced still further.[39]

Autres Régimes, Autres Mœurs?

Over the past decade an extensive academic debate has arisen over the links between foreign policy and the actual nature of a regime, beyond broad constitutional structure and principles. This is the 'democratic peace' hypothesis, which harks back to Kant and was formulated by Michael Doyle.[40] It states that democracies are a force for peace, or at least that democracies 'feel guilty about the use of force'.[41] The arguments which have raged since the mid-1980s have usefully brought empirical and normative political science together, just as they have joined up International Relations, Political Philosophy and Comparative Politics. Strangely, they have not attracted many foreign policy analysts, despite the fact that the problem of the extent to which the internal nature of a state determines foreign policy is a central question for FPA.[42] The subject had identified the issue empirically but had become bogged down in behavioural attempts to give a definitive answer.[43]

If it can be established that democracies are less war-prone, or more cooperative, or indeed display any particular pattern of external behaviour, then it would demonstrate conclusively that the domestic factor is of central importance in international relations – *pace* Kenneth Waltz and other 'international structuralists'.[44] Unfortunately the question is not quite so straightforward as it seems, to say nothing of the answer. There are two major *caveats* to note before any conclusions can be drawn.

The first is that it is possible to formulate the problem in subtly different ways, with the result that much debate takes place over whether findings are commensurable. Some consider whether or not democracies are *intrinsically* pacifistic; others only how they behave towards each other. Some restrict their interest to the problem of war; others are interested in whether democracies are as 'constitutional', or respectful of law, in their external relations as they are in internal affairs. Lurking behind the whole debate, but not so often brought into central focus, are the issues of whether historical period makes a difference, and of the differences between proselytizing and non-intervening democracies in world affairs. Thus there exist various possible lines of argument, some much more ambitious than others. All, however, presuppose a link of some kind between domestic regime and foreign policy behaviour.

The second *caveat* is that the categories of 'democracy' and 'non-democracy' (for the debate necessarily involves the discussion of non-democracies) are wider and more elusive than might be supposed. Despite the common tendency to include classical Athens in the former category, and to talk as if the democratic era began in 1816, it is highly dubious as to whether we can justify talking about established democracies until after the First World War. This is because of the *de facto* disenfranchisement of the black population in the United States (which arguably continued until the 1960s), the lack of votes for women in Britain (and even of votes *by right* for men) before 1918, and the strongly authoritarian nature of Wilhelmine Germany. Republican France would qualify as a democracy if women were written out of the script.[45] Thus we have barely a century's experience to go on, a period in which war regularly led to the suspension of normal rights, and in which the number of new, unsteady states was rapidly growing.

Defining democracy also raises the problem of what kind of democracy, and how much of it. We may decide without difficulty that we mean here liberal democracy, with its stress on political competition, individual rights and a free economy, rather than the one-party democracy claimed by socialist states. But that still leaves a great deal of variety to take into account – between degrees of mass suffrage (may we only count systems where women have the vote?), between degrees of efficacy, and between systems where the economy is wholly 'free' and those where the state controls some or all of the movement of capital, goods, persons, information and services. Is modern Russia, with a rip-roaring, Klondyke capitalism grafted onto the old nomenklatura of communism, truly a democracy? Is Singapore, with its paternalist guided democracy of efficiency and clean-living, to be counted in the same category as messy, individualistic Britain or stable, participatory Canada? Non-democracies make an equally wide category, not least because there is such a grey area between the two. So many states are in transition, or display elements of autocracy and liberalism simultaneously. And can any group which contains the murderous tyranny of Pol Pot's Cambodia and the relatively benign monarchy of Hashemite Jordan really be a good basis for generalization?

Despite these difficulties, there are three conclusions to be drawn from the democratic peace debate and which tell us something about the role of domestic factors in foreign policy. The first is often seen as the most 'robust' empirical finding in all International Relations, namely that established democratic states do not (so far) tend to fight each other. This proposition can only be qualified at the margins, by including minor affairs like the four Anglo–Icelandic 'cod wars', which in truth are exceptions that prove the rule, since neither side wanted an all-out shooting war with a like-minded neighbour and NATO ally. The reasons why democracies should not wish to fight each other can be speculated over at length, but it is highly unlikely that international factors, such as the need for unity against a common enemy, can explain the persistence and universality of the norm. Clearly certain aspects of democratic life predispose towards peaceful conflict resolution with others of the same kind. These aspects do not relate only to the political regime. It is quite probable that civil society and the way it constrains executives (or, is thought to constrain them) are at least as important.

The second finding is that democracies do not hold back in their willingness to use violence against those they regard as 'others': that is, not of their own type. Although such statements subsume complicated debates about the responsibility of starting the major wars of the past century, what can be said is that democratic states have been willing to declare wars, that they may sometimes have created the conditions in which war was likely, and that they have often pursued war with grim vigour – as the tragic slaughters on the Somme, in Korea and in Vietnam testify – when it was not so infeasible to consider a negotiated peace.[46] This argument has been put even more strongly; that the self-styled democracies are hypocritical in their foreign policies, since they often treat non-westerners in a ruthless, even racist way, and continue to engage in various forms of oppressive imperialism.[47] At the least one must conclude that the proposition that democracies have an intrinsic aversion to war as such is simply wrong.

This does not mean that foreign policies towards non-democracies are the result of international rather than domestic factors, viz., that democracies suddenly switch into cynical realism when they step outside the freemasonry of relations between 'like-minded' states. Domestic factors also have a part to play here, in that the conviction of rectitude so common in liberal states, can lead to a determination to pursue a civilizing mission, an anti-communist crusade or a struggle against a would-be hegemon (the enemy is usually bent on hegemony; one's own side is naturally defending the right). This has been one of the most paradoxical aspects of the western debate about Kosovo. War has moved from being the epitome of failure or domination to being a necessary instrument of humanitarianism. It is a switch which has left many, particularly on the left, confused. Either way, the use of force by western states is likely to be powerfully affected by domestic political argument for the foreseeable future.

The third and last foundation on which to build future work is the finding that non-democracies do not necessarily engage in aggressive or uncooperative behaviour internationally, however unpleasant they may be towards their own people. That they were inherently dangerous was a common assumption among western scholars at the height of the Cold War, especially those who identified 'totalitarianism' as a distinct phenomenon, and those hawks who saw the Soviet Union and its Third World friends as the successors to the Third Reich in posing a threat to world peace and to democracy (usually equated). After a pause during détente there is now a similar tendency evident in relation to democratization. Those who resist the Hegelian spirit of history, it seems, are likely to be a danger to the international community as well as to their own people.

In practice this is a political position. There is no convincing evidence which suggests that autocracies pursue their ends internationally through aggression, terrorism or general uncooperativeness. Because some examples can easily be found of tyrants who do so behave does not justify the larger statement. There are just as many cases, perhaps indeed a majority, where a deeply illiberal regime has behaved with great caution, even propriety, in its foreign relations. Many Latin American states in the 1960s and 1970s, Spain under Franco and Iran under the Shah are examples. The People's Republic of China has been another, although it took the United States 22 years to accept that it could conduct normal diplomatic business with Peking, partly no doubt because of the prevalent belief that left-wing autocracies exported danger in a way that right wing autocracies did not.[48] Military regimes, likewise, are far from being inherently militarist. The armed forces increase defence spending, to be sure, and usually degrade the societies they control, but on balance they are more cautious over external adventures than are their civilian counterparts.[49] It is easier to suppress the enemy within – usually the reason for taking power in the first place – than to unleash unpredictable international conflicts.

The result of this survey of the democratic peace problem is one positive statement – that democracies shy away from war with each other – and two negative propositions, about democracies not displaying any particular pattern of behaviour towards other states, and non-democracies not behaving in a distinctive, let alone a uniformly aggressive, manner. The latter two tend to suggest that the nature of a regime is only significant in the relatively narrow circumstances of inter-democratic relations. This would, however, be too restricted a conclusion. Foreign policy is not only about the war problem, and the nature of a regime also matters in terms of how closely states are prepared to work together – contrary to traditional views of the inconstancy of democracies, it may be that they are capable of considerable continuity in their alliances and other commitments.[50]

When we move beyond the single-factor approach and add in a sensitivity to historical period or to the extent to which the regime in question has universalizing aspirations (as some do, independently of their democratic or undemocratic character), we may see that the nature of any domestic political system does help to determine the direction of a foreign policy. In part this is merely to impart the truism that when governments change there may well be an impact on foreign policy; more profoundly, it suggests that certain regimes evolve historically, through the very interplay of domestic and external forces, into international actors which are assertive or introverted, cooperative or domineering, ineffectual or responsible. And once institutionalized, this mix of regime and policy will take time to change even if the current pressures for democratization assume that the domestic is the key, and that political engineering is possible. Ultimately, domestic and international factors together represent a powerful, evolving matrix, determining a country's 'place in the world', as with the limits on modern Germany's foreign policy activism. It follows that too much external pressure will prove counterproductive at both levels. The post-Cold War regime in Russia, for example, will not conform to a western model for a long time (if ever) and it will take decades for its Soviet characteristics to fade completely. Its foreign policy is then a key point at which the domestic system encounters external influences and expresses its identity in a suddenly more overweaning world. Regimes need foreign policies.

Class, Development and Foreign Policy

Beyond regimes, constitutions and politics lies the broader social and economic context of a state. Its possible impact on external activity is both a neglected subject and one too large to do more than introduce here. But foreign policy cannot be fully understood if it is abstracted from the society and productive system which it serves, particularly as economic goals are central to modern governments' concerns and since civil society now has an international dimension. In the sketch which follows of the most relevant elements, the main focus will be on class and on levels of development, but some reference will also be made to the great socio-political forces of nationalism, religion and gender.

The twentieth century produced a great deal of talk about 'socialist' or 'bourgeois' foreign policies – evolving from John Bright's nineteenth-century view that it was 'a gigantic system of outdoor relief for the aristocracy'.[51] Most of this was mere rhetoric. It is difficult to imagine that any foreign policy, given the complex of pressures and influences which act upon it, could be the simple arm of any given dominant *class*, always assuming one could be identified. Even the fact that foreign policy, like most other aspects of government, is usually handled by an internationally mobile and sophisticated elite of *dirigeants*, and that their perceptions and judgements will be crucial to its outcomes, does not mean that foreign policy will reflect the interests of a particular social class. This has been a familiar problem in the debate over Marxian analyses of society in general, and few would now argue for a straightforward relationship between class and politics in any area. The most that could be said is that foreign policy-making is often the preserve of a sub-class, or specialized elite familiar with other languages and 'abroad'. This may or may not be nested within a persistent 'ruling class'. On the other hand, it stretches a point to assume, as it is all too often by liberal commentators, that the masses have by definition their views represented in democratically elected governments. It is rare to find a person of working-class culture (or even extraction) in high office and dealing with foreign policy.

In the immediate aftermath of a successful revolution, a different social class may enter power. It will then wish to put its stamp on foreign policy – perhaps most particularly, given the association of diplomacy with a narrow caste. The fact of having to deal with the continuing dominance of that caste across the rest of the international system tends to diminish the ardour of the purge sooner rather than later, but in the period before acculturation takes place some unusual moves may be made. It took Libya almost twenty years to relinquish its self-styled radicalism and use of the 'People's Bureaux' as bases for terrorism. The Soviet Union soon learned to play the diplomatic game after Trotsky's early threat to 'shut up shop', but continued for some time to behave as if diplomacy was a supplement to secret intelligence, rather than vice versa. The style of Chinese diplomacy after the 1949 revolution, rather more than the substance, was parochial, ideological and somewhat hectoring, at least until after Mao's death in 1976.[52] Given the experiences of the men who had fought long and hard to overthrow from below the feudal order in China, a more cosmopolitan approach was hardly likely. The same is true of the ZANU-PF regime in Zimbabwe.

Class is not the only way in which to approach the sociology of the domestic environment of foreign policy. Nationalism, religion and gender are prominent elements in most societies, and all have the potential to bear on foreign affairs – the first directly, and the latter two by virtue of their transnational qualities. All have been written about extensively by IR scholars, but rarely in specific relation to foreign policy.

Nationalism and populism by definition figure prominently in the history of foreign policies. It is not difficult to think of examples where assertive, even xenophobic, campaigns have been conducted against other states, or have undermined attempts at international cooperation. The Balkans is only the latest in a series of outbreaks over the past two centuries. Some of this can be put down to the cynical exploitation by elites of the popular factor so as to justify acts of aggression, and/or to distract their disgruntled populations. But whether domestic movements inherently sweep foreign policy up in their tide is another matter. The beginnings of European nationalism were associated with the creation of conscript armies and the idea of 'the nation in arms', while national-ism, as opposed to the nationality principle, is a sociological phenome-non with a mass element.[53] Moreover, although the idea that our nation is the highest good need not entail xenophobia, it is difficult for profes-sional diplomats to contain its effects. Within their own states poor immigrants are always the first victims, on the streets, of any national-ist resurgence. Foreign policy is structurally vulnerable to the same process, as two recent examples illustrate.

In India the dominance of the Congress Party after independence produced a foreign policy of pacifistic non-alignment, qualified only by a powerful assertiveness where borders were in question, whether in Kashmir, Bengal or the Himalayas. There seemed no interest in becom-ing a great power or in acquiring the relevant military strength. The inequalities and problems of domestic society were also managed in a surprisingly quietist mode. From the late 1980s, however, the Congress Party, weakened by the failings of any dynastic order, and by the sharp-ening contradictions of modernization, came increasingly under chal-lenge from the Bharatiya Janata Party (BJP), which eventually came to power in 1996. This militant Hindu party arose from nowhere on a tide of discontent with corruption and stagnation, but it also soon developed a distinctive foreign policy, in part genuine and in part an effective way of accusing the old order of not having defended India's interests. The result, by 1998, was that India had taken the momentous step to explode a nuclear device. This immediately led to a tit-for-tat Pakistani explo-sion, but it was wildly popular in India. The nationalism of the BJP had thus taken India's foreign policy very rapidly down a new and risky path, compelling other parties to jump on the bandwagon if they wished to survive.[54]

Almost as dramatic was the emergence of the far-right nationalist Jörg Haider in Austria. Although Haider is only Governor of the province of Carinthia, his populist appeals to a notion of a pristine Austria free from the contamination of immigrants and other forms of external 'interfer-ence' meant that his Freedom Party gained 27 per cent of the vote and was taken into the governing coalition in February 1999. This in itself would not have changed Austrian foreign policy, but the strong reactions from fellow Member States of the European Union, and their imposition of sanctions on Austria (in the form of exclusion from meetings), not surprisingly evoked a further nationalist reaction in the country itself which has weakened Austria's support for the enlargement policy of the

Austria + India.

Union, and even for the EU as such. The Defence Minister Werner Fassalend (from the conservative People's Party) immediately replied that 'we absolutely reject the possibility of accepting that foreigners can make decisions over us'.[55]

Nationalism, therefore, by its nature spills over into foreign policy even when it is not violent or does not spring directly from international problems. The connections between the two phenomena are revealing and would repay further research, especially in the context of the new post-Cold War nationalisms of the Balkans and Transcaucasus. The same is true of religion, although as argued in Chapter 8, this is mostly a force for transnationalism. Occasionally a state will become theocratic, as Iran still is in important respects more than 20 years after the revolution of 1979, and as Saudi Arabia has always been in part. Israel is more an ethnie-state than a theocracy, but it is possible to imagine it in the hands of Orthodox Jewry. Under right-wing Republicans the United States can come close to vitiating its constitutional church–state separation and to institutionalizing the evangelical agenda. In these circumstances foreign policy will always be affected, largely because of the projection of particular codes of morality abroad, but also through the blurring together of the instruments of foreign policy. Italy under the Christian Democrats sometimes harnessed its foreign policy to that of the Vatican, and in Iran's pursuit of the *fatwa* against Salman Rushdie it was almost impossible to distinguish the roles of politicians and *imam*. German Catholics had some influence over Germany's concern to recognize Croatia. When religion is important domestically, there will always be a limit to what can be tolerated abroad. As with Britain and the Bulgarian atrocities of 1877, if fellow members of the community seem in danger of persecution, there will be pressure on the government to act. Muslim states cannot be indifferent to the sufferings of Bosnia, or to the Palestinian position on Jerusalem. This is, however, a long way from saying that they will act, even in a crisis, while for the routine business of foreign policy religion is mostly a background factor.

Gender is a social dimension which can bear on foreign policy, but even more indirectly. The concern with gender which has burgeoned in IR studies over the past fifteen years has primarily been a normative and philosophical one. There are important cases to be made about the differential sufferings of women in development, and about their neglected part in war. The view that orthodox thinking about international relations has been too suffused with masculinist values also has a great deal to be said for it.[56] In terms of an analytical approach to the impact of the gender dimension from within particular states on foreign policy, however, there is less of interest to be said. Women and men do not divide on gender lines in terms of attitudes to war or any other foreign policy issue, although opinion polls sometimes show a limited (and variable) degree of differentiation. It is true that 'women's issues' have started to force their way onto foreign policy agendas. In particular, the Greenham Common women's movement against nuclear weapons had a wide impact on public attitudes, and well beyond Britain. The United Nations has promoted awareness of gender-specific human rights concerns. For the most part, however, discourse changes more than facts. The sadness of the mothers of the disappeared young people in Argentina or of the sailors drowned in the *Kursk* submarine, is only acknowledged after the event, and at best helps to forge better intentions for the future.[57] The scandal of sex tourism to the Third World is publicized, but left largely untouched. It should not be forgotten, either, that there are just as many fathers mourning their lost sons, from Verdun through Stalingrad to the Iran–Iraq war, and that men, women and children suffer equally the horrors of invasion, displacement and civil war. The issue then becomes less that of the impact of gender on foreign policy, than whether there is any scope at all for 'the voice from below'.[58]

Development is another point at which domestic society and foreign policy can intersect, and another where a vast literature fails to give much coverage to the intersection. Notwithstanding this neglect it is important to say something about two issues, the relationship between *levels* of development and foreign policy, and the impact of the *type of socio-economic system* on foreign policy.

In terms of the level of development the question can be focused further by asking whether or not less developed countries (LDCs) manifest particular kinds of foreign policies. Although there is an argument to be had as to whether the widening of the category since the 1970s to include the Newly Industrializing Countries (NICs) at one end and the Least Less Developed Countries (LLDCs) at the other does not invalidate it, there is still a big enough gap between the income levels of the OECD states and those of the poor, agricultural states to justify a hypothesis about differential behaviour.

These poor states constitute all but about 70 of the 189 members of the UN, and have a per capita income (GDP) of less than $5000 a year. As a result they are structurally on the defensive. Not only do they lack the resources to be pro-active in international affairs, intervening far from home or helping to shape the milieu as a whole, but they also find it difficult to protect themselves from external interference. Their foreign policy is dominated by the need for economic development and financial assistance. Diplomacy in these circumstances is successful if it can widen the negotiating margin of manoeuvre of a supplicant even a little. Although many of these states have wasted precious resources on building armed forces, there is little which can in fact be done with the military instrument, except engaging in ruinous wars, such as those which plague the Horn of Africa.

These generalizations do not do justice to all LDCs or to all phases f their history. Countries like Nigeria, particularly when oil-rich, Egypt or India are in a distinct category as states with huge potential, and some actual clout. But many others, whether Angola or Zambia, Vietnam or Bangladesh, Guatemala or Cuba, are in very difficult situations. They may not, as the 1960s conventional wisdom had it, exist in a complete condition of 'dependency' on particular rich states or on the dictates of global capitalism in general, but their foreign policies persistently display passivity and highly restricted choice. Jamaica's Michael Manley in the 1970s consciously reacted against the perception of dependence, and attempted to use foreign policy to break out of it, as had Fidel Castro, Kwame Nkrumah and Julius Nyerere, but with the same largely counterproductive results.[59] LDCs do not have the options of the average developed state, that is of a relaxed independence, with more or less free choice over association and cooperation with other states. Their domestic situation presents them in theory with five options, but in practice often only with the first – that of accepting the disciplines of structural adjustment presented by international economic institutions, and not seeking to rock the boat by political activism. The other four are all unattractive or costly in various ways: (1) international trades unionism, or combining in a strategy of resistance with other poor states. This looked like the way forward in the 1970s with the Group of 77; now the divisions within the group are too great. (2) Confrontation, rhetorical or practical: this was a line pursued variously by Libya, Cuba, Iran, China and Iraq. The costs can only be borne by states with secure sources of funds, and an impregnable domestic basis. (3) Clientelism, or attaching the fate of the state to a more powerful friend. Cuba, North Korea and South Vietnam have all followed this path, only to discover their vulnerability to changes in external patterns of power or in the regime of the patron. (4) Isolation, which we dealt with more generally in Chapter 7.

All of these options are relatively extreme, and illustrate how LDCs have to make big sacrifices if they wish to assert their political values and independence. It is not surprising that most do not try, or are forced to change course after a costly attempt. More often than not while poverty combined with a relatively pitiless external environment (witness the dragging of feet over the cancellation of Third World debts) ensure limited choices in public policy, it is the elite rather than the people of these states who determine which trade-off to go for and who will incur its costs.

This said, it should not be assumed that the LDCs do not also face the same general foreign policy issues as other states, that is, security, regionalism, balancing the internal with the external, and ideology. It is just that their constraints are more pressing, and that foreign policy may also have to be used more frequently for nation-building, or consolidating the borders and structure of the new state itself. In time, the same kind of decision-making issues and domestic pressures will occur in LDCs as in richer states: bureaucratic politics, groupthink, domestic factionalism and even press criticisms are not the preserve of the developed alone. All foreign policy-making is prone to a greater or lesser degree to these syndromes.[60] They are just more spasmodic and embryonic in the poorer countries, whose domestic and international environments tend to blur into one around the needs of development. When poverty coincides with potential importance and geopolitical position, however, the resulting 'pivotal states' may generate foreign policies of great consequence for themselves and for others.[61]

The issue of the impact of the *type* of economic system, as opposed to its level of development, in a way boils down to whether capitalism produces different foreign policies from communism. This issue was so sullied by the political disputes of the Cold War that it is difficult to separate it out from that of the responsibilities of the USA and the USSR. It also tends to merge into the more contemporary debate as to whether the spread of capitalism will itself promote democracy, and in time therefore also a more peaceful, post-military world – two giant steps for logical argument. The answer to that lies in the future, although we can all make our best guesses. It is also to some extent beside the point, now that the major alternative to capitalism has collapsed. Of more use here is a brief demonstration of the fact that political regime and socio-economic system cannot always be kept analytically apart, and that in certain circumstances their mutual interplay will have a dramatic impact on foreign policy.

The history of imperialism, for example, has raised huge controversy over the relative parts played by domestic and international factors in pushing or pulling the European states into the scramble for Africa and other territories at the end of the nineteenth century. Within the domestic category there have also been debates about whether or not economic forces were decisive. The propositions of Hobson and then Lenin that surplus production capacity led the Europeans to acquire new markets overseas were eventually refuted by the work of historians like David Fieldhouse who showed both that the arguments over surplus capacity were exaggerated and that the new territories were the least promising places to absorb it – most exports going to places where industrialization was already underway, such as the United States or Russia.[62] Nonetheless, this does not mean that socio-economic factors have no role in imperialist foreign policies. At the least one can say that if imperialism is pursued its form will be related to the socio-economic system of the metropole. England acquired far-flung colonies not just because it was an island with a strong navy but also because its Crown was one of the first to make deals with private adventurers and then to encourage joint-stock companies like the East India Company or Hudson's Bay. In our own epoch, now that colonialism has been discredited, 'informal empires' are enabled through the many subtle processes made available by advanced capitalism. What governments lose in political control they gain in reduced responsibility and visibility. Thus the United States has never needed to have colonies in central America, as its economic interests already penetrate deep into most states of the region. By the same token it has inexorably supplanted British and French influence in the Caribbean. Meanwhile, the Europeans have retained influence in many parts of the Third World via a combination of private capital and the European Union's association agreements with the 78 ACP countries.

Imperialism has hardly been a preserve of the capitalist countries. Accordingly communist states, or more broadly state-trading countries, have their own mode of seeking external control. They can use barter trade or tied currencies up to a point, but have had mostly to rely on military force and formal occupation on the one hand, or informal penetration through party connections on the other.[63] Thus the Soviet Union created a huge, territorially contiguous empire which when it fell apart between 1989–91 had far more fundamental consequences for the Soviet state than the collapse of the European empires had had for their mother countries. Involvement further afield also required large commitments of men and *matériel* which fostered bloody wars (as in Angola and Ethiopia) with largely counterproductive results. For their part, of course, the capitalist countries can also play this game, but more deniably and not as their only instrument. Capitalism does not always generate informal empire – as the histories of Switzerland, Denmark and Canada show – but it certainly makes it possible.

Fascism is another major historical phenomenon of great interest to the student of domestic factors in foreign policy. Was fascism generated by a particular type of economic and class configuration which *required* aggressive imperialism to sustain it? This is an enormously complex problem which cannot be done justice to here. Even if fascism historically was expansionist, is that because of a particular ideology or were there deeper, inherent forces at work? Was Nazism the classic case, or a critical variant? Although we have (thankfully) few cases to base conclusions on, it seems likely that fascism is far more than a matter of regime. It goes beyond autocracy and one-partyism to engage in violence, messianic nationalism/racism, and mass mobilization behind a crusading disrespect for pluralism.[64] Probably fascism was an historical phenomenon of a particular period, but there is always the possibility that it could return in some form. In that event we should always be alert to any state in which there is considerable domestic upheaval, demanding *lebensraum* or producing a racist, xenophobic regime. That would be very likely to have contempt for its neighbours and for any notion of international society. By definition fascists are not interested in realpolitik and co-existence. They are revolutionaries with a commitment to an aesthetic of violence, at home and abroad.[65] Their sense of historical rectitude and supremacy means that their agitation is unlikely to stop at their own frontier.

Foreign Policy as Output – and Choice

The domestic environment undoubtedly shapes foreign policy regularly, and importantly. But it does so in interaction with international factors. Both are filtered through the decision-making process, which makes its own contribution to outcomes. This process then produces a set of positions and attitudes which amount together to a foreign policy tradition, which might also be described as a matrix, or a discourse, according to taste. They represent the continuity of foreign policy and to some extent become institutionalized in processes, language and institutions.[66]

From this point of view foreign policy can be seen as an *output*, sometimes deriving principally from domestic sources. Certainly it will be the domestic setting which will seem to embody foreign policy traditions, even if they have not been primarily generated at home, given that their rationale is primarily national. Often they will also be severely constrained by domestic factors and actors. None of this, however, is enough to justify generalizations about the 'primacy of domestic politics' for single countries or particular periods, let alone across the board. The domestic factor is frequently central to our ability to understand foreign policy, and in some sense it always provides the key starting-point, in relation to ultimate purpose, as we shall see in Chapter 11. Nonetheless, foreign policy is 'foreign' policy and it cannot be regarded simply as the external face of pre-determined state positions. The interplay between the domestic and the international is perpetual, and complex, to the point that in terms of causation the two sets of pressures cannot always be fully disentangled. This is evident from a number of examples, such as fascism, or what are increasingly known as 'transitional states', where the very process of constitution or re-constitution involves simultaneous attention to problems of borders, recognition, regime, aid and nation-building, all of which have both 'inside' and 'outside' connotations.[67]

A concern with the domestic dimension ultimately goes beyond questions of influence, explanation and determinism, which may be analysed with some pretensions to neutrality. It also directs us to the question of choice; that is, how far can a polity, a people, control their own foreign policy executive, and how much influence can they exert over the content of policy? What are the most important means by which domestic participation is made possible – and how far does practice vary? These are matters for informed analysis, but they also bring us close to the realm of political and normative debate, from which foreign policy should not be abstracted. In dealing with them, the chapter which follows thus prepares the ground for the book's conclusion, which attempts to make sense of the changing place of foreign policy in our political and ethical life.

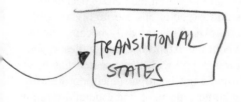

TRANSITIONAL STATES

10

The Constituencies of Foreign Policy

[handwritten margin notes: "Society ; responsibility ;"]

A democratic decision-maker is always aware of being responsible to the society which lies behind the political process. Even autocrats are not always insensate in this respect. But responsibility is ambiguous and relational, because there are many constituencies which must be borne in mind simultaneously: at home there are colleagues in government, the party machine, the constituency voters who brought you to power in the first place, sponsors of various kinds, and ultimately the electorate as a whole. In the international realm there are allies, neighbours and colleagues in a network of similar parties, together possibly with 'the international community'. All this is to say nothing of future generations, whether at home or abroad.

It is a matter of practical and theoretical importance as to whom decision-makers feel responsible, and to whom they are expected to be responsible. Yet these feelings and expectations are highly variable, according to individuals and contexts. This is partly because of the obscure nature of the evidence about the extent to which domestic populations are concerned about foreign policy. Little research has been done on this question, although much has been presumed, not least by politicians. While it is clear that some aspects of domestic and foreign policy have come to be intertwined, and therefore that certain groups have come to have stakes in external policy which they did not previously possess, at the same time there is much which remains specialized, arcane and remote to the silent majority still rooted in one particular society – until it smashes unexpectedly into their lives, as so literally and horribly happened to the people of New York on 11 September 2001.

Even under the impact of such events we cannot assume that there is necessarily a steadily growing international awareness. The tragic upheavals of war and totalitarianism destroyed or rearranged the lives of hundreds of millions between 1914–89. Yet the children and grandchildren of those who suffered, perhaps precisely because of a painful awareness of the past, are only too happy to sink back into a routine existence, whose essential parochialism remains unchallenged by occasional travel to foreign beach resorts or real-time news of crises in exotic countries of which they know little. To an extent this is a Eurocentric perspective. The populations of the Middle East, Indo-China and parts of Africa know only too well how the international can tear into their lives, through war, environmental degradation, alien ideologies and the continuing consequences of imperialism. Yet by the same token they resent the incursions and hold the more fiercely onto their local identity. Only a few are able to embrace globalization or to harvest its benefits.

Given these uncertainties about what the sovereign people might want, expect and need their governments to do in relation to the world beyond their immediate community, this chapter investigates the relationship between foreign policy and the political constituencies which lie behind it. A path is steered between the traditional paternalist assumption of a necessarily elite-run foreign policy on behalf of the general good, and the implication of globalization theory that foreign policy is an empty vessel, incapable of delivering any goods, general or particular. The questions are posed: for whom is foreign policy conducted, in principle and in practice? Who lays claim to it, and by what means are decision-makers held to account? And a version of the old question, *cui bono*, who sees themselves as benefiting from foreign policy? The analysis begins with the formal mechanisms of foreign policy accountability, building on the discussion of constitutional structures in Chapter 9. This is followed by discussion of the key institutions connecting decision-makers to wider society, namely public opinion, interest groups and the mass media, leading to an assessment of the view that since civil society and domestic politics themselves are constituted by foreign policy activity, they cannot be seen as independent constraints. The chapter ends by showing how leaders increasingly feel the need to engage in dialogue with foreign publics as well as their own, which tells us something about the evolving meaning of responsibility in the modern era, and about how the constituencies of foreign policy have become more extensive, and more complex.

Accountability versus the Security State

Accountability is not the same as responsibility. Responsibility is about the awareness of acting for others as well as oneself; it begins with perceptions and values. Accountability is more formal, and refers to the ability to make someone answerable for their actions, and to pay a penalty if, according to the prevalent rules, their account is unsatisfactory.[1] In foreign policy the issue of accountability has been widely discussed since the First World War (and in the United States for much longer). In few countries, however, have very clear mechanisms been established, and even where they have, actual practice often does not live up to theory. Indeed, it can be argued that provisions for accountability have often been deliberately sacrificed in the presumed interests of security and an effective executive – and that legislators have been all too willing to go along with the attenuation of their powers. When one adds in the dimension of the enormous growth in the apparatuses of foreign, defence and intelligence policy-making in the twentieth century, we can see how difficult democratic accountability is to achieve in practice against the presumptions of the 'security state', all too often bloated, secretive and prepotent.

The discussion of accountability primarily involves liberal democratic states, which make it an article of faith to restrain executive power and to seek a popular consensus for public policy. Even one-party systems, however, usually have formal provisions for some degree of answerability and participation in foreign policy-making. The Supreme Soviet had powers over the ratification of treaties, and the Chinese National People's Congress (NPC) likewise. That in practice they performed the function of rubber-stamps does not mean that their constitutional powers could not have been asserted more, with meaningful debates and more genuine transmission of views upwards from local party representatives.[2] The political systems of the Soviet Union and of the People's Republic were forged in war and revolution and never evolved beyond their original command culture, at least on foreign policy. In many other states parliaments are equally ineffective – unrepresentative, cowed or suspended *sine die*.

Since 1989 there has, nonetheless, been a general move towards democratization, which means that it is particularly important to examine the experience of pluralist states. Here formal accountability has two main aspects: *parliamentary control* and the verdict of the electors. These things are inter-related since legislatures consist of elected representatives who then exercise powers in the light of the views of the voters who gave them power, but members of parliament in a representative system follow the dictates of party and conscience, the first of which in particular tends to take precedence. In foreign policy-making in any case they generally have few constitutional levers to pull because of the presumption in most constitutions that the executive needs free hands if the state is to be effectively protected. Yet parliaments are powerful symbols of popular political control and are focal points for both insurgents and nervous leaders – as Boris Yeltsin revealed when suspending and shelling the Russian Supreme Soviet in 1993.[3] It is worth asking in the context of the contemporary triumph of liberal democracy whether even foreign policy is now becoming more open to democratic influences – or if not, why not?

Always the exception, as we saw in the last chapter's discussion of constitutional structures, has been the United States. In terms of basic powers over foreign policy-making the US Congress has no rival. The constitution gives it the right to declare war, to raise and to support armed forces and to ratify treaties (by a two-thirds majority of the Senate – and of those present). It also has the crucial power of the purse; appropriations for foreign policy purposes are not excluded (as in Britain) from the general requirement to be specified in a budget with legislative approval. This is vital given the immense size of the military–industrial complex and of the United States' global presence. Finally, the Senate's approval is required for senior ambassadorial appointments.[4] In the past thirty years the Congress has extended these nineteenth-century powers by approving the War Powers Resolution (in 1973) which sets limits on the period in which the presidency can pursue an undeclared war, and by requiring the secretary of state to give the Congress the texts even of executive agreements (previously the way around Congressional powers over treaties) within sixty days of their signature.[5]

Other democratic systems, mature or not, do not have these provisions for parliamentary control. In some the executive tends to be extremely cautious about not running too far ahead of the legislature, for historical reasons. The Federal Republic of Germany is a case in point, where the Basic Law of 1949 does not in so many words forbid the use of troops 'out of area', but where the conventional political interpretation until the Constitutional Court ruling of 1994 was that it did.[6] The French National Assembly voted down the European Defence Community in 1954 just as the US Senate had done with the League of Nations thirty-five years before. The Japanese Diet in 1955 threw out the idea of an extension of the Japanese–American security treaty, despite Foreign Minister Shigemitsu having signed a joint communiqué agreeing to it.[7] The House of Commons has given British governments a very hard time over every treaty relating to accession to the European Communities and their development.

What is common to these cases is not the formal powers which parliaments have over foreign policy; these vary considerably, not least in their implementation. More important is the interpretation of the law, which itself depends partly on general political culture and partly on particular circumstances. Given the number of occasions when even the parliaments with relevant powers do not assert themselves to halt treaties or to interrogate the foreign and defence budgets, it is clear that it will take an unusual combination of circumstances for the executive to have its agreement with another state overturned by parliament at home. Even in the United States there will need to be both a deep lack of confidence in the government of the day plus a high degree of salience and concern about the foreign policy issue concerned – probably as the result of a long sequence of frustrations which have brought things to boiling point. Thus both President Carter and the Congress had had enough of Soviet behaviour in the Third World by the time they ended the SALT II negotiations after the Soviet invasion of Afghanistan in December 1979. But the Congress was ready to throw out a treaty whatever Carter decided, and it is the knowledge of its *potential* power which is most inhibiting to a president.

At times, given these are always two-level games, the potential obstruction is useful to an executive. When the European states were reluctant to go along with American sanctions against Iran in April 1980 they pointed out that since any action would have to be ratified by the nine national parliaments involved, they would therefore only apply to new contracts and not to existing ones. This was a successful delaying tactic, although arguably short-sighted in terms of its effect on the United States.[8] At other times, the blind eye tactic suits the legislature itself. The Congress was generally opposed to President Reagan's covert actions with the Contras in Central America, but at much the same time was prepared to overlook the arming of the *mujahideen* in Afghanistan. More constructively, where a legislature has a significant role in foreign policy-making, as with the Danish Folketing, it creates a greater certainty, both at home and abroad, that commitments entered into are legitimate and will hold.[9]

One sensitive point where legislative activism can generally be expected is where a treaty, or agreement, has implications for sovereignty, in terms of ceding powers or territory, or both. The Israeli Knesset passed a law in 1999, at the behest of the settlers in the Golan Heights, specifying that no territory can be ceded to another country without a majority in the 120-member house.[10] This is the ultimate power of a parliament which makes any democratic leader cautious; legislators exist to make law, and sometimes they do, thus even moving the goalposts in foreign affairs. In the US *only* the Congress can acquire or cede territory. The UK government, well aware only two years after the Falklands War of how sensitive an issue the cession of Hong Kong to China would be, ensured that the Westminster Parliament had plenty of opportunities to discuss the Sino–British Agreement, even though only the Queen's signature was constitutionally required for ratification of a treaty, which technically this was not.[11] Apart from legal considerations, parliamentary divisions stimulate public awareness and pressures on government. When legislation was sought in the New Zealand parliament to enshrine in law the ban on visits by nuclear-armed ships, it stirred up debate and precipitated a serious clash with the United States. The outcome was that the US suspended its guarantees, and the ANZUS Treaty, between 1986–94.[12] Similarly, once the European Parliament had acquired in 1987 the 'power of assent' over association agreements concluded by the European Community, debate on the policy-making of external relations became notably more substantial.

Against these cases, however, may be set many more, equally 'high politics' in character, where executives have been able to circumvent parliamentary powers without difficulty, or simply to drive a coach and horses through the gaps not covered by the constitution. With hubris, the law may simply be broken, as Reagan did when continuing to arm the Contras in defiance of the Boland Amendment, or as Nixon and Kissinger had done through the secret bombing of Cambodia – which certainly breached the spirit, if not the letter, of the War Powers Resolution.[13] At least the latter had closed the loophole exploited by President Johnson nine years before, in 1964, when he got almost unanimous Congressional support for the Tonkin Gulf Resolution, and thus a free hand to prosecute a war against North Vietnam, on the basis of the most flimsy, indeed fabricated *casus belli*.[14] Much will depend in the United States on whether the president's party has a majority in Congress and/or on whether he is already in difficulties with Congress. In Britain and France, by contrast, war may still be undertaken by executive *fiat*, although the lofty disregard of parliamentary support may later come home to haunt leaders, as during the Suez crisis of 1956–7. Mrs Thatcher was wise enough to allow an emergency debate in the House of Commons on a Saturday (3 April 1982) before sending a Task Force to the Falklands three days later. Had the debate gone wholly against a military response it would have been difficult for the Prime Minister to have ignored it.

It will be clear from the above that even the power over the purse strings may be circumvented – this is precisely what Colonel Oliver North was doing for President Reagan in arranging the secret arms deal with Iran which funded the Contras in Nicaragua.[15] The British government, when it decided to upgrade the Polaris missile system at a time of considerable public support for the Campaign for Nuclear Disarmament in 1977, simply slipped through the necessary funding in the general Defence Estimates placed before the House of Commons, without drawing attention to it.[16] The Italian government moved in the 1990s to being one of the major contributors to UN peace-keeping efforts with the Chamber of Deputies barely noticing.[17] In Malaysia in 1988 the Leader of the Opposition demanded that full details of a proposed $1 billion arms deal with Britain be made public; his speech in the budget debate was not even reported in the local media.[18]

On a day-to-day level, parliaments relate to foreign policy less through the exercise of formal powers than through supervision, scrutiny and investigation. Here too their capacity to constrain and participate is limited, but it can be expected to grow as foreign policy becomes ever more central to normal political life, and as the presumption of bipartisanship breaks down. In the first place, representatives usually have some means of questioning the executive on its activities. In the Westminster model, still in use in many ex-colonies, this occurs through scheduled question and answer sessions. Unfortunately, civil servants soon become skilled in briefing ministers on how not to give away information, and on how to use the occasion for sending signals to other states as much as to their own citizens – insofar as foreign policy is ever the focus of questioning.[19] Elsewhere, foreign ministers may be brought more regularly under the spotlight and cross-questioned on particular themes. But this will normally rely on the existence of a lively and independent foreign affairs committee (FAC).

It is only in the past twenty years that it has become normal for legislatures to have a committee specializing in foreign affairs on the American model (both chambers in Washington have such a committee, and more besides, relevant to external policy). All member states of the European Union, for example, now have FACs, and they are also well-established in the major Commonwealth democracies and in Japan. This should not lead us to conclude that the committees consistently act like Senator Fulbright's Foreign Relations Committee in the 1960s, which for a time was in the eye of the storm over the Vietnam War. Even for the United States this was exceptional. All too often they are perceived as 'a nice club of honoured personalities who are satisfied to have regular exchanges of views with the foreign minister without claiming directly to control and influence the government's strategy'.[20] They also provide opportunities to travel abroad, leading to reports which all too often go unnoticed or are out of date by the time they appear. As in the relatively infrequent plenary debates which take place on foreign policy in national assemblies, it is all too evident that only a small proportion of members is informed and interested about foreign affairs, while some of those will be pursuing special interests, such as the need to gain a particular defence contract for their own constituency.

Granted the deficiencies of parliamentarians in relation to foreign policy, it is the FACs which represent the best hope of exerting sustained pressure on an executive. They are more able to build up expertise over time with which to challenge the diplomatic specialists. They may, if able to insist on the presence of ministers (and even better, the release of documents), expose errors and dissimulations through cross-questioning and written analysis. Their reports – especially those investigating policy fiascoes – carry the weight of a public body and will often be taken up by journalists and scholars. If at times they provoke sharp controversy, unwelcome to decision-makers, this is essential for quality control and shows they are doing their job. So long as the committees can avoid being recruited into the process of diplomacy itself – for example by acting as spokesmen abroad – and if they can find themselves an air pocket, free from the control of party managers, then they will at least be able to engage the executive in a meaningful dialogue. Although the foreign relations committees of the US Congress are now less in the public eye than during the Vietnam War, together with others such as the committees on Appropriations, Armed Services, Commerce, and Intelligence, they keep up a remorseless pressure on the White House, which knows that if it wants to get measures approved it needs to invest in a major political effort, involving side-payments and concessions. This is particularly evident in foreign trade policy, where the lobbies proliferate, but it can also happen on purely political matters, since key groups can exert a veto on official policy simply by the threat of publicity and filibustering.

No other national system yet has the resources to rival the US effort (the total staff of Congress is nearly 30 000), or indeed the political culture which requires it, but most parliaments are coming to realize that detailed forensic work through committees is the essential precondition of plenary debate and ultimately of the very principle of democratic control. Otherwise such control as exists ends up in the hands of special interests, which claim all too easily to be representing 'the national interest'. This was the case with the Falkland Islands in the late 1970s and early 1980s, when a small group in the House of Commons were able to talk out a government proposal for a negotiated solution with

Argentina. The British government simply decided not to invest the political effort in over-ruling them, and paid the price later with a major crisis. If parliaments do master the details on a regular basis they keep governments looking over their shoulder, as with the Netherlands, which suggested to its European partners in the last Intergovernmental Conference that it should have one more vote than the other middle-ranking countries, in order to prevent trouble in their parliament in The Hague.[21]

The second way in which formal accountability is exercised over foreign policy is through *the verdict of the electors,* who can make governments pay the price for errors or simply decide to change direction by voting in a new party or coalition. At one level it is difficult to see how elections do give citizens a role in foreign policy. They take place only every four to seven years, and represent crude choices between the large package deals offered by the main parties. Voters seem to be concerned principally with tax and welfare issues, and in any case the parties either do not talk much about foreign policy, or do not differ significantly in the options they present. In periods of war, when voters might actually wish to have a say in the foreign policy questions deciding their fate, elections are often suspended. At best there will be pressure not to undermine the government by voting for peace parties.

It is not surprising if the outcomes of elections usually seem to have little to do with foreign policy. In the 1983 German election, for example, the conservative CDU/CSU party was returned to government at a time when there was considerable unrest in the country over the Euromissiles affair. Whether this was a vote of confidence in the missiles policy, or simply a demonstration of the irrelevance of foreign policy to voting behaviour, is difficult to tell. In 1992 and 1996 Bill Clinton deliberately campaigned on domestic issues alone, partly because he genuinely wished to concentrate on internal priorities but partly because he correctly deduced that foreign policy was not a strong suit for the Democrats in general, and (certainly in 1996) for himself in particular.[22] The case can be made generally that conservative parties find it easier to 'wrap themselves in the flag' and to portray progressive parties as 'soft' on the national interest. On the other hand this would suggest that conservatives ought to campaign on foreign policy questions more frequently than seems to be the case, and it does not allow for bipartisanism. Moreover, the arrival of human rights concerns on the foreign policy agenda may have reversed this advantage.

At times voters do seem willing to distinguish between foreign and domestic policy issues and to favour the former – and in making such distinctions they show themselves to have the capacity for judgement, even if detailed knowledge is lacking. In 1945 the world was astonished to see the British people vote out of office, in a landslide victory for the Labour Party, the war hero Winston Churchill. This result did not arise from any disapproval of Churchill's conduct of the war – he remained popular with people of all parties for that – but was the product of years of discontent with the old social and political order. Having made the huge effort for victory, the British people were determined to reap some reward at home. In that they thought that the war had been brought on by the failures of the Chamberlain government in 1938–9, voters were also punishing the Conservative Party, and not Churchill, who had himself been marginalized in the 1930s.[23] This kind of sophistication was also evident in the election of Clinton in 1992, which was a slap in the face for the Republican presidents who had been in office from 1981, and who had 'won the Cold War' so dramatically. On the other hand the low US electoral turn-out (*c.* 50 per cent) and the cyclical nature of party successes qualifies any generalization about American popular attitudes.

Only in countries with (1) active foreign policies, and (2) well-established democracies will any effective foreign policy debate be possible at election time. It is the kind of higher order activity that is difficult to achieve even in mature systems. What is true is that 'foreign policy is … a prism through which voters judge the basic soundness of a candidate to govern the country'.[24] The ability to run a foreign policy safely and successfully in a dangerous world is an attribute valued widely, and one which contributes significantly to general images of competence. This attribute is therefore played on by the spin-doctors who have dominated elections since at least the arrival of President Kennedy's 'Camelot' in 1960. Of course Kennedy, however glamorous, was inexperienced and untried in foreign policy at perhaps the most dangerous time of the Cold War, and that weakness was reflected in his victory over Richard Nixon by the narrowest of margins (some indeed have said that the result was fixed by malpractice in Chicago, and that Nixon was the true victor). Other American elections, such as that of Eisenhower in 1952, and Reagan in 1980, were also determined in part by the wish of the voters to have a president who could resolve difficulties in foreign policy – the Korean War, and the humiliations of Carter by Iran and the USSR, respectively.[25] More recently Vladimir Putin won the office of president in Russia largely by emphasizing that he would win the war in Chechnya and thereby restore Russia's international image as a country to be reckoned with.[26] In Singapore in 1997 Prime Minister Goh Chok Tong argued, less than credibly, that his word

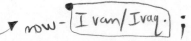
now – I van/Ivaq. ;

would count for less in international circles if a particular opposition candidate were returned who had questioned the predominance of English-speakers in the Singapore Cabinet.[27] Elections are always an opportunity to play up the gravitas that comes with office and the opportunities for international statesmanship.

It may be just as well that personality and foreign events both have their roles, for there are very few occasions when voters actually get a choice on key issues. In 1968 there was a crucial opportunity for the two main American parties to offer the voters a choice of strategies at the most difficult time in the Vietnam War, when Lyndon Johnson had withdrawn from the race in a funk, and the best way forward was genuinely uncertain. In the event, neither Nixon nor Humphrey gave a clear lead as to peace or war; both promised vaguely to achieve both peace and honour, but without specifying the policy implications. In office Nixon then escalated the war while trying to scale down the number of US troops. This was a major failure for democracy. Foreign policy does not need to dominate elections often, but this was the obvious exception. Neither party trusted the American people, or indeed itself.

The same is true in other states. The United Kingdom has had 14 general elections since the war. Arguably in three of them (1964, 1983 and 1987) the Labour Party was damaged by having an image of being unreliable on defence, in particular through association with the Campaign for Nuclear Disarmament. The second two of these were lost, not least because the two leaders of the time, Michael Foot and Neil Kinnock, were presented (mostly by the media) as being particularly unsound on defence. Foot held few cards on foreign policy; he was proud of never even having visited the United States, and Mrs Thatcher had just conducted the victorious campaign in the Falklands. Thus defence was used largely as a means of strengthening the image of the Conservative Party. Labour ran scared and actively tried to avoid giving the voters a clear foreign policy choice. In all the other elections, despite the obvious possibilities for debates on international matters (Korea in 1950 and 1951, Suez in 1959, east of Suez in 1970, the Middle East in 1974) the campaigns were almost wholly domestic in tone and voters would have had difficulty in obtaining information on the parties' foreign policy differences.[28]

It is clear that there are structural limits on the extent to which foreign policy accountability can be achieved through democratic elections, and these are both inherent in the complexity of the process and the product of a security state ethos among elites. There are, however, some signs of change which might tend to raise the profile of foreign policy at elections. One is the way in which the politicization of foreign policy weakens both bipartisanism and internal party discipline, aided by the end of the Cold War but predating it in origin. This means that external issues can cut across parties and sometimes lead to severe internal divisions, as with the British political parties over European integration since 1959. This may make for less than effective decisions from the viewpoint of outsiders, but it certainly opens up the political space for prolonged internal debate. The same has been true in Germany, over the use of military force for humanitarian interventions. The result may not favour clear electoral choices, but it does weaken the ability of parties to manage the argument.

The second relevant development is the way foreign and domestic issues are now generally intimately interconnected; a domestic issue often has a foreign dimension, and vice versa. This means that it will not be easy to focus an election wholly on domestic issues, or to seal off foreign policy into a separate, bipartisan compartment. The prolonged Zimbabwean election campaign of 1999–2000, in which President Mugabe encouraged his supporters to occupy white farms as a way of appealing to the landless poor, inevitably had a foreign dimension. The white farmers appealed to Britain, the United States and the European Union for help both in upholding the law and ensuring fair elections. For its part Mugabe's ZANU-PF party combined anti-white with anti-British rhetoric throughout as a way of reawakening anti-colonialist sentiment. The President was no doubt delighted when the British government, in the form of FCO Minister Peter Hain, rose to the bait and engaged in an angry public slanging-match.[29]

Elections may, therefore, offer more platforms for the politics of foreign policy in the future. But debate will remain general, and voters will be able to do little more than to indicate broad preferences and to make judgements on their leaders' performances of the kind familiar in a Roman amphitheatre – thumbs up, or down. They act as a backup to the more formal powers of parliaments, themselves difficult to establish, assert and implement. At least both elections and legislators possess enough ammunition to keep an executive guessing. It is striking how most foreign policy-makers still take care to avoid riding roughshod over the processes of accountability, even if they well exploit the lacunae they find there. For democratic politicians and officials an embarrassing row over foreign policy, in parliament or at election time, is a prospect to be feared and avoided. US foreign policy virtually shuts down in an election year.[30] Whether justifiably or not, public opinion looms large in their minds as a potential constraint.

Public Opinion

Politicians often argue that their hands are tied by public opinion, or at the least that they have to work within the limits set by it. Campaigners also set store by this belief. Martin Dent, who is both an academic and an activist for Third World debt relief, rests his hopes on the claim of the *Anti-Slavery Review* in the nineteenth century that public opinion was 'the steam which [would] enable Parliament to extinguish slavery in one massive stroke'.[31] Political scientists tend to be sceptical and side more with those radical critics who claim that public opinion is paid lip-service to but in practice ignored. All these positions need scrutinizing within the special context of foreign policy.

The concept of public opinion is difficult to pin down. It refers at once to an actor in the political process and to an object of influence. Michel Tatu says it is 'both an instrument and a factor in the conduct of foreign policy'.[32] In this, however, it resembles a number of problems in social life, and academic writing has done a good deal to establish the parameters of the problem over the past forty years. On that basis there are four preliminary conclusions which may be drawn.

First is the fundamental distinction between mass and attentive opinion, particularly important in relation to any issue which is remote from everyday life and which cannot even be conceptualized without specialized knowledge (unlike, for example, the state of the nation's hospitals). This is not the same as a distinction between the educated and the lumpen, as mass opinion includes all sections of society, from the illiterate to Nobel Prize winners. But it does differentiate between the whole, which will only rarely be sufficiently focused on a foreign policy issue as to display a collective animus, and the minority which takes a persistent and knowledgeable interest in international affairs.[33] The latter will vary in size according to the location, culture and degree of development of a country, but even in western Europe it is unlikely to be more than 20 per cent of the adult population, and may be much less. Yet in one opinion poll in 1984, 60 per cent of Europeans said that they almost never thought about the Third World, which means that 40 per cent did reflect on the matter from time to time, and 10 per cent even said they would be prepared to give up 1 per cent of their income for development assistance.[34] It is not that the majority of the population is never concerned; only that interest goes up and down according to the issue and to its degree of perceived urgency or moral importance. The 'attentive' group can swell quickly, especially in times of crisis. More routinely there is a contrast between the basic importance which the mass of people attribute to domestic affairs, compared to the generally more internationalist attentive public. According to a series of American focus groups in 1996, most people believed that 'domestic needs have been neglected at the expense of foreign affairs'. In a separate poll, 84 per cent of 'the elite' were willing to go to war to defend South Korea from an invasion by North Korea, but only 45 per cent of the general public took the same view.[35] Whether this is judged to be parochial isolationism, or historical memory of the costs of war, is a matter of political taste.

The second proposition which most students of foreign policy would accept is that there is a widespread degree of ignorance about the details of international affairs. This even applies to the basics of geography. It is difficult to form an opinion about the European Union if you do not know the names of its member states, or where to find them on a map.[36] In the midst of the arguments raging in the early 1970s about Britain's entry into the European Communities only 17 per cent of those questioned in the UK knew that the EEC had nine members and the location of its headquarters.[37] At the end of the decade, in 1979, only 60 per cent correctly identified what the initials EEC stood for. The figures for NATO and the IMF were even lower, at 33 per cent and 44 per cent respectively, although interestingly the UN was identified by 85 per cent of people and the IRA, whose actions were very much closer to home, by 75 per cent.[38]

In the United States, the National Geographic Society commissioned a Gallup poll in 1988 to measure geographical knowledge and to compare with a similar poll from 1947–8. Not only did they discover that there had been a distinct falling off over time, but the actual levels of ignorance were alarming. One in five could not name a single European country, one in two could not find South Africa on the map (at a time when the issue of support for the black majority was a big political issue in the US) and only one in three could find Vietnam, where nearly 60 000 Americans had died.[39] Respondents from other countries, notably Sweden and West Germany, displayed better knowledge, but it would be a mistake to assume that these data can be explained by Anglo-Saxon insularity.

Most people do not have the knowledge of geography and world politics taken for granted by diplomats and journalists, just as they do not seek to find out how their car works unless compelled by circumstances. Of course ignorance does not stop people having opinions or making judgements, nor should it. In a developed democracy, at least, people can improve their knowledge quite quickly if they so wish. But lack of knowledge does undermine individuals' confidence in their ability to participate in the political process, and to heighten the elite perception of a hopelessly ill-informed mass whom it would be irresponsible to trust with decisions. When Mikhail Gorbachev started to liberalize the Soviet Union, one of his key ideas was *glasnost*, or openness. *Glasnost*, however, only applied to domestic affairs.[40] Despite the importance of issues such as the war in Afghanistan and the negotiations with the West on intermediate nuclear forces, the taboo on entrusting the people with a debate on foreign and security policy remained in force – until the point where the people intervened with direct action.

 For at times, even on foreign policy, public opinion bursts forth with unexpected vigour and impact. This is actually the consequence of the third of our general conclusions, that the public is usually a follower, not a leader, when it comes to shaping policy. The combination of ignorance, apathy and other priorities means that the general public is often passive, and therefore able to be ignored, divided or used by the politically active, whether in governmental or NGO circles. The public's instinct is not necessarily to trust leaders but to be fatalistic about the possibilities of change.[41] Indeed decision-makers hold four vital cards: (i) the power of initiative; (ii) the capacity to define external threats; (iii) control over information and propaganda; (iv) the ultimate power of the state to coerce. Leaders issue the cues and the public tends to pick them up. The prime example of this remains the sad spectacle of millions of men accepting their fate in the First World War, condemned by the rigidity of their military high commands and their blinkered politicians.[42]

On rare occasions this norm breaks down. The apparently content and suggestible public turns out to have been taken for granted. In 1999 the UN conducted what it claimed was 'the largest survey of public opinion ever conducted – of 57 000 adults in 60 countries, spread across all six continents'. This found that while most people thought elections in their country were fair, 'two-thirds of all respondents considered that their country was not governed by the will of the people. This opinion held even in some of the oldest democracies in the world'.[43] This shows that the conditions of distrust and cynicism exist for occasional resistance. When a government ignores the actual feelings of its people, as opposed to its perceptions of their views, a political earthquake can ensue, with unpredictable consequences, even over foreign policy.

 When this happens it is because of the impact of the last of our four parameters of the relationship between government and public opinion: the tendency on the part of the former to confuse the voice of the public with a particular channel through which it is being transmitted. Decision-makers naturally look to the most articulate elements in society for evidence of what the public is thinking, especially in foreign policy, which is rarely touched on in opinion polls. They may assume that silence means consent, or they may take the hubbub in press and television to be widely representative – a transmission belt of democratic feeling, rather than one particular source of opinion. The same is true for members of parliament, who exist to 'represent' their constituencies.[44] In modern conditions leaders are particularly likely to interpret the activity of attentive opinion, in the form of pressure groups, as the voices which matter most. Pluralist theories of politics tend to make the same assumption.

Steven Lukes and others have shown that this distorts the truth.[45] MPs, journalists and pressure groups may have a better idea than most as to grassroots opinion (and the methodological obstacles to anyone being able to generalize about public opinion are enormous), but they also have their own special interests and perceptual blinkers. It is all too easy for decision-makers and their privileged interviewers to embrace in a closed circle of complacency as to what politics is about. Thus, on occasions, they all get taken by surprise.[46] The bitter outpourings in Russia in the summer of 2000 against the arrogance of the military in not seeking foreign help early enough to save the crew of the foundering submarine *Kursk* was a sharp lesson for Vladimir Putin, previously insulated from the people by his past as a KGB officer and by his facile entry into office. The greatest lesson of all was administered by the peoples of eastern Europe when they finally managed to throw off Moscow-imposed communism through peaceful revolution. That this was possible in 1989, and had not been earlier, for example in the abortive risings of 1956 in Hungary and 1968 in Czechoslovakia, tells us something about the need for conditions to be ripe before popular resistance can succeed. But it also demonstrated the immense strength of the people when united, and facing a government whose will to use force had been weakened through loss of legitimacy. It was spectacular evidence of how even elites disposing of the fullest apparatus of internal surveillance can misperceive the feelings of their own citizens. Their sonar picked up 'merely the echo of their own propellors'.[47]

It will always be the case that some decision-makers are misled by their own values or vanity to interpret public opinion wrongly. Neville Chamberlain was so entranced by the welcome he received at Heston Airport on his return from Munich in October 1938, and by his overwhelmingly favourable postbag, that he came to believe in the myth of his own ability to know what the people wanted. Thus when he received a critical postbag after taking Britain into war in September 1939, he interpreted it as the product of an unrepresentative minority. He could not believe that the majority had not followed his own change of direction.[48]

Some indicators of public opinion are evidently more objective than others. Unless amounting to wholescale revolution, demonstrations will always be subject to the kind of rationalizations employed by Anthony Eden in 1956, when citing a bus-driver's letter to the effect that 80 per cent of a hostile demonstration in London over Suez was composed of foreigners, and therefore did not count.[49] Referenda and opinion polls, however, are more difficult to overlook, and they have been used increasingly after 1945, as party managers have sought to know how to please voters before elections, and how to stave off embarrassing media criticisms.[50] Referenda are still unusual on foreign policy issues, and they always contain the dangers of manipulation and populism, but in that turn-out tends to be high they are evidently welcomed by citizens. The results set the outline of policy for the medium term and make backsliding by government difficult. The Swiss, for whom referenda are a way of life, could not possibly enter the EU without popular approval in a referendum. Indeed, in 1985 75 per cent of the poll voted against Switzerland even entering the United Nations, with all 26 cantons voting against. After that few could be in any doubt as to public opinion on the issue, until the question was raised again in 1997, leading to acceptance of entry in the referendum of 2002. The narrow vote in 1992 against joining the European Economic Area, headed off any possibility of accession to the EU, just as the two votes in Norwegian referenda against EC/EU entry, of 1972 and 1994, made it impossible for the more integration-minded elites in Oslo to push on strongly with their project. Referenda in Denmark, Ireland and France on aspects of European integration, including defence, also forced the governments of these countries to take on board the greater caution of their populations.[51]

It is true that after such setbacks governments then become even more cautious about embarking on referenda, and about their wording, and they pursue other means of getting the same result – so that Denmark, for example, has now signed up to a European defence force, after the softening of domestic opposition. Still, a referendum made legitimate by a good turn-out makes it impossible for a government to interpret the public's wishes on that issue in a cavalier way, and will always increase their circumspection. That is why the supporters of the settlers in the occupied territories have ensured that any cession of Israel's territory in future will require not only a parliamentary majority, but approval in a popular vote. As the Head of the Golan Heights Residents' Committee, Avi Zeira, pointed out, 'the decision is not in the hands of the prime minister, it's in the hands of people'.[52] Even a close result may be a humiliation for a government, as De Gaulle decided when he resigned in 1969 after failing to win the support he expected in a referendum that turned into a vote of confidence.

Attention to opinion polls represents either a fetishizing of the *vox populi* or a fiendish instrument of political spinning, according to one's point of view. Polls, like any statistics, are certainly not inherently neutral and reliable. In 1987 Jerzy Urban, the Polish Foreign Minister cited a poll done for Polish radio and TV in 1985 in which 73 per cent judged the USSR a friendly country – this after the rise of Solidarity and only four years before the overthrow of communism. More accurate, paradoxically, were the police reports on censored letters which Mussolini saw in 1942–3, and which showed clearly the extent of popular disillusion with his rule.[53] Although opinion polling, which George Gallup began in the United States in 1935, has become a refined and indispensable instrument of government in the past few decades, it is rarely used to measure views on foreign policy, except in crises where the Vietnam syndrome, of the fear of haemorrhaging support from TV spectators appalled at the sight of body bags, is all too evident. When foreign policy becomes a test of the government's competence, image or leadership qualities, opinion polls will be used incessantly. When foreign issues drop below the horizon of daily visibility, whatever the polls say on international issues will be secondary to other factors.

There are transnational elements to governments' concern for public opinion. Israeli Prime Minister Benjamin Netanyahu's advisers concluded that his best chance of reaching the Russian immigrants in his country was to appear on the Russian-language TV shows most of them watch on cable. Accordingly Netanyahu's trip to Georgia, the Ukraine and Moscow in March 1999 was 'first and foremost a campaign trip'. Given the forthcoming general election, and the tendency of the large number of immigrants from the ex-Soviet Union to vote in blocs, this was crucial, and reaped dividends in terms of the 'reams of articles, stacks of photographs and many minutes of campaign time dedicated to Netanyahu and his pitch'.[54] Diasporas play important roles in and for particular countries. Otherwise, however, decision-makers tend to perceive public opinion as being firmly part of their own and others' domestic environments. Thus it is very common to come across discussions of how Europeans and Americans may be growing apart because of divergences in their respective public opinions, or of how US foreign policy may be forced in this direction or that by popular pressure.[55] Whatever the truth of transnational coalitions, or public lack of interest, decision-makers still conceptualize public opinion as being important because it is so distinctively national.

Ultimately conceptualizations matter, for public opinion is a 'notional constraint'.[56] By this is meant a constraint which exists at least as much in the minds of decision-makers as it is embodied in substantive elements like law, institutions, demonstrations. It is what is now termed a 'constructed' reality. On any given foreign policy issue decision-makers will have an image of the public's view and degree of interest which may or may not be supported by 'the facts'. Indeed the nature of the facts will be particularly contestable, given that the public is large, amorphous, divided and reliant on transmission belts. There may thus be a tendency to over-rely on the 'scientific' evidence of opinion polls and focus groups, or on personal impressions. If the view of what the public wants is held strongly enough it may become a self-fulfilling prophecy in that decision-makers will feel inclined to bow the knee, and the myth of an influential public is born. This happened during the Vietnam War, where the US is commonly thought to have withdrawn because of opposition at home, but where there is evidence to show that public opinion was not ahead of official decisions, and indeed was generally permissive.[57]

Thus leaders do not always exploit the inherent incapacity of the public to mobilize the general will as ruthlessly or as effectively as theories of elitism might lead us to believe. They are, after all, fallible human beings themselves, as immersed in their country's political culture as anyone else, and often convinced democrats. In other guises they, too, are members of the public. They want and need to believe in accountability both because it relieves them of some responsibility, and because it avoids the cognitive dissonance which would result from speechifying about democracy while behaving like Stalin. On any given occasion this does give the alert politician the opportunity to have it both ways, but for the most part decision-makers tend to keep a close eye on the shadow which flickers in the cave behind them.

Interest Groups and the Mobilization of Civil Society

Even attentive public opinion requires organization, if it is to be an actor in the policy process as well as an object of it. Broadly speaking there are three major ways for public opinion to exert an active influence over foreign policy: through populist political movements, whether parties or less structured demonstrations; in crises, through heightened awareness and direct pressure on politicians; and through preparation and full-time organization. Risse-Kappen's study concluded that in established democracies the more decentralized the system and the stronger the social groups capable of mobilizing public opinion, the more opportunities the latter had for influencing policy-makers.[58] It is evident that the groups seeking to influence foreign policy have multiplied since 1945, even if they are hardly as new a phenomenon as is often assumed. They are more visible, and they have acquired a degree of informal legitimacy in the political systems of complex societies, where governments require dialogue with their citizens on an increasing range of issues.[59] Unfortunately the serious study of the impact of societal groups on foreign policy has only just begun.[60]

Societal groups should not be regarded only as transmission belts for the conveyance of mass opinion to the centre. They perform that function, but also have their own specific concerns, relating to particular 'stakes' in society or distinctive cherished values. A double distinction must be made at the outset, between interest groups and pressure groups, and between interest groups and cause groups. Pressure groups by definition exist to exert pressure on government policy. Many interest groups will wish to influence policy and are therefore also pressure groups. But some exist simply to enable citizens to mobilize themselves around common interests – sporting federations are a good example – and they will only occasionally need to take on the role of pressure group. Cause groups also exist in order to change the world, but instead of relating to stakes which the members hold jointly, whether as dock workers or athletes, they arise out of common value positions, and a desire to achieve a given good independent of their connection to it. Those groups in rich countries which devote themselves to helping developing countries are a prime case in point. Thus cause, interest and pressure groups are overlapping but distinct categories.[61]

Many of these groups have developed considerable expertise, resources and (as we have seen in Chapter 8), transnational scope. It can no longer be concluded, as Milbraith did in relation to the United States in the late 1960s, that their influence is even weaker than slight.[62] The more important, like Oxfam, Amnesty, or the Stockholm Peace Research Institute, do not target only the government of their host country, and their influence must therefore be assessed on a regional or global basis. Furthermore, interest and cause groups, in contrast to pressure groups, act more on civil society, nationally or transnationally, than on governments. The Foreign Policy Association of the United States, which does a huge amount of work to spread knowledge of international issues

among schools, colleges and citizens' groups, is a foremost example –
even if it is fighting an uphill battle.[63]

In terms of individual issue-areas, pressure groups can be effective,
although there is much variability according to historical and national
context. British overseas aid levels rose (temporarily) after the huge
publicity obtained by Bob Geldof in creating BandAid in 1984, and
the European Nuclear Disarmament movement (END) pushed west
European members of NATO into a much less enthusiastic stance *re* the
modernization of theatre nuclear weapons and the countering of Soviet
SS20s. Although END failed to get the installation of Cruise and
Pershing missiles unilaterally reversed, it compelled the SPD government in Bonn to make arms control and détente their first priority.
Indeed, Helmut Schmidt's famous speech in London in 1977 which
started the whole debate, did not in fact mention the SS20s, and stressed
non-military security, out of deference to his domestic anti-militarists.[64]

Groups in particular sectors where the government either rates the
issue low on its agenda, or is concerned not to engage in a public struggle, may have a veto on the way in which policy develops. Various
national and ethnic groups within the United States are seen as having
this capacity, particularly the Cubans, the Irish, the Jews, the Poles and
the Greeks, although matters are rarely so simple. While these groups
may well be better organized and have more electoral clout, than, say,
the native American population, it is by no means clear that US policy
in relation to their concerns would be any different without their input.
In any case, the more a group's influence is celebrated, by itself or others, the more a government will wish to show its independence. This is
beginning to happen with both the Cuban and the Jewish lobbies, and
the Turkish lobby, set up to counterbalance Athens, has certainly not
gone unheard in Washington, as is clear from US pressure on the EU to
admit Turkey.[65] In a pluralist system groups compete in the political
market and can cancel each other out. This is particularly true of economic groups, which are amongst the most active now that economic
policy almost always has an international dimension.[66]

Even powerful lobbies may be outflanked by governments when they
choose to ride out a public storm, as they often can, given the relative
infrequency of elections. All American presidents have to tread carefully when they consider withdrawing support from Israel, but this does
not mean to say that the American Israel Public Affairs Committee
(AIPAC) always has a veto on US policy in the Middle East – even leaving aside the fact that American Jews are far from being of one mind on
foreign policy. Ronald Reagan's sale of AWACs aircraft to Saudi Arabia

in the early 1980s was strenuously opposed by AIPAC but went ahead regardless. Nonetheless, such disputes helped to forge Jewish unity in the USA and AIPAC's organizational strength. According to *Fortune* magazine in 1997 it was the only foreign policy group in the top 25 lobbies, and the second most powerful in the country after the American Association of Retired Persons.[67] As a result, the Jewish lobby is widely *believed*, especially outside the US, to determine American policy on the Arab–Israel dispute, a perception which has important consequences.

When key values are at stake, or where there is a risk of serious upheaval, some groups will have to be heard. No Greek government could have ignored the nationalist outrage against the former Yugoslav Republic of Macedonia, for having taken the name of Macedonia on independence. Similarly, it was impossible even for the centre–left elements in the government of Concertación Democrática in Chile in 1999 not to protest to the British government over the arrest of General Pinochet. In a dangerously divided country, the organized right was simply too strong to be allowed the luxury of painting the government in anti-patriotic colours.[68] On anything less central to the character of the state, governments have many ways of averting pressure from sectoral or cause groups.

It is in their collective impact that societal groups have most impact on foreign policy. Pluralist democracy means both freedom for individual actors and a web of common activity, in which governments as well as interest groups get caught, and in which a number of groups may be acting in broadly the same direction even if not in an actual coalition. In foreign policy this has produced a number of examples of the significant, cumulative impact of different groups operating simultaneously and giving a government no rest. Thus the Conservative administrations of Stanley Baldwin and Neville Chamberlain in the 1930s came to adopt the quietist policy of appeasement under persistent pressure from organized groups reminding them of the need to avoid another war and to follow the road of agreement rather than force. This was despite their huge majority in the House of Commons.[69] Likewise the French right, acting through various extra-parliamentary groups, some involved in violence, others not, brought down the Fourth Republic over the Algerian crisis. The number and extent of the foreign aid lobbies in the Netherlands and Scandinavian countries make it difficult for those countries to reduce their ODA spending down to, say, Spanish levels, to say nothing of the huge range of companies, trades unions and towns with a vested interest in the continuance of a global military role for the

United States. Their collective pressure does not even need to be brought to bear on policy. It is so structural as to be a given.[70]

Organized opinion has the advantage of being able to get close to the seat of power. By the same token it may be drawn in too close, and lose some of its independence. If this becomes a permanent arrangement groups become what has been called 'parastate organizations', effectively serving the functions of the state while remaining private.[71] In such form they may be subsidized directly or indirectly by the state, and develop common definitions of problems and solutions. Inderjeet Parmar and others have argued from a Gramscian perspective that while ideas, groups and individuals make a difference, if they come to share the same 'state spirit', the necessary tensions between those in power and those seeking accountability will become lost in a form of intellectual (and sometimes institutional) corporatism.[72] It is certainly no accident that in most countries the principal institute of foreign affairs is close to government, and often significantly subsidized by it. Even when not, as is currently the case with the Royal Institute of International Affairs in London, it is difficult not to take cues from officialdom, in terms of research projects, conferences and visiting speakers.

Such institutes are perceived abroad as staffed by what Chadwick Alger has called 'external bureaucrats'.[73] The Council of Foreign Relations in New York is the most studied example, and indeed one which has been important in creating and reproducing consensus over American foreign policy, particularly during the move away from isolationism and during the Cold War. Such a privileged position, however, carries with it the inevitable risk of becoming detached from wider society, and overtaken by powerful new ideas and groups. Thus the Council of Foreign Relations was seen by the radical right as part of the very east coast establishment which needed supplanting in the late 1970s, and struggled to have influence over the Reagan administration and its newly assertive foreign policy.

Each era tends to produce its own activist groups, some of which gradually get drawn into the process of policy-making. They thus exchange influence for compromise, and a certain distancing from their own roots. They also create for decision-makers the sense of being in touch with public opinion, when in practice the boundary between ins and outs may simply have been moved a little further out. This process, ineluctable more than dishonourable, can be seen in the way the Blair government in Britain encouraged human rights and development groups to enter into structured dialogues with officialdom, and has come to rely on them for help with policy implementation in the Third

World. The risk, as with the Green Party in Germany which entered the governing coalition in 1998, is that the process of taking responsibility alienates natural supporters without convincing general opinion. The whole point about interest groups is that they offer alternative definitions of responsible behaviour; once in partnership with decision-makers they imperceptibly change roles and the pressure for accountability must come from elsewhere.

If there are to be democratic struggles over the direction of foreign policy, expert officials can only be engaged by those with a degree of knowledge and professionalism. Accordingly, pressure groups become a career choice like everything else, and their permanent staffs can end up in too cosy a relationship with their erstwhile targets. Nonetheless, on foreign policy the general public has little choice but to rely on these groups to keep governments up to the mark and aware of attitudes within the society which they serve. The same is true of an even more important social institution.

The Media as Gatekeepers

In the age of television the mass media look like kings. They seem to be the key to influence over public opinion, and they have the ear and eye of government. With real-time broadcasts from even remote spots in the world to the homes of hundreds of millions, the 'CNN effect' – of foreign policy shaped by the latest media feeding frenzy – seems palpable. If the press was the 'fourth estate' so radio, and in particular television, are now the fifth – the constituency which holds most informal power.

Despite this there have been few serious studies produced of the relationship between the media and foreign policy.[74] As with much of the domestic environment, commentators are long on opinion and short on evidence. It is not surprising if many journalists exaggerate their own importance, or if politicians like to paint themselves as boxed in by constant media pressure, but academics can use a wider angle lens. In this respect, such work as has so far been done tends to qualify the picture of the dominant media.

Historically the 'age of the masses' and the growing importance of the media go hand in hand, the one fostering the other. If print was important in fostering first the emergence of the state, and then the 'imagined communities' of nationalism, the development of rapidly published and widely disseminated broadsheets was fundamental to the organization of modern industrial society, both liberal and totalitarian.[75]

The daily newspaper was soon recognized as a key instrument of the dissemination of information and the mobilization of the mass, whether for constructive or manipulative purposes. Nor did it take long to become apparent that the flow of influence went in two directions – from the public via the press to government, as well as from the top down – or that the press itself could be a formidable independent factor in politics. The arrival of press barons like Beaverbrook, Rothermere and Northcliffe had a major impact in the British Commonwealth countries between the two world wars, just as William Randolph Hearst dominated the press in the United States, exerting a powerful influence for isolationism and nationalism. As early as 1922 there was an example of a politician using the press, when Lloyd George let journalists know during the Chanak crisis that he would be calling on Canadian and Australian troops – this without informing the government of either country, while exploiting the advantage of time zones and print deadlines. The resulting storm may have gone beyond what Lloyd George intended, but it certainly exerted pressure in favour of the principle of imperial loyalty.[76]

With the proliferation of war correspondents, diplomatic correspondents, film crews and 'star' reporters this kind of 'media event' has become commonplace. A constant struggle takes place for advantage between the press corps (used here to refer to journalists of all kinds) and those responsible for official policy. At one moment the former will have the advantage, creating embarrassment or setting the agenda. The next moment, those we now call 'spin-doctors' will be planting a story or distracting attention from the real issue of the day. It also happens not infrequently that the two sides develop a common way of looking at the world, even common interests, and behave in an incestuous way which closes the circle against public involvement. Each of these three patterns of relationship bears some further examination.

The power of the media is exerted in two distinct ways: over public opinion, and then over decision-makers, including indirectly via the political class. There is no doubt that in the relatively restricted area of foreign policy – however widely we define it – the media have an almost exclusive gatekeeping role with respect to the public. Only very few individuals even in a highly educated society are in a position to acquire information or to express their views on international relations without relying on the media – although the internet may transform this in the future. Such public debate as exists on foreign policy is almost entirely focused on the noticeboards provided by newspapers and television. Public meetings, word of mouth and interest groups produce a *samizdat* literature which may have a long-run impact, but even they never exist in isolation from the dominant discourse conducted at the national, indeed often transnational, level by the big battalions. It is not difficult to think of cases where the media have created almost out of nothing a public mood of concern which has then rebounded onto government. African famines have produced many such moments in western societies, but probably the most revealing of recent times was the publicizing of the plight of Kurdish refugees in northern Iraq at the end of the Gulf War, which led first the British, then other governments, into a commitment to 'safe havens' from Iraqi attack and thus a *de facto* policy of intervention inside northern Iraq.[77] Since journalists and editors have their own news values, and are also restricted by circumstances in their access (it was easier for them to film in northern Iraq, via Turkey, than in the south, where the Shias were also in revolt) they only publicize certain problems, and to a large extent their selectivity determines public debate.

On the other hand although the media appear to have almost monopolistic access to the public, there are limitations to their impact. For one thing even the serious newspapers only devote between 33–45 per cent of their space to international affairs.[78] Television news does the same, but as Theodore Sorensen points out, '45 per cent of the 22 minutes of news contained in a 30 minute newscast does not convey enough words to fill one-third of one page of a standard-size newspaper'.[79] Image therefore predominates over information and analysis. This is not always a superficial matter, since an emotional and visual appeal can leave a more lasting effect than metres of the written word. But it is usually evanescent, and leaves the watcher ill-equipped to do more than telephone in a credit card donation. This is particularly the case given that the evidence suggests that most readers and viewers are not much interested in foreign affairs. Distance counts, in the sense that without some involvement of 'our people' (usually co-nationals) only the most massive events will halt the tendency to switch off, literally, or more likely, psychologically. Thus much of the media will play up the simplistic and even the xenophobic aspects of their coverage to ensure the attention their proprietors and advertisers require.[80] This does have a dumbing-down effect on the audience. More insidious is the opportunity cost of denying clear information and analysis to the mass of people, who are far from being as coarse or as incapable as cynical journalists assume. The public is thus not quite so moulded by the media as it might seem, but nor is it empowered.

The more direct power of the media, as an actor in the policy-making process, is exerted both through personal contacts and through providing a means of communication between foreign policy professionals and the attentive public, particularly those inner rings which might be politically active. Decision-makers do not have much time to read the press or watch television, and at times they affect not to do so. But they employ advisers to summarize who is saying what and anything which shows a weakness or starts a trend is soon spotted. Key opinion-formers, like Josef Joffe of the *Süddeutschezeitung* in Germany, or Stanley Hoffmann in both France and the United States, do not go unheard. In this respect the media have the capacity to influence political argument, by ventilating debate which might otherwise stay behind closed doors, by subjecting the official line to critical scrutiny and by tilting the balance in favour of one position over another. Even on what was for the average citizen the arcane subject of NATO enlargement it was not possible to take policy forward without an extensive debate in the press on both sides of the Atlantic. This interacted with argument in Congress (and no doubt inside western ministries) to ensure that the policy did not escape interrogation. The same ordeal by fire may have contributed to President Clinton's decision in August 2000 not to go ahead with the Nuclear Missile Defence system he had previously announced. The combination of difficulties with Russia, and strenuous opposition within NATO countries, made him calculate that it was too big a political risk to leave the policy hanging round the neck of Al Gore (the Vice President, hoping to be elected to the White House in his turn).

In democracies many other cases of media influence over foreign policy can be found, but there are an equal number where their role has been exaggerated. This is the conclusion of Halliday's study of the Gulf War, and of Carruthers' survey of other cases in the 1990s, including Somalia, Yugoslavia and Rwanda.[81] It is also the view taken of television in the research done by Nik Gowing, himself a distinguished TV reporter.[82] If we look at the other big enlargement issue of the 1990s, for example, that of the European Union, we find that there has been little serious debate, and that the press coverage has been muddling and diffuse. This is because the issue is less clear-cut, and the timetable much longer than that of the NATO enlargement, where there was polarization around one more or less clear proposition. With respect to the EU, the timetable is long and shifting, the permutations endless and the issues multiple – and difficult for all actors to synthesize. In this situation the serious press, to say nothing of television and the tabloids, has failed even to identify the main outlines of a debate, let alone to insist on one taking place. The problem is compounded by the need for a Europe-wide debate, whereas the press is still predominantly national in its focus, and by the tendency in a complex issue to take cues from governments – which in this case, although for diverse reasons, have manufactured a consensus in favour of the principle of enlargement. The issue is presented as closed, with only implementation at stake. The media have thus failed to ensure that a massive question of public interest and accountability is properly debated, and no other institution has been able to do any better. Given the number of constituencies affected by enlargement this neglect could lead to a considerable political backlash in the future.

Not only do the media often fail to rise to the occasion, but they can be more easily manipulated by policy-makers than the general public realizes. The press has long been used to launch diplomatic trial balloons, and not infrequently information is released which has only the most tenuous relationship to the truth. Particularly in war-time, actual disinformation is frequently reported faithfully by the media. Whole squads of public relations experts have now moved into the foreign policy area in order to present parties in the best policy light. Many foreign trips are essentially media events, designed to use press, radio and television as instruments of projection, at home and abroad.[83] The expertise and continuity of public officials as opposed to the short newspaper memory caused by the torrent of deadlines, gives the former a great advantage. The media lack both stamina and *gravitas* when it comes to pursuing complex foreign issues over time, compared to parliamentary committees, disadvantaged in a different way.[84] Both also tend to chase the game. As James Reston said, 'we will send 500 correspondents to Vietnam after the war breaks out ... but we will not send five reporters there when the danger of war is developing'.[85]

It is also evident that the relationship between the media and government in many respects suits both sides very well. Publicity and the two-way transmission of information are exchanged for privileged access and (often) seats on the presidential or prime ministerial plane. Some critics have concluded from this element of collusion that the press corps is structurally rotten and part of the self-serving elites it is supposed to be scrutinizing.[86] It is certainly true that some journalists have subverted their own independence by acting as diplomatic 'couriers', or even as actual spies. Nervous governments often assume that foreign journalists are agents of influence. Systematic subordination is a serious problem in autocracies, but in democracies it is a relatively trivial problem compared to the structural difficulty of developing foreign policy themes in an ever more commercial and trivializing environment. In any case, in the post-Cold War era it is not clear what the ideology of a power elite means when applied to foreign policy, unless it is the simple injunction not to criticize official policy, which holds little water. On many of the problems confronting us, like the future of Taiwan, the Middle East peace process and Third World debt, it is simple-minded to suppose that there is an obvious line which serves the interests of the most powerful. Complexity produces divided opinion inside both officialdom and the media. The latter could be much more alert, sceptical and creative in their approach to the reporting of international affairs, but anyone familiar with *Le Monde*, *The International Herald Tribune* or the BBC's 'Newsnight' programme (watched extensively in Belgium and the Netherlands as well as the UK) will not think that western governments, at least, have things all their own way.[87]

The media are hardly a flawless example of a pluralism in action, given the power of the big proprietors like Murdoch, Berlusconi and Springer, and the real problem is the excessively narrow range of options which journalists tend to consider as 'realistic'. This is less a matter of radical writers being denied platforms – which does happen – than of conventional thinking within a self-regarding media world. It is true that there is still competition in the treatment of foreign policy issues, and that various functions are performed for political debate: between them press, radio and TV can bring new issues to the public's attention, transmit opinion back to the centre, act as noticeboards for discussion, conduct informal diplomacy, make transnational links between national debates and put governments under pressure. The difficulty is that the process is hit and miss, with few being sure as to which function is being served at any one time, and little continuity. Some pressures merely cancel out, leaving governments freer to go their own way. Popularizing can lead to a crude jingoism which serves no-one's interests.

More significantly, the short-termism of the media means that fundamental or long-term questions are rarely pursued, and the basic assumptions of decision-makers too often go unquestioned. The debate about foreign policy will often take place within too narrow limits, with both policy-makers and commentators accepting the same conventional wisdoms. The media may, therefore, be gatekeepers between politicians and their domestic environment, but in so doing they do not serve democracy particularly well. That there is some variety evident between different capitalist countries – as between British tabloid culture, which affects even the broadsheets, and the more serious Dutch or German press – suggests that this is not an inevitable outcome. But the costs of running modern mass media mean that once a pattern of ownership, and a culture, has been established, it can be changed only slowly, if at all.

The Rise of Public Diplomacy

An important new dimension of the domestic environment in recent decades has been the emergence of public diplomacy. This is the process whereby governments by-pass their equivalents in another country and target the wider political process, including civil society. They do this on the assumptions that opinion matters, that transnationalism is unavoidable and that they can influence outcomes by direct intervention in another country – not least because of the increased freedom of movement of capital, goods and people governments themselves have signed up to. States therefore have to work out strategies both of public diplomacy and of coping with others' activity behind their own backs.

As a result of this deliberate crossing of the public/private boundary, there can be some confusion as to the nature of the actors and actions involved. Mark Leonard and Vidhya Alakeson argue that 'people [are] at the heart of the agenda rather than states' but the key word here is 'agenda'. Most of the discussion arising from the soft power paradigm is directed to the necessity for governments to understand that 'people' are now a necessary target, and that they must be drawn into the diplomatic process. This is a different thing from the *direct* people-to-people contacts which we discussed in Chapter 8, which create a new environment for states independent of their attempts at controlling it.[88] Public diplomacy involves a government deliberately attempting to manipulate (even if at times, with benign intentions) a foreign society. This is little different in principle from the familiar uses of propaganda to target morale or belief in another state. Yet public diplomacy is more subtle than the megaphone operations of the Cold War, and is generally perceived as more legitimate. This is because it builds upon an implicit recognition of shared, or at least over-lapping, constituencies between separate states. Issues such as reparations for war-time crimes (for instance the theft of Jewish gold), the future of genetically modified food, or the treatment of refugees from the Balkans play differently in different societies, but they stimulate enough of a common debate for governments to accept that they are involved in dialogues not just with their own public opinion, but with opinion more broadly.

In its more manipulative, or coercive, modes public diplomacy may actively seek advantage in the decisions taken within a foreign political process or even to undermine a government. The western allies attempted the latter during the Kosovo war by using the internet. This proved unworkable, because the authorities in Belgrade were able to flood the NATO server and put it out of action for ten days.[89] China and

Singapore too have proved adept at limiting their citizens' access to foreign information on the web. More usual is the simple attempt to gain access to another state's decision-making process. Thus foreign governments employ not just their own lobbyists but also professional marketing firms in Washington, sometimes advised by those who have recently left positions of responsibility in the US government. The number of firms involved grew from 468 in 1967 to 824 in 1986, and the number of new foreign clients from 118 in 1987 to 453 in 1987.[90] These hired guns are part of an increasingly professional approach in the work which diplomats are doing within a foreign society. Ambassadors were already rare among functionaries in having any kind of public profile, with their occasional appearances on television in their host country, but they are now much more active in reaching out to the regions and to citizens' groups. They have to work with marketing and opinion survey specialists, as well as to take rather more seriously the functions of cultural diplomacy, seen during the Cold War as something of a poor relation.

One aspect of this is a curious revival of statism in this age of globalization. A state has become something to sell, through an image which effectively promotes its strengths and downplays its weaknesses. States with obvious image problems, like Rhodesia in the 1970s, or Malaysia in 1999, have tried to improve their reputations by such means as hiring image consultants or advertising their economic achievements in western newspapers. But there is a limit as to what can be achieved in the face of obviously negative messages coming from what Manheim calls 'historical reality' – that is, problems of human rights or incompetent management which just cannot be kept out of the news.[91] With less problematic behaviour, matters become easier. 'Old states' wishing to escape from outdated images, like Britain and the City gent, or Germany and the jackboot, may take active measures to rectify them. Thus the campaigns for 'cool Britannia' and 'cool Germania'. Conversely, new states without 'name recognition', like the Baltic states, may have an urgent need to raise their profile, not just at the popular level but also among elites, given their wish to enter the European Union at the earliest opportunity. Slovenia has been particularly active in marketing its brand, and in distinguishing itself from the other ex-Yugoslav republics as a modern and peaceable country which would fit easily into the EU.[92]

Striking as this kind of activity is at first sight, it is clear that only limited progress is possible through re-branding.[93] Much more effective than marketing are substantive achievements, such as Ireland's self-transformation from a poor agricultural backwater to thriving post-modern economy and centre of youth culture. Word of mouth has transmitted this new image around the world, with the aid of diasporas. What is more, an excessive enthusiasm for a new image, as in Britain, invites a satirical response from the sophisticated, and is superfluous for those who know about the country in the first place. The fashion for this kind of public diplomacy, however, does reveal both the continued differentiation of national approaches, and a certain anxiety about how to pursue national economic goals in an era of privatization. The various paradoxes which public diplomacy thus presents do at least help us to understand the changing nature of foreign policy instruments, and their increasingly close ties with civil society.

Finally, the rise of public diplomacy presents us with two interesting moral issues. The first is about the public's right to know. If we take seriously the need for information and accountability, then citizens need to have access to the views of other governments than their own, and not just filtered through their own diplomats or national media. Well-grounded political systems have little to fear from this cross-fertilization, but they are not, unhappily, in the majority.

The second issue revolves around the ethics of intervening in the internal affairs of another state. Hiring a public relations firm might seem innocuous enough, but when it involves senior figures recently retired from the host country's civil service, tensions soon arise. Even advertising campaigns or cultural diplomacy can seem acts of aggression to some regimes. Yet more problematic were the moves by the Libyan leader Colonel Gaddafi to improve his international image by helping to liberate hostages in the Philippines. The paying of ransoms did not delight the western states, which nonetheless had to express public thanks for having got their citizens back.[94]

In Conclusion

If Chapter 9 dealt with the issue of how far foreign policy was primarily a domestic formation, this chapter has been concerned with the more directly political dimension of decision-makers' answerability to their domestic constituents. It is evident that with respect to foreign policy the function of intermediary institutions between government and public is even more significant than usual. Individual citizens, usually aggregated under the heading of public opinion, have few opportunities to get to grips with the substance of foreign policy, for all the conventional talk of the 'vetoes' or 'limits' imposed on those who make it. Apart from constitutional procedures, they have to rely on their parliamentary representatives, pressure groups and the media, all of whom take on the role of speaking for public opinion with relish but less concern for accuracy. Thus decision-makers have to deal with a range of different institutions and interests, in which concern for the common weal is continuously blurred with special interests.

The foreign policy process is broadly pluralist, even where societies are not fully developed economically or liberal in their politics. Except under conditions of terror there will always be some domestic inputs from those with special degrees of concern for, or knowledge about, the outside world. Yet this is not at all to say that even in established democracies the processes of foreign policy scrutiny work well. They do not. Formal accountability usually amounts to a light and loose set of obligations on the executive, and the day-to-day influence of interest groups and the media works only in a patchy, indirect and post hoc way. Actual participation in ongoing foreign policy decision-making is still immensely difficult even for the informed and articulate, who continue to be in a small minority on all but exceptional occasions. Politicians and officials do internalize an ideology of responsibility, even democracy – what I have called 'the notional constraint' – and as a result they sometimes aim off for fear of anticipated opposition or accusations of illegitimacy. Nonetheless, they enjoy considerable space in which to interpret the needs of their people, and they rarely live up to their own self-image of responsiveness.

This Gramscian picture, of elitism fleshed out by a sense of duty and the need for consensus, must be qualified in two ways to fit modern conditions. First, the relationship between foreign policy-making and its domestic constituencies is unpredictable, and can erupt in ways which disturb both the governing elite and the pattern of international relations. Although even the foreign policy professionals among the attentive public usually struggle to shape or restrain policy, at times a conjuncture of forces will occur which empowers parts of the citizenry and cuts decisively across the normal pattern. This is why decision-makers tend to look nervously over their shoulders, even when there seems little to be concerned about. Secondly, historical (and geographical) contexts matter a great deal, and it seems clear that there is now a trend towards greater domestic interest in foreign policy in some states, not least because the scope of foreign policy has expanded to include much of what is familiar in everyday life. We thus observe a heightened activism in liberal democracies, and some other states, deriving from a generally reduced sense that foreign policy is a reserved domain, protected from normal politics, and with its own distinctive (a)moral ambience. Foreign policy always mattered to us all. It is now increasingly seen to matter.

11

On Purpose in Foreign Policy: Action, Choice and Responsibility

On the face of things the 'changing politics' of foreign policy involves a shift from the realism of the great power conflicts of the twentieth century into the ideas of liberal interdependence which many policy-makers came to espouse in the 1990s, after two decades of discussion in academic and business circles. This book has attempted to go beyond such simplicities, not least in contesting a clear correspondence between changes in thought about international relations and changes in the pattern of world politics. The association of foreign policy with real-ism has been challenged at a more fundamental level: not only is realism itself a broad church, but since foreign policy is an activity rather than an outlook it may be harnessed to all kinds of political posi-tions, from crusading parochialism to abstract cosmopolitanism, of which realism is merely one. This has become gradually more apparent over a much longer period than the decline and fall of the Cold War.

All the central notions of modern politics are implicated in the con-duct of foreign policy, and it is always a mistake to regard the latter as some specialized form of conduct, sealed away from the rest of public life. Civil society, the state and the values which they serve are shapers of foreign policy and may be shaped by it in turn. In an era where every society is affected by globalization and democratization this is even more true. Foreign policy faces the challenge of coping with the impact of structural economic forces which if left to themselves would have an homogenizing effect, but which individual political communities have the capacity to mediate and diversify. It must also cope with not just an increased public interest in external policy but also an increasingly

283

direct participation by citizens in international relations, fuelled by the knowledge that legitimate 'domestic' concerns are to some extent dependent on international and transnational contexts. This heightens the responsibilities of foreign policy-makers as well as making more complex the technical, managerial tasks they face.

This chapter seeks to pull the argument of the book together by making sense of the changing place of foreign policy in our political and ethical life, which starts in the state but does not finish there. It does this by focusing on three concepts: action, choice and responsibility. Action is the missing link in contemporary accounts of international relations, which tend to focus on system-wide trends while dismissing what can be done by individual units. Choice is the central issue in any consideration of decision-making, itself a concept which western social science brought to public life after the Second World War, as part of a new scepticism over formal appearances and rhetorical claims, and a desire to probe beneath the surface. Responsibility is a crucial notion because it connects technical issues of democratic accountability to wider concerns over the consequences of public policy, in this case for those outside the constituency of a particular state.

Those conducting foreign policy, as well as the rest of us, who know that governments dispose of considerable assets in the protection of our interests and/or the promotion of our values, have to consider where and how they may *act*, and with what effect. They have to *choose* between those problems in which they might make a difference and those where their involvement might prove counterproductive. And they need some reasonably coherent notion as to whom, in a chaotic world of competing claims and demands, they are *responsible* and to what degree. Since the state has no choice but to work with others towards most of its ends, and since some of its citizens identify with other human beings outside their own community, foreign policy is a perpetual process of engaging in forms of multilateralism. It is also political theory in perpetual motion, inasmuch as principles over intervention, genocide or development tend to be forged through individual events in which interests and values jostle confusingly for all concerned. Only the distance attained by theory, or the historian's rear-view mirror, provide some eventual clarity of vision.

At the time, immersed in the swirling events and conflicts which make up politics, leaders are faced with the need to locate the decisional space on a given issue – that is, what is to be decided, and in which forum – and to insert themselves into it as much as possible whenever their primary concerns (and those of their fellow citizens) are at stake.

They may not always be aware that this involves judgements about the purpose of foreign policy, and its role in linking a society to the wider world community, but it does. What is more, their actions in the foreign policy arena may well turn out to have significant implications for the kind of polity, even the kind of society, they are developing at home. War in the Balkans has helped extend European integration into the field of defence; conflicts with the United States and France over nuclear power had radicalizing effects on domestic politics in New Zealand.

Foreign policy is, ultimately, purposive action with a view to promoting the concerns of a single community, even if it often falls short in so doing. The concerns will often be particular and self-regarding but they will also frequently relate to the wider milieux, or structures, in which the state is located. The hopes, fears and values which lie behind such purposes will overlap with those of other political communities and occasionally may even reflect a majority view. Thus analysing foreign policy is an important intellectual task. It involves outlining the parameters of the extent to which actions and choices are intended (that is, done 'on purpose') and of the ways in which polities formulate their underlying purposes in relation to the wider world – not just how their primary concerns translate into international activity, but how far their very purposes or senses of themselves are derived from interactions with 'abroad'. It also involves continually bearing in mind the issue of the *proper* purposes of foreign policy, where philosophers and public debate set the tone. Here some kind of balance has to be struck between communitarian concerns (which all communities generate, by definition) and cosmopolitan concerns (which can no longer be ignored). Foreign policy has to be at the cusp of this great debate, as acknowledged by theorists of international justice like John Rawls, who set himself the task of elaborating the 'foreign policy of a liberal people'.[1]

Whatever a country's size or weaknesses, its conduct of foreign policy can 'make a difference'.[2] Both realists and liberal globalists have underestimated this capacity, with their respective emphases on military force and market integration. Decision-makers, by contrast, have few doubts. Australia's first White Paper on foreign and trade policy, for example, (despite its concern with global economic trends), stressed the 'contribution that foreign and trade policy makes to the advancement of Australia's core national interests: the security of the Australian nation and the jobs and standard of living of the Australian people'.[3] And this from one of the most progressive foreign policy elites, which since 1972 has stressed the need to abandon the old defence-based verities.[4]

For their part, states like Germany and Italy in Europe, or Argentina and Brazil in Latin America, have been rediscovering the importance of foreign policy in making it possible to realize goals through partnership as much as competition. For those carrying public responsibility, foreign policy is an even more critical site of action and choice than ever before.

Action

All states, but only certain transnational actors, have a foreign policy in some form. Thus states are the main players in the realm of foreign policy. What is more, since there are now nearly four times as many states as there were in 1945, there are proportionately more foreign ministries, more diplomatic missions and more diplomats employed across the world.[5] Nor is this the end of the story. The proliferation of multilateral institutions has created a huge need for the coordination of national positions, while the expansion of the contents of international relations (prefigured by the UN Charter, which stressed the importance of the economic and social conditions of peace) has implicated the majority of domestic ministries in the 'foreign policy process'.[6] International cooperation, together with the internationalization of domestic politics, has placed more of a premium on foreign policy, not less.

Quantitative changes of this magnitude can amount to qualitative change, and it is understandable that some should have perceived the dissolution of foreign policy in the outflanking of professional diplomats by functional experts and bureaucratic rivals. Certainly the idea that foreign policy-making is a discrete area with sharply distinct boundaries must be abandoned. It is, rather, a broad area of interface between the public policies of one state or community and the external environment, which itself has many different dimensions. Regular attempts will be needed to pull together the strands of these myriad external relations, and the general image or 'brand' of a country provides another stimulus to achieve a broad foreign policy. Distinctive historical, regional and ethical concerns push in the same direction. But it is wholly anachronistic to imagine that foreign policy is only what foreign ministries do and that the latter constitute gatekeepers between a government (let alone a society) and the world.

One significant difficulty for the modern study of foreign policy has been the apparent need to conclude from the diversification of governmental and societal actors involved in 'external relations' that the state has become atomized and no longer has a meaningful international

sequitur ;

presence. This is, however, a non sequitur of a high order. States vary –
in size, development, coherence and power – and many are capable of
sustaining significant actions such as war-making, maintaining complex
programmes of international assistance or building an alliance. Some
are capable of none of these things but still manage to pursue consistent
damage-limitation strategies of various kinds. Only a very few are so
splintered or ineffectual, perhaps through external interference and/or
civil war, that they have no foreign policy worth the name.

What, then, does 'the state' mean in today's foreign policy context?
The extensive debates about the nature of the state internally, in the
international system, historically or in particular contexts like that of
the EU, have touched surprisingly rarely on issues of foreign policy.[7]
One has almost to start from first principles. If we take it as given that
the territorial state 'has not succumbed to transnational or localist influences', that it still provides an 'arena in which individuals can decide
or at least influence their collective fates', then it follows that some
collective means of relating to other such arenas will be necessary.[8] The
state furnishes a people, a society or a community, whichever term is
preferred, with a means of bundling their concerns together when that
might be necessary in dealings with outsiders – at its most extreme in
war, but more routinely in discussions over borders, travel, trade and
various kinds of joint enterprise, reaching up to the heights of diplomacy on nuclear non-proliferation or global warming. Very often full
bundling will not be necessary, but that does not mean that the separate
parts of a state, bureaucratic or regional, will be free to conduct their
own, private foreign policies. Empirical work shows that they do often
achieve degrees of autonomy which then pose problems for the coherence of 'staatspolitik', but as a matter of principle this is regarded by
most participants as pathological unless constitutionally authorized,
as is the case to a limited degree with the German Länder and other
sub-state units.[9]

The growth of the world economy, and of the private sector within it,
has tended to obscure this fact. Even those who study 'international
political economy' or 'foreign economic policy' tend to be at arm's
length from political scientists studying FPA, with the regrettable result
that the divide between economics and politics is preserved. But it is
evident both that states and firms are deeply intertwined in the mutual
pursuit of prosperity and that classical problems of security or diplomacy have always had an economic dimension – witness the debate
over economic reparations in the 1920s, the history of CoCom during
the Cold War, or the importance of oil in naval rivalries before the First

state – arena in which individual can
decide their collective fate(s)

World War. That there are problems in interrelating the economic and political complexities of these issues, and indeed the action/structure dimensions, is not a reason for deprecating foreign policy. International organizations and transnational enterprises have their own problems in this same regard, but with a different balance of strengths and weaknesses with which to confront them.

It is not necessary, therefore, before taking a position on foreign policy, to choose between the liberal, nightwatchman version of the state and a realist emphasis on collective strength and identity.[10] The first requires the state to perform some external political functions, such as ensuring stability and the honouring of agreements, but also helping to promote domestic enterprises abroad and what Rosecrance calls 'supervising and protecting the market'[11]. Conversely the second, even in a neo-Hegelian form where the state might seem to embody the national will, must allow for mediation between internal and external dynamics, and variation across issue-areas – which is where foreign policy comes in, not as a robotic arm of state power but as a formal means whereby societies engage with each other, and cope with their differences.[12]

For its part, a focus on foreign policy can tell us things about the state which 'inside' perspectives are likely to miss. Among the more important are:

- The creation of a *military–industrial complex,* whereby parts of society might become dependent on the armed services and the production of weapons. This can even lead to internal repression through the formation of a *security state*, or worse, through the hostile reactions of outsiders, to a *garrison state.*
- The *disproportionate bearing of the costs* of the international system, through, for instance, having a reserve currency or acting as a world policeman. Here the notion, implicit in liberal contract theory, that the state, and therefore its foreign policy, exists primarily to serve its own citizens, gets reversed.
- *The relieving of external pressures* which threaten the state, by helping to build a safer, more durable milieu, thus in its turn enabling new domestic developments.
- *The reinforcement – or destabilizing – of a particular regime*. This might happen through direct intervention, the spread of revolution, or mere distraction, as when Kwame Nkrumah was overthrown in Ghana in 1966 while visiting Peking.
- *The mediation of new political trends – or forms of polity*. This is the case inside the EU, and even the Commonwealth. The Concert of

Europe was in part a foreign policy mechanism for dealing with transnational political change.[13]

- *The taking on of new obligations, or orientations,* through alliances, treaties, even foreign friendships. Spain's agreement with the United States to provide nuclear bases in 1953 set the path for an eventual accession to NATO in the post-Franco years, despite contemporary public opinion.[14] British military conversations with France from 1905 on virtually tied the hands of the House of Commons over a decision for war in August 1914.[15]

- *The mediating of new values and culture from abroad.* There are limits to what state policy can do to help or to hinder this process, but the clashes in the World Trade Organization over audiovisual trade, and the Asian Values debate about resistance to western human rights pressure are both examples of how states have become deeply implicated in it. Foreign policy, indeed, is in the front line of the new cultural issues in international relations, from the G8 and globalization to the accounts given in Japanese schoolbooks of the war in Korea.[16]

- *The weakening of state cohesion through the development of sub-state foreign policies,* or more conventionally, the ability of other states to find interlocutors other than central government. If, for example, outsiders prefer, and are able to talk directly to the military, by-passing civil government, then constitutionalism is undermined. Conversely, if the regions develop a significant ability to conduct something which seems to resemble official foreign policy, then we may reasonably suspect that fault lines are opening up in the very construction of the state.

This last development is noteworthy because it might indeed represent a challenge to the idea of a central foreign policy. If a state, federal or otherwise, could prosper without central government insisting on a monopoly over foreign policy, and without disintegrating, as Hobbesians would predict, into a plurality of smaller states, then it would represent a revolution in the theory and practice of statehood (International Relations theory has already canvassed the possibility). As it is, sub-state 'foreign policies' are not yet worthy of the name. Quebec was the exception which proved the rule, in that its challenge to Canadian sovereignty through relations with France quickly led to a reassertion of federal competence. The German Länder have important powers within the European Communities, but no significant role in the Common Foreign and Security Policy or in Germany's bilateral political relationships.

The Australian states have a profile independent of the Canberra government, including offices overseas, but their activity is almost wholly limited to trade and tourism promotion. The Chinese provinces are increasingly important points of contact for foreign consulates and business but their capacity for external affairs stops well short of anything political or controversial.[17] The same is broadly true of the states of the American Union, despite their long heritage. The shadow of the Civil War still has its disciplining effects.

Foreign policy from below, therefore, is more an intermittent impulse than a widespread reality. To the extent that it represents a genuine desire to be free of a metropole then it reinforces the notion of foreign policy by showing how much it matters to be able to conduct separate relations with third parties. This in turn could have a profoundly solvent effect on a state. The United Kingdom is now at the point where resistance to a nuclear weapons policy associated with London might conceivably push Scotland (where British nuclear submarine bases are located) into full independence – although a government in Edinburgh could only envisage such a momentous step under the shelter of a common European defence policy. Small units often want distinctive foreign policies, and can achieve them – but they are ill-advised not to find means of systematic cooperation with like-minded neighbours or allies.

Actions in international relations still occur significantly through foreign policies, despite their highly pluralist environment. The state itself is constantly engaged in a process of internal debate, sometimes fragmenting and coming together again through bureaucratic politics, sometimes deliberately using multiple entities to engage with the outside world. Some pressures for devolved diplomacy exist within certain states and certainly the many international organizations in which states and NGOs now participate produce pressures for coordination. In developed systems like those of the EU this may amount to foreign policy from above, with a new layer of diplomatic activity superimposed on (but not replacing) that of the nation–states, and the external relations engaged in by sub-state units and transnational actors. Other intergovernmental organizations, like ASEAN, are following the same path more cautiously, and yet others, like NAFTA or MERCOSUR, will have at some point to decide whether they too might not develop a political capacity.

Foreign policy is thus now a far more contested and complex area, but it is far from disappearing. Indeed, the lack of clear paths for action in the current international system has placed a premium on organized, legitimate political actions beyond borders. There is no need to assume that this complexity will soon resolve itself into any simpler structure; foreign policy is at the heart of the ways in which separate societies are trying to reframe their identities in a testing, evolving world, but it is a means, not a solution.

Transnational actors, as we saw in Chapter 8, are now major factors in the environments of states. Their ability to dispose of resources complicates state foreign policies, and to some extent they have their own international strategies which are the virtual equivalent. Nonetheless, they operate alongside states not in place of them. As Lord Marshall, Chairman of British Airways, has insisted, big companies have no desire to run society or to take on any other political functions.[18] They act upon all levels of world politics, from national societies through governments and international organizations to the management of the global economy. But their capacity to take responsibility for actions, structures and consequences is profoundly limited. Since foreign policy is about the latter, and therefore a prime site of politics, the power of transnational actors is of no more (or less) significance than the power represented by ideology, class or religion in previous eras. To see the two phenomena as rivals is to make a category mistake.[19]

States and their foreign policies have a crucial role to play in knitting together the burgeoning activities of the international system. The world is politically pluralist in the sense that it consists of multiple actors operating in many different kinds of forum. Moreover, the system has no true hegemon or commanding set of rules. Thus the means of expression of the major actors and the nature of their inter-relationships are of critical importance. The actual conduct of foreign policy cannot be evaluated through scientific measurement, but actions can be analysed with a view to identifying the most effective, and the most risky, patterns of behaviour.[20] Chapters 5 and 6 argued that foreign policy necessarily involves the pursuit of many goals simultaneously, with no simple way of ordering them; similarly, that there are no rules of thumb for employing the instruments of foreign policy. What is decisive is the context. On the one hand the criteria have to involve certain elements from classical realism, such as balance, flexibility, self-preservation, prudence and the need to ensure the resources to back up aspirations. On the other hand, they must also involve empathy and imagination, the ability to understand what can be achieved through cooperation, and the capacity to make cooperation work, bilaterally and multilaterally. This means understanding where possessional goals must be folded into milieu goals, as well as the limits of joint action, and the stripping away of illusions about who does or does not share the same values. It is at this point that advice about foreign policy action must engage with debates about the ethics of foreign policy. We shall come to this when discussing the last theme, that of responsibility. Before immersion in the normative dimension, however, it is necessary to consider *how* foreign policy choices tend to be made.

Choice

The making of choices is central to modern economics and to much political science. In the latter, the theories of rational choice and public choice have come to dominate American scholarship and are steadily extending their sway elsewhere.[21] They have not, however, made much impact on foreign policy analysis. In part this is a matter of training and basic preference; yet there are also some good reasons why the insights of these individualist approaches provide only limited insights for students of foreign policy.

It is not that formal methods might not in principle be useful. Game theory evidently helps us to understand patterns of conflict and cooperation, and the strategy required in structured, limited-participant negotiations. Where voting and coalition-building is a principal activity, as in the United Nations or the EU General Affairs Council, the problems of collective action, such as free-riding, which public choice theory addresses, must be high on the research agenda. The problem lies in the fact that such activities are only one part of foreign policy, and a relatively small one at that. The character of a policy arena, the number of parties, and the nature of the problems which it presents between them determine the kind of social science which is most illuminating.

If, for example, we take the problem of preference formation so central to political science, we run straight into the question of 'whose preferences?' The work of Neustadt, Allison and others in the 1960s laid to rest the notion that the state was generally a unitary, 'rational actor' in international affairs. At the very least, foreign policy is subject to competition from differing parts of the national bureaucracy, so that even in monolithic systems like that of the Soviet Union during the Cuban missile crisis one cannot assume that leadership will be consistently exerted. Of course the bureaucratic politics model was itself based on a form of methodological individualism which assumes that individuals, or even political sub-units, might follow the precepts of rational choice.[22] But subsequent work in International Relations has made it clear that understanding foreign policy requires far more than aggregating the preferences of individual decision-makers. There are too many of them, and the values at stake are difficult to simplify, involving as they do few obvious pay-offs and diffuse notions such as international stability, prestige and historical memory. On the occasions when governments do take decisions on the basis of a conventional rationalism, as arguably Israel did in relation to Syria and the Lebanon in 1982, they risk disastrous miscalculations.[23]

Since the nature and sources of preferences in foreign policy cannot be taken as given it follows that choice is a complex matter – certainly much too complex for the old-fashioned notion of pursuing the national interest. The environments in which it is conducted (including the domestic) have no clear structure, and are characterized by perpetual flux, if not actual anarchy. States and the international organizations or regimes they have manufactured provide some points of reference, but since the internal affairs of states are just as much part of the environment as is diplomacy the world presents a cosmopolitan challenge. The range of differences which exists between societies and polities rules out making policy on the basis of a single, parsimonious set of criteria.

Making rational choices in the area of foreign policy means in the first instance not making irrational choices, as by pursuing personal obsessions or relying on stereotypes of 'people of whom we know nothing', to adapt Neville Chamberlain's famous words. It also means having the flexibility to adjust policy within the framework created by the broad strategies which are indispensable if any kind of intellectual order is to be maintained and progressive change achieved. Hardly any actor believes that the international system is satisfactory as it is, and so there is a persistent pressure towards change. This movement represents risks as well as possibilities, as some believe that they possess the secret of remaking the world and may take on too much in the attempt to hasten events. Some will adopt the ostrich posture in a spasm of suspicious conservatism. Furthermore, this variety of attitudes is to be found in every regional and micro context as well as the macro frame of the system as a whole.

Foreign policy decision-making thus needs to start from the assumption that even more than in any other area choices are a very different matter from outcomes. Leads and lags are exceptionally long, whether in relation to nuclear missile defence or the enlargement of the European Union. Almost every strategy needs negotiating with a wide range of other actors, many of them bewildering and intractable in their conduct. Even if it makes little sense not to have any planning function, built in to any idea of implementation must be an acceptance that the eventual outcomes may be unrecognizable to their initiators, or simply null. Certainly they are unlikely to be 'final', for international relations are made mainly in minds and on paper. Some institutions achieve physical presence, but in general the outcomes of foreign policy are contingent and perpetually contestable. Attempts to fix matters through measures such as iron curtains or forced migration just attract opposition.

The issue of how to choose is closely tied to that of how much choice exists. The emphasis thus far on the complexity of the environment has probably given the impression that the margins of manoeuvre in foreign policy are barely perceptible. But this is by no means the whole story. For one thing, the lack of homogeneity and ramshackle structure of the international system create air pockets in which individual players may operate relatively undisturbed. One good example is small states. An extensive literature has demonstrated that smaller states have often enjoyed a surprising latitude of choice, resisting both powerful neighbours and apparently irresistible forces.[24] The continuity of Swiss policy in the face of the diverse challenges of war and European integration is a case in point, but North Vietnam, Cuba, Romania, Finland and Yugoslavia managed to plough their own furrows during the Cold War, and Burma, Singapore and Taiwan provide other kinds of example today. The decision-makers in these countries have benefited from self-fulfilling prophecies. Because some degree of independence has been asserted in the past, their options seem wider in the present and they may consider themselves to have the luxury of choice.

This is in part a matter of the continuum between voluntarism and determinism which is an inherent part of the human experience. It is a truism that even for powerful states, foreign policy lies closer to the latter end of the continuum than the former. Yet this does not mean that choice is so restricted as to become politically or intellectually uninteresting. Foreign policy exists always on the cusp between choice and constraint. Depending on the actor, the moment and the situation, opportunities are constantly being carved out from unpromising circumstances, producing actions which then constrain both the self and others in the future. The attainment from time to time of a *decisional space*, in which choices may be considered and made with some sense of freedom, is a precondition of having a foreign *policy*, rather than a mere set of pressurized reactions to external events. Choices and constraints, exercised by the multiple exponents of foreign policy, are in a continuous process of making and remaking each other. To put it in conventional social science terms, foreign policy is not a dependent variable. That is to say, it is not *always* a dependent variable, just as the domestic and external environments cannot be taken always as independent variables. A reasonable observer must surely agree that while at times foreign policy is at the mercy of various kinds of circumstances, conversely it may also be the site of significant initiatives with the capacity to shape aspects of both domestic and international systems.

This dialectical relationship may be seen as structurationism applied to foreign policy analysis: structures shape actors, and actors make structures. Yet such an observation should be a starting point and not an end itself. Empirical research is the only way to show how interaction takes place, and when opportunities are real or illusory. It is also the means by which we do justice to historical periods, and analyse which actors make most contribution to shaping structures, as well as their own fates – the answers are often far from obvious, as with Slovenia's role in the break-up of Yugoslavia. Furthermore, just because actors and structures are tied together in endless systemic loops does not mean that they dissolve into each other. The existence of identifiable foreign policy-making processes tells us where attempts at choosing and self-assertion are being made. For example, the claims for, and institutions of, an EU foreign policy also enable us to analyse the extent to which a collective diplomacy is genuinely emerging in parallel to that of the Member States, and to measure its degree of independent impact on the international environment. The degree to which attempts at choice are effective is beside the point, except in the special case of client states, as with East German foreign policy during the Cold War, when rhetoric and reality diverged almost completely.[25]

At times states may perceive too much freedom of choice. There are many examples of decision-makers asserting themselves, often when newly entered into office, by restructuring their countries' foreign policies.[26] Not all of these are successful. Either the policy turns out to have been the product of mere *hubris* or the external environment is itself in the process of becoming less malleable through other dynamics. An example which combines the two is Anwar Sadat's reorientation of Egyptian foreign policy in 1977 so as to make peace with Israel. This succeeded in its immediate goal, and indeed relations between the two countries remain normalized, but it cost the President his own life in 1981 and Egypt has had to pay high maintenance costs ever since both on the domestic front and in the wider Arab world.

There is, ultimately, no need to make a choice between actors and structures in terms of the main sources of explanation of foreign policy, nor yet to take refuge in an undifferentiated process of structuration. Robert Gilpin has provided a notable version of the realist 'solution' to this problem, whereby all states have to adapt to living in a hostile, lawless world, but some have the capacity to shape the system in their own image, with the consequence that the weak do 'as they must' – in Thucydides' timeless formulation.[27] More open-ended, and allowing for the possibility of interplay between the triad of international system, decision-makers and domestic environment, is Wolfram Hanrieder's unjustly neglected schema. Hanrieder saw foreign policy as needing both consensus and compatibility: consensus in the sense of support for a policy in the domestic context, where it is generated, and compatibility in terms of it being a feasible move in the outside world, where it has to be implemented.[28] If it failed on the first criterion then achievement on the other would be undermined, and vice versa. Ideally some sort of equilibrium would be reached between internal and external demands, even if at times one might be particularly pressing and the other relatively insignificant. Over a period of years, however, it would be dangerous to conduct foreign policy as if it were primarily about either domestic politics or international affairs.[29] In their different ways both Richard Nixon and Bill Clinton discovered the truth of this.

The two big issues in relation to choice in foreign policy are the way choices get framed (decision-making) and the extent to which choice is illusory (determinism). They are interrelated in that policy-makers always have to estimate how much room for creativity they have, and that will have some impact on whose views are heard or how many options are considered. Conversely, gambles sometimes come off and an apparently constricting situation can be loosened by particular initiatives (witness the use of the oil weapon in 1973). More commonly, ambitious efforts to make a mark on history are reeled in remorselessly, not by opposition from any one adversary, but by the unbreakable force of circumstance. In the event of particularly dire failure, foreign policy can bring down a leader or even a regime.

Foreign policy-makers have to have some broad guidelines (which they will conventionally cast in the unhelpful language of 'national interest'). On the one side will be factors arising from the very existence of the state for which they are responsible, like self-preservation, independence, security and prosperity. On the other will be the interesting but more problematical matter of domestic values, by which is meant the particular set of principles which the government asserts, as well as those which society as a whole (or the 'nation') seems to embody. Both will involve taking the foreign policy positions which seem most likely to promote the preferred way of life, at home and abroad. And these positions will automatically contain judgements about how counterproductive any particular external action might be – will it be too costly, or draw the enmity of a powerful neighbour, or distract from other, less grandiose priorities, and so on. In that sense foreign policy choices are entangled with those of domestic society and both are sub-sets of some notion, however ill thought-out, of a desirable world. In this, however, they run into the difficult obstacle of how much responsibility to take, and for whom. In any country's foreign policy, the practical and the ethical converge inexorably.

Responsibility

Good foreign policy analysis must find ways of doing justice, in explanatory as well as prescriptive terms, to this convergence. It is a persistent challenge and there is no panacea. But the notion of responsibility does give us a useful handle on the problem. It enables us to ask who is responsible for what (and why) thus bringing together formal considerations of accountability and statehood with the issue of the best approach to the international milieu. Like power, responsibility is a relational concept in that it does not make sense if applied to a person or an actor in isolation. Foreign policy-makers have little option but to juggle multiple constituencies and competing criteria; they are no more able to suspend the practical procedures within which they work than to avoid having norms implicit in their actions. But in this at least they are grappling with real political problems, in contrast to the undifferentiated pursuit of 'global responsibilities' held up as a totem by Third Way politicians and anti-globalization protesters alike. They have particular responsibilities – even if too often they do not live up to them.

What does 'responsibility' mean? There are two linked parts to any definition. First are the formal *duties* which a person has to others by virtue of their *role*. For example a doctor has a responsibility to all those patients listed on his or her list. But this is only within reasonable limits. If the doctor comes across a road accident then professional duty instinctively leads him or her to take charge. On the other hand, no-one would expect doctors to accept responsibility for the health care of all their friends and neighbours. The relational element here is both official and personal, in terms of the trust which is naturally placed in someone who is responsible – the French word '*responsable*' also means '*digne de confiance*', or worthy of trust. Either way, someone who 'has a responsibility' for something knows that he or she must live up to their office and take into account the needs of specified others.

The second aspect of responsibility is the internalized sense of duty found in '*un responsable*'. Taking responsibility for oneself means not blaming others for one's mistakes; it is often taken to be a definition of adulthood. The captain of a sinking ship is the last to leave – the buck stops with him. In this sense responsibility means accepting the burden of taking decisions together with their consequences, however unjust. Conversely, behaving irresponsibly means ignoring any actual obligations one might have to others and being carefree in relation to consequences – even for oneself.[30]

In the context of foreign policy the above definitions alert us to the formal responsibilities which decision-makers take on by virtue of their role, for their own citizens but also – depending on ideology and political tradition – for certain features of the international system. These could be 'leadership of the free world', the relief of poverty, debts incurred through war guilt or many other things. In other words the state apparatus creates clear and heavy responsibilities but they are by no means confined within its frontiers. Furthermore, an internalized sense of responsibility adds further ideas about international commitments according to the individual and the elite within which they are located. Some are all too eager to take on the weight of decision-making for a wider constituency; others will take a minimalist view. This is by no means determined only by the geopolitical situation of the state, as a realist might presume. It also depends on the interactions between domestic and world politics.

A list of the likely constituencies of responsibility perceived by democratic foreign policy-makers would be extensive. It would begin with the constitutional remit to serve the sovereign people and its political equivalent, public opinion. It would include the responsibilities felt to government and to party colleagues, and would then move outside the state to the links with allies or privileged partners. The list would extend to some elements of the 'international community', as democratic politicians usually feel some responsibility to observe international law, to participate in international organizations and to take note, at least, of the erratic expressions of world opinion. More abstractly, foreign policy-makers are very likely also to have some sense of responsibility to their own conscience, to history (in the sense both of past generations who have made sacrifices and grandchildren yet unborn) and even to humanity as a whole, although these latter categories will vary greatly in their content and relative importance.

It might have seemed self-evident in the past as to whom statesmen were responsible – their own countrymen. But what was a simplification then has turned into a wholly inadequate notion now. There may be no clear advice to be given on how to reconcile these many, competing responsibilities, but at least the extent of the challenge should be more apparent. States and TNAs will naturally look to their own members first, while they will vary in their positions on any given third party problem because of their diverse internal characteristics. What is more, every particular focus of responsibility may be understood better by reference to three key dimensions: legitimacy, identity and ethics. To the extent that a constituency is perceived as (i) having legitimate rights to ask for action on its behalf; (ii) being part, in some sense, of one's own group, and (iii) having a strong moral claim, it is very likely to attract foreign policy support. Where it is perceived as lacking something on one or more of these criteria, it will struggle to do so.

In this context *legitimacy* involves the two-way relationship between those making foreign policy and those on whose behalf the policy is being made. Although decision-makers get their basic legitimacy from the constitutional position in their state or organization, the international system will also have an important say through the need for recognition. The leaders of Taiwan, for example, while clearly legitimate internally, represent problems for other governments who also wish to deal with the People's Republic of China.[31] Accordingly their foreign policy is more restricted than it would otherwise be. Conversely, if support is being considered for a group (such as the Kosovan Albanians) whose right to independence or to help against oppression is regarded with some ambivalence, the foreign policy being constructed may be fatally undermined. Thus both policy-makers and the objects of policy need to be seen as legitimate.

The most basic legitimacy problem occurs when leaders' rights to govern are contested within their own country, although ironically they may be seen as legitimate abroad. This was the case for the Spanish Republican government in 1936, and it was soon brought down in civil war, assisted by the ideological divisions which were spilling across every European frontier. A less extreme but still serious case is Northern Ireland, where the representatives of Sinn Féin contest the right of what they always refer to as 'the British (sic) government' to speak for the Catholic community on the world stage. Indeed, they have managed very effectively to assert that right themselves, and to impede the capacity of the UK to speak with one voice, which is the traditional presumption of national foreign policy.

Where both internal and external legitimacy exists a government can, and indeed should, act internationally to exercise its responsibilities.

Where neither exists to any great degree an actor may enjoy a superficially attractive freedom from responsibility, but will almost certainly be marginalized in the process. The Taliban regime in Afghanistan contemptuously dismissed outside opinion over many things, from women's rights to the destruction of Buddhist statues. This succeeds only up to the point where the regime needs cooperation from others in order to achieve its goals, or where the patience of outsiders is exhausted. Then the weakness of a self-regarding foreign policy becomes apparent. The same is true of the present Israeli government's determination to ignore the widespread condemnation of its treatment of the Palestinians. Only the United States' continued support protects Israel from having to face some deeply difficult international dilemmas.

The twin aspects of legitimacy, internal and external, connote the structure within which foreign policy operates. In Martha Finnemore's words, 'states are embedded in an international social fabric that extends from the local to the transnational'.[32] The patterns of this fabric may resemble those of a kaleidoscope, but they are much more easily identifiable than those of globalization, where neither agents nor structures can be identified with any confidence, and where the sites of political decision are accordingly absent. The current chaos, whereby protesters assume that the G8 rules the world, while the G8 itself has no other form of accountability than to respond to street protest, is partly the result of the neglect of foreign policy, and its role in international organizations, by party politicians, parliaments, and intellectuals, who have glibly assumed that (the United States apart) not much can be done through foreign policy.

Legitimacy fosters a sense of responsibility because it is a two-way relationship. Thus if democracy, much talked about but little specified in the globalization debate, is to have an international meaning beyond the proliferation of national democracies, it will need to be anchored to sites of decision-making which have legitimacy, and which entail particular responsibilities. Rosecrance has said that the rise of the virtual state 'portends a crisis for democratic politics ... because national governments have insufficient jurisdiction to deal with global problems'.[33] On the other hand, he also concludes that 'democracy does not exist in any other place [than the nation–state] – religious, corporate or cultural'.[34]

Foreign policy certainly represents our only serious means of holding to account those who negotiate in the international arena. It is at last attracting more sustained interest from domestic publics and is now accepted as an integral part of public policy, rather than a world apart.

Direct action and transnational pressure groups have an important role in placing and keeping issues on the political agenda, but they are a necessary rather than a sufficient condition of democratic participation. Multinational parliaments like the NATO Assembly are at best gatherings of specialists and at worse excuses for political tourism. 'Cosmopolitan democracy' resembles the latest version of idealist internationalism far more than a working model of popular sovereignty at the global level. However unpalatable it may be, the way the US Congress obstructs the UN is an example of democracy influencing events through the foreign policy process. Amnesty International's campaign against capital punishment world-wide is not – it represents, rather, the vital freedom *enabled* by democracy to raise the level of civilized discourse about politics, which is another matter. The familiar challenge is therefore to ensure that democracy has its voice while attempting to provide leadership in an international environment in which there will be robust differences of view.

A balancing act of this kind is most likely to succeed where both subjects and objects of foreign policy share some sense of common *identity*. Ultimately this should mean simultaneous feelings of citizenship and common humanity for all of us, world-wide, but for the present the ambition must be more limited. Responsibility is likely to be felt more keenly where there is a clear sense of roots, or loyalty. Even where mechanisms for foreign policy accountability are inadequate (as is mostly the case), internalized 'notional constraints' of the kind referred to in relation to public opinion (in Chapter 10) represent important anchor points. Accepting responsibility means both acknowledging the obligation on the subject (in this case, the foreign policy decision-maker) and the attachment to the object, which can be certain groups of 'foreigners', as well as domestic constituents.[35]

If there is no such identification, policy will be personalized and unreliable. Too much attachment is just as big a problem. Hitler and Mussolini both began by asserting the superiority of their own *volk* and history, but ended with bitter contempt for the way their own peoples had 'failed' them. It is also important not to take a crudely majoritarian view, which can lead to the suppression of minority needs, thus pushing some groups in the direction of foreign help – as with the Algerian or Turkish governments, which assert a particular identity for the country at the expense of internal Islamic parties, and of ethnic groups such as the Berbers and the Kurds. On the other side of the coin, Fidel Castro's persistent hopes for international revolution led him to expend scarce resources on armed forces which in 1985 ranked third in size behind only the US and Brazil in the Americas, and on entanglements in Angola, the Congo and a number of Latin American trouble spots. Allowing for the evident uncertainty about US intentions, this still meant that he neglected his responsibility for the well-being of his own people.[36]

David Campbell has argued that while 'identity is an inescapable dimension of being' it is also 'a site in which political struggles are enacted'.[37] He also distinguishes between 'foreign policy' (the representational practices of a general kind which lead us to dichotomize relationships between self and 'other') and 'Foreign Policy', which is the 'conventional' phenomenon associated with the state. In his view the latter is a privileged discourse which reproduces the boundaries of identity already achieved by the persistent association in any society of dangers and enmity with outsiders.[38] Either way, 'foreign' policy is a key means of ensuring that an 'us and them' mentality, an exclusive rather than inclusive form of identity, is perpetuated within the sovereign states out of which it has grown.

The position of this book is significantly different. The argument here is that the changing politics of both state and international relations have drawn foreign policy-makers in many states to reconfigure their approaches, given that the sense of identity of themselves and their fellow citizens is no longer uncomplicatedly confined within the paradigm of the nation–state (if, indeed, it ever was). Accordingly it is neither possible nor desirable to define just in domestic terms the particular set of concerns which lie behind every foreign policy – a given 'solution' will almost always involve changes in other states or in the international system as a whole. Identification with outsiders, however intermittent or partial, changes the nature of the game and means that responsibilities also come to be perceived as extending outside the formal boundaries of the state. Yet identity certainly is a 'site for political struggles', many of which occur precisely over the extent to which identity might be transnational and over the role of official policy in encouraging or restricting change (the aforementioned Australian arguments over how far the country should be seen as Asian is a prime example). It is just that these struggles do not always go the way of the exclusivists and dichotomizers. Indeed it is arguable that modern foreign policy is unavoidably about a society coming to terms with how to live *in* the world, rather than despite it, about how an agent must be understood as embedded *within* its structures, not separate from them. The subjects and objects of foreign policy are far from always sharing the same sense of identity, but to the extent that there is an overlap, the ties of responsibility will be strengthened.

Some decision-makers have already articulated practical versions of these conclusions, notably Tony Blair and Robin Cook in Britain – not surprisingly given the access of Tony Giddens, the author of Third Way politics, to Downing Street. In doing so they have given *ethics* a much more prominent place in the spectrum of their foreign policy responsibilities.[39]

The content of an ethical foreign policy is a problem which goes beyond the ambitions of this book. It has generated an extensive and sophisticated political theory literature.[40] Certain contextual comments are, however, in order. Firstly, foreign policy cannot but have an ethical dimension, even if it is only discussed overtly at certain junctures. The Thousand Year Reich was, in its grotesque way, an ethic pursued through foreign policy. Foreign policy always has consequences for others, and even apparently technical agreements, such as those over fishing rights, make implicit judgements about the rights of one community over another.[41] Secondly, if ethical concerns are to be acted upon in international relations there are few other sites available than foreign policy. It is a true optimist who has faith in the self-executing properties of cosmopolitan democracy.

Thirdly, it is also true that by definition foreign policy cannot be wholly cosmopolitan in its ethic. It exists, in the first instance, as the instrument of a very particular political process and set of concerns – which is why, in the current wave of cosmopolitan enthusiasm, foreign policy has often been dismissed as inherently reactionary. Foreign policy has to be about many other things than the strictly ethical. Fourthly, however, these 'concerns' are precisely not synonymous with, or confined to, self-regarding interests. They will also include ideas about preferred ways of living in which the nation–state in question may simply be one part of a wider whole, as in the European Union. They will often include more particular goals which are still difficult to tie to clear self-interests, as with Denmark's persistent support for the anti-apartheid movement in South Africa.

Fifthly, therefore, the old antithesis between interests and morals in foreign policy must finally be put to rest. Every community has many concerns which are particular and some which are general (but possibly more important). This is Wolfers' key distinction between possessional and milieu goals. Furthermore, the two types cannot always be sharply distinguished, as a number of possessional goals will either be identical with those of some other states, or will significantly overlap with them. What may seem a pure 'interest' can indeed shade into a general principle. Nor is this always a matter of gradually creating a bigger unit through integration. Often the overlapping will be with states or groups beyond the partners in a regional grouping, and/or it will be partial and intermittent. If international relations imposes many cross-cutting cleavages, foreign policy can be about the obverse: creating cross-binding. There will thus be a real sense of ethical responsibility towards outsiders, if without clear boundaries or structure. The idea of 'good international citizenship', formulated by Gareth Evans when Australian Foreign Minister, is to be welcomed as an attempt to provide guidelines from the perspective, for once, of the actors who have to use them.[42]

At the highest level of generality foreign policy can be seen as a means of mediating between community and cosmopolis, each of which entails choices over resources, values and privileged partners. It is rarely used simply as a battering ram for maximizing national interests regardless of the wider impact. While hard choices have sometimes to be made and subtle strategies are invariably at work, national diplomats get criticized at home precisely because they are necessarily immersed in the international environment, and have to represent its needs to a domestic audience quite as much as vice versa. They are therefore in a double bind: of having responsibilities to a number of different constituencies but possibly the backing of none. This is a formidable ethical and practical challenge.

Hopes and Prospects

As the twenty-first century begins, foreign policy is in the situation of having both too little and too much expected of it. Academic specialists in International Relations have been so taken with rediscovering their subject as a fully-fledged social science, with all the epistemological and theoretical scaffolding required, that too many have tended to see foreign policy as part of the prehistory of the subject. In the United States, where the focus is predictably more on agency, the majority is either preoccupied with the unique nature of the American position, or works on the basis of the limiting assumptions of rational choice. To practitioners such questions matter little, but here too there is a tendency to see foreign policy as the *chasse gardée* of professional diplomats, and therefore increasingly cut off from the 'realities' of finance, trade and information technology.

In the world of political argument, by contrast, too much is often expected of foreign policy. Certainly for liberal states the default setting is to take on ever more external responsibilities, and 'isolationism' is virtually a term of abuse. Citizens are increasingly told by elites that they must make new sacrifices for the sake of international order.[43] Yet 'ordinary' men and women do not always fall into line. Ambitions for foreign policy often run beyond what can actually be achieved and/ or sustained in terms of domestic support as well as capabilities provided.[44]

Over-extension, however, is not just a matter of what might be called the Atlas complex of the powerful – the intermittent temptation to run crusades, to remake the world in their own image. More common is the desire to do *something* to respond to the challenges of an ever-changing and all-encompassing world, out of the control of even the most assertive of actors. The existential reaction to global determinism is wholly understandable. Foreign policy has an indispensable part to play in helping human beings to assert some control over their own fates. As we have seen, it is a key route-centre where different issues meet and trade-offs are made. Yet it also represents one of the few opportunities for organized communities to express their distinctive identities and concerns in a common context.

The United Nations Organization is the established forum for international discussion, and much of what takes place there is foreign policy. But as is well known, it also suffers from such severe limitations that expectations have almost fallen below the organization's actual capability.[45] Foreign policy may be renamed 'global strategy', and ministries of foreign affairs 'departments of world politics' so as to fill this vacuum, but it will not change the reality that no world organization (let alone 'global governance') is capable of delivering *in and of itself* serious and specific decisions on change. It is the actors, primarily states, which do that by reaching collective agreement – sometimes in international organizations, but just as often outside them. Until the world no longer consists of self-standing, constitutionally independent communities which have a perpetual need to engage in systematic relations with each other, then there will always exist something with the substance of foreign policy, if not its title.

The purposes of foreign policy are articulated by elites and to some extent are shaped by mass society. As stated, they usually seem banal. Yet beneath the surface this is one of the most creative, demanding and exciting of human activities, worthy of the most serious intellectual attention. It is probably the principal site of political action and choice in international affairs. It carries the heaviest responsibilities for the lives of ordinary people across the planet, in terms of their vulnerability not just to the war and devastation of which we have seen so much in the last hundred years, but also to environmental degradation, population pressure, economic dislocation and ideological conflict. These problems cannot be 'solved', but they have to be managed. Agreements reached through foreign policy, which is a channel for negotiation precisely because it derives from the expression of diverse perceptions and competing interests, are the only way forward. Foreign policy and international organization (including INGOs as well as IGOs) are necessary but not sufficient conditions of international order. They are partners, not opposites.

The political strategies of international actors confront, *mutatis mutandis*, the same great challenge as politics within a single community, which has exercised political philosophers down the centuries: how to reconcile 'our' legitimate needs and preoccupations, whether as individuals or sub-groups, with (i) the equivalent concerns of others; (ii) the less tangible issues of collective goods and structures; (iii) obligations to future generations (abstract), including our children and grandchildren (compelling). In its fundamentals, foreign policy is about these first order questions, which is why theorists like Walzer and Rawls have been drawn inexorably outwards, to reflect on the nature of 'liberal foreign policy'.

Globalization has provoked a generalized sense of anxiety in states.[46] They feel their independence and governing capacities threatened, not least because the 'decline' of the state, or its transmogrification into the 'virtual' state, is the orthodoxy of the day. Accordingly some have borrowed the strategies of business by reinventing or 'rebranding' themselves. Even the Quai d'Orsay in France produced a new magazine whose title may be loosely translated as 'Brand France'.[47] Much of this is ephemeral in the extreme, but when taken together with the revived interest in 'public diplomacy' (discussed in Chapter 10) it can be seen as part of a process of perpetual evolution. Foreign policy has to respond to change in the world and in the demands of citizens. A recognition of the importance of perceptions and the mass market is simply the latest manifestation of this fact.

For some global activists and students of International Relations foreign policy is the enemy – the embodiment of necessarily reactionary state policies in a world which will soon render them as redundant as the principle of absolute monarchy. A more reasonable view is to compare foreign policy to Michelangelo's great unfinished statue 'The Prisoners', where the human form is visible emerging from the great blocks of stone but remains trapped within them – truly a metaphor in itself.[48] Foreign policy is emerging from the bonds of realism, and contains within it the potential for use by many different political approaches. It does not have to be a discourse or a practice of fear and antagonism. Foreign policy serves our hopes, as well as our understandable insecurities.

Notes and References

Preface

1. Joseph Frankel, *The Making of Foreign Policy* (London: Oxford University Press, 1963).
2. Lloyd Jensen, *Explaining Foreign Policy* (Englewood Cliffs, NJ: Prentice Hall, 1982); Michael Clarke and Brian White (eds), *Understanding Foreign Policy: the Foreign Policy Systems Approach* (Aldershot: Edward Elgar, 1989). Further very useful surveys are to be found in P.A. Reynolds, *An Introduction to International Relations*, 3rd edn (London: Longmans, 1994), Parts II & IV, and Margot Light, 'Foreign policy analysis', in A.J.R. Groom and Margot Light, *Contemporary International Relations: a Guide to Theory* (London: Frances Pinter, 1994). An example of a good country-study is Charles W. Kegley and Eugene R. Wittkopf, *American Foreign Policy: Patterns and Process*, 5th edn (London: Macmillan, 1996), while a classic of middle-range theory is Graham T. Allison, *Essence of Decision: Explaining the Cuban Missile Crisis* (Boston: Little, Brown, 1971, with a 2nd edn in 1999).
3. Any such list would include (in alphabetical order): Graham Allison, David Baldwin, James Barber, Michael Brecher, Walter Carlsnaes, Bernard C. Cohen, Adeed Dawisha, Karen Dawisha, Jean-Baptiste Duroselle, Lawrence Freedman, Alexander George, Fred Halliday, Brian Hocking, Kalevi Holsti, Ole Holsti, Irving Janis, Robert Jervis, Roy Jones, Miles Kahler, Robert Keohane, Baghat Korany, Ned Lebow, Margot Light, Ernest May, Marcel Merle, Richard Neustadt, Pierre Renouvin, Philip Reynolds, Thomas Risse, James Rosenau, Avi Shlaim, Michael Smith, Steve Smith, John Steinbruner, Yaacov Vertzberger, Ole Wæver, William Wallace.

   This list reflects my own approach and is not exhaustive. It is dominated by American names, as is FPA itself, but there are enough Europeans to show that the subject has some healthy roots elsewhere.
4. See in particular Arnold Wolfers' classic set of essays *Discord and Collaboration* (Baltimore: Johns Hopkins University Press, 1962), and Stanley Hoffmann's more recent collection *Essays on Sisyphus: Essays on Europe 1964–94* (Oxford: Westview, 1995).

Chapter 1

1. The Cold War encouraged this belief, but so, unfortunately, has its demise – witness events in the Balkans, Chechnya, the Gulf, West and Central Africa and Afghanistan.
2. For further discussion see Christopher Hill, 'Foreign policy', in Joel Krieger (ed.), *Oxford Companion to World Politics* (New York: Oxford University Press, 1993, and Revised Edition, 2001).
3. Definitions of foreign policy have been offered surprisingly rarely. For a recent attempt to wrestle with the problem, defining foreign policy as 'attempts by governments to

influence or manage events outside the state's boundaries', see Ian Manners and Richard G. Whitman (eds), *The Foreign Policies of European Member States* (Manchester: Manchester University Press, 2000) p. 2.

4. David Baldwin makes pertinent criticisms of the way in which the distinction leads both economics and politics to be undervalued at various times. See his *Economic Statecraft* (Princeton, NJ: Princeton University Press, 1985) p. 61. The distinction itself derives from functionalist approaches. See Stanley Hoffmann, 'Obstinate or obsolete? The fate of the nation-state and the case of Western Europe', *Daedalus*, vol. XCV, no. 3, 1966, pp. 862–915; Edward L. Morse, *Foreign Policy and Interdependence in Gaullist France* (Princeton, NJ: Princeton University Press, 1973) pp. 5–6; and William Wallace, *The Foreign Policy Process in Britain* (London: Royal Institute of International Affairs, 1975) pp. 11–15.

5. Michael Smith has argued in relation to the EU that the concept of foreign policy does not do justice to the increased interpenetration of domestic and foreign affairs, and that 'external relations' is the better term to use. See, for example, Brian Hocking and Michael Smith, *Beyond Foreign Economic Policy: the United States, the Single Market and the Changing World Economy* (London: Pinter, 1997) pp. 21–2; also Michael Smith, 'Does the flag follow trade? "Politicisation" and the emergence of a European foreign policy', in John Peterson and Helene Sjursen (eds), *A Common Foreign Policy for Europe: Competing Visions of the CFSP* (London: Routledge, 1998) pp. 77–94.

6. See D.C. Watt, *Personalities and Policies: Studies in the Formulation of British Foreign Policy in the Twentieth Century* (London: Longmans, 1965), and *What about the People? Abstraction and Reality in History and the Social Sciences: An Inaugural Lecture* (London: LSE, 1983).

7. See Christopher Hill, 'History and International Relations', in Steve Smith (ed.), *International Relations: British and American Perspectives* (Oxford: Basil Blackwell, 1985), and 'The Study of International Relations in the United Kingdom', in *Millennium: Journal of International Studies*, vol. 16, no. 2, Summer 1987, reprinted in Hugh Dyer and Leon Mangasarian (eds), *The Study of International Relations: the State of the Art* (London: Macmillan, 1989). Good examples of the spirit of collaboration in the United States are Paul Lauren (ed.), *Diplomacy: New Approaches in History, Theory and Policy* (New York: Free Press, 1979); Ernest May and Richard Neustadt, *Thinking in Time: the Uses of History for Decision Makers* (New York: Free Press, 1986); and Colin Elman and Miriam Fendius Elman (eds), *Bridges and Boundaries: Historians, Political Scientists and the Study of International Relations* (Cambridge, Mass: the MIT Press, 2001).

8. The notable exception, of course, was Raymond Aron. See his *Imperial Republic: the United States and the World* (London: Weidenfeld & Nicolson, 1975). Christopher Coker has also written tellingly from an external standpoint, in *Reflections on American Foreign Policy* (London: Pinter, 1989).

9. The relevant national works here are too many to list. On the groups, see, for example, Stephen Wright (ed.), *African Foreign Policies* (Boulder, Col: Westview Press, 1999) and Christopher Hill (ed.), *The Actors in Europe's Foreign Policy* (London: Routledge, 1996).

10. Some of these gaps are being filled. Michael Leifer's *The Foreign Policy of Singapore: Coping with Vulnerability* (London: Routledge, 2000) is an authoritative treatment of an 'exceptional state' whose external impact is disproportionate to its size, while Jim Broderick, Gary Burford and Gordon Freer (eds), *South Africa's Foreign Policy* (London: Palgrave, 2001) updates the story of another key state regarded as a model by many.

11.   For examples of recent work which qualify the stereotypes in this respect see Timothy
      Dunne, *Inventing International Society: a History of the English School* (Basingstoke:
      Macmillan, 1998) and Michael Cox (ed.), *E.H. Carr: a Critical Appraisal* (Basingstoke:
      Palgrave, 2000). The relevant writings of the writers listed are: E.H. Carr, *The Twenty
      Years' Crisis: an Introduction to the Study of International Relations*, first published in
      1939 but reissued with an Introduction by Michael Cox (Houndmills, Basingstoke:
      Palgrave Macmillan, 2001); Hans J. Morgenthau, *Politics Among Nations* (New York:
      Alfred P. Knopf, 1948); Reinhold Niebuhr, *Christian Realism and Political Problems*
      (New York: Charles Scribner's Sons, 1953); Martin Wight, *Power Politics*, first published
      in 1946 but reissued with an Introduction by Hedley Bull and Carsten Holbraad
      (Leicester: Leicester University Press, 1978); Arnold Wolfers, *Discord and Collaboration:
      Essays on International Politics*, with a Foreword by Reinhold Neibuhr (Baltimore: Johns
      Hopkins University Press, 1962).
12.   A point made effectively by Brian White in his *Understanding European Foreign Policy*
      (London: Palgrave, 2001) pp. 32–6.
13.   It is an elementary error, for example, to suppose that because realists study foreign
      policy, all those who study foreign policy are realists. John Vasquez comes close to
      this position in his *The Power of Power Politics: a Critique* (London: Pinter, 1983)
      pp. 47–79 and 205–15.
14.   Kenneth Waltz, *Theory of International Politics* (Reading, Mass: Addison-Wesley, 1979).
15.   Barry Buzan and Richard Little, *The Logic of Anarchy in International Relations:
      Neorealism to Structural Realism* (New York: Columbia University Press, 1993).
16.   Kenneth Waltz, *Foreign Policy and Democratic Politics: the American and British
      Experience* (Boston: Little, Brown, 1967).
17.   For a contrary view, see Colin Elman and Kenneth Waltz, 'Horses for courses: why *not*
      a neo-realist theory of foreign policy?' *Security Studies*, vol. 6, no. 1, Autumn 1996.
18.   David Lake, 'Realism', in Joel Krieger (ed.), *Oxford Companion to World Politics*,
      Revised Edition (New York: Oxford University Press, 2001) p. 716.
19.   Michael Nicholson, in *Formal Theories in International Relations* (Cambridge:
      Cambridge University Press, 1989) pp. 206–15, recognizes this and makes an ingenious
      attempt to overcome the simplification by reference to satisficing, hypergames and cog-
      nitive maps. See also Nicholson's *Rationality and the Analysis of International Conflict*
      (Cambridge: Cambridge University Press, 1992), especially pp. 53–7 and 138–41.
20.   David Campbell, *Writing Security: United States Foreign Policy and the Politics of
      Identity* (Minneapolis: University of Minnesota Press, 1992; Revised Edition, 1998);
      Henrik Larsen, *Foreign Policy and Discourse Analysis: France, Britain and Europe*
      (London: Routledge, 1997); Ole Waever, 'The language of foreign policy', *Journal of
      Peace Research*, vol. 27, no. 3, 1990, and 'Resisting the temptation of post foreign
      policy analysis', in Walter Carlsnaes and Steve Smith (eds), *European Foreign Policy:
      the EC and Changing Foreign Policy Perspectives in Europe*, *op.cit.*; Roxanne Doty,
      Imperial Encounters: the Politics of Representation in North–South Relations
      (Minneapolis: University of Minnesota Press, 1996); Roxanne Doty, 'Foreign policy as
      social construction: a post-positivist analysis of U.S. counter-insurgency in the
      Philippines', *International Studies Quarterly*, vol. 37, no. 3, 1993.
21.   For example, Larsen, *Foreign Policy and Discourse Analysis*, p. 198: 'the framework of
      meaning around the political processes remains national'.
22.   For surveys of FPA and its evolution see Christopher Hill, 'The credentials of foreign
      policy analysis', *Millennium: Journal of International Studies*, Autumn 1974;
      Steve Smith, 'Foreign policy analysis and International Relations', in Hugh Dyer and

Leon Mangasarian, *The Study of International Relations: the State of the Art* (London: Macmillan in association with *Millennium: Journal of International Studies*, 1989); Valerie M. Hudson, with Christopher S. Vore, 'Foreign policy analysis yesterday, today and tomorrow', *Mershon International Studies Review* (1995) p. 39.

23. For a fair-minded but inevitably defensive account of the work done in CFP see Charles F. Hermann and Gregory Peacock, 'The evolution and future of theoretical research in the comparative study of foreign policy', in Charles F. Hermann, Charles W. Kegley Jr and James N. Rosenau (eds), *New Directions in the Study of Foreign Policy* (London: George Allen & Unwin, 1987) pp. 13–32.

24. On middle-range theories see Margot Light, 'Foreign policy analysis', in A.J.R. Groom and Margot Light (eds), *Contemporary International Relations: a Guide to Theory* (London: Pinter, 1994) pp. 97–100. Also Ole Waever, 'Thinking and rethinking in foreign policy', *Cooperation and Conflict*, XXV, 1990, p. 152. Middle-range theories were first discussed by Robert Merton. See Charles Reynolds, *Theory and Explanation in International Politics* (London: Martin Robertson, 1973) pp. 51–88.

25. 'Weak theory' is what the 'Scandinavian school' wishes to promote, in contrast to 'over-ambitious American grand theory and/or raw empiricism [and] the English middle-range theory and/or historical studies'. It focuses on 'a specific *idea, thesis, problematique*'. See Ole Wæver, 'Resisting the temptation of post foreign policy analysis', in Carlsnaes and Smith, *European Foreign Policy, op.cit.*, p. 251. Apart from Wæver himself, he names Carlsnaes, Hans Mouritzen and Kjell Goldmann as members of the school. Waever invented the school in his 'The language of foreign policy', *Journal of Peace Research*, vol. 27, no. 3, 1990, p. 335.

26. See Michael Clarke and Brian White (eds), *Understanding Foreign Policy: the Foreign Policy Systems Approach* (Aldershot: Edward Elgar, 1989). Systems theory too has been unjustly neglected in recent years. For a strong recent reevaluation, see Robert Jervis, *System Effects: Complexity in Political and Social Life* (Princeton: Princeton University Press, 1997), in particular Chapter 7, 'Acting in a system'. The best example of systems theory used for empirical work on foreign policy, and one which has influenced many subsequent case-studies, is Michael Brecher's *The Foreign Policy System of Israel: Setting, Images, Processes* (London: Oxford University Press, 1972); also Michael Brecher, *Decisions in Israel's Foreign Policy* (London: Oxford University Press, 1974).

27. Fred Halliday, *The World at 2000* (London: Palgrave, 2001) pp. 19–22.

28. See Robin Niblett, 'France and Europe at the end of the Cold War: resisting change', and Christopher Hill and Filippo Andreatta, 'Struggling to change: the Italian state and the new order', both in Robin Niblett and William Wallace (eds), *Rethinking European Order: West European Responses, 1989–1997* (London: Palgrave, 2001).

29. The major works have been orchestrated by David Held. See David Held, Anthony McGrew, D. Goldblatt and J. Perraton, *Global Transformations: Politics, Economics and Culture* (Cambridge: Polity Press, 1999) and David Held *et al.* (eds), *The Global Transformations Reader* (Cambridge: Polity Press, 2000). In the combined 995 pages of these well-indexed and valuable volumes, foreign policy gets not a single reference. The same is true of Jan Art Scholte's *Globalization: a Critical Introduction* (Basingstoke: Palgrave, 2000). These authors are much more cautious than the 'hyperglobalists' about the likely impact of the changes they chart on the state and its political capacity. Yet their main theme is system transformation, with little interest in engaging with the major issue of foreign policy, or even agency.

30. Peter Hain, *The End of Foreign Policy? British Interests, Global Linkages and Natural Limits* (London: Fabian Society, Green Alliance and the Royal Institute of International

312 Notes and References to pp. 13–23

Affairs, 2001). A close reading reveals that the question-mark in this apparently dramatic title (from a serving UK foreign minister) is crucial. The call is really for an internationalist, multilateral foreign policy, based on the idea of global commons. This is in no way incompatible with the idea of a national foreign policy.

31. A point made powerfully by Tony Smith in his survey of the influence of special ethnic interests over American foreign policy. Tony Smith, *Foreign Attachments: the Power of Ethnic Groups in the Making of American Foreign Policy* (Cambridge, Mass: Harvard University Press, 2000) for example, pp. 7–8.

32. On Blair's proposal, made in his Chicago speech during the Kosovo war in April 1999, see Christopher Hill, 'Foreign policy', in Anthony Seldon (ed.), *The Blair Effect* (London: Little, Brown, 2001). Also Rhiannon Vickers, 'Labour's search for a third way in foreign policy', in Richard Little and Mark Wickham Jones (eds), *New Labour's Foreign Policy: a New Moral Crusade?* (Manchester: Manchester University Press, 2000) pp. 41–2.

33. Authoritative commentaries on this development are to be found in Nicholas J. Wheeler, *Saving Strangers: Humanitarian Intervention in International Society* (Oxford: Oxford University Press, 2000), and Chris Brown, *Sovereignty, Rights and Justice: International Political Theory Today* (Polity, 2002).

34. See Steve Smith and Michael Clarke (eds), *Foreign Policy Implementation* (London: George Allen & Unwin, 1985). The groundwork had been laid in Graham T. Allison, *Essence of Decision: Explaining the Cuban Missile Crisis* (Boston: Little, Brown, 1971) which is, in essence, a study of implementation problems. See also the second, revised edition, with Philip Zelikow (New York: Longman, 1999) which relates the original rational actor model to subsequent rational choice work, as well as using the vast amount of new historical material which has emerged since 1971.

35. The concept of legal personality entails recognition on the part of states and international organizations of the right to participate in negotiations, to be an 'interlocuteur valable'. Some entities, like the European Union (cf. the European Communities), still lack this legal capacity but evidently enjoy political personality in the sense that they are generally acknowledged to have the capacity to make decisions and to impact on others. See Nanette A.E.M. Neuwahl, 'A partner with a troubled personality: EU treaty-making in matters of CFSP and JHA after Amsterdam', *European Foreign Affairs Review*, vol. 3, no. 2, Summer 1998, pp. 177–95.

36. Stanley Hoffmann, *Duties beyond Borders: On the Limits and Possibilities of Ethical International Politics* (Syracuse, New York: Syracuse University Press, 1981).

37. By 'direct engagement' is meant either attempting to influence a foreign government directly, without going through one's own government, or forming a transnational social movement. For an early survey of such activities, see Peter Willetts (ed.), *Pressure-groups in the Global System: the Transnational Relations of Issue-Oriented Non-Governmental Organizations* (Oxford: Pinter, 1982); see also Peter Willetts (ed.), *The Conscience of the World: the Influence of Non-Governmental Organizations in the UN System* (London: Hurst, 1995); Katsuya Kodama and Unto Ves (eds), *Towards a Comparative Analysis of Peace Movements* (Aldershot: Dartmouth, 1990); and Jan Aart Scholte, *International Relations of Social Change* (Buckingham: Open University Press, 1993).

38. Valerie M. Hudson, with Christopher S. Vore, 'Foreign policy analysis yesterday, today and tomorrow', *Mershon International Studies Review* (1995), vol. 39, p. 210.

39. Raymond Aron, *Peace and War: A Theory of International Relations* (London: Weidenfeld & Nicolson, 1966) p. 17.

40. Fred Halliday, *Rethinking International Relations* (London: Macmillan, 1994) pp. 13–14.
41. Thus the argument of the book is broadly 'structurationist'. This is explained further in the first pages of Chapter 2.

Chapter 2

1. This debate is best approached through Colin Hay's 'Structure and agency', in David Marsh and Gerry Stoker (eds), *Theory and Methods in Political Science* (London: Macmillan, 1995) pp. 189–206. Alexander Wendt, *Social Theory of International Politics* (Cambridge: Cambridge University Press, 1999) is a rich discussion of the problem in the context of International Relations. See also Gil Friedman and Harvey Starr, *Agency, Structure and International Politics: From Ontology to Empirical Enquiry* (London: Routledge, 1997). One of the first to articulate these issues was P.G. Cerny, in *The Changing Architecture of Politics: Structure, Agency and the Future of the State* (London: Sage, 1990).
2. 'Meta-ontology' because the debate largely focused on philosophical issues such as the nature of 'free' agency without confronting 'the first-order' questions of what entities, actors, units to admit of in world politics. Alexander Wendt, both in *Social Theory of International Politics* and in his earlier 'Bridging the theory/meta-theory gap' (*Review of International Studies*, vol. 17, no. 4, October 1991), stresses the need to get down to substantive or first-order argument.
3. For Giddens' notion of structuration, whereby agencies help to form structures and structures agencies, see Anthony Giddens, *Central Problems in Social Theory: Action, Structure and Contradiction in Social Analysis* (London: Macmillan, 1979) pp. 69–73.
4. Philip G. Cerny, 'Political agency in a globalizing world: towards a structurational approach', *European Journal of International Relations*, vol. 6, no. 4, December 2000, p. 438.
5. As Martin Hollis and Steve Smith showed in their 'Roles and reasons in foreign policy decision-making', *British Journal of Political Science*, (1986), vol. 16, no. 3.
6. Barry Buzan, 'The levels of analysis problem in International Relations reconsidered', in Ken Booth and Steve Smith (eds), *International Relations Theory Today* (Oxford: Polity Press, 1995); Walter Carlsnaes, 'The agency–structure problem in foreign policy analysis', *International Studies Quarterly* (1992) vol. 36, no. 3; Walter Carlsnaes, 'In lieu of a conclusion: compatibility and the agency–structure issue in foreign policy analysis', in Walter Carlsnaes and Steve Smith (eds), *European Foreign Policy: the EC and Changing Perspectives in Europe* (London: Sage, 1994) pp. 274–87. See also the exchanges in the *Review of International Studies*, i.e. Alex Wendt, 'Bridging the theory/meta-theory gap in international relations', vol. 17, no. 4, pp. 383–92; Martin Hollis and Steve Smith, 'Beware of gurus: structure and action in international relations', vol. 17, no. 4, pp. 393–410; Alex Wendt, 'Levels of analysis vs. agents and structures: Part III', vol. 18, no. 2, pp. 181–5; Martin Hollis and Steve Smith, 'Structure and action: further comment', vol. 18, no. 2, pp. 187–8.
7. The levels of analysis model was based on Kenneth Waltz's *Man, the State and War* (New York: Columbia University Press, 1959) and explicated in J. David Singer, 'The level of analysis problem in International Relations', in Klaus Knorr and Sidney Verba (eds), *The International System: Theoretical Essays* (Princeton: Princeton University Press, 1961).

8. Martin Hollis and Steve Smith, *Explaining and Understanding International Relations* (Oxford: Clarendon Press, 1990). As Walter Carlsnaes puts it, if 'we define the agency–structure issue as a question not of combining two accounts but rather of the need for a *single integrative conceptual framework* in terms of which the *empirical interaction* of agential and structural factors in social behaviour can be properly analysed, then we can escape the implications of this harsh logic'. Carlsnaes, 'In lieu of a conclusion', in Carlsnaes and Smith, 1994, p. 280.

9. This is obviously close to the position of Karl Popper, who argued that theories should be falsified empirically, yet without denying the sociological factors which mean that the 'intellectual market' is coloured by its time – a view arising from the work of Thomas Kuhn. For the debate between the two see Imre Lakatos and Alan Musgrave (eds), *Criticism and the Growth of Knowledge* (Cambridge: Cambridge University Press, 1970).

10. The early works of foreign policy decision-making theory are particularly open to this criticism. See Richard C. Snyder, H.W. Bruck and Burton Sapin, *Foreign Policy Decision-Making* (New York: Free Press, 1962), and Glenn Paige, *The Korean Decision: June 24–30 1950* (New York: Free Press, 1968).

11. A point made by Charles Reynolds, *Theory and Explanation in International Politics* (London: Martin Robertson, 1973) pp. 339–54. See also the revised edition, *The World of States: an Introduction to Explanation and Theory* (Aldershot: Edward Elgar, 1992) pp. 41–5.

12. For 'weak theory' see note 25 in Chapter 1.

13. But see Roy E. Jones, *The Principles of Foreign Policy: the Civil State in its World Setting* (Oxford: Martin Robertson, 1979) for example, pp. 84–5, where the difference that can be made by a 'constitutional state' is explored.

14. To a lesser extent this has also involved the constructivist–positivist debate. See Cynthia Weber, *Simulating Sovereignty: Intervention, the State and Symbolic Exchange* (Cambridge: Cambridge University Press, 1995) Richard Ashley, 'The poverty of neo-realism', *International Organization*, vol. 38, no. 2, Spring 1984; Richard Ashley and R.B.J. Walker, 'Reading dissidence/writing the discipline: crisis and the question of sovereignty in international studies', *International Studies Quarterly*, vol. 34, no. 3, September 1990. For the classical approach see Alan James, *Sovereign Statehood: the Basis of International Society* (London: George Allen & Unwin, 1986). Unfortunately 'debate' is not a correct description. The two schools of thought carefully avoid ever having to talk to each other, a fact illustrated by Walker's bizarre claim that writers like F.H. Hinsley existed 'somewhere in the more obscure margins of the literature'. R.B.J. Walker, 'The concept of the political', in Ken Booth and Steve Smith (eds), *International Relations Theory Today* (Oxford: Polity Press, 1995) p. 318.

15. While theoretically absolute, in practice there are various examples of states coping with divided or pooled sovereignties. The EU Members are cases in point, while West Germany provides a prominent example before 1989 and even, arguably, afterwards. See Peter Katzenstein, *Policy and Politics in West Germany: the Growth of a Semi-Sovereign State* (Philadelphia: Temple, 1987), and William E. Paterson, 'Beyond semi-sovereignty: the new Germany in the new Europe', *German Politics*, vol. 5, no. 2, August 1996.

16. The origins of the modern doctrine of sovereignty are well traced in Alexander Passerin D'Entrèves, *The Notion of the State: an Introduction to Political Theory* (Oxford: Clarendon Press, 1967), but for the international meaning see F.H. Hinsley, *Sovereignty* 2nd edn (Cambridge: Cambridge University Press, 1986) pp. 158–235.

17. One of the most sophisticated treatments is still Kenneth Dyson's *The State Tradition in Western Europe* (Oxford: Martin Robertson, 1980).

18. This is also the approach of Georg Sørensen's insightful *Changes in Statehood: the Transformation of International Relations* (Houndmills: Palgrave, 2001).

19. See John A. Hall, *Powers and Liberties: the Causes and Consequences of the Rise of the West* (London: Penguin, 1992) pp. 133–41.

20. The importance of military power in the evolution of the modern state is discussed in detail in Charles Tilly (ed.), *The Formation of National States in Europe* (Princeton, NJ: Princeton University Press, 1975), and Michael Mann, *The Sources of Social Power*, two volumes (Cambridge: Cambridge University Press, 1986 and 1993), especially vol. II.

21. See, for example, Vendulka Kubálková and Albert Cruickshank, *Marxism and International Relations*, 2nd edn (Oxford: Clarendon Press, 1985).

22. For analysis of the genesis of nationalism in the context of international relations, see Anthony D. Smith, *Nationalism and Modernism* (London: Routledge, 1998), pp. 70–96, and James Mayall, *Nationalism and International Society* (Cambridge: Cambridge University Press, 1990).

23. The *prebendal state* is a notion coined by Richard Joseph, adapting the ideas of Max Weber. See James Mayall, 'The variety of states', in Cornelia Navari (ed.), *The Condition of States: a Study in International Political Theory* (Milton Keynes: Open University Press, 1991) pp. 53–6 and 60. See also James Mayall, *Nationalism and International Society* (Cambridge: Cambridge University Press, 1990) pp. 35–49, and Robert H. Jackson, *Quasi-States: Sovereignty, International Relations and the Third World* (Cambridge: Cambridge University Press, 1993), Chapter 1.

24. The bluntest form of this view is that held by anarchists, but Marxists, realists and elitists have all held it in varying forms, often in reaction to the perceived dangers from the external environment. See Dyson, *The State Tradition in Western Europe*, pp. 101–7.

25. Max Weber is the founder of this modernist conception of the state. See, for example, his 'Politics as a Vocation', in trans., intro. and eds H.H. Gerth and C. Wright Mills. *From Max Weber: Essays in Sociology* (London: Routledge and Kegan Paul, 1948) pp. 80–2 and p. 95.

26. Alan James, *Sovereign Statehood*, pp. 147–8 and p. 271 (for recognition as a political act); also Adam Roberts and Benedict Kingsbury (eds), *United Nations, Divided World: the UN's Roles in International Relations*, 2nd edn (Oxford: Clarendon Press, 1993), pp. 56–7; Ian Brownlie, *Principles of International Public Law* (Oxford: Clarendon Press, 1966) pp. 80–7; and M.N. Shaw, *International Law* (Cambridge: Cambridge University Press, 1991), pp. 138–42 and 242–75.

27. Articles 4 and 18 of the UN Charter provide for admission of a state by a two-thirds vote in the General Assembly, on the recommendation of the Security Council (where the veto would apply). Recognition of a new *regime* in any given state is a more piecemeal matter, and depends on bilateral relations as well as the UN. On recognition in this sense see Stephen D. Krasner, *Sovereignty: Organized Hypocrisy* (Princeton: Princeton University Press, 1999) pp. 14–20.

28. See, for example, David Campbell, *Writing Security: United States Foreign Policy and the Politics of Identity* (Minneapolis: University of Minnesota Press, 1992) p. 56: 'Both the state and the church require considerable effort to maintain order within and around themselves, and thereby engage in an evangelism of fear to ward off internal and external threats, succumbing in the process to the temptation to treat difference as otherness'.

29.   On liberal realism, see Christopher Hill, '1939: the origins of liberal realism', *Review of International Studies*, vol. 15, no. 4, October 1989. Also, John H. Herz, 'Political realism revisited', and comments by Inis Claude and Herz, again, *International Studies Quarterly*, vol. 25, no. 2, June 1981, pp. 182–203.

30.   This section draws in part on the author's 'What is left of the domestic? A reverse angle view of foreign policy', in Michi Ebata and Beverly Neufeld (eds), *Confronting the Political in International Relations* (London: Palgrave Macmillan, 2000).

31.   Robert D. Putnam, 'Diplomacy and domestic politics: the logic of two-level games', in *International Organization*, 42 (Summer 1988) pp. 427–60, reprinted in Peter B. Evans, Harold K. Jacobson and Robert D. Putnam (eds), *Double-Edged Diplomacy: International Bargaining and Domestic Politics* (Berkeley: University of California Press, 1993).

32.   R.B.J. Walker, *Inside/Outside: International Relations as Political Theory* (Cambridge: Cambridge University Press, 1993) p. 25; Cynthia Weber, *Simulating Sovereignty*) pp. 10 and 6.

33.   I have developed this point in ' "Where are we going?" International Relations and the voice from below', *Review of International Studies*, vol. 24, no. 1, January 1999.

34.   See James N. Rosenau, *Along the Domestic–Foreign Frontier: Exploring Governance in a Turbulent World* (Cambridge: Cambridge University Press, 1997). This forms a continuity with Rosenau's other works in the 1990s focusing on the difficulty of separating micro and macro levels of international political causation. See his *Turbulence in World Politics: a Theory of Change and Continuity* (Hemel Hempstead: Harvester Wheatsheaf, 1990) pp. 141–77.

35.   Susan Strange, *States and Markets: an Introduction to International Political Economy* (London: Pinter, 1988).

36.   Murdoch has been so keen to adapt and to do business with China that he removed the BBC World TV station from his Astra satellite, and his papers are generally judged to have toned down criticisms of the Beijing regime.

37.   Cf. David Held, *Democracy and the Global Order: from the Modern State to Cosmopolitan Governance* (Cambridge: Polity Press, 1995), who sees globalization as challenging the state so firmly that only a new 'cosmopolitan democracy' can preserve liberty, through embedding common principles in the multiple system of authority which characterizes international relations.

38.   The last two decades have seen the welcome development of an extensive literature on ethics in international relations. Not all of it is targeted on the morality of state foreign policy, and indeed the location of responsibility – individual, government, region, UN – is often ducked. Still, a great deal of it does in fact deal with the problem of ethics in foreign policy. For the first influential works see Michael Walzer, *Just and Unjust Wars* (New York: Basic Books, 1977), Stanley Hoffmann, *Duties beyond Borders: On the Limits and Possibilities of Ethical International Politics* (Syracuse, New York: Syracuse University Press, 1981), and Chris Brown, *International Relations Theory: New Normative Approaches* (Hemel Hempstead: Harvester, 1992). There is a usefully clear statement in Christopher Brewin, 'Liberal states and international obligations', in Cornelia Navari (ed.), *The Condition of States: a Study in International Political Theory* (Milton Keynes: Open University Press, 1991).

39.   James Rosenau was the first to conceptualize the 'domestic sources of foreign policy'. See his book of the same name published in New York by the Free Press in 1967. Historians such as Fritz Fischer and Pierre Renouvin, however, were emphasizing the domestic factor from the 1950s, following in the footsteps of Eckart Kehr's pioneering

study of German naval policy before the First World War: *Schlachtflottenbau und Parteipolitik 1894–1902* (Berlin, 1930). Gordon Craig brought this back into prominence more than forty years later. See his edition of Eckart Kehr, *Economic Interest, Militarism and Foreign Policy: Essays on German History* (Berkeley: University of California Press, 1977). Peter Gourevitch initiated the study of the international sources of domestic politics. See his 'The second image reversed: the international sources of domestic politics', *International Organization*, vol. 32, no. 4, 1978, pp. 881–912.

40. In November 1996. Malta and Cyprus had both been offered, at the Madrid European Council of December 1995, a start to negotiations on entry six months after the end of the forthcoming Intergovernmental Conference. The position was reversed in September 1998 once the Nationalist Party returned to power in Malta. See Ulrich Sedelmeier and Helen Wallace, 'Eastern enlargement: strategy or second thoughts?', in Helen Wallace and William Wallace (eds), *Policy-Making in the European Union* 4th edn, (Oxford: Oxford University Press, 2000) pp. 445 and 459.

41. See John Stopford and Susan Strange, with John Henley, *Rival State, Rival Firms: Competition for World Market Shares* (Cambridge: Cambridge University Press, 1991) pp. 211–27.

42. *Ibid.*, p. 224.

43. Adeed Dawisha (ed.), *Islam in Foreign Policy* (Cambridge: Cambridge University Press, 1985).

44. See Edward Luttwak, 'The missing dimension' and Barry Rubin, 'Religion and international affairs', in Douglas Johnston and Cynthia Sampson (eds), *Religion, the Missing Dimension of Statecraft* (New York: Oxford University Press, 1994) pp. 8–19 and 20–34 respectively.

45. On regions, see Brian Hocking (ed.), *Managing Foreign Relations in Federal States* (London: Leicester University Press, 1993), and on international pressure groups note 37 in Chapter 1 above.

46. For a useful treatment, which does not, however, focus much on agency, see Thomas Risse-Kappen (ed.), *Bringing Transnational Relations Back In: Non-State Actors, Domestic Structures and International Institutions* (Cambridge: Cambridge University Press, 1995).

47. On the Union of Democratic Control see Sally Harris, *Out of Control: British Foreign Policy and the Union of Democratic Control 1914–18* (Hull: University of Hull Press, 1996). On the different views taken about what and for whom foreign policy is for, see Martin Ceadel, *Thinking about Peace and War* (Oxford: Oxford University Press, 1987).

48. R.J. Vincent, *Human Rights and International Relations*, and the same author's edited volume *Foreign Policy and Human Rights* (both Cambridge: Cambridge University Press, 1986).

49. Justin Rosenberg, *The Empire of Civil Society: a Critique of the Realist Theory of International Relations* (London: Verso, 1994), and Stefano Guzzini, *Realism in International Relations and International Political Economy: the Continuing Story of a Death Foretold* (London: Routledge, 1994).

50. The concept is that of Arnold Wolfers, who contrasted goals which aimed at changing the external environment (the milieu) with those which were 'possessional', or deriving from the actor's particular needs. See Arnold Wolfers, *Discord and Collaboration: Essays on International Politics* (Baltimore: Johns Hopkins Press, 1962) pp. 73–7.

51. For this concept see Christopher Hill, 'The capability-expectations gap, or conceptualising Europe's international role', *Journal of Common Market Studies*, vol. 31, no. 3,

September 1993, reprinted in Simon Bulmer and Andrew Scott (eds), *Economic and Political Integration in Europe: Internal Dynamics and Global Context* (Oxford: Blackwell, 1994).

52. For representative examples see Sheila Harden, *Small Is Dangerous: Micro-States in a Macro World* (London: David Davies Institute, 1985); Christopher Clapham (ed.), *Foreign Policy Making in Developing States* (Farnborough: Saxon House, 1977); Carsten Holbraad, *Middle Powers in International Politics* (London: Macmillan, 1984).

53. On the democratic peace debate see Chapter 9 below, pp. 11–13. The discussion of state–society relations derives from the study of international political economy. See Peter Katzenstein, 'International Relations and domestic structures: foreign economic policies of advanced industrial states', *International Organization*, vol. 30, no. 1, Winter 1976; Stephen Krasner, *Defending the National Interest: Raw Materials, Investments and U.S. Foreign Policy* (Princeton: Princeton University Press, 1978) focused explicitly on the concept of weak and strong states. Dyson, *The State Tradition in Western Europe* (1980) also discusses the problem, although not in the context of foreign policy. Thomas Risse-Kappen refines the categories in his 'Public opinion, domestic structure and foreign policy in liberal democracies', *World Politics*, vol. 43, no. 1, October 1990.

54. See Georg Sørensen, *Changes in Statehood: the Transformation of International Relations*, pp. 87–91, and Robert Cooper, *The Post-Modern State and the World Order* (London: Demos, 1996). John Ruggie, however, was one of the first to write in this vein, using the concept of 'unbundled territoriality'. See his 'Territoriality and beyond: problematizing modernity in International Relations', *International Organization*, vol. 47, no. 1, 1993.

Chapter 3

1. This term was first coined by Lincoln Bloomfield in his *The Foreign Policy Process: a Modern Primer* (New York: Prentice Hall, 1982).

2. For example, General Geisel, head of state and government in Brazil between 1974–9 led the whole foreign policy process, even if Itamatary, the Foreign Ministry, usually initiated the process. See Leticia Pinheiro, *Foreign Policy-making under the Geisel Government: the President, the Military and the Foreign Ministry*, unpublished PhD thesis, London School of Economics and Political Science, 1995.

3. Although Mény and Knapp point out that von Weizsäcker took 'a back seat ... in the rush to unification'. Yves Mény with Andrew Knapp, *Governments and Politics in Western Europe: Britain, France, Italy, Germany*, 2nd edn (Oxford: Oxford University Press, 1993) pp. 240–1. Von Weizsäcker could not help but be involved in some of the delicate diplomacy of that period, however. See Philip Zelikow and Condoleezza Rice, *Germany Unified and Europe Transformed: A Study in Statecraft* (Cambridge, Mass: Harvard University Press, 1997), pp. 32–4. Also p. 153 on the President's attempts to calm fears over the Polish frontier.

4. For multinational corporations' decision-making structures see J.M. Stopford and L.T. Wells, *Managing the Multinational Enterprise: Organisation of the Firm and Ownership of the Subsidiaries* (London: Longman, 1972); M.J. Taylor and N.I. Thrift, 'Models of corporate development and the multinational corporation', in Michael Taylor and Nigel Thrift (eds), *The Geography of Multinationals: Studies in the Spatial Development and Economic Consequences of Multinational Corporations*

(London: Croom Helm, 1982) pp. 14–32; and Ian M. Clarke, *The Spatial Organisation of Multinational Corporations* (London: Croom Helm, 1985) pp. 40–60. John Stopford stresses that transnational corporations need to be 'diplomats' in protecting their global interests in the political realm, not least in relations with governments. See his 'Interdependence between TNCs and governments', in *Companies without Borders: Transnational Corporations in the 1990s* (London: International Thomson Business Press on behalf of UNCTAD, 1996) pp. 255–79.

5.   Jeremy Howells and Michelle Wood, *The Globalisation of Production and Technology, a Report Prepared for the Commission of the European Communities* (London: Belhaven, 1993) p. 153. For example Japanese companies tend to follow a pyramidal structure, and European/American companies a flatter and broader one.

6.   Jonathan Power, *Like Water on Stone: the Story of Amnesty International* (London: Allen Lane, The Penguin Press, 2001).

7.   See Nelson Mandela, *Long Walk to Freedom* (London: Abacus, 1995) pp. 347 and 731. Mandela himself refers to Tambo as 'the best possible ambassador' for the ANC.

8.   The concept of the 'foreign policy executive' derives from Christopher Hill, *Cabinet Decisions in Foreign Policy: the British Experience, September 1938–June 1941* (Cambridge: Cambridge University Press, 1991) pp. xviii and 224–47.

9.   For example, Russian Foreign Minister Yevgeny Primakov has known Saddam Hussein of Iraq for more than thirty years as the result of his various posts, and can thus always put himself forward as an intermediary in crises. See, 'Fingerprints on Iraqi accord belong to Albright', *New York Times*, 25 February 1998. Jimmy Carter and Henry Kissinger have been even more prominent examples.

10. A crisis (in any walk of life) may be defined as deriving from: a threat to basic values, a finite time for response, and a sense of compelled choice – the status quo is not an option. This definition builds on, but significantly amends (in that it omits the criterion of the likelihood of war), that authoritatively provided by Michael Brecher. See his *Decisions in Crisis: Israel, 1967 and 1973*, with Benjamin Geist (Berkeley, California: University of California Press, 1980), Chapter 1.

11. See Graham Allison and Philip Zelikow, *Essence of Decision: Explaining the Cuban Missile Crisis*, 2nd edn (New York: Addison-Wesley, 1999) pp. 113–14; Adam Roberts and Philip Windsor, *Czechoslovakia 1968: Reform, Repression and Resistance* (London: Chatto and Windus for IISS, 1969) pp. 62–78; also Karen Dawisha, *The Kremlin and the Prague Spring* (Berkeley: University of California Press, 1984).

12. Hill, *Cabinet Decisions in Foreign Policy*, *op.cit.*, pp. 48–84.

13. William Wallace, *Opening the Door: the Enlargement of NATO and the European Union* (London: Centre for European Reform, 1996) pp. 1–29.

14. Fred I. Greenstein, *Personality and Politics: Problems of Evidence, Inference and Conceptualization*, 3rd edn (Princeton, New Jersey: Princeton University Press, 1987) pp. 40–62; but also Fred I. Greenstein, *The Presidential Difference: Leadership Style from FDR to Clinton* (New York: Martin Lessler Books, 2000) p. 193, where Greenstein argues (*re* the Middle East) that 'Carter provides a reminder that presidents need not simply respond to circumstances. They can make opportunity their servant, engaging in acts of political creativity.'

15. Ellen Reid Gold, 'Politics by word power: Ronald Reagan and the art of rhetoric', *Times Higher Education Supplement*, 28 October 1988.

16. The infrequency of summits has led to what is called 'funeral diplomacy', or the conducting of business while attending the funerals of major world figures, such as Brezhnev or Indira Gandhi. See Geoffrey Berridge, 'Diplomacy after death: the rise of the

working funeral', *Diplomacy and Statecraft*, vol. 4, no. 2, July 1993, pp. 217–34, and 'Funeral summits', in David H. Dunn (ed), *Diplomacy at the Highest Level* (London: Macmillan, 1996) pp. 106–17. Also Hans-Dietrich Genscher, *Rebuilding a House Divided: a Memoir by the Architect of Germany's Reunification* (New York: Broadway, 1998) pp. 174–5, 206.

17. This figure comprises two years of Lenin after his strokes, seven years for Stalin after his first stroke, seven for Brezhnev after his stroke in 1975, and the two years of Andropov and Chernenko, both seriously ill. All of these figures died in office, the product, as in modern China, of an ossifying gerontocracy. See Hugh L'Etang, *Ailing Leaders in Power, 1914–1994* (London: Royal Society of Medicine, 1995).

18. Lionel Barber, 'All the world has been his stage', *Financial Times*, 27 December 1991. On the Attlee Report of 1957, see file PREM 11/2351 in the Public Record Office, Kew, UK. It was brought to public attention by Peter Hennessy in 'The Whitehall man's burden', The *Independent*, 25 July 1989. On how one foreign minister dealt with overwork by discreetly arranging regular, group meetings with his French, American and British colleagues, see Hans-Dietrich Genscher, *Rebuilding a House Divided*, *op.cit.* p. 116. For an extract from Robin Cook's crowded diary, see Kevin Theakston, 'The changing role of the British Foreign Secretary', in Kevin Theakston (ed.), *British Foreign Secretaries since 1974* (London: Frank Cass, forthcoming).

19. This has not been uncommon, especially in developing countries. In 1965, 22 of the world's 123 heads of government also held the position of foreign minister. Data from George Modelski, cited in P.J. Boyce, *Foreign Affairs for New States: Some Questions of Credentials* (St Lucia: University of Queensland Press, 1977) p. 60. Silvio Berlusconi did the same in 2002 after the resignation of his respected foreign minister Renato Ruggiero.

20. Peter Riddell, 'Blair as Prime Minister', in Anthony Seldon (ed.), *The Blair Effect: the Blair Government 1997–2001* (London: Little, Brown, 2001) p. 37. Also Peter Hennessy, *The Prime Minister: the Office and its Holders since 1945* (Harmondsworth: Allen Lane, The Penguin Press, 2000) pp. 476–523.

21. Avi Shlaim, Peter Jones and Keith Salisbury, *British Foreign Secretaries since 1945* (Newton Abbot: David & Charles, 1977) pp. 20–2; also Evelyn Shuckburgh, *Descent to Suez: Diaries 1951–56* (London: Weidenfeld & Nicolson, 1986), for example, pp. 28, 41, and 74–8.

22. Paul Preston and Denis Smyth, *Spain, the EEC and NATO*, Chatham House Papers 22 (London: Royal Institute of International Affairs and Routledge & Kegan Paul, 1984), pp. 76–8.

23. The *Independent*, 24 September 2001.

24. Samaras was sacked on 13 April 1992 and created his new party ('Political Spring') on 30 June. See Aristotle Tziampiris, *Greek Foreign Policy: EPC and the Macedonian Question* (Aldershot: Ashgate, 2000) pp. 109–35.

25. On these three resignations, see Keith Middlemas, *Diplomacy of Illusion: the British Government and Germany, 1937–39* (London: Weidenfeld & Nicolson, 1972) pp. 151–4; Barry Rubin, *Secrets of State: the State Department and the Struggle over US Foreign Policy* (New York: Oxford University Press, 1985) pp. 194–6; Peter Calvert, *The Foreign Policy of New States* (Brighton: Wheatsheaf, 1986) p. 96.

26. See Howe's memoirs, *Conflict of Loyalty* (London: Macmillan, 1994), especially pp. 581–676 and Thatcher's *The Downing Street Years* (London: HarperCollins, 1993). Howe regarded Eduard Shevardnadze as a hero for his courage and impact on events. See 'Heroes and villains: Eduard Shevardnadze' by Sir Geoffrey Howe, The *Independent Magazine*, 3 August 1991, p. 46. For his part Shevardnadze valued his friendship with James Baker: 'I had 35 meetings with [George] Schultz. With Baker I've lost

count ... when we meet we feel like friends first and politicians second'. Interview between Shevardnadze and Eugenio Scalfari of *La Repubblica*, translated in The *Independent*, 20 March 1991.

27. Paul Schott Stevens, 'The National Security Council: past and prologue', *Strategic Review*, Winter 1989, pp. 55–62.

28. Saddam Hussein kept his colleagues in order through physical fear – he is supposed to have shot one minister personally outside the meeting room after a disagreement. Fortunately this is not the rule in cabinet government.

29. R.A.W. Rhodes, 'From prime ministerial power to core executive', in R.A.W. Rhodes and Patrick Dunleavy (eds), *Prime Minister, Cabinet and Core Executive* (New York: St Martin's Press, 1995) pp. 11–37.

30. Peter Hennessy, *Cabinet* (Oxford: Basil Blackwell, 1986) stresses the overload problem; Thomas T. Mackie and Brian W. Hogwood, 'Decision-making in cabinet government' and 'Cabinet committees in context', in Thomas T. Mackie and Brian W. Hogwood (eds), *Unlocking the Cabinet: Cabinet Structures in Comparative Perspective* (London: Sage, 1985) pp. 1–15 and 31–5; also Jean Blondel and Ferdinand Müller-Rommel, *Cabinets in Western Europe*, 2nd edn (London: Macmillan, 1997) p. 275.

31. These were only the most prominent examples. Amintore Fanfani, Giuseppe Saragat, Emilio Colombo and others fit the same pattern. Data computed from Appendix II of Luigi Vittorio Ferraris (ed.), *Manuale della politica estera italiana 1947–1993* (Rome-Bari: Laterza, 1996) pp. 517–21.

32. The Privy Council itself is a formalistic body. On 4 August 1914 it met to declare war on Germany in the presence of the King, one minister and two court officials. A.J.P. Taylor, *English History 1914–1945* (Oxford: Oxford University Press, 1965) p. 2.

33. Max Hastings and Simon Jenkins, *The Battle for the Falklands* (London: Pan, 1983) pp. 378–9.

34. Douglas Porch, *The French Secret Services: from the Dreyfus Affair to the Gulf War* (London: Macmillan, 1996) pp. 465–7, and 494–5.

35. On 1939, see Hill, *Cabinet Decisions, op.cit.*, pp. 85–99. On Suez, opinions still differ as to whether Eden's ill-health was the occasion or the cause of his going. See Keith Kyle, *Suez* (London: Weidenfeld & Nicolson, 1992) pp. 532–3; Anthony Gorst and Lewis Johnman, *The Suez Crisis* (London: Routledge, 1997) pp. 147–9; Evelyn Shuckburgh, *Descent to Suez, op.cit.*, pp. 365–6.

36. The text of the President's resignation address to the nation is to be found in: 'I am being ignored by ministers serving in my cabinet', *Financial Times*, 15 August 1989.

37. Keith Wilson, 'Grey', in Keith M. Wilson (ed.), *British Foreign Secretaries and Foreign Policy: from Crimean War to First World War* (London: Croom Helm, 1987) pp. 172–97.

38. Geoffrey Hosking, *A History of the Soviet Union, 1917–1991* (London: Fontana, 1992) pp. 270–3.

39. Gradually, the principle of Politburo collective responsibility was re-established, becoming a powerful norm even in the late Brezhnev years.

40. See Bert Edström, *Japan's Evolving Foreign Policy Doctrine: from Yoshida to Miyazawa* (Basingstoke: Macmillan, 1999), pp. 119–30; also Mitsumi Hirano, *The Implications of History Education for External Relations: A Case Study of the Japanese History Textbook Disputes in the 1980s* (London School of Economics and Political Science PhD thesis, 2001) p. 138.

41. It has grown in importance since 1940. See Reginald Hibbert, 'Intelligence and policy', *Intelligence and National Security*, vol. 5, no. 1, January 1990, pp. 110–28. See also p. 126: 'The secret intelligence agencies have become actors on the diplomatic stage, with something more than walk-on parts'.

42. As often asserted by some of those once involved themselves in intelligence operations. See, for example, Anthony Verrier, *Through the Looking Glass: British Foreign Policy in an Age of Illusions* (London: Cape, 1983) and Peter Wright, *Spycatcher: the Candid Autobiography of a Senior Intelligence Officer* (New York: Viking, 1987). It is almost impossible to check how much of this kind of gaff-blowing is itself disinformation.

43. For an excellent analysis of the risks involved in intelligence forecasts, see Avi Shlaim, 'Failures in national intelligence estimates: the case of the Yom Kippur war', *World Politics*, vol. 28, no. 3, April 1976, pp. 348–80.

44. See Charlie A. Beckwith and Donald Knox, *Delta Force: the US Counter-Terrorist Unit and the Iranian Hostage Rescue Mission* (London: Arms and Armour Press, 1984), and Zbigniew Brzezinski, *Power and Principle: Memoirs of the National Security Adviser, 1977–1981* (London: Weidenfeld & Nicolson, 1983) pp. 491–500. Of course the hostage mission failure was not the only reason for Carter's defeat. On the other hand, had it gone well, his popularity would undoubtedly have soared.

45. Christopher Andrew, 'Churchill and Intelligence', in Michael I. Handel (ed.), *Leaders and Intelligence* (London: Cass, 1989) pp. 181–93. Also Michael Handel in the same volume, pp. 6–8.

46. Douglas Porch, *The French Secret Services*, pp. 473–4.

47. *Ibid.*, pp. 450–1; John Tower *et al.*, *The Tower Commission Report* (New York: Bantam Books and the New York Times, 1987) especially pp. 102–48. And see Anne Armstrong, 'Bridging the gap: intelligence and policy', *Washington Quarterly*, Winter 1989, pp. 28–9.

48. See, for example, the Franks Report on the failure of British intelligence to predict the invasion of the Falkand Islands in 1982. This, like most such exercises, showed little interest in probing too deep. Lord Franks, *Falklands Islands Review: Report of a Committee of Privy Councillors, Cmnd 8787* (London: Pimlico edition, 1992, with introduction by Alex Danchev), also William Wallace, 'How frank was Franks?', *International Affairs*, vol. 59, no. 3, Summer 1983, pp. 453–8. The French report on responsibility for the sinking of Greenpeace's 'Rainbow Warrior' in Auckland harbour in 1985 was brazenly mendacious. See Porch, *The French Secret Services*, p. 462.

49. Handel, in his own *Leaders and Intelligence*, *op.cit.*, pp. 27–8. In the same volume Jay Lavas shows that in very different times Napoleon was able to combine these functions. See his 'Napoleon's use of intelligence: the Jena campaign of 1805', pp. 4–54. Compare Shlomo Gazit, 'Intelligence estimates and the decision-maker', pp. 261–81, which recounts how Golda Meir accidentally became aware of how small a proportion of actual intelligence reports she was seeing (pp. 271–2).

50. 'The only groups which understood the need for reform – without, however, being prepared to embrace the remedy – were the security services.' Henry Kissinger, *Diplomacy* (London: Simon and Shuster, 1994) p. 797.

51. Seweryn Bialer and Michael Mandelbaum (eds), *Gorbachev's Russia and American Foreign Policy* (Boulder: Westview, 1988) pp. 277–8.

52. Probably this happened with R.A. Butler, the senior Conservative politician that many expected to become party leader, after his indiscretions on peace moves in 1940 and other rumours of personal problems.

53. The growth of academic interest among historians and political scientists over the past decade has made it possible to talk on a more informed basis about a previously taboo

subject. An example is the journal *Intelligence and National Security*, which first appeared in 1986.

54. Indeed Hibbert, a former British diplomat of some seniority, asks, 'would it not be healthy to try to manoeuvre the secret intelligence agencies a little more to the margin of affairs?', Hibbert, 'Intelligence and policy', p. 126.

55. Shlomo Gazit, 'Intelligence estimates and the decision-maker', *op.cit.*, p. 262.

56. Max Weber's other two ideal-types were traditional and charismatic leadership. The latter is not uncommon even today in foreign policy, as the examples of Gaddafi, Gorbachev and Mandela all show, although Gorbachev's charisma was more effective outside his own country than in.

57. This is a version of the Paul Kennedy over-stretch hypothesis, formulated before the end of the Cold War. Paul Kennedy, *The Rise and Fall of the Great Powers: Economic Change and Military Conflict from 1500 to 2000* (London: Unwin Hyman, 1988). After cataloguing the Soviet Union's problems, Kennedy noted that 'this does *not* mean that the USSR is close to collapse ... it *does* mean that it is facing awkward choices' – a statement which shows that even if a particular prediction goes awry, a general thesis may still retain its explanatory power.

Chapter 4

1. The increasing personalization of trust between politicians and bureaucrats is explored in a pioneering comparative study, which unfortunately does not extend into foreign policy. See Edward C. Page and Vincent Wright (eds), *Bureaucratic Elites in Western European States: a Comparative Analysis of Top Officials* (New York: Oxford University Press, 1999).

2. Writing in the midst of war in 1917, Weber looked back on an uneasy combination of efficient administration and court politics, unbuffered by a responsible class of democratic politicians. See 'Rule by officials in foreign policy', section IV of Weber's 'Parliament and government in Germany', reproduced in Peter Lassman and Ronald Spiers (eds), *Weber: Political Writings* (Cambridge: Cambridge University Press, 1994) pp. 196–209. Also pp. 145–6, and 161.

3. The public sphere has historically often been confused with that of the political. See Hannah Arendt, *The Human Condition* (Chicago: University of Chicago Press, 1958) pp. 28–37, 50–8.

4. Weber saw modern administration as having originated in Renaissance Italy and as having been developed by the logic of capitalism. See 'The profession and vocation of politics' (1919) in Peter Lassman and Ronald Spiers (eds), *Weber: Political Writings*, p. 322. He drew personally on the writings of Moisie Ostrogorski. See Lassman and Spier's 'Introduction', pp. xvii–xx.

5. For invaluable historical analysis see Zara Steiner (ed.), *The Times Survey of Foreign Ministries of the World* (London: Times Books, 1982). On the USA in particular see William I. Bacchus, *Staffing for Foreign Affairs: Personnel Systems for the 1980's and 1990's* (Princeton, New Jersey: Princeton University Press, 1983) pp. 3–6; also Graham Allison and Peter Szanton, *Remaking Foreign Policy: the Organizational Connection* (New York: Basic Books, 1976) pp. ix–xiv, 24–43.

6. Cited by Teddy J. Ulricks, 'The Tsarist and Soviet Ministry of Foreign Affairs', in Zara Steiner (ed.), *The Times Survey of Foreign Ministries of the World*, p. 531.

7. Anthony Adamthwaite, *France and the Coming of the Second World War* (London: Frank Cass, 1977) pp. 152–3. François-Poncet was as significant as the more notorious Nevile Henderson as an engineer of appeasement.

8. In the United States, the term 'official' covers both politicians and administrators. Here the term is used in its European sense, and refers just to the latter.

9. In the USSR the foreign ministry, unlike other ministries, was directly responsible only to the Politiburo. Arkady Shevchenko, *Breaking with Moscow* (London: Cape, 1985) p. 188. In both the USSR and China we are limited by our lack of knowledge of policy processes at certain periods. See Carol Lee Hamrin, 'Elite Politics and the Development of China's Foreign Relations', in Thomas W. Robinson and David Shambaugh (eds), *Chinese Foreign Policy: Theory and Practice* (Oxford: Clarendon Press, 1995). Also Lu Ning 'The central leadership, supraministry coordinating bodies, State Council ministries and party departments', in David M. Lampton (ed.), *The Making of Chinese Foreign and Security Policy, 1978–2000* (Stanford: Stanford University Press, 2001), especially pp. 45–60. Ning argues (p. 60) that the rise of economic issues and the decline of world communism has led to 'the subtle shift in power from the central political leadership to the foreign affairs establishment', with the Party's International Liaison Department the biggest loser.

10. See Patrick Keatinge, 'Ireland and common security: stretching the limits of commit-ment?' and Pierre-Louis Lorenz, 'Luxembourg: new commitments, new assertiveness', in Christopher Hill (ed.), *The Actors in Europe's Foreign Policy* (London: Routledge, 1996) pp. 208–25 and 226–46 respectively.

11. On Germany, see Kurt Doss, 'Germany: the history of the German Foreign Office', in Zara Steiner (ed.), *The Times Survey of Foreign Ministries of the World*, pp. 244–6.

12. See Simon Nuttall, 'The Commission and foreign policy-making', in Geoffrey Edwards and David Spence (eds), *The European Commission*, 2nd edn (London: Cartermill, 1997) pp. 303–19.

13. Steven Everts, 'Coming to terms with Germany: the slow and arduous adjustment of Dutch foreign policy after 1989', in Robin Niblett and William Wallace (eds), *Rethinking European Order: West European Responses, 1989–97* (Houndmills: Palgrave, 2001) pp. 172–4.

14. R.P. Barston, *Modern Diplomacy*, 2nd edn (London: Longman, 1997) pp. 11–31.

15. Cook spent only five hours in the Turkish capital, and some of that time was taken up with a photo-call at the bedside of a human rights activist wounded in a shooting. *Financial Times*, 19 May 1998.

16. Andrés Rozental, 'Mexico: change and adaptation in the Ministry of Foreign Affairs', in Brian Hocking (ed.), *Foreign Ministries: Change and Adaptation* (New York: St Martin's Press, 1999) p. 151, note 24. The total resources of these units exceeds the Ministry of Foreign Affairs' budget by 20 per cent! They can also engage in direct foreign relations with their equivalents in other states. On such transgovernmentalism, see Anne-Marie Slaughter, 'The real new world order', *Foreign Affairs*, September–October 1997, vol. 76, no. 5, pp. 183–97.

17. See Lauri Karvonen and Bengt Sundelius, *Internationalization and Foreign Policy Management* (Aldershot: Gower, 1987) pp. 30–1.

18. William I. Bacchus, *Staffing for Foreign Affairs*, p. 28.

19. It does, however, depend on the state. In Japan, where image and good relations have been vital since 1945, the foreign ministry has been relatively privileged in terms of resources. Kyoji Komachi, 'Japan: towards a more pro-active foreign ministry', in Brian Hocking (ed.), *Foreign Ministries: Change and Adaptation* (Basingstoke: Macmillan, 1999) p. 103.

20. A point presciently made by a Pakistani diplomat criticizing the US reliance on the CIA in Afghanistan while cutting back on conventional diplomacy. Letter to The *Independent*, 12 October 1987.

21. Henry Kissinger, *Diplomacy* (London: Simon and Schuster, 1994) p. 9.

22. Samuel Williamson, *The Politics of Grand Strategy: Britain and France Prepare for War 1904–1914* (Cambridge, Mass: Harvard University Press, 1969) pp. 59–88.

23. Richard K. Betts argued that 'military advice has been most persuasive as a veto of the use of force and least potent when it favored force', but admits that in 1965 politicians did not heed military warnings about the scale of commitment involved to achieve victory in Vietnam. See his *Soldiers, Statesmen and Cold War Crises* (Cambridge, Mass: Harvard University Press, 1977) pp. 209–12.

24. Lauri Karvonen and Bengt Sundelius, *Internationalization and Foreign Policy Management.*

25. *Ibid.*, 'Findings', pp. 153–7. In both Norway and Sweden there has been a history of to-ing and fro-ing between independent economic ministries and an inclusive foreign ministry, with Norway usually following the Swedish lead. At present the fashion is for independent Trade and Industry ministries. The situation in the two countries has been studied more than most. See, apart from Karvonen and Sundelius above, the many works of M.A. East, for example 'The organizational impact of interdependence on foreign policy-making: the case of Norway', in C.W. Kegley Jr and Patrick McGowan (eds), *The Political Economy of Foreign Policy Behaviour* (London: Sage, 1981). Also Iver Neumann, 'The Foreign Ministry of Norway', in Brian Hocking (ed.), *Foreign Ministries: Change and Adaptation* (New York: St Martin's Press, 1999) pp. 152–69.

26. Graham Allison, *Essence of Decision: Explaining the Cuban Missile Crisis* (Boston: Little, Brown, 1971). The theory had first appeared in an article in the *American Political Science Review* of 1969 (vol. 63, 3: 'Conceptual models and the Cuban missile crisis').

27. Morton Halperin, *Bureaucratic Politics and Foreign Policy* with the assistance of Priscilla Clapp and Arnold Kanter (Washington D.C.: the Brookings Institution, 1974); and Robert Gallucci, *Neither Peace Nor Honour: the Politics of American Military Policy in Vietnam* (Baltimore: Johns Hopkins University Press, 1975). The second edition of *Essence of Decision* (New York: Addison-Wesley, 1999) in which Allison was joined by Philip Zelikow to assess the flood of historical and theoretical literature which had emerged since 1971, is a rich source and the best place to start.

28. For discussion of the bureaucratic politics model, see, *inter alia*, Alan C. Lamborn and Stephen P. Mummie, *Statecraft, Domestic Politics and Foreign Policy Making: the El Chamizal Dispute* (Boulder, Colorado: Westview, 1988) pp. 22–36; Steve Smith, 'Perspectives on the foreign policy system: bureaucratic politics approaches', in Michael Clarke and Brian White (eds), *Understanding Foreign Policy – the Foreign Policy Systems Approach* (Aldershot: Edward Elgar, 1989) pp. 109–34; Christopher Hill, 'A Theoretical Introduction', in William Wallace and W.E. Paterson (eds), *Foreign Policy Making in Western Europe: a Comparative Approach* (Farnborough, Hants.: Saxon House, 1978) pp. 7–30; Jerel A. Rosati, 'Developing a systematic decision-making framework: bureaucratic politics in perspective', *World Politics*, vol. XXXIII, no. 2, January 1981, pp. 246–52; and Lawrence Freedman, 'Logic, politics and foreign policy processes', *International Affairs*, vol. 52, no. 3, July 1976, pp. 434–49.

29. Lamborn and Mummie, *Statecraft, Domestic Politics and Foreign Policy Making*, pp. 24 and 32. They argue that the great omission in Allison's theoretical discussion is any reference to the problem of the non-transitivity of social choice, highlighted by Kenneth Arrow.

30. Allison, *Essence of Decision*, p. 164.
31. Halperin, *Bureaucratic Politics and Foreign Policy*, Chapters 1 and 16.
32. Rosati, 'Developing a systematic decision-making framework', pp. 246–52.
33. Martin Hollis and Steve Smith, 'Roles and reasons in foreign policy decision making', *British Journal of Political Science*, vol. 16, part 3, July 1986, pp. 269–86.
34. The central point of Freedman, 'Logic, politics and foreign policy processes', pp. 434–49.
35. Halperin, *Bureaucratic Politics and Foreign Policy*, p. 311.
36. William Wallace, 'Old states and new circumstances: the international predicament of Britain, France and Germany', in Wallace and Paterson (eds), *Foreign Policy Making in Western Europe*, pp. 31–55 and Hill, 'Theoretical introduction', pp. 7–30 in the same volume; Karvonen and Sundelius, *Internationalization and Foreign Policy Management*, *op.cit.*; Karen Dawisha, 'The limits of the bureaucratic politics model: observations on the Soviet case', *Studies in Comparative Communism*, vol. XIII, no. 4, 1980, pp. 300–26.
37. Fred Halliday, private communication. cf. Michael Donovan, 'National intelligence and the Iranian revolution', in Rhodri Jeffreys-Jones and Christopher Andrew (eds), *Eternal Vigilance: Fifty Years of the CIA* (London: Frank Cass, 1997) pp. 143–63. Donovan argues that bureaucratic game-playing, particularly by NSC Adviser Zbigniew Brzezinski, paralysed US policy at the critical time.
38. Allison and Zelikow, *Essence of Decision*, 2nd edn, pp. 353–4. Khrushchev accused Castro of responsibility for shooting down the U2, but the most likely explanation is confusion, with Moscow being unable properly to control its forces on the ground.
39. Richard Neustadt, *Alliance Politics* (New York: Columbia University Press, 1970). This pioneering book started life as a confidential report for Kennedy on what had gone wrong and why for Anglo-American relations in the Suez and Skybolt crises.
40. Shevchenko, *Breaking with Moscow*, pp. 189–90.
41. See Shlomo Gazit, 'Intelligence estimates and the decision-maker', in Michael I. Handel (ed.), *Leaders and Intelligence* (London: Cass, 1989) p. 266. On Italy, see 'Forze italiane a Kabul: scontro Ruggiero-Martino', *La Repubblica*, 15 November 2001.
42. Lisette Andreae and Karl Kaiser, 'The "foreign policies" of specialized ministries', in Wolf-Dieter Eberwein and Karl Kaiser (eds), *Germany's New Foreign Policy: Decision-Making in an Interdependent World* (London: Palgrave, 2001) pp. 38–57.
43. On complex system-induced compromises, see Robert Jervis, *System Effects: Complexity in Political and Social Life* (Princeton, New Jersey: Princeton University Press, 1997), especially Chapter 1.
44. Richard Betts, *Soldiers, Statesmen and Cold War Crises*, p. 209.
45. William I. Bacchus, *Staffing for Foreign Affairs*, p. 50. Of course the chicken and egg problem occurs here: did key interests in the US government ensure that the relevant department was weak, because they were hostile to a law of the sea agreement in the first place?
46. Martin Walker, 'Mission implausible', The *Guardian*, 14 April 1997. The problem seems to have been in the different spellings of 'Khamisiyah', which impeded an effective computer search.
47. Alexander Dallin, *Black Box: KAL 007 and the Superpowers* (Berkeley: University of California Press, 1985).
48. James Joll, *The Origins of the First World War* (London: Longman, 1984) pp. 12, 82–4, 87; also Samuel R. Williamson Jr, 'Theories of organizational process and foreign policy outcomes', in Paul Gordon Lauren (ed.), *Diplomacy: New Approaches in History,*

Theory and Policy (New York: Free Press, 1979) pp. 151–4; and David Stevenson, *The First World War and International Politics* (Oxford: Clarendon Press, 1988) pp. 23, 29, 33.

49. Patience finally snapped in British circles. Commissioner Chris Patten initiated change with even more overt criticisms than those contained in UK Secretary of State Clare Short's *Eliminating World Poverty: Making Globalisation Work for the Poor – White Paper on International Development*, Cm 5006 (London: HMSO, December 2000) pp. 95–6.

50. 'Una Farnesina a misura d'Europa', *Il Sole-24 Ore*, 24 December 1998.

51. The communist collapse is the *locus classicus* for examples of bureaucratic, political and psychological rigidity. One almost poignant result was that when policy finally changed, with East German leader Egon Krenz signing an order to permit his people to make trips abroad, his administration could hardly believe it, and there was a serious risk that border guards would fire on the many fellow-citizens who were thronging the Berlin wall. Fortunately the guards themselves sensed the *zeitgeist*. 'The day the wall fell: a series of historic accidents', *International Herald Tribune*, 9 November 1990.

52. Margaret Thatcher, *The Downing Street Years* (London: HarperCollins, 1993) p. 309.

53. The same accusation has been made against British diplomats and soldiers involved in the Balkans in the early 1990s. See Brendan Simms, *Unfinest Hour: How Britain Helped to Destroy Bosnia* (Harmondsworth: Allen Lane, The Penguin Press, 2001).

54. Henry A. Kissinger, 'Domestic structure and foreign policy', in Harold Karan Jacobson and William Zimmerman (eds), *The Shaping of Foreign Policy* (New York: Atherton Press, 1969) p. 144.

55. A problem discussed in Vincent A. Auger, *The Dynamics of Foreign Policy Analysis: The Carter Administration and the Neutron Bomb* (Lanham, Md.: Rowland and Littlefield, 1996) p. 4 and *passim*. This is a study of a case which became unusually public, and where the president eventually cancelled the project. Still, his decisions were only taken with great difficulty and the neutron bomb has become a classic 'fiasco' of foreign policy analysis.

56. Steve Smith and Michael Clarke (eds), *Foreign Policy Implementation* (London: George Allen & Unwin, 1985).

57. Roger Hilsman, *The Politics of Policy Making in Defense and Foreign Affairs: Conceptual Models and Bureaucratic Politics* (Englewood Cliffs: Prentice Hall, 1987). Hilsman first sketched this approach in his *To Move a Nation: the Politics of Foreign Policy in the Administration of John F. Kennedy* (New York: Doubleday, 1964).

Chapter 5

1. Michael Nicholson, 'The continued significance of positivism?' in Steve Smith, Ken Booth and Marysia Zalewski (eds), *International Theory: Positivism and Beyond* (Cambridge: Cambridge University Press, 1996) pp. 138–40.

2. For an insightful survey see Miles Kahler, 'Rationality in International Relations', in Peter J. Katzenstein, Robert O. Keohane and Stephen D. Krasner (eds), *Exploration and Contestation in the Study of World Politics* (Cambridge, Mass: MIT Press, 1999) pp. 285–6.

3. Martin Wight, *International Theory: the Three Traditions*, ed. Gabriele Wight and Brian Porter (Leicester: Leicester University Press, 1991) pp. 37–40; and also Andrew Linklater, *The Transformation of Political Community* (Cambridge: Polity Press, 1998) pp. 59–60, 209–10.

4. David Dessler, 'Constructivism within a positivist social science', *Review of International Studies*, vol. 25, no. 1, January 1999, pp. 123–37.
5. Ole Wæver, 'Resisting the temptation of post foreign policy analysis', in Walter Carlsnaes and Steve Smith (eds), *European Foreign Policy: the EC and Changing Perspectives in Europe* (London: Sage, 1994) p. 256.
6. Robert Nozick, *The Nature of Rationality* (Princeton, NJ: Princeton University Press, 1993) pp. 64–5.
7. Herbert Simon, 'From substantive to procedural rationality', in Anthony G. McGrew and M.J. Wilson (eds), *Decision Making: Approaches and Analysis* (Manchester: Manchester University Press, 1982) pp. 87–96. Simon had first published ideas along these lines in 1945, in 'A behavioral model of rational choice', *Quarterly Journal of Economics*, February 1955, reprinted in Herbert A. Simon, *Models of Man: Social and Rational Mathematical Essays on Rational Human Behavior in a Social Setting* (New York: John Wiley, 1957/1967) pp. 240–60; the terms 'process' and 'outcome' are used by Yaacov Y.I. Vertzberger, *The World in their Minds: Information Processing, Cognition and Perception in Foreign Policy Decisionmaking* (Stanford: Stanford University Press, 1990) pp. 39–40 and 367.
8. Vertzberger, *ibid.*, p. 367.
9. Leslie Gelb and Richard Betts, *The Irony of Vietnam: the System Worked* (Washington: Brookings Institution, 1979).
10. For an interesting discussion of this general problem, which concludes that 'it is not possible … to understand human behaviour simply at the level of the individual', see Richard Little, 'Belief systems in the social sciences', in Richard Little and Steve Smith (eds), *Belief Systems and International Relations* (Oxford: Basil Blackwell in association with the British International Studies Association, 1988) pp. 37–56.
11. This is related to 'Arrow's paradox' about voting in democracies, whereby the economist Kenneth Arrow showed in 1954 that aggregating individual preferences runs the risk that no clear preference will emerge, or that the majority's preference will not win out. See M. Carley, 'Analytic rationality', in McGrew and Wilson, *Decision Making*, p. 63.
12. As Herbert Simon argued, 'the difference in direction of the individual's aims from those of the larger organization is just one of those elements of non-rationality with which [the] theory must deal'. He went on to say that the basic task of administration is to provide every employee with a decision environment 'such that behaviour which is rational from the standpoint of this environment is also rational from the standpoint of the group values and the group situation'. He gave the example of a soldier in combat, taking orders which have the potential to be disastrous for himself. Herbert A. Simon, *Administrative Behavior*, 3rd edn (New York: Free Press, 1976, first published 1946) pp. 41 and 243–4.
13. On the other hand, because the president did not dare to declare his hand, the preparations for war were at best incremental. See David Braybrooke and Charles E. Lindblom, *A Strategy of Decision: Policy Evaluation as a Social Process* (New York: Free Press, 1963) pp. 75–7.
14. Kenneth Waltz, *Foreign Policy and Democratic Politics: the American and British Experience* (Boston, Mass: Little, Brown, 1967).
15. As Vertzberger says, 'the norms of rationality are culture-bound'. He gives the example of how a Korean official describes lack of response to criticism as an indication of a sense of guiltlessness, rather than the opposite, as would be the case in the West. Vertzberger, *The World in their Minds*, p. 270.

16. Thomas Schelling, *The Strategy of Conflict* (Cambridge, Mass: Harvard University Press, 1960) pp. 187–203.

17. Simon, *Administrative Behaviour*, pp. xxvii. Classical rationality is sometimes referred to as the synoptic method.

18. As Braybrooke and Lindblom point out, there is much talk of planning, especially in one-party states, but the rhetoric rarely matches the reality. See *A Strategy of Decision*, p. 77.

19. The metaphor was originally Lord Salisbury's, Foreign Secretary and then Prime Minister of Britain at the end of the nineteenth century. See F.S. Northedge, 'The nature of foreign policy' in his edited book *The Foreign Policies of the Powers* (London: Faber & Faber, 1968) pp. 9–38. Also James Joll (ed.), *Britain and Europe: Pitt to Churchill 1793–1940* (London: Nicholas Kaye, 1950), especially the 'Introduction' and various speeches by Foreign Secretaries Canning and Palmerston.

20. Bruno Bettelheim, *A Good Enough Parent* (London: Thames & Hudson, 1987).

21. Robert Keohane, *After Hegemony: Cooperation and Discord in the World Political Economy* (Princeton: Princeton University Press, 1984), Chapter 7, 'Bounded rationality and redefinitions of self-interest', pp. 110–32.

22. For a full account of this theory see Brayrooke and Lindblom, *A Strategy of Decision*, pp. 81–110, and Charles E. Lindblom, 'Still muddling, not yet through', *Public Administration Review*, vol. 39, 1979, pp. 517–26, reprinted in an abridged version in McGrew and Wilson (eds), *Decision Making*, pp. 125–38. The original article dates from 1959: Charles E. Lindblom, 'The science of muddling through', *Public Administration Review*, vol. XIX, no. 2, Spring 1959, pp. 79–88.

23. After the 'Glorious Revolution' of 1689 John Locke began to emphasize the importance of a political system which could adapt to change. But it was Burke who gave voice to the natural instincts of the English ruling class, with its ambivalent attitudes towards central authority, in his *Reflections on the Revolution in France*, edited and Introduction by Conor Cruise O'Brien (Harmondsworth: Penguin Books, 1969, first published 1790).

24. Simon, *Administrative Behavior*, pp. xxix–xxxiv.

25. Note the ambivalent language of 'muddling through' and 'disjointed' incrementalism. Lindblom himself recognized that this was 'pejorative and deliberately awkward' – presumably as a provocation. *A Strategy of Decision*, p. 105. See also G. Smith and D. May, 'The artificial debate between rationalist and incremental models of decision-making', in McGrew and Wilson, *Decision Making*, p. 118.

26. Susan Strange, *Sterling and British Policy: A Study of an International Currency in Decline* (Oxford: Oxford University Press, 1971); Philip Darby, *British Policy East of Suez, 1947–1968* (Oxford: Oxford University Press, 1973).

27. Glenn D. Hook, Julie Gilson, Christopher W. Hughes, Hugo Dobson, *Japan's International Relations: Politics, Economics and Security* (London: Routledge, 2001) pp. 7, 132–6, 458.

28. John D. Steinbruner, *The Cybernetic Theory of Decision* (Princeton: Princeton University Press, 1974).

29. Avi Shlaim, *The United States and the Berlin Blockade 1948–1949: a Study in Crisis Decision-Making* (Berkeley: University of California Press, 1982) pp. 242–6.

30. Roberta Wohlstetter, *Pearl Harbor: Warning and Decision* (Stanford: Stanford University Press, 1962).

31. The original work was done by Peter Bachrach and Morton Baratz, *Power and Poverty: Theory and Practice* (New York: Oxford University Press, 1970). Steven Lukes'

Power: a Radical View (1974) and Matthew A. Crenson's *The Un-politics of Air Pollution: a Study of Non-Decisionmaking in the Cities* (Baltimore: Johns Hopkins University Press, 1971) are also important sources.

32. *The Times*, 1 October 1980, cited in Fred Halliday, *Revolution and World Politics: the Rise and Fall of the Sixth Great Power* (Houndmills: Palgrave Macmillan, 1999) p. 256.

33. David Stevenson, *The First World War and International Politics* (Oxford: Clarendon Press, 1988) pp. 87–138; Victor Rothwell, *British War Aims and Peace Diplomacy 1914–1918* (Oxford: Clarendon Press, 1971); Christopher Hill, *Cabinet Decisions on Foreign Policy: the British Experience October 1918–June 1941* (Cambridge: Cambridge University Press, 1991) pp. 188–223.

34. E.E. Schattschneider, *Semi-Sovereign People: a Realist's View of Democracy in America* (Hinsdale, New Jersey: The Dryden Press, 1975) p. 69.

35. On elite theory, and its nineteenth-century roots in both realism and Marxism, see Geraint Parry, *Political Elites* (London: George Allen and Unwin, 1969). Little work has been done on foreign policy elites, but see Inderjeet Parmar, 'The Carnegie Endowment for International Peace and American public opinion 1939–1945', *Review of International Studies*, vol. 26, no. 1, January 2000, pp. 35–48.

36. The first relevant work was Kenneth Boulding's *The Image* (Ann Arbor: University of Michigan, 1956), followed by Joseph De Rivera, *The Psychological Dimension of Foreign Policy* (Columbus, Ohio: Merrill, 1968), and Robert Jervis, *Perception and Misperception in International Politics* (Princeton: Princeton University Press, 1976). The Department of International Relations at the London School of Economics and Political Science was the first, to my knowledge, to run a university course on 'the Psychological Aspects of International Relations', from 1951 under the tutelage of Charles Manning and then F.S. Northedge. See *Department of International Relations: a Brief History, 1924–1971* (unpublished mss, 1971) p. 15.

37. Alfred Cobban, *A History of Modern France, Vol. 1: 1715–1799,* 3rd edn (Harmondsworth: Penguin, 1963) p. 157.

38. T.W. Adorno, E. Frenkel-Brunswick, D.N. Levinson and R.N. Sanford, *The Authoritarian Personality* (New York: Harper, 1950).

39. A succinct discussion is to be found in Vertzberger, *The World in their Minds*, pp. 172–3.

40. Alexander L. George and Juliet L. George, *Woodrow Wilson and Colonel House* (New York: John Den, 1965). Many would say that the opportunity of 1919 was missed mainly because of failings in Wilson's character. Others would stress the difficulties of making an intelligent peace in the context of Congressional isolationism, French hostility to Germany and British preoccupations with other problems. See also Miles Kahler, 'Rationality in International Relations', in Katzenstein, Keohane and Krasner (eds), *Exploration and Contestation in the Study of World Politics*, pp. 285–6.

41. Erik H. Erikson, *Young Man Luther: A Study in Psychoanalysis and History* (New York: Norton, 1958); Robert Waite, *Kaiser and Führer: A Comparative Study of Personality and Politics* (Toronto: University of Toronto Press, 1998); Doris Kearns, *Lyndon Johnson and the American Dream* (London: Deutsch, 1976); Leo Abse, *Margaret, Daughter of Beatrice: a Politician's Psychobiography of Margaret Thatcher* (London: Cape, 1989).

42. Fred I. Greenstein, 'The impact of personality on politics: an attempt to clear the under-brush', *American Political Science Review*, vol. 61, 1967, pp. 629–41, and *Personality and Politics: Problems of Evidence, Inference and Conceptualisation* (New York: Norton, 1975).

43. William H. Dray, 'Was Collingwood an historical constructionist?', in David Boucher (ed.), *Collingwood Studies*, vol. I, 1994, *The Life and Thought of R.G. Collingwood*

(Swansea: Collingwood Society, 1994) pp. 59–75; also Charles Reynolds, *Theory and Explanation in International Politics*.

44. Vertzberger, *The World in their Minds*, p. 40.

45. This crucial distinction was formalized by Harold and Margaret Sprout. See their 'Man–milieu' hypotheses in both their *Foundations of International Politics* (Princeton, New Jersey: D. Van Nostrand Co., 1962) pp. 122–35 and in *The Ecological Perspective on Human Affairs* (Princeton: Princeton University Press, 1965).

46. The research behind these and other examples is analysed extensively in both Vertzberger, *The World in their Minds*, pp. 7–50, and Jervis, *Perception and Misperception in International Politics*, *passim*.

47. Christopher Hill, 'Reagan and Thatcher: the sentimental alliance', *World Outlook* (Dartmouth College, New Hampshire), vol. 1, no. 2, Winter 1985–6.

48. Robert F. Kennedy, *Thirteen Days: the Cuban Missile Crisis* with forewords by Harold Macmillan and Robert McNamara (London: Pan Books, 1969).

49. It was the philosopher D.C. Dennett who suggested we might all be 'pretty rational'. See Richard Little, 'Belief systems in the social sciences', in Little and Smith (eds), *Belief Systems and International Relations*, *op.cit.*, pp. 53–4.

50. See Lawrence Freedman and Virginia Gamba-Stonehouse, *Signals of War: the Anglo–Argentine Conflict of 1982* (London: Faber and Faber, 1990).

51. Leon Festinger, *A Theory of Cognitive Dissonance* (Stanford: Stanford University Press, 1957).

52. Hansard, 25 November 1988. Healey said: 'She finds herself practically alone now in the Western European Union, by pressing for the modernisation of tactical nuclear weapons. I understand there is a medical term for the condition from which she suffers. It is known as cognitive dissonance – a psychiatric condition in which the patient finds it impossible to accept a reality which conflicts with his or her prejudices or vanity.'

53. Robert Axelrod (ed.), *Structure of Decision: the Cognitive Maps of Political Elites* (Princeton: Princeton University Press, 1976); Irving L. Janis and Leon Mann, *Decision Making: A Psychological Analysis of Choice, Conflict and Commitment* (New York: Free Press, 1977) pp. 212–18.

54. Norman Dixon, *On the Psychology of Military Incompetence* (London: Cape, 1976) pp. 164–8, 245.

55. Steinbruner, *Cybernetic Theory of Decision*, p. 139.

56. See Tam Dalyell, 'Holding policy-makers to account: the problem of expertise', in Christopher Hill and Pamela Beshoff (eds), *Two Worlds of International Relations: Academics, Practitioners and the Trade in Ideas* (London: Routledge, 1994) pp. 118–35.

57. R.F. Harrod, *The Prof: a Personal Memoir of Lord Cherwell* (London: Macmillan, 1959) p. 217.

58. Michael Donelan, *The Ideas of American Foreign Policy* (London: Chapman & Hall, 1963) pp. 59–66; Charles W. Kegley Jr and Eugene R. Wittkopf, *American Foreign Policy: Pattern and Process*, 3rd edn (Houndmills: Macmillan Education, 1987) pp. 78–9.

59. Irving L. Janis, *Victims of Groupthink: a Psychological Study of Foreign Policy Decisions and Fiascoes* (Boston: Houghton Mifflin, 1972); the second edition is *Groupthink: Psychological Studies of Foreign Policy Decisions and Fiascoes* (Boston: Houghton Mifflin, 1982). See also his *Crucial Decisions: Leadership in Policy-Making and Crisis Management* (New York: Free Press, 1989).

60. The most important work in this respect has been done by Paul 't Hart and a group of colleagues. See Paul 't Hart, Eric K. Stern and Bengt Sundelius (eds), *Beyond Groupthink: Political Group Dynamics and Foreign Policy-making* (Ann Arbor: University of

Michigan Press, 1997). This book puts groupthink sympathetically in context and extends considerably its importance by the very fact of not presenting it as a single-factor explanation.

61. Janis, *Victims of Groupthink, op.cit.*, pp. 102–6; Hill, *Cabinet Decisions on Foreign Policy*, pp. 19–46.

62. See David Dilks, *The Diaries of Sir Alexander Cadogan, 1938–1945* (London: Cassell, 1971) pp. 27–9.

63. Miriam Steiner, 'The search for order in a disorderly world: worldviews and prescriptive decision paradigms', *International Organisation*, vol. 37, no. 3, Summer 1983, p. 413.

64. See B. Ripley, 'Psychology, foreign policy and international relations', *Political Psychology*, vol. 14, pp. 403–16. Smith and May, 'The artificial debate between rationalist and incrementalist models of decision making', are less convinced. They regard 'intuition' and 'experience' as 'disconcertingly vague variables' (p. 121); rationality provides a good prescription and incrementalism a good description. The problem is how to bridge the gap.

65. Ernest R. May, *'Lessons' of the Past: the Use and Misuse of History in American Foreign Policy* (Oxford: Oxford University Press, 1973) p. 179.

66. Robert Jervis, *Perception and Misperception in International Politics, op.cit.*, pp. 217–82; Lloyd Etheredge, *Can Governments Learn?* (Elmsford: Pergamon Press, 1985); Yaacov I. Vertzberger, 'Foreign policy decision-makers as practical-intuitive historians: applied history and its short-comings', *International Studies Quarterly*, vol. 30 (1986) pp. 223–47 and reprinted in an expanded form in *The World in their Minds, op.cit.*, pp. 296–341; Michael Howard, *The Lessons of History* (Oxford: Oxford University Press, 1991).

67. Richard E. Neustadt and Ernest R. May, *Thinking in Time: the Uses of History for Decision Makers* (New York: Free Press, 1986).

68. These distinctions are further explored in Christopher Hill, 'The historical background: past and present in British foreign policy', in Michael Smith, Steve Smith and Brian White (eds), *British Foreign Policy: Tradition, Change and Continuity* (London: Unwin Hyman, 1988) pp. 25–49.

69. James N. Rosenau, 'The national interest', in *The Scientific Study of Foreign Policy* (New York: The Free Press, 1971) pp. 239–49. Some writers, notably Joseph Frankel in *The National Interest* (London: Macmillan, 1970) and Donald Nuechterlein, in 'National interests and foreign policy: a conceptual framework for analysis and decision-making', *British Journal of International Studies*, vol. 2, no. 3, October 1976, pp. 246–66, have tried to resuscitate the notion of national interest, but they have only succeeded in highlighting the variety of uses of the term.

70. *The Independent*, 15 November 1990.

71. The phrase comes from Lord Franks, who as Oliver Franks was British Ambassador in Washington between 1948–1952. The remark was made in his Reith Lectures of 1954 (cited in Alex Danchev, *Oliver Franks* [Oxford: Oxford University Press, 1993] p. 145) a propos of Britain's right to sit at the top table, which only shows how quickly what James Joll called the 'unspoken assumptions' can come under challenge. James Joll, *The Unspoken Assumptions: An Inaugural Lecture at the London School of Economics and Political Science* (London: Weidenfeld & Nicolson, 1968).

72. Arnold Wolfers, 'The goals of foreign policy', in his *Discord and Collaboration: Essays on International Politics* (Baltimore: Johns Hopkins University Press, 1962) pp. 67–80.

73. *Ibid.*, 'The pole of power and the pole of indifference', pp. 81–102.

74. Multiple advocacy is the notion, invented by Alexander George, that the provision of competing voices, and in particular devil's advocates, should be institutionalized in decision-making, in order to ensure that bad arguments are not protected by an autocratic or excessively collegial atmosphere. However, it is not difficult to think of circumstances in which multiple advocacy might lead to delays and overly mechanistic discussions, thereby falling into disrepute. It is not rational to pursue multiple advocacy independent of circumstance. Alexander George, 'The case for multiple advocacy in making foreign policy', *American Political Science Review*, 66, pp. 751–85, and *Presidential Decision-making in Foreign Policy: the Effective Use of Information and Advice* (Boulder: Westview Press, 1980); 't Hart *et al.*, *Beyond Groupthink*, pp. 328–31; Robert O. Keohane, 'International multiple advocacy in US foreign policy', in D. Caldwell and T.J. McKeown (eds), *Diplomacy, Force and Leadership* (Boulder: Westview, 1993) pp. 285–304.

75. Andrew Linklater, *The Transformation of Political Community* (Cambridge: Polity Press, 1998) p. 211.

76. Vertzberger, *The World in their Minds*, p. 361.

77. This is a version of the general position of Jürgen Habermas. See his critique of both positivism and post-modernism in *The Philosophical Discourse of Modernity: Twelve Lectures* (Cambridge: Polity and Basil Blackwell, 1987).

Chapter 6

1. This was a high-risk strategy, which worked insofar as the visibility of the Cyprus question, and the perceived need to allow Cyprus into the EU, were both heightened, A way of not buying the missiles was eventually found. Clement H. Dodd, *The Cyprus Imbroglio* (Huntingdon: The Eothen Press, 1998) pp. 98–100.

2. This point is expanded in a number of interesting ways in Raymond Cohen, *Theatre of Power: the Art of Diplomatic Signalling* (London: Longman, 1987).

3. Hans J. Morgenthau, *Politics Among Nations: the Struggle for Power and Peace* (New York: Alfred A. Knopf, 1948/1950); George Modelski, *A Theory of Foreign Policy* (London: Pall Mall Press, 1962).

4. There are more permutations possible, as with the nine meanings of the balance of power. See Martin Wight, 'The balance of power', in Herbert Butterfield and Martin Wight (eds), *Diplomatic Investigations: Essays in the Theory of International Politics* (London: George Allen and Unwin, 1966) pp. 149–75. The triad used here is not so far from that of Kenneth Boulding in his *Three Faces of Power* (Newbury Park, California: Sage, 1989) but Boulding concentrates on relational aspects. His three faces are: coercion (threat power); exchange (economic power); and persuasion (integrative power).

5. Harold Lasswell and Abraham Kaplan, *Power and Society: a Framework for Political Inquiry* (New Haven: Yale University Press, 1950), cited in Arnold Wolfers, *Discord and Collaboration: Essays on International Politics* (Baltimore: Johns Hopkins University Press, 1962) p. 84.

6. See Alan Bullock, *Hitler and Stalin: Parallel Lives* (London: HarperCollins, 1991), and Ian Kershaw, *Hitler: 1889–1936: Hubris* (Harmondsworth: Allen Lane, The Penguin Press, 1998), for example, pp. xxviii–xxx.

7. Adeed I. Dawisha, *Egypt in the Arab World: the Elements of Foreign Policy* (London: Macmillan, 1976) pp. 102–7; and see P.J. Vatikiotis, *Nasser and his Generation* (London: Croom Helm, 1978) pp. 325–47, who notes some western idealization of Nasser.

8. Arnold Wolfers, 'The pole of power and the pole of indifference', in *Discord and Collaboration*, pp. 81–102. This essay was first published in *World Politics* in October 1951 (vol. IV, no. 1).

9. *Ibid.*, p. 89.

10. *Ibid.*, p. 84. John Herz formalized 'the security dilemma' in *Political Realism and Political Idealism: a Study in Theories and Realities* (Chicago: University of Chicago Press, 1951). It was subsequently reformulated and developed as the Cold War waned, notably by Barry Buzan in his *People, States and Fear: the National Security Problem in International Relations* (Brighton: Harvester Wheatsheaf, 1983), especially chapters 6 and 7.

11. George Modelski, *A Theory of Foreign Policy*, pp. 27–30. See also Klaus Knorr, *Power and Wealth* (London: Macmillan, 1973).

12. See in particular Susan Strange's distinction between relational and structural power in her *States and Markets: an Introduction to International Political Economy* (London: Pinter, 1988).

13. But see Alan Sked's *The Decline and Fall of the Habsburg Empire 1815–1918* (London: Longman, 1989), where he argues that only the war policy of 1914 brought down the Empire.

14. See Malcom Muggeridge (ed.), *Ciano's Diary 1939–1943* (London: Heinemann, 1947), and Macgregor Knox, *Mussolini Unleashed, 1939–1941: Politics and Strategy in Fascist Italy's Last War* (Cambridge: Cambridge University Press, 1982), for example, pp. 46–9.

15. Henry Kissinger, *Diplomacy* (London: Simon & Schuster, 1994) p. 731.

16. The 'wider context' has been usually called 'the external environment' in foreign policy analysis, following on from the work of Harold and Margaret Sprout. See their *The Ecological Perspective on Human Affairs – with Special Reference to International Politics* (Westport, Connecticut: Greenwood Press, 1965/1979).

17. Thanks largely to the work of Professor Joseph Nye. See his *Bound to Lead: the Changing Nature of American Power* (New York: Basic Books, 1990) pp. 29–35 and 'Soft power', *Foreign Policy*, no. 80, Fall 1990, pp. 153–71.

18. Nye, 'Soft power', p. 167.

19. *International Herald Tribune*, 22 February 1999.

20. Alan Chong and Jana Valencic (eds), *The Image, the State and International Relations: Conference Proceedings* (London: London School of Economics and Political Science, EFPU Working Paper No. 2001/2, 2001).

21. Pierre Renouvin and Jean-Baptiste Duroselle, *Introduction to the History of International Relations* (London: Pall Mall Press, 1968).

22. Donald J. Puchala, *International Politics Today* (New York: Harper & Row, 1971) pp. 176–84.

23. If it is doubted that soft power can include the military instrument, consider the Partnership for Peace system set up by NATO to help educate the military of the ex-Warsaw Pact into western approaches to civil–military relations and confidence-building measures.

24. For various good treatments of diplomacy see Cohen, *Theatre of Power*; Ronald Barston, *Modern Diplomacy*, 2nd edn (London: Longman, 1997); Keith Hamilton and Richard Langhorne, *The Practice of Diplomacy: its Evolution, Theory and Administration* (London: Routledge, 1994); Adam Watson, *Diplomacy: the Dialogue between States* (London: Eyre Methuen, 1982); G.R. Berridge, *Diplomacy: Theory and Practice* (Hemel Hempstead: Harvester/Wheatsheaf, 1995); G.R. Berridge and Alan James, *A Dictionary of Diplomacy* (Houndmills: Palgrave, 2001). See also the country-study of Philip Everts

and Guido Walraven (eds), *The Politics of Persuasion: Implementation of Foreign Policy by the Netherlands* (Aldershot: Avebury, 1989).

25. As do private groups and individuals, sometimes in loose harness with states. See Raymond Cohen, 'Putting diplomatic studies on the map', *DSP Newsletter* (University of Leicester: Centre for the Study of Diplomacy, no. 4, May 1998), and George Kennan, 'Diplomacy without diplomats', *Foreign Affairs*, September–October 1997.

26. Ambassador Karl Prinz was expelled because Germany was protesting more than other donors about government abuses in Sierra Leone.

27. Harold Nicolson, *Diplomacy*, with new introduction by Lord Butler, 3rd edn (London: Oxford University Press, 1969 – first published in 1939).

28. Robert Jervis, *The Logic of Images in International Relations* (Princeton: Princeton University Press, 1970), especially pp. 18–40.

29. Another Canadian example is provided by Prime Minister Pierre Trudeau, who wore trainers when he reviewed a Brazilian Guard of Honour. The insult to Brazil was almost certainly unintentional, but diplomacy to mend the broken fences was given a stern test. Cohen, *Theatre of Power*, p. 21.

30. For the complex issues involved, see, among many others, James Joll, *The Origins of the First World War*, cited earlier; Philip M.H. Bell, *The Origins of the Second World War in Europe*, 2nd edn (London: Longman, 1997); Gerhard L. Weinberg, *A World at Arms: a Global History of World War II* (Cambridge: Cambridge University Press, 1994) pp. 6–47; Donald Cameron Watt, *1939: How War Came* (London: 1989).

31. Kissinger, *Diplomacy*, pp. 719–30.

32. Uriel Dann, *King Hussein's Strategy of Survival* (Washington, DC: Washington Institute for Near East Policy, 1992).

33. Michael Yahuda, *Hong Kong: China's Challenge* (London: Routledge, 1996); Percy Cradock, *Experience of China* (London: John Murray, 1994), Part III; also Cradock's *In Pursuit of British Interests: Reflections on Foreign Policy under Margaret Thatcher and John Major* (London: Murray, 1997) pp. 203–5.

34. Marco Pedrazzi, 'Italy's approach to UN Security Council reform', *The International Spectator*, vol. XXXV, no. 3, July–September 2000, pp. 49–56.

35. Hadley Arkes, *Bureaucracy, the Marshall Plan and the National Interest* (Princeton: Princeton University Press, 1972) pp. 52–5.

36. As it did for Douglas Hurd with the Pergau Dam affair, in which development aid to Malaysia was given in order to secure £1.3 billion worth of arms orders. *Financial Times*, 3 and 8 March 1994.

37. The *Independent*, 2 December 1993.

38. Delighting the 350 000 Armenian community in France, however. *The Times*, 19 January 2001.

39. Alexander L. George and William E. Simons, *The Limits of Coercive Diplomacy*, 2nd edn (Boulder, Col: Westview Press, 1994). The influential first edition, with the same title and authors (plus David K. Hall), was published in Boston by Little, Brown, in 1971. Although the term coercive diplomacy includes both blackmail and defensive reactions (that is, attempts to stop an adversary doing something unwelcome by counter-threats) George *et al.* restrict themselves to studying the second aspect. Their cases also deal exclusively with American foreign policy.

40. Charles Lockhart, *Bargaining in International Conflicts* (New York: Columbia University Press, 1979) p. 146, cited in Paul Gordon Lauren, 'Coercive diplomacy and ultimata: theory and practice in history', in George and Simons, *The Limits of Coercive Diplomacy* (1994) p. 45.

41. The literature on the Cuban crisis is now voluminous and revealing. See in particular Graham Allison and Philp Zelikow, *Essence of Decision*, 2nd edn (New York: Longman, 1999); Ernest R. May and Philip D. Zelikow, *The Kennedy Tapes: Inside the White House During the Cuban Missile Crisis* (Cambridge: Harvard University Press, 1997); Raymond L. Garthoff, *Reflections on the Cuban Missile Crisis*, revised edn (Washington, DC: Brookings Institution, 1989); James G. Blight, Bruce J. Allyn and David A. Welch, *Cuba on the Brink: Castro, the Missile Crisis and the Soviet Collapse* (New York: Pantheon Books, 1993); Alexander George, 'The Cuban missile crisis: peaceful resolution through coercive diplomacy', in *The Limits of Coercive Diplomacy* (1994) pp. 111–32.

42. *The Limits of Coercive Diplomacy* (1994) p. 291.

43. See Robert J. Art and Kenneth N. Waltz (eds), *The Use of Force: International Politics and Foreign Policy* (Boston: Little, Brown, 1971), especially Part I; F.S. Northedge (ed.), *The Use of Force in International Relations* (London: Faber, 1974).

44. Gregory F. Treverton, *Covert Action: the CIA and the Limits of Intervention in the Postwar World* (London: Tauris, 1987).

45. State-fostered terrorism should be distinguished from that which is primarily transnational and which embarrasses most governments. See Lawrence Freedman *et al.*, *Terrorism and International Order* (London: Routledge and Kegan Paul for the Royal Institute of International Affairs, 1986) and Grant Wardlaw, *Political Terrorism: Theory, Tactics and Counter-Measures* (Cambridge: Cambridge University Press, 1989).

46. Buzan, *People, States and Fear*, and also Barry Buzan *et al.*, *The European Security Order Recast: Scenarios for the Post-Cold War Era* (London: Pinter, 1990) pp. 3–10.

47. This sub-title derives from David Baldwin's *Economic Statecraft* (Princeton, NJ: Princeton University Press, 1985). Baldwin makes the fundamental points (i) that political economy can and should be looked at from a foreign policy perspective; (ii) that economic instruments should be assessed on the same criteria as tools of statecraft, no more, no less; (iii) that instruments, unlike capabilities, are always relational in character, that is, their functioning depends on the interaction of actor and target.

48. The distinction between foreign policy and foreign economic policy is not, of course, always so clear. See Chapter 1, and also Brian Hocking and Michael Smith, *Beyond Foreign Economic Policy: the United States, the Single European Market and the Changing World Economy* (London: Pinter, 1997), especially pp. 7–22 and 180–3.

49. This is a simplification of a complex series of problems, and of a huge literature. For a valuable perspective, see Charles S. Maier, 'The politics of productivity: foundations of American international economic policy after World War II', in Peter J. Katzenstein (ed.), *Between Power and Plenty: Foreign Economic Policies of Advanced Industrial States* (Madison: University of Wisconsin Press, 1978) pp. 23–49.

50. See Gary Clyde Hufbauer, Jeffrey J. Schott and Kimberly Ann Elliott, *Economic Sanctions Reconsidered* (two volumes, Washington: Institute for International Economics, 1990). Also Margaret Doxey, *International Sanctions in Contemporary Perspective*, 2nd edn (London: Macmillan, 1996); Kimberly Ann Elliott, 'The sanctions glass: half full or completely empty?', and Robert A. Pape's reply, 'Why economic sanctions *still* do not work', both in *International Security*, vol. 23, no. 1, Summer 1998, pp. 50–77.

51. See James Barber, 'Economic sanctions as a policy instrument', *International Affairs*, vol. 55, no. 3, July 1979, pp. 367–84.

52. It is important to distinguish between sanctions as an instrument of collective security, used by the League of Nations and the United Nations (where they have almost always

proved a failure) and sanctions as an instrument of foreign policy, where they have been a qualified success in a number of cases despite the smaller number of enforcing states.

53. Stephen D. Krasner, *Structural Conflict: the Third World Against Global Liberalism* (Berkeley: University of California Press, 1985).

54. Robert Cassen, *Does Aid Work?* (Oxford: Clarendon Press, 1986) pp. 1–18.

55. Karen E. Smith, 'The use of political conditionality in the EU's relations with the third world', *European Foreign Affairs Review*, vol. 3, no. 2, Summer 1998.

56. Juichi Inada, 'Japan's aid diplomacy: economic, political or strategic?', *Millennium*, vol. 18, no. 3, Winter 1989.

57. The classical works on this theme are Susan Strange, *Sterling and British Policy* (Oxford: Oxford University Press, 1971), and Paul Kennedy, *The Rise and Fall of the Great Powers: Economic Change and Military Conflict from 1500 to 2000* (London: Unwin Hyman, 1988).

58. Philip M., Taylor, *Munitions of the Mind: a History of Propaganda from the Ancient World to the Present Day* (Manchester: Manchester University Press, 1995).

59. Hitler made this remark in April 1941, just before the invasion of the USSR. See David Irving, *Hitler's War 1939–1942* (London: Macmillan, 1977) p. 142. Goering's remark is cited in Wolfers, *Discord and Collaboration*, p. 94 n. Given the early successes of Nazi propaganda it was not surprising that E.H. Carr should have devoted ten pages of *The Twenty Years Crisis* to 'power over opinion'.

60. James N. Rosenau, *Linkage Politics* (New York: The Free Press, 1969).

61. The West itself fell sometimes into the same trap in the early Cold War. See Garry D. Rawnsley, *Radio Diplomacy and Propaganda: the BBC and the VOA in International Politics, 1956–64* (London: Macmillan, 1996).

62. For a general survey of cultural diplomacy, see James Mitchell, *International Cultural Relations* (London: Allen & Unwin, 1986). Much more up to date, including recent image-making perspectives, is Michael Kunczik, *Images of Nations and International Public Relations* (Mahwah, NJ: Lawrence Erlbaum Associates, 1997).

63. Frances Stonor Saunders, *Who Paid the Piper? The CIA and the Cultural Cold War* (London: Granta, 1999). See also Donald Cameron Watt's review article, 'The proper study of propaganda', *Intelligence and National Security*, vol. 15, no. 4, Winter 2000, pp. 143–63. Professor Watt excoriates Ms Saunders for selective criticisms of CIA funding. If governments fund intellectual magazines secretly, however, they must expect distaste when discovered.

64. Dawisha, *Egypt in the Arab World*, pp. 164–77. Radio has been a powerful medium in the twentieth century, not least because TV ownership is still not so diffused in poor countries as some imagine. See Julian Hale, *Radio Power* (London: Elek, 1975) and Donald R. Browne, *International Radio Broadcasting: the Limits of the Limitless Medium* (New York: Praeger, 1982).

65. The reasons for the collapse of the USSR are subject to much debate. For a limpid summary see Ian Clark, *Globalization and Fragmentation: International Relations in the Twentieth Century* (Oxford: Oxford University Press, 1997) pp. 172–9.

Chapter 7

1. Hedley Bull, *The Anarchical Society* (London: Macmillan, 1977).

2. Joseph Frankel, *The Making of Foreign Policy* (Oxford: Oxford University Press, 1963) p. 63.

3. On the 'English School', see Brunello Vigezzi, 'Il "British Committee on the Theory of International Politics" 1958–1985', in the Italian translation of Hedley Bull and Adam Watson, i.e. *L'Espansione della Società Internazional: L'Europa e il mondo dalla fine del medioevo ai nostri tempi* (Milano: Editoriale Jaca Book, 1994) pp. xi–xcv; also Tim Dunne, *Inventing International Society* (London: Macmillan, 1998). The School came into being in the 1950s, but was not so named until Roy E. Jones's article, 'The English School of International Relations: a case for closure', *Review of International Studies*, vol. 7, no. 1, 1981, pp. 1–14.

4. Kenneth Waltz, *Theory of International Politics* (Reading, Massachusetts: Addison-Wesley, 1979).

5. *Ibid.*, pp. 122–3.

6. Waltz's only book on foreign policy argued that the US foreign policy-making system was more effective than the British. See *Foreign Policy and Democratic Politics: the American and British Experience* (Boston: Little, Brown, 1967). Its starting-point is the 'capabilities of democracies in the realm of foreign policy' (p. 1) and it argues that success equates to setting 'sensible goals ... what interest requires and resources permit' (p. 15). The impact of democracy on foreign policy is thus reduced to the capacity to cope with the balance of power.

7. Colin Elman, 'Horses for courses: why *not* neo-realist theories of foreign policy?', *Security Studies*, vol. 6, no. 1, Autumn 1996, pp. 38–9. Elman's theories have very little to do with explaining complex foreign policy behaviour. He focuses on the straw man of prediction and does not descend to cases.

8. Waltz, *Theory of International Politics*, p. 118.

9. The main proponent of the idea of cosmopolitan democracy, that is, that since the state is no longer capable of maintaining a healthy democracy in the age of globalization, we should build a sense of solidarity among the *peoples* of the world, is David Held. See his *Democracy and the Global Order: from the Modern State to Cosmopolitan Governance* (Oxford: Polity Press, 1995). Others broadly associated with advocating cosmopolitan democracy under the mantle of globalization include Boutros Boutros-Ghali, Johan Galtung and Richard Falk. See their respective contributions in Barry Holden (ed.), *Global Democracy: Key Debates* (London: Routledge, 2000).

10. A sophisticated example of this approach is the work of Michael Brecher. See, for example, his *The Foreign Policy System of Israel: Setting, Images, Process* (Oxford: Oxford University Press, 1972). The idea of systems was made familiar in IR by Morton Kaplan's *System and Process in International Politics* (New York: Wiley, 1957) and first related to foreign policy by Richard Snyder, H.W. Bruck and Burton Sapin, in *Foreign Policy Decision-Making: an Approach to the Study of International Politics* (New York: Free Press, 1962).

11. Chris Brown, 'Moral agency and international society', *Ethics and International Affairs*, vol. 15, no. 2, 2001, pp. 87–98.

12. For a helpful discussion, *inter alia*, of the extent to which the international system should be regarded as a physical phenomenon, see Hidemi Suganami, 'Agents, structures, narratives', *European Journal of International Relations*, vol. 5, no. 3, September 1999.

13. The work of R.J. Vincent is the most notable here. See his edited book *Human Rights and International Relations* (Cambridge: Cambridge University Press in association with the Royal Institute of International Affairs, 1986), and *Foreign Policy and Human Rights: Issues and Responses* (Cambridge: Cambridge University Press in association with the Royal Institute of International Affairs, 1986). Also relevant are a number of

essays in Hedley Bull and Adam Watson (eds), *The Expansion of International Society* (Oxford: Clarendon, 1984).

14. Alexander Wendt, 'Anarchy is what states make of it: the social construction of power politics', *International Organisation*, 46, 1992, pp. 391–426; see also Wendt's book, *Social Theory of International Politics* (Cambridge: Cambridge University Press, 1999), especially Chapter 6 (pp. 246–312), 'Three cultures of anarchy'; and Tim Dunne, 'The social construction of international society', *European Journal of International Relations*, I, pp. 367–89. Michael Donelan, *Elements of International Political Theory* (Oxford: Clarendon Press, 1984) makes both the normative and the epistemological points through its erudite 'conversation' between traditions of thought.

15. Christopher Hill, '1939, or the origins of liberal realism', *Review of International Studies*, vol. 15, no. 4, October 1989.

16. Robert Cooper, *The Post-Modern State and the World Order*, 2nd edn (London: Demos, 2000).

17. Influential in shaping the current understanding of a tension between the community of states and the cosmos of peoples, have been Andrew Linklater's *Men and Citizens in the Theory of International Relations*, 2nd edn (London: Macmillan, 1990) and Chris Brown's *International Relations Theory: a New Normative Approach* (Hemel Hempstead: Harvester Wheatsheaf, 1992).

18. Susan Strange, *States and Markets* (London: Pinter, 1993) pp. 235–40.

19. Regimes are 'implicit or explicit principles, norms, rules and decision-making procedures around which actor expectations converge in a given area of international relations.' Stephen D. Krasner, 'Structural causes and regime consequences: regimes as intervening variables', *International Organization*, vol. 36, no. 2, Spring 1982, p. 186.

20. James N. Rosenau and Ernst-Otto Cziempel (eds), *Global Changes and Theoretical Challenges: Approaches to World Politics for the 1990s* (Lexington, Massachusetts: Lexington Books, 1989), and James N. Rosenau, *Turbulence in World Politics: a Theory of Change and Continuity* (Princeton: Princeton University Press, 1990). One of the first works to focus on change was Barry Buzan and R.J. Barry Jones (eds), *Change and the Study of International Relations: the Evaded Dimension* (London: Pinter, 1981).

21. In the past fifty years states have extended their territorial waters from three to twelve miles, and asserted their rights to have 'exclusive economic zones' up to 200 miles from their coasts. The 'global commons' have thus shrunk in extent as well as being diminished by over-use.

22. The fires which blocked two Alpine tunnels between 1999–2002 threatened European trade, a factor which has also been a great pressure on an unhappy Switzerland to allow the passage of heavy lorries.

23. For a good general account of geopolitics and its influence, see W.H. Parker, *Mackinder: Geography as an aid to Statecraft* (Oxford: Clarendon Press, 1982).

24. Alfred Mahan lived from 1840–1914. His major work was *The Influence of Seapower Upon History 1660–1783* (Boston, 1890) which took its cue from the rise of Britain to supremacy in the nineteenth century.

25. Sir Halford Mackinder (1861–1947) was Director of the London School of Economics and Political Science from 1903–8. His main book in this context was *Democratic Ideals and Reality: a Study in the Politics of Reconstruction* (London: Constable and Company, 1919). Like Mackinder, Klaus Haushofer was a professor of Geography, who founded in Munich in 1924 the influential journal *Zeitschrift für Geopolitik*.

26. Despite the occasional attempts to launch the 'new geopolitics' particularly in South America and in Italy. See Carlo Jean, *Geopolitica* (Roma-Bari: Editori Laterza, 1995).

27. Cited in Harold and Margaret Sprout, 'Environmental factors in the study of international politics', in James N. Rosenau (ed.), *International Politics and Foreign Policy* (New York: Free Press, 1969) p. 45. In a way this gets to the heart of the debate about constructivism. Advocates of the latter perspective might well argue that Switzerland is a standing rebuttal to Pate.

28. The Sprouts used a continuum between determinism, through free-will environmentalism, possibilism, cognitive behaviouralism and probabilism, not even bothering to consider voluntarism, where existential free will resides. *Ibid.*, pp. 44–6.

29. See, for example, the journal *Geopolitics* (London: Frank Cass).

30. Frances Cairncross, *The Death of Distance: How the Communications Revolution Will Change Our Lives* (London: Orion Business Books, 1997).

31. Iceland does not apply for membership of the EU largely because adhesion to the Common Fisheries Policy would destroy its main source of income.

32. Ellsworth Huntington (1876–1947) in his *Civilisation and Climate* (New Haven: Yale University Press, 1924) argued that average temperatures of 18–21 Centigrade promoted civilization because peoples spent less time fighting the elements and disease, citing ancient Babylon and the then cooler climate in the Tigris–Euphrates valley in evidence. There has been speculation on climate's impact on civilization since Herodotus. See Arnold Toynbee, *A Study of History*, One Volume Edition (London: Thames & Hudson, 1972) for example, pp. 95–6.

33. Data from Mark Zacher's essay on 'International Organizations', in Joel Krieger (ed.), *The Oxford Companion to Politics of the World* (New York: Oxford University Press, 1993) p. 451.

34. Traditionalist scholars like Aron, Bull and Northedge did not trouble themselves with the problem of how we know whether or not a system or structure exists. It was enough for them that it was axiomatic, and that intelligent observers, including participating decision-makers, could agree on its existence.

35. Indeed, economics and security should be seen as part of a 'seamless web'. See Michael Mastanduno, 'Economics and security in statecraft and scholarship', in Peter J. Katzenstein, Robert O. Keohane and Stephen D. Krasner (eds), *Exploration and Contestation in the Study of World Politics* (Cambridge, Mass: MIT Press, 1999) pp. 185–214.

36. The definition of interdependence as involving mutual sensitivity and vulnerability comes from Robert Keohane and Joseph S. Nye, *Power and Interdependence* (Boston: Little, Brown, 1977) pp. 11–19.

37. David Armstrong, *Revolution and World Order* (Oxford: Clarendon Press, 1993); Fred Halliday, *Revolution and World Politics* (Houndmills: Palgrave Macmillan, 1999). Armstrong and Halliday represent different positions on the important issue of whether the international system socializes revolutionary states into conformity (Armstrong) or is itself shaped by the socio-economic dynamics underlying both revolution and capitalist order (Halliday).

38. Michael Leifer, *ASEAN and the Security of South-East Asia* (London: Routledge, 1989).

39. In the mid 1970s the UK subscribed to 126 separate international organizations, from the Commonwealth Secretariat to the International Municipal Parking Congress. Most other rich middle-range states are just as involved in the web of international organizations. *Review of Overseas Representation: Report by the Central Policy Review Staff [the Berrill Report]* (London: HMSO, 1977) p. 408.

40. Daniel Keohane, 'Realigning neutrality? Irish defence policy and the EU' (Paris: Western European Union Institute for Security Studies, Occasional Paper No. 24, March 2001).

41. Cited in Antonio Cassese, 'International law', in Joel Krieger (ed.), *The Oxford Companion to Politics of the World* (New York: Oxford University Press, 1993) p. 442.

42. Louis Henkin, *How Nations Behave: Law and Foreign Policy*, 2nd edn (New York: published for the Council on Foreign Relations by Columbia University Press, 1979).

43. Even in such a setpiece of power politics as the Cuban Missile Crisis. See Abram Chayes, *The Cuban Missile Crisis* (London: Oxford University Press, 1974).

44. As Mikhail Gorbachev recognized. On entering power in 1985 he let it be known that the Soviet Union wished to change tack in foreign policy and to share responsibilities as a full member of the international community. Michael McGwire, *Perestroika and Soviet National Security* (Washington, DC: Brookings Institution, 1991) pp. 174–86.

45. Immanuel Kant, 'Perpetual peace: a philosophical sketch', in *Kant: Political Writings*, ed. Hans Reiss, second edition (Cambridge: Cambridge University Press, 1991) p. 126.

46. For a detailed analysis of the meaning of world opinion, see Christopher Hill, 'World opinion and the empire of circumstance', *International Affairs*, vol. 72, no. 1, January 1996.

47. See Frank Louis Rusciano and Roberta Fiske-Rusciano, 'Toward a notion of "world opinion"', in Frank Louis Rusciano with Roberta Fiske-Rusciano, Bosah Ebo Sigfredo A. Hernandez and John Crothers Pollock, *World Opinion and the Emerging International Order* (Westport, Connecticut: Praeger, 1998) pp. 13–28.

48. While foreign policy aggression usually implies a form of domestic tyranny, the contrary is far from true.

49. Lyndon Johnson explained in 1966, 'we are not trying to wipe out North Vietnam ... we are trying to make them ... realize the price of aggression is too high' (cited in Henry Kissinger, *Diplomacy*, London: Simon & Schuster, 1994, pp. 661–2). And in this, for once, he was probably not being disingenuous.

50. In this sense the lesson of the Suez crisis of 1956, only two years before the first Cod War, was that of post-modern image-making – don't look like a bully.

51. John Burton, *Systems, States, Diplomacy and Rules* (Cambridge: Cambridge University Press, 1968) and *World Society* (Cambridge: Cambridge University Press, 1968). As Chris Brown has pointed out, Burton saw the society of states and world society as incompatible, rather than, as here, necessarily interwoven. Chris Brown, 'World society and the English School: an "International Society" perspective on world society', *European Journal of International Relations*, vol. 7, no. 4, December 2001.

52. See Deon Geldenhuys, *The Diplomacy of Isolation: South Africa's Foreign Policy-Making* (London: Macmillan, 1984), and *Isolated States: a Comparative Analysis* (Cambridge: Cambridge University Press, 1990).

53. K.J. Holsti with Miguel Monterichard *et al. Why Nations Realign: Foreign Policy Restructuring in the Postwar World* (London: Allen and Unwin, 1982).

54. In this context it should be noted that the associations of the United Kingdom with 'splendid isolation' and the United States with 'isolationism' are so misleading as to put them in a wholly different category.

55. Jacob Berkovitch (ed.), *ANZUS in Crisis: Alliance Management in International Affairs* (London: Macmillan, 1988).

Chapter 8

1. For an historical perspective on transnationalism see F.S. Northedge, 'Transnationalism: the American illusion', *Millennium*, vol. 5, no. 1, Spring 1976, and Stephen D. Krasner, 'Power politics, institutions and transnational relations', in Thomas Risse-Kappen (ed.),

Bringing Transnational Relations Back In: Non-State Actors, Domestic Structures and International Institutions (Cambridge: Cambridge University Press, 1995).

2.   The two principal works in this respect were James N. Rosenau, *Linkage Politics* (New York: Free Press, 1969) and Joseph S. Nye and Robert Keohane (eds), *Transnational Relations and World Politics* (Cambridge: Harvard University Press, 1971). See also R.W. Mansbach *et al.*, *The Web of World Politics: Non-State Actors in the Global System* (London: Prentice Hall, 1976). More recent, and with detailed case-materials, is Daphne Josselin and William Wallace (eds), *Non-State Actors in World Politics* (Basingstoke: Palgrave, 2002).

3.   The reference is to Raymond Vernon's early book *Sovereignty at Bay: the Multinational Spread of US Enterprises* (Harlow: Longman, 1971), which set the tone for much subsequent work on the 'decline' of the state.

4.   In this I broadly follow Ian Clark, in his 'Beyond the Great Divide: globalization and the theory of international relations', *Review of International Studies* (1998), vol. 24, no. 4, pp. 479–98, although I think that Clark exaggerates the historical tendency to separate the domestic and the international.

5.   Nye and Keohane, *Transnational Relations and World Politics*, p. xi.

6.   David Held, Anthony McGrew, David Goldblatt and Jonathan Perraton, *Global Transformations: Politics, Economics and Culture* (Cambridge: Polity Press, 1999) pp. 1–28. See also Ian Clark's historical contextualization in his *Globalization and Fragmentation* (Oxford: Oxford University Press, 1997), and analysis in *Globalization and International Relations Theory* (Oxford: Oxford University Press, 1999). For a powerful critique of the paradigm, see Justin Rosenberg, *The Follies of Globalisation Theory: Polemical Essays* (London: Verso, 2000).

7.   Marshall McLuhan, the Canadian media studies pioneer, is now virtually relegated to the status of curiosity. Some of his ideas, however, were insightful and innovative. See *Understanding Media: the Extensions of Man* (London: Routledge, 1964), and *The Global Village: Transformations in World Life and Media in the 21st Century* (New York: Oxford University Press, 1989).

8.   The speeches of Tony Blair, notably in Chicago in April 1999, to the Labour Party Conference in October 2000, and in Bangalore on 5 January 2002, arguably constitute the most serious attempt yet to articulate what globalization implies for foreign policy.

9.   Chris Brown, 'Moral agency and international society', and Toni Erskine, 'Assigning responsibility to institutional moral agents: the case of states and quasi-states', both in *Ethics and International Affairs*, vol. 15, no. 2, 2001.

10. For an excellent discussion of globalization and the problem of causation see R.J. Barry Jones, 'Globalization and change in the international political economy', in *International Affairs* (1999), vol. 75, no. 2, pp. 357–66.

11. Adam Watson, *The Evolution of International Society: a Comparative Historical Analysis* (London: Routledge, 1992); see, for example, p. 318.

12. The sociology of Amitai Etzioni prefigured the understanding of international relations as more complex than either balance of power or world society models would suggest. He emphasized 'the need to treat social units and their change as multilayer phenomena, including at least a performance, a power (or control) and a communication layer'. Amitai Etzioni, 'The epigenesis of political communities at the international level', *American Journal of Sociology*, LXVIII, (1963), p. 421. Reprinted in James N. Rosenau (ed.), *International Politics and Foreign Policy* (New York: Free Press, 1969) pp. 346–58.

13. Brian Hocking and Michael Smith, *Beyond Foreign Economic Policy: the United States, the Single European Market and the Changing World Economy* (London: Pinter, 1997)

p. 13. Hocking and Smith to some extent follow Seyom Brown's idea of 'global polyarchy' in the latter's *New Forces, Old Forces, and the Future of World Politics* (New York: HarperCollins, 1995).

14. The World Economic Forum, in Davos, Swizerland, is attended by the world's business elite, private and public. See http://www.weforum.org/ For the transnational anti-globalizers see François Houtart and François Polet (eds), *The Other Davos: the Globalization of Resistance to the World Economic System* (London: Zed Books, 2001).

15. James Mayall, 'The variety of states', in Cornelia Navari (ed.), *The Condition of States: a Study in International Political Theory* (Milton Keynes: Open University Press, 1991) pp. 44–60.

16. On the PLO see Barry Rubin, *Revolution until Victory: the Politics and History of the PLO* (Cambridge, Mass: Harvard University Press, 1994). On the ANC see Scott Thomas, *The Diplomacy of Liberation: the Foreign Relations of the ANC since 1960* (London: Tauris Academic, 1995).

17. Brian Hocking has pioneered work in this area. See his *Localizing Foreign Policy: Non-Central Governments and Multilayered Diplomacy* (London: Macmillan, 1993) and *Managing Foreign Relations in Federal States* (London: Leicester University Press, 1993). See also Heidi Hobbs, *City Hall Goes Abroad: the Foreign Policy of Local Politics* (Thousand Oaks, CA: Sage, 1994).

18. On the Länder, see Karl H. Goetz, 'National governance and European integration: inter-governmental relations in Germany', *Journal of Common Market Studies*, vol. 33, no. 1, 1995, pp. 91–116.

19. Chad Alger has long been associated with the study of cities in international relations. See his ' "Foreign" policies of US publics', *International Studies Quarterly*, vol. 21, no. 2, June 1977, pp. 277–318; and 'The world relations of cities – closing the gap between social science paradigms and everyday human experience', *International Studies Quarterly*, December 1990, vol. 34, no. 4, pp. 493–518. On twin-towning, see J.E. Farquharson and S.C. Holt, *Europe from Below: an Assessment of Franco-German Popular Contacts* (London: George Allen & Unwin, 1975). It is often actively promoted by governments, as with the EU funding and sponsorship of arrangements between western Europe and the former USSR under the TACIS aid scheme.

20. I lean here on Douglas Johnston and Cynthia Sampson (eds), *Religion, the Missing Dimension of Statecraft* (New York: Oxford University Press for the Center for Strategic and International Studies, 1994), and in particular on the contributions by Henry Wooster, 'Faith at the ramparts: the Philippine Catholic Church and the 1986 revolution' and Douglas Johnston, 'The churches and Apartheid in South Africa'.

21. Barry Rubin, 'Religion and international affairs', in Johnston and Sampson, *op.cit.*

22. Fred Halliday has insisted on this truth for many years, in the face of much prejudice. See his *Islam and the Myth of Confrontation* (London: I.B. Tauris, 1996), and *Nation and Religion in the Middle East* (London: Saqi Books, 2000); see, for example, pp. 129–36.

23. The three principal foundations are: the Friedrich Ebert Foundation (SPD), the Konrad Adenauer Foundation (CDU), and Friedrich Naumann Foundation (FDP). Foundations for the Greens and the ex-Communists of the DDR are also becoming established as international actors. The foundations were active in democracy-building ventures in Spain and Portugal in the 1970s, in central America in the 1980s and in Eastern Europe in the 1990s. The German state provides funding, and party competition is supposed to ensure independence from government. See Sebastian Bartsch, 'Political foundations: linking the worlds of foreign policy and transnationalism', in Wolf-Dieter Eberwein and

Karl Kaiser (eds), *Germany's New Foreign Policy: Decision-Making in an Interdependent World* (Houndmills: Palgrave, 2001).

24. See Donatella Viola, *European Foreign Policy and the European Parliament in the 1990s: An Investigation into the Role and Voting Behaviour of the European Parliament's Political Groups* (Aldershot: Ashgate, 2000).

25. See Peter Haas's keynote article in *Knowledge, Power and International Policy Coordination*, the special issue of *International Organisation*, vol. 46, no. 1, Winter 1992, and book with the same title (Columbia, SC: University of South Carolina Press, 1997).

26. On the CNN effect see Nick Gowing, 'Instant TV and foreign policy', *The World Today*, October 1994.

27. Margaret E. Keck and Kathryn Sikkink, *Activists beyond Borders: Transnational Advocacy Networks in World Politics* (Ithaca, New York: Cornell University Press, 1998); Thomas Risse, Stephen C. Ropp and Kathryn Sikkink (eds), *The Power of Human Rights: International Norms and Domestic Change* (Cambridge: Cambridge University Press, 1999); Daniel C. Thomas, *Boomerangs and Superpowers: the 'Helsinki network' and Human Rights in US Foreign Policy* (Florence: European University Institute, 1999) EUI Working Paper, RSC 99/23.

28. Matthew Evangelista, 'Transnational relations, domestic structures and security policy in the USSR and Russia', in Thomas Risse-Kappen (ed.), *Bringing Transnational Relations Back In: Non-State Actors, Domestic Structures and International Institutions*, pp. 146–88.

29. Thomas Risse-Kappen, 'Ideas do not float freely: Transnational coalitions, domestic structures, and the end of the Cold War', *International Organization*, vol. 48, no. 2, Spring 1994, pp. 185–214.

30. A summary of this complex issue, which has rumbled on for more than two decades, is to be found in David Armstrong, 'Law, justice and the idea of a world society', *International Affairs*, vol. 75, no. 3, July 1999, pp. 566–7.

31. By functionalism is meant the integrative consequences of transnational contacts between specialists, and indeed peoples, working together. See Paul Taylor, 'Functionalism: the theory of David Mitrany', in Paul Taylor and A.J.R. Groom (eds), *International Organisation* (London: Pinter, 1978) pp. 236–52.

32. Samuel Huntington, 'Transnational Organisations in World Politics', *World Politics*, vol. 25, April 1973, pp. 333–68.

33. See Chapter 3, above, Note 48.

34. Peter Katzenstein and Yutaka Tsujinaka, ' "Bullying", "buying" and "binding": US–Japanese transnational relations and domestic structures', in Risse-Kappen (ed.), *Bringing Transnational Relations Back In*, p. 79.

35. Samuel Huntington, 'Transnational organisations in world politics'. It should be noted that Huntington's analysis is in part flawed by his insistence on including organizations like the USAAF in the category of transnational actors. The US Air Force is guilty of bureaucratic politics, but that is another category.

36. A conclusion which the excellent case studies in Adeed Dawisha (ed.), *Islam in Foreign Policy* (Cambridge: Cambridge University Press, 1983) make irresistible.

37. They are 'nasty ... they defend themselves when attacked'.

38. John Stopford and Susan Strange, *Rival States, Rival Firms: Competition for World Market Shares* (Cambridge: Cambridge University Press, 1991).

39. James N. Rosenau, *Linkage Politics*.

40. See William Wallace, 'Issue linkage among Atlantic governments', and Ann-Margaret Walton, 'Atlantic bargaining over energy', both in *International Affairs*, vol. 52, no. 2, April 1976.

41. Rosenau, *Linkage Politics*, p. 45.

42. Rosenau proposed a matrix of up to 3888 cells, each to be studied independently. To do this he multiplied six kinds of external environment by 24 domestic variables, then again by three kinds of linkage and nine different kinds of output. Even he found this too exhausting to follow up. *Linkage Politics*, pp. 49–51.

43. E.L. Woodward, *The Age of Reform 1815–1870* (Oxford: Oxford University Press, 1954) pp. 236–9. A.J.P. Taylor, *The Trouble Makers: Dissent over Foreign Policy 1792–1939* (London: Pimlico, 1993) pp. 58–9. Austria was seeking to extradite Kossuth from Turkey and Palmerston sympathized with the popular hostility in England to this – much to the fury of his prime minister, Lord Russell. Another incident which inflamed Anglo-Austrian relations saw General Haynau roughly handled by London brewery workers.

44. *Boston Globe*, 23 June 1999. Other states followed suit. See also Brannon P. Denning and Jack H. McCall, 'States' rights and foreign policy: Some things should be left to Washington', *Foreign Affairs*, vol. 79, no. 1, January/February 2000.

45. This third diagram resembles quite closely, but coincidentally, Figure 3 in Ian Clark's 'Beyond the great divide: globalization and the theory of international relations', *Review of International Studies* (1998), vol. 24, p. 496.

46. They are, however, partly contingent on international circumstances. For example, various attempts at Sino–Japanese cultural and trade links were crushed by the Cold War. J.S. Hoadley and S. Hasegawa, 'Sino–Japanese relations 1950–1970: an application of the linkage model of international politics', *International Studies Quarterly*, June 1971. On the other hand Anglo-Soviet commerce and cultural contacts grew in the 1960s–70s despite bad intergovernmental relations, largely because no explicit linkages (that is, sanctions) were attempted. Duncan Wilson, 'Anglo-Soviet relations: the effect of ideas on reality', *International Affairs*, vol. 50, no. 3, July 1974, pp. 380–93.

47. M. Giro, 'The Community of San Egidio and its peace-making activities', *The International Spectator*, vol. XXXIII, no. 3, 1998.

Chapter 9

1. As further developed in Christopher Hill, 'Introduction: the Falklands War and European foreign policy', in Stelios Stavridis and Christopher Hill (eds), *Domestic Sources of Foreign Policy: Western European Reactions to the Falklands Conflict* (Oxford: Berg, 1996) pp. 5–11.

2. Pipes quoted in *Corriere della Sera*, 9 August 2000 (my translation). Alexander Wendt, *Social Theory of International Politics* (Cambridge: Cambridge University Press, 1999) p. 2.

3. Eckart Kehr, *Economic Interest, Militarism and Foreign Policy* (Berkeley: University of California Press, 1977), with Introduction by Gordon Craig.

4. James N. Rosenau (ed.), *The Domestic Sources of Foreign Policy* (New York: Free Press, 1967).

5. Robert D. Putnam, 'Diplomacy and domestic politics: the logic of two-level games', *International Organization*, vol. 42, Summer 1988, pp. 427–60; reprinted in Peter B. Evans, Harold K. Jacobson and Robert D. Putnam (eds), *Double-Edged Diplomacy: International Bargaining and Domestic Politics* (Berkeley: University of California

Press, 1993). The work of Andrew Moravcsik on European integration has carried this work further. See his *The Choice for Europe: Social Purpose and State Power from Messina to Maastricht* (New York: Cornell University Press, 1998). The extra EU dimension arguably creates a third board on which the game must be played.

6. Andrew Moravcsik, 'Introduction: integrating international and domestic theories of international bargaining', in Evans, Jacobson and Putnam (eds), *Double-Edged Diplomacy*, p. 23.

7. For a compelling analysis of these critical interactions, see Fred Halliday, *Revolution and World Politics: the Rise and Fall of the Sixth Great Power* (London: Macmillan, 1999), especially chapter 5, 'The antimonies of revolutionary foreign policy'.

8. Peter B. Evans, 'Building an integrative approach to international and domestic politics: reflections and projections', in Evans, Jacobson and Putnam (eds), *Double-Edged Diplomacy*, pp. 402–3.

9. The concentric circles model of policy-making was introduced by Roger Hilsman, in his *To Move a Nation: the Politics of Foreign Policy in the Administration of John F. Kennedy* (New York: Delta, 1964) pp. 541–4. Hilsman acknowledges his debt to Gabriel Almond's model of public opinion and foreign policy.

10. The Rabbi was Ovadiah Yosef. See *The Guardian*, 8 August 2000.

11. See Chapter 2, note 23.

12. For an overview of foreign policy – domestic relations, see Avner Yaniv, 'Domestic structure and external flexibility: a systemic restatement of a neglected theme', *Millennium: Journal of International Studies*, vol. 8, no. 1, Spring 1979.

13. Israel could not pursue its assertive and highly militarized stance in the Middle East without the uniquely unconditional underwriting of its debts from the USA. The Argentine military junta in 1982 sought to escape from its chronic financial difficulties with a self-justifying war over the Falkland Islands, only to be forced to face realities in the most humiliating fashion through military defeat.

14. See Warren I. Cohen, *America in the Age of Soviet Power* (Cambridge: Cambridge University Press, 1993) pp. 198–201.

15. For a plausible version of the stronger view, that the United States actively sought the division of Cyprus, and cynically engineered it, see Brendan O'Malley and Ian Craig, *American Espionage and the Turkish Invasion* (London: I.B. Tauris, 1999).

16. On Greece, see Thanos Veremis, *Greece's Balkan Entanglement* (Athens: Hellenic Foundation for European and Foreign Policy, 1995).

17. Frank L. Klingberg, *Cyclical Trends in American Foreign Policy Moods* (Lanham, Md: University Press of America, 1983). Also Jack E. Holmes, *The Mood/Interest Theory of American Foreign Policy* (Kentucky: University Press of Kentucky, 1985).

18. John Keegan, 'The ordeal of Afghanistan', *The Atlantic Monthly*, November 1985, pp. 94–105. Two important articles in *Review of International Studies*, vol. 25, no. 4, October 1999, concentrate on the extraordinary impact of the Afghanistan War of 1979–89 on the Soviet Union and the Cold War: Fred Halliday, 'Soviet foreign policy-making and the Afghanistan war: from "second Mongolia" to bleeding wound', *Review*, pp. 675–91; Rafael Reuveny and Aseem Prakash, 'The Afghanistan war and the breakdown of the Soviet Union', *Review*, pp. 693–708.

19. Rudolph J. Rummel, 'The relationship between national attributes and foreign conflict behaviour', in J. David Singer (ed.), *Quantitative International Politics: Insights and Evidence* (New York: Free Press, 1968) p. 208. Pitirim Sorokin was the noted sociologist of conflict. Rummel cites his *Social and Cultural Dynamics* (New York: America Book, 1937).

20. Geoffrey Blainey, *The Causes of Wars* (London: Macmillan, 1973) pp. 70–1.
21. Miles Kahler, 'Introduction: liberalization and foreign policy', in Miles Kahler (ed.), *Liberalization and Foreign Policy* (New York: Columbia University Press, 1997) p. 12.
22. Halliday identifies four phases of relations between a revolutionary power and the outside world: a period of grace; confrontation; accommodation; longer-run heterogeneous conflict. Halliday, *Revolution and World Politics* (Houndmills: Macmillan, 1999) pp. 135–40. Whoever has the responsibility for these events, it is certainly striking that of the major states of the Westphalia system to have undergone violent revolution, the majority (Britain, America, France, Russia, China and Iran) have found themselves engaged in serious warfare in the decade after their revolution succeeded.
23. Richard Little, *External Intervention in Civil Wars* (London: Martin Robertson, 1975).
24. On Italy, see Carlo M. Santoro, *La Politica Estera di Una Media Potenza* (Bologna: Il Mulino, 1991) pp. 177–246. On France, Dorothy Pickles, *The Fifth Republic*, 2nd edn (London: Methuen, 1962).
25. On 'policy modes' see Helen Wallace, 'Analysing and explaining policies', in Helen Wallace and William Wallace (eds), *Policy-Making in the European Union*, 4th edn (Oxford: Oxford University Press, 2000) pp. 71–2. Professor Wallace acknowledges a debt to the earlier work of John Peterson.
26. For the nineteenth-century concept of the 'constitutional state', but with particular reference to foreign policy, see Roy E. Jones, *Principles of Foreign Policy* (Oxford: Martin Robertson, 1979), for example, pp. 83–7.
27. Uwe Leonardy, 'Federation and *Länder* in German foreign relations: power-sharing in treaty-making and European affairs', in Brian Hocking (ed.), *Foreign Relations and Federal States* (Leicester: Leicester University Press, 1993) pp. 236–51. The quotation (p. 249) is from Bismarck's speech to the *Reichstag* of the North German Confederation on 16 April 1869, and is itself a citation from German sources.
28. Leonardy, *op.cit.*, especially pp. 237–41.
29. A point made by Brian Hocking, in his 'Patrolling the "frontier": globalization, localization and the "actorness" of non-central governments', *Regional and Federal Studies*, vol. 9, no. 1, 1999, pp. 17–39.
30. The sanctions have been imposed through public policies of disinvestment or elective procurement at the NCG level. See John M. Kline, 'Managing intergovernmental tensions: shaping a state and local role in US foreign relations', in Hocking (ed.), *Foreign Relations and Federal States*, p. 111; also Chapter 8 above.
31. See Hocking (ed.), *Foreign Relations and Federal States, passim*. Also Michelmann and Soldatos (eds), *Federalism and International Relations* (Oxford: Oxford University Press, 1990). The early history of Nigeria provides examples of the regional governments going their own way. See Lloyd Jensen, *Explaining Foreign Policy* (Englewood Cliffs, NJ: Prentice Hall, 1982) p. 116; also Stephen Wright and Julius Emeka Okolo, 'Nigeria: aspirations of regional power', in Stephen Wright (ed.), *African Foreign Policies* (Boulder: Westview, 1999) especially pp. 123–4. In India, Hyderabad and Kerala have been opting out of international agreements on power-station installations (I am grateful to Tien-Sze Feng for this information).
32. Stuart Harris, in 'Federalism and Australian foreign policy', in Hocking (ed.), *Foreign Relations and Federal States*, pp. 90–104, makes it clear that the Australian states have tended to have a diminished direct role in international dealings as they have come to cooperate more with the Commonwealth (central) government (p. 103).
33. See Charles de Gaulle, *Memoirs of Hope* (London: Weidenfeld & Nicolson, 1971) p. 319.

34. There were 48 Italian governments between 1946–92. Even after 1992, when the process of reform began, little changed until 2001, when the electoral victory of Silvio Berlusconi seemed to presage a four-year term of office. For the image of Italy abroad, see the account of one of the country's few specialized diplomatic correspondents: Dino Frescobaldi, *Con gli occhi degli altri* (Florence: Le Lettere, 2000).

35. Avi Shlaim and Avner Yaniv, 'Domestic Politics and Foreign Policy in Israel', in *International Affairs*, vol. 56, no. 2, Spring 1980, pp. 256 and 262. See also Yael Yishai, 'Domestic inputs into foreign policy-making: the case of the settlement issue', *Review of International Studies*, vol. 8, no. 3, July 1982.

36. The 'Founding Act on Mutual Relations, Cooperation and Security between NATO and the Russian Federation' was signed on 27 May 1997.

37. On the links between domestic continuity and international success, see T.J. Pempel, 'Japanese Foreign Economic Policy: the Domestic Bases for International Behaviour', in Peter J. Katzenstein (ed.), *Between Power and Plenty: Foreign Economic Policies of Advanced Industrial Countries* (Madison: University of Wisconsin Press, 1978) especially pp. 145–57.

38. This two-way process was reinforced by transgovernmental, inter-elite ties. See Peter Katzenstein and Yutaka Tsujinaka, ' "Bullying", "Buying" and "Binding": US–Japanese Transnational Relations and Domestic Structures', in Thomas Risse-Kappen (ed.), *Bringing Transnational Relations Back In* (Cambridge: Cambridge University Press, 1995). Another example of elections returning the same party for decades is Mexico, where the People's Revolutionary Party (PRI) was in office from 1929 until expelled by the voters in 2000.

39. Stephen Wright, 'The Changing Context of African Foreign Policies', in Stephen Wright (ed.), *African Foreign Policies*, pp. 10–19.

40. Michael Doyle, 'Kant, liberal legacies and foreign affairs', *Philosophy and Public Affairs*, vol. 12, no. 3–4, Summer–Autumn 1983, pp. 205–35 in no. 3 and pp. 323–53 in no. 4. Also his 'Liberalism and world politics', *American Political Science Review*, vol. 80, no. 4, December 1986, pp. 1151–69. Immanuel Kant made the original argument in 'Perpetual peace: a philosophical sketch' in 1795. This is most easily available in Hans Reiss (ed.), *Kant: Political Writings* (Cambridge: Cambridge University Press, 1991) pp. 93–130.

41. Laurence Martin, *The Two-edged Sword: Armed Force in the Modern World* (London: Weidenfeld & Nicolson, 1982) p. 90.

42. The main works since Doyle have been Bruce Russett's *Grasping the Democratic Peace: Principles for a Post-Cold War World* (Princeton, NJ: Princeton University Press, 1993); Thomas Risse-Kappen, 'Democratic peace – warlike democracies? A social constructivist interpretation of the liberal argument', *European Journal of International Relations*, vol. 1, no. 4, December 1995, pp. 491–517; R.J. Rummel, 'Democracies ARE less warlike than other regimes', *European Journal of International Relations*, vol. 1, no. 4, December 1995, pp. 649–64; Robert Latham, 'Democracy and war-making: locating the international liberal context', *Millennium: Journal of International Studies*, vol. 22, no. 2, Summer 1993; Michael E., Brown, Sean M., Lynn-Jones, and Steven E. Miller, (eds), *Debating the Democratic Peace* (Cambridge, Mass: MIT Press, 1996); Miles Kahler (ed.), *Liberalization and Foreign Policy*.

43. For one of the clearer examples see Erich Weede, 'Democracy and war involvement', *Journal of Conflict Resolution*, vol. 28, no. 4, December 1984, pp. 649–64.

44. Kenneth Waltz, *Man, the State and War* (New York: Columbia University Press, 1959), and *Theory of International Politics* (Reading, Mass: Addison-Wesley, 1979). It is not

just the neo-realists who stress the importance of international structures over the domestic. See Christopher Hill, 'Introduction: the Falklands War and European foreign policy', in Stelios Stavridis and Christopher Hill (eds), *Domestic Sources of Foreign Policy*, pp. 6–11. Brian White picks up on this point in his 'The European Challenge to Foreign Policy Analysis', *European Journal of International Relations*, vol. 5, no. 1, January 1999, p. 38.

45. British male householders had the vote from 1885, but not all males over 21 until 1918. In the same year women over 30 gained the vote. Women had to wait until 1928 for equal enfranchisement with men. In France universal male suffrage came and went between 1793–1848, when it returned for good. Women, however, did not get the vote until 1944.

46. Britain and France declared war on Germany in both 1914 and 1939, without having been attacked by her. They must share some responsibility at least for the tensions which led to war in 1914, as must the United States for those before Pearl Harbor. Examples of failures to consider compromise peaces are more contestable but it is striking how the idea was regarded as unthinkable, even treasonable, in Britain in 1916–17 (over Lord Lansdowne's peace initiative), or in the United States in 1951–2 (McCarthyism) and 1965–8.

47. This thesis is propounded vigorously in the many writings of Noam Chomsky and John Pilger. For an application of it to a single country, see Mark Curtis, *The Ambiguities of Power: British Foreign Policy since 1945* (London: Zed Books, 1995).

48. This was the doctrine notoriously enunciated by Jean Kirkpatrick, Ronald Reagan's Ambassador to the UN. See her *Dictatorships and Double Standards: Rationalism and Realism in Politics* (New York: Simon and Shuster, 1982). The eponymous article of the title first appeared in *Commentary*, November 1979, as a critique of Jimmy Carter's foreign policy.

49. Lloyd Jensen, *Explaining Foreign Policy*, pp. 130–5.

50. As argued by Kurt Taylor Gaubatz, 'Democratic states and commitment in International Relations', in Miles Kahler (ed.), *Liberalization and Foreign Policy*, pp. 28–65.

51. Speech by John Bright on 'Foreign policy', Birmingham, 29 October 1858, in *Selected Speeches of the Rt. Honourable John Bright MP on Public Questions* (London: J.M. Dent & Sons, 1907) p. 204.

52. See Steven I. Levine, 'Perception and ideology in Chinese foreign policy', and Paul H. Kreisberg, 'China's Negotiating Behaviour', both in Thomas W. Robinson and David Shambaugh (eds), *Chinese Foreign Policy: Theory and Practice* (Oxford: Clarendon Press, 1994).

53. William R. Polk, *Neighbours and Strangers: the Fundamentals of Foreign Affairs* (Chicago: University of Chicago Press, 1997) pp. 118 and 226.

54. See Bhabani Sen Gupta, 'Forget ideology, Give them onions!', *The World Today*, February 1998, vol. 54, no. 2, pp. 40–1.

55. The *Independent*, 2 February 2000.

56. For the first key work on feminist approaches to IR see Rebecca Grant and Kathleen Newland (eds), *Gender and International Relations* (Milton Keynes: Open University Press, 1991); also Jill Steans, *Gender and International Relations: an Introduction* (Cambridge: Polity Press, 1998). Gender theorists are building on work already begun in psychoanalysis about repression, control and violence. See Wilhelm Reich, *The Sexual Revolution: Towards a Self-Governing Character Structure* (London: P. Nevill, 1951) and Norman Dixon, *On the Psychology of Military Incompetence* (London: Cape, 1976).

57. This is not to undervalue the role of the 'madres de la Plaza de Mayo' in Argentina, or any of those who struggle against powerlessness. In modern conditions of reduced labour and role differentiation, however, men are increasingly in the same position.

58. Christopher Hill, '"Where are we going?" International Relations and the voice from below', *Review of International Studies*, vol. 25, no. 1, January 1999, pp. 107–22. See Chapter 10 below.

59. Pamela Beshoff, *Structuralist and Realist Perspectives in Jamaican Foreign Policy 1972–1980* (London School of Economics and Political Science, unpublished PhD thesis, 1988).

60. Christopher Hill, 'Theories of foreign policy-making for developing countries', in Christopher Clapham (ed.), *Foreign Policy-Making in Developing Countries* (London: Saxon House, 1977). For an alternative view see Bahgat Korany *et al.*, *How Foreign Policy Decisions are Made in the Third World: a Comparative Approach* (Boulder: Westview, 1985).

61. For the concept of pivotal states, see Robert Chase, Emily Hill and Paul Kennedy (eds), *The Pivotal States: a New Framework for US Policy in the Developing World* (New York: W.W. Norton, 1999) pp. 1–11. The cases considered are Indonesia, India, Pakistan, Turkey, Egypt, South Africa, Brazil, Algeria and Mexico.

62. See D.K. Fieldhouse, *Economics and Empire, 1830–1914* (London: Macmillan, 1984).

63. Andrew M. Scott, *The Revolution in Statecraft: Intervention in an Age of Inter-dependence* (Durham, NC: Duke University Press, 1982). On the difficulties which Moscow sometimes had with sister communist parties, see Eric Hobsbawm, 'The "Moscow line" and international communist policy', in Chris Wrigley (ed.), *Warfare, Diplomacy and Politics: Essays in Honour of A.J.P. Taylor* (London: Hamish Hamilton, 1986) pp. 163–88.

64. For important aspects of the extensive historical debate on the origins, definition and meaning of fascism, see S.J. Woolf (ed.), *The Nature of Fascism* (London: Weidenfeld & Nicolson, 1968), which contains a seminal piece by Tim Mason ('The primacy of politics – politics and economics in National Socialist Germany').

65. It may be objected that the Brazilian para-fascist Vargas actually declared war on the Axis in 1942 and sent troops to fight them in Italy. What is interesting about this, however, is not only the geopolitical factor (a wish not to fight the USA) but also the inability to stay out of war.

66. Accordingly differences between these traditions can lead to diplomatic misunderstandings. See Raymond Cohen, 'Resolving conflict across languages', *Negotiation Journal*, vol. 17, no. 1, 2001, pp. 17–34.

67. This important question is developed in Ayla Gol, *The Place of Foreign Policy in the Transition to Modernity: Turkish Policy towards the South Caucasus, 1918–1921* (London School of Economics and Political Science, PhD thesis, 2001).

Chapter 10

1. Responsibility is discussed further in Chapter 11. It is worth noting that despite the distinctions evident in English usage, in both French and Italian the same word (responsable/responsabile) may be used for both 'accountable' and 'responsible', because in these cultures the concept of trust is central to both.

2. On the Supreme Soviet, see Vernon Aspaturian, *Process and Power in Soviet Foreign Policy* (Boston: Little, Brown, 1971) pp. 592–5 and 676–83. On China there is little written, but see David Shambaugh, 'Patterns of interaction in Sino-American relations', in Thomas W. Robinson and David Shambaugh (eds), *Chinese Foreign Policy: Theory and Practice* (Oxford: Clarendon Press, 1994) p. 215. The NPC is beginning to become involved on issues such as human rights, the environment and information, but works

mainly through committees and is hardly a forum for open debate. See Elizabeth Economy and Michel Oksenberg (eds), *China Joins the World: Progress and Prospects* (New York: Council of Foreign Relations Press, 1999).

3. Margot Light, 'Democracy, democratisation and foreign policy in post-socialist Russia', in Hazel Smith (ed.), *Democracy and International Relations: Critical Theories/Problematic Practices* (Basingstoke: Palgrave Macmillan, 2000) pp. 90–107.

4. The literature on Executive–Congressional relations in foreign policy is voluminous. Particularly useful for their comparative range are Stephen E. Ambrose, 'The Presidency and foreign policy', *Foreign Affairs*, vol. 70, no. 5, Winter 1991–2; Michael Lee, 'Parliament and foreign policy: some reflections on Westminster and Congressional experience', *Irish Studies in International Affairs*, vol. 2, no. 4, 1988; Eugene R. Wittkopf and James M. McCormick (eds), *The Domestic Sources of American Foreign Policy: Insights and Evidence* (Lanham, Md: Rowman & Littlefield, 1998).

5. This was the Case Act of 1971. For that and the War Powers Act, see Francis O. Wilcox, and Richard A. Frank (eds), *The Constitution and the Conduct of Foreign Policy* (New York: Praeger, 1976) pp. 83–138.

6. Rainer Baumann and Gunther Hellmann, 'Germany and the use of military force: "total war", the "culture of restraint" and the quest for normality', in Douglas Webber (ed.), *New Europe, New Germany, Old Foreign Policy?* Special Issue of *German Politics*, vol. 10, no. 1, April 2001, pp. 68–74. Also Alan Sked, *Cheap Excuses, or Life, Death and European Unity* (London: the Bruges Group, 1991). Whatever the exact legal position, the Court's ruling helped create a new political consensus, previously hindered by differing legal interpretations.

7. I.M. Destler *et al.*, *Managing an Alliance: the Politics of US–Japanese Relations* (Washington: Brookings Institution, 1976) p. 15, cited by Raymond Cohen, *Negotiating across Cultures: International Communication in an Interdependent World*, rev. edn (Washington, DC: United States Institute of Peace Press, 1997) p. 132.

8. Christopher Hill and James Mayall, 'The Sanctions Problem: International and European Perspectives', EUI Working Paper no. 59, European University Institute, Florence, July 1983.

9. The point made in Lisa Martin's *Democratic Commitments: Legislatures and International Cooperation* (Princeton, NJ: Princeton University Press, 2000).

10. 'Peace nears, but selling it is Barak's test', *The Guardian*, 10 December 1999.

11. The Chinese side, taking the view that Hong Kong was their territory in the first place, and therefore did not require a 'treaty', insisted on referring to the deal as merely 'an agreed announcement'. Harold C. Hinton, 'China as an Asian Power', in Thomas W. Robinson and David Shambaugh (eds), *Chinese Foreign Policy: Theory and Practice*, p. 355; Percy Cradock, *Experiences of China* (London: John Murray, 1994) pp. 214–16.

12. Keith Jackson and Jim Lamare, 'Politics, public opinion and international crisis: the ANZUS issue in New Zealand politics', in Jacob Bercovitch (ed.), *ANZUS in Crisis: Alliance Management in International Affairs* (London: Macmillan, 1988) pp. 175–6.

13. Stephen E. Ambrose, 'The Presidency and foreign policy', *Foreign Affairs*, vol. 70, no. 5, Winter 1991–2, p. 127.

14. Stephen Ambrose, *Rise to Globalism: American Foreign Policy since 1938*, 7th edn (London: Penguin, 1993) pp. 199–201.

15. John Tower *et al.*, *Tower Commission Report* (New York: Bantam Books and New York Times, 1987).

16. This was the Chevaline warhead enhancement project. See Lawrence Freedman, *Britain and Nuclear Weapons* (London: Macmillan, 1980). On this occasion the British government's news management, in terms of keeping the issue unremarked, was particularly successful.

17. Filippo Andreatta and Christopher Hill, 'Italy', in Jolyon Howorth and Anand Menon (eds), *The European Union and National Defence Policy* (London: Routledge, 1997) pp. 78–9.

18. 'Malaysia Supplement', *Financial Times*, 14 November 1988, p. 21. In cases like this it is rather more likely that a decision-maker will talk to a foreign journalist, than to his own members of parliament.

19. Charles Carstairs and Richard Ware (eds), *Parliament and International Relations* (Milton Keynes: Open University Press, 1991).

20. This is the observation of Elfriede Regelsberger about Germany, in Stelios Stavridis and Christopher Hill (eds), *Domestic Sources of Foreign Policy: Western European Reactions to the Falklands Conflict* (Oxford: Berg, 1996), p. 71.

21. Private interview, 6 February 1998. Dutch negotiators told foreign colleagues that they would have settled for parity but the Parliament was afraid that the Netherlands would eventually end up with fewer votes than Romania. This may have been merely a negotiating tactic.

22. It has been argued that in the United States foreign policy is generally to the advantage of the Republicans. See William A. Galston and Christopher J. Makins, 'Campaign '88 and foreign policy', *Foreign Policy*, Summer 1988, pp. 3–21.

23. Paul Addison, *The Road to 1945: British Politics and the Second World War* (London: Cape, 1975), for example, pp. 266–9. See also Angus Calder, *The People's War* (London: Granada, 1971).

24. William A. Galston and Christopher J. Makins, 'Campaign '88 and foreign policy', *Foreign Policy*, Summer 1988, p. 4.

25. *Ibid.*, pp. 3–4.

26. Margot Light, 'Information war', *The World Today*, February 2000.

27. The *Independent*, 1 January 1997.

28. This is obvious from a study of the invaluable Nuffield Election Studies, produced after every general election by David Butler and colleagues. See for example, David Butler and Michael Pinot-Duschinsky, *The General Election of 1970* (London: Macmillan, 1971).

29. 'The complex world of Peter Hain', *The Economist*, 24 June 2000.

30. The election of 2000 did not stop President Clinton continuing to mediate between Israel and the Palestinians. But it did lead the US to inform other members of the UN Security Council that it would permit an end to sanctions against Sudan – but only once the elections were over. *Financial Times*, 29 June 2000.

31. Mr Dent was a Lecturer in International Relations at the University of Keele, and a distinguished Africanist, when he launched his campaign for a Millennial amnesty for poor countries' debt, together with ex-diplomat Bill Peters. The campaign snowballed, culminating in extensive demonstrations at the G7 summit in Birmingham in 1998. Dent and Peters drew the lesson from the anti-slavery campaign that influence was only possible on the basis of 'a simple and radical goal', and they succeeded in moving official opinion. *Independent on Sunday*, 17 May 1998.

32. Michel Tatu, 'Public opinion as both means and ends for policy-makers', in *The Conduct of East–West Relations in the 1980s: Part III: Papers from the IISS 25th Annual Conference, Summer 1984* (London: International Institute of Strategic Studies, 1984) pp. 26–32.

33. The distinction was originally made by Gabriel Almond, in his *The American People and Foreign Policy* (New York: Harcourt and Brace, 1950).

34. *The ACP–EEC Courier* (Brussels: European Commission), No. 8, November/December 1984.

35. Cited in Eric Alterman, 'Reading foreign policy: are those journals talking to *us*?', *The Nation*, 27 October 1997.

36. A contestant on a British TV general knowledge quiz, on being asked *twice* 'in which European country is Mount Etna?' answered first 'Japan' and then 'Mexico'. *Private Eye*, no. 1047, 8–21 February 2002, p. 8.

37. Roger Jowell and James D. Spence, *The Grudging Europeans: a Study of British Attitudes towards the EEC* (London: SCPR, 1975) pp. 1–7. Remarkably, given subsequent events only 33 per cent thought the issue of UK membership 'very important' – a figure which rose only to 52 per cent when the category of 'important' was added.

38. MORI poll (D) s/s 2022, in Elizabeth Hann Hastings and Philip K. Hastings (eds), *Index to International Public Opinion, 1979–1980* (Oxford: Clio Press, 1981) p. 89. The Strategic Arms Limitation Talks (SALT) were identified correctly by only 16 per cent. Interestingly there was a significant gender split in the results, with men being better informed than women, and also a clear class split, with information levels falling geometrically. For example the EEC was identified by 72 per cent of men and 50 per cent of women, by 76 per cent of social class AB, 71 per cent of C1, 61 per cent of C2 and 44 per cent of DE.

39. Reported in *The Economist*, 30 July 1988. In a *Washington Post–ABC News* poll of 14–18 October 1981, 53 per cent of Americans had not been able to answer correctly the question 'which country, the United States or the Soviet Union, is a member of NATO?' *Washington Post*, 21 October 1981.

40. Edward Mortimer, 'Parts that glasnost fails to reach', *Financial Times*, 22 September 1987.

41. As Yves Mény says, 'we have probably gone too far insulating the people from politics, except in rather conventional, ritualistic exercises such as elections. The populism which is once again appearing on the stage might be understood as a signal, as the call and need for major involvement of the civil society'. Yves Mény, *The People, the Elites and the Populist Challenge*, Jean Monnet Chair Paper 47 (Fiesole: Robert Schuman Centre at the European University Institute, 1998) p. 22.

42. It is not surprising that mutinies broke out in 1917–18, or that they were suppressed. It is a testimony both to the power of the state and the demoralization of the troops that there were not more. See Leonard V. Smith, *Between Mutiny and Obedience: the French Fifth Infantry Division during World War I* (Princeton, NJ: Princeton University Press, 1994) pp. 175–214; and David Englander, 'Discipline and morale in the British Army 1917–18', in John Horne (ed.), *State, Society and Mobilization in Europe during the First World War* (Cambridge: Cambridge University Press, 1997) pp. 125–43.

43. *We the Peoples: the Role of the United Nations in the Twenty-First Century*, A/54/2000 (New York: UN General Assembly, 27 March 2000) pp. 9–11.

44. In theory this means, following Burke's classical formulation, that they precisely do not just act as a megaphone for their constituents, but are free to follow judgement and conscience. Edmund Burke, 'Speech at the Conclusion of the Poll in Bristol, 3 November 1774', in Paul Langford (ed.), *The Writings and Speeches of Edmund Burke. Vol. III: Party, Parliament, and the American War, 1774–1778* (Oxford: Clarendon Press, 1996) pp. 63–70. In practice they follow the Whips more than the voters.

45. Pluralism assigns political power to the self-assertive, the active and articulate, and assumes that the introverted, the passive, and the silent are content to act as spectators to

democracy. This omits to address the issues of agenda-setting, education and access. Steven Lukes, in *Power: a Radical View* (London: Macmillan, 1974).

46. This is the result, as Cynthia Enloe has pointed out, of assuming that 'margins stay marginal, the silent stay voiceless and ladders are never turned upside down'. Cynthia Enloe, 'Margins, silences and bottom rungs: how to overcome the underestimation of power in the study of international relations', in Steve Smith, Ken Booth and Marysia Zalewski (eds), *International Theory: Positivism and Beyond* (Cambridge: Cambridge University Press, 1996) p. 189. See also Christopher Hill, '"Where are we going?" International Relations and the voice from below', *Review of International Studies*, vol. 25, no. 1, January 1999, pp. 107–22.

47. This metaphor is taken from Bernard C. Cohen, *The Public's Impact on Foreign Policy* (Boston: Little, Brown, 1973) pp. 178–9. Ironically Cohen took it from the perplexed Captain of the US destroyer *Maddox*, the ship involved in the Gulf of Tonkin incident.

48. 'In three days last week I had 2450 letters and 1860 of them were stop the war in one form or another' (Neville Chamberlain, letter to his sister Ida, 8 October 1939, NC 18/1/1071-91, University of Birmingham Library). See also the Cabinet Minute of 7 October 1939 (CAB65/1 WM 39 [4], Public Record Office), which shows that he took the letters to indicate that only 'a small section of society' was pacifist.

49. Anthony Eden, *Memoirs: Full Circle* (London: Cassell, 1960) p. 546. Eden went on to cite other evidence, including opinion polls, but all to the effect that the majority had come to swing round behind him. A guess may be hazarded that the strain of the cognitive dissonance and denial contributed to his worsening physical health.

50. It was one conclusion of the three-volume collective study on foreign policy and public opinion in Europe between 1870 and 1981 that 1945 constituted a decisive break-point, in that 'la notion de légitimité est totalement remise en cause'. Philippe Levillain, 'Opinion publique et politique extérieure de 1870 à 1981', in *Opinion publique et politique extérieure, III 1945–1981* (Rome/Milan: Università di Milano/Ecole Française de Rome, 1985) pp. 310–12.

51. Viz., the very close vote in favour of the Maastricht Treaty in France in 1992, that in Denmark which actually rejected the Treaty and compelled a Danish opt-out, and that in Ireland in 2001 which cast the ratification process of the Treaty of Nice into doubt.

52. *The Guardian*, 10 December 1999. The pressure was reinforced by demonstrations. Two hundred thousand people were estimated to have demonstrated in Tel Aviv on 9 January 2000 against handing over the Golan. 'Israelis show increasing reluctance to give up Golan', *The Guardian*, 12 January 2000.

53. Polish poll cited by Jerzy Urban in his lecture to the Royal Institute of International Affairs, London, 17 February 1987, on 'the relationship between domestic and international factors in Polish foreign policy'. The police censorship reports for 1942–3 were cited in the Italian TV Channel RAI 3's 'L'Ultimo Mussolini' of 4 September 2000. See also Malcolm Muggeridge (ed.), *Ciano's Diary, 1939–1943* (London: Heinemann, 1947) pp. 519 and 527.

54. Danna Harman, 'Addressing the audience back home', *Jerusalem Post*, 23 March 1999. Netanyahu harvested the Soviet immigrant votes but still lost the election.

55. Andrew J. Pierre (ed.), *Domestic Change and Foreign Policy: a Widening Atlantic?* (New York: Council on Foreign Relations, 1986).

56. Christopher Hill, *The Decision-Making Process in Relation to British Foreign Policy, 1938–1941*, unpublished D.Phil. thesis, University of Oxford, 1979, p. 378.

57. George C. Herring, 'The War in Vietnam', in Robert A. Divine (ed.), *The Johnson Years Volume I: Foreign Policy, the Great Society and the White House* (Lawrence: University

Press of Kansas, 1987) pp. 39–55. Herring refers to a contemporary study of poll data, viz. Sidney Verba *et al.*, 'Public opinion and the war in Vietnam', *American Political Science Review*, vol. 61, June 1967, pp. 317–33.

58. Thomas Risse-Kappen, 'Public opinion, domestic structure and foreign policy in liberal democracies', *World Politics*, vol. 43, no. 41, July 1991, pp. 479–512.

59. Certainly the number of individuals involved in international NGO activity has risen enormously. It is estimated that 2600 representatives attended the Fourth World Conference on Women in Beijing in September 1995, and no fewer than 35 000 the unofficial forum held in parallel. See James A. Paul, 'Non-governmental organizations', in Joel Krieger (ed.), *Oxford Companion to Politics of the World*, 2nd edn (New York: Oxford University Press, 2001) pp. 598–601.

60. As pointed out by Heidi Hobbs in her review article of a book which seeks to rectify this, viz., David Skidmore and Valerie M. Hudson (eds), *The Limits of State Autonomy: Societal Groups and Foreign Policy Formulation* (Boulder, Col: Westview, 1993). Heidi Hobbs, 'Theoretical evolution in foreign policy analysis', *Mershon International Studies Review*, vol. I, no. 1, 1994, pp. 158–60.

61. For further problems of definition, see Lester Milbraith, 'Interest groups in foreign policy', in James N. Rosenau (ed.), *The Domestic Sources of Foreign Policy* (New York: Free Press, 1967).

62. *Ibid.*, p. 251.

63. The FPA was founded in 1918 and is non-partisan and non-profit-making. Its election briefings, special 'Headline Series' of briefings, and 'Great Decisions' annual publications draw attention to the foreign policy issues facing the citizenry in a way no other country manages to equal – except possibly France, with its high quality press coverage of foreign affairs. See the FPA's website at www.fpa.org.

64. Diana Johnstone, *The Politics of Euromissiles: Europe's Role in America's World* (London: Verso, 1984); Thomas Risse-Kappen, *Cooperation among Democracies: the European Influence on US Foreign Policy* (Princeton, NJ: Princeton University Press, 1995), especially pp. 188–91. The previous controversy over the 'neutron bomb' had sensitized public opinion and strengthened the organization of peace groups.

65. Tony Smith, *Foreign Attachments: the Power of Ethnic Groups in the Making of American Foreign Policy* (Cambridge, Mass: Harvard University Press, 2000) pp. 63–4, 107.

66. It is interesting that the protests against the World Trade Organization in Seattle in November 1999 were based on the coordination of thirty national movements, which continue to press for their own countries to withdraw from the WTO. The transnational and the national dimensions should not therefore be seen as opposites. See 'Lori's war', an interview with Lori Wallach, the Director of the US consumer organization Public Citizen's offshoot Global Trade Watch. *Foreign Policy*, no. 118, Spring 2000.

67. Tony Smith, *Foreign Attachments*, pp. 110–15.

68. See, on Chile, Emilio Menesis. 'The military vote', *The World Today*, vol. 55, no. 12, December 1999, pp. 23–5; and on Macedonia, Thanos Veremis, *Greece's Balkan Entanglement* (Athens: Hellenic Foundation for European and Foreign Policy, 1995).

69. For information on these groups see Martin Ceadel, *Pacifism in Britain, 1914–45: the Defining of a Faith* (Oxford: Clarendon Press, 1980).

70. As with the 'military–industrial complex', a term first coined by Eisenhower in his farewell address to the American people. The balance within the complex may be shifting, with trends towards an ever more capital-intensive and high-tech arms industry, the state ever more dependent on private enterprise, and a less 'militarized' society. See David Held and Anthony McGrew, David Goldblatt and Jonathan Perraton, *Global*

Transformations: Politics, Economics and Culture (Cambridge: Polity Press, 1999) pp. 137–9.

71. The term is used by Eldon Eisenach, in his *The Lost Promise of Progressivism* (Lawrence: University Press of Kansas, 1994) cited by Inderjeet Parmar, ' "Mobilizing America for an internationalist foreign policy": the role of the Council on Foreign Relations', *Studies in American Political Development*, vol. 13, Fall 1999, pp. 337–73.

72. *Ibid.*

73. Chadwick Alger, 'The external bureaucracy in United States foreign affairs', *Administrative Science Quarterly*, vol. 7, June 1962, cited in Inderjeet Parmar, 'The issue of state power: the Council of Foreign Relations as a case study', *Journal of American Studies*, vol. 29, no. 1, 1995, p. 73. Mr Parmar is almost alone in researching the important theme of foreign policy and expert opinion.

74. For a useful early set of essays, mostly on the US, see Simon Serfaty (ed.), *The Media and Foreign Policy* (London: Macmillan, 1990). Serfaty's conclusion that the media are 'neither hero nor villain' is a useful reminder not to discount the wider political context.

75. Benedict Anderson, *Imagined Communities* (London: Verso, 1991).

76. The Dominion governments at the time were in the process of enlarging their foreign policy independence from London. I am indebted for this example to the one-time diplomatic correspondent of The *Guardian*, Mr Patrick Keatley, and his seminar to the LSE's Foreign Policy workshop entitled 'The Press and the Diplomats'.

77. See Susan L. Carruthers, *The Media at War: Communication and Conflict in the Twentieth Century* (London: Palgrave Macmillan, 2000) pp. 210–13; and Nicholas J. Wheeler, *Saving Strangers: Humanitarian Intervention in International Society* (Oxford: Oxford University Press, 2000) pp. 165–6. As Wheeler points out, it would be wrong to account for the safe havens in terms just of media influence – or any single factor – but the media, at a minimum, helped to legitimize the policy at home.

78. Michael Clarke, *British External Policy-Making in the 1990s* (London: Macmillan, 1992), Appendix on 'The British press and international affairs', pp. 319–28.

79. Theodore C. Sorensen, 'A changing America', in Andrew J. Pierre (ed.), *Domestic Change and Foreign Policy: A Widening Atlantic?* p. 92.

80. Carruthers, *The Media at War*, pp. 231–4. Also Sorensen, pp. 92–3, summarizing his work with public opinion surveys.

81. Carruthers, *op.cit.*; Fred Halliday, 'Neither treason nor conspiracy: reflections on media coverage of the Gulf War 1990–91', *Citizenship Studies*, vol. 1, no. 2, 1997, pp. 157–72.

82. Nik Gowing, 'Real-time television coverage of armed conflicts and diplomatic crises: does it pressure or distort foreign policy decisions?' (Cambridge, Mass: Joan Shorenstein Working Paper, 94/1, Harvard University, 1994) – summarized in Nik Gowing, 'Instant TV and foreign policy', *The World Today*, vol. 50, no. 10, October 1994; see also Nik Gowing, 'Real-time television coverage from war: does it make or break government policy?' in J. Gow, R. Paterson and A. Preston (eds), *Bosnia by Television* (London: British Film Institute, 1996).

83. John Dickie, *Inside the Foreign Office* (London: Chapman, 1992) pp. 82–5, 247–8; and see note 54 above on Netanyahu's trip to Russia.

84. Important and honourable exceptions are individuals like Daniel Ellsberg, who achieved the release of the Pentagon Papers by expertise and persistence, and Robert Fisk of *The Independent* in London, known throughout the Middle East for his ability to keep certain themes in the public eye. For most newspapers, however, 'the age of the foreign correspondent' has passed.

85. Quoted by Simon Serfaty, in his *The Media and Foreign Policy*, p. 14.
86. For example, Edward S. Herman and Noam Chomsky, *Manufacturing Consent: the Political Economy of the Mass Media* (London: Vintage, 1994); John Pilger, *Distant Voices* (London: Vintage, 1992).
87. This still leaves many countries where debate, while ostensibly free, is thin or manipulated, as in Putin's Russia. Encouragingly, however, there was some media criticism in India of the explosion of a nuclear weapon, a sensitive issue in any country. See Frank Louis Rusciano, 'A world beyond civilisations: using global opinion theory to explain international order', in *International Journal of Public Opinion Research*, January 2001. Also Keith Hindell, 'The influence of the media on foreign policy', *International Relations*, vol. 12, no. 4, April 1995.
88. Mark Leonard and Vidhya Alakeson, *Going Public: Diplomacy for the Information Society* (London: The Foreign Policy Centre, 2000) p. 59.
89. As reported by NATO's press spokesman Jamie Shea at a seminar of the Foreign Policy Centre, the BBC World Service, the British Council and Design Council, London, 16 May 2000.
90. The data is from Jarol B. Manheim, *Strategic Public Diplomacy and American Foreign Policy: the Evolution of Influence* (New York: Oxford University Press, 1994) pp. 15–16 and pp. 165–6.
91. Manheim, *Strategic Public Diplomacy*, pp. 145–7; on Malaysia see Wally Olins, *Trading Identities: why countries and companies are taking on each others' roles* (London: The Foreign Policy Centre, 1999) p. 17.
92. Olins, *passim*. See also Alan Chong and Jana Valencic (eds), *The Image, the State and International Relations:* (London: London School of Economics and Political Science, 2001, EFPU Working Papers 2001/2).
93. 'A positive image cannot be forced nor bought, and once it has been built it needs continuous cultivation'. Michael Kunczik, *Images of Nations and International Public Relations* (Mahwah, NJ: Lawrence Erlbaum Associates, 1997) p. ix.
94. 'Il volto nuovo del Colonnello' (the new face of the Colonel), *La Repubblica*, 28 August 2000.

Chapter 11

1. John Rawls, *The Law of Peoples* (Cambridge, Mass: Harvard University Press, 1999) p. 82. See also Michael Walzer, *Just and Unjust Wars: A Moral Argument with Historical Illustrations* (New York: Basic Books, 1977).
2. 'Foreign policy is one of the few things where being President [of the USA] matters', *The Economist*, 6 May 2000.
3. *In the National Interest: Australia's Foreign and Trade Policy* (Canberra: Department of Foreign Affairs and Trade, 1997), Foreword by Alexander Downer, Minister for Foreign Affairs, and Tim Fischer, Deputy Prime Minister and Minister for Trade, p. ii.
4. The change in Australian foreign policy initiated by Gough Whitlam tended to increase the emphasis on geography, by asserting that the country's future now lay with the Asia-Pacific region. This was paradoxical given that geography was associated with realism, at that time distinctly unfashionable. See the scathing critique of Australian foreign policy 1972–99 in David Martin Jones and Mike Lawrence Smith, *Reinventing Realism: Australia's Foreign and Defence Policy at the Millennium* (London: Royal Institute of International Affairs, 2000).

5. For example the 15 Member States of the EU now have between them c. 1377 embassies around the world, not counting the 123 European Commission missions – an average of *c*.92 each. Figures from a paper submitted to the Evian General Affairs Council, 2–3 September 2000 by the Secretary-General/High Representative, Javier Solana, and reproduced in Antonio Missiroli (ed.), *Coherence for European Security Policy: Debates–Cases–Assessments* (Paris: West European Institute for Security Studies, Occasional Paper No. 27, May 2001) Annex B.1, p. 57. This document does not contain figures for Greece and so I have added the current figure of 78. Compare the average of 81 embassies for the then nine at the end of the 1970s, provided in Christopher Hill and William Wallace, 'Diplomatic Trends in the European Community', *International Affairs*, January 1979, p. 58.

6. A term first given prominence by William Wallace in his *The Foreign Policy Process in Britain* (Oxford: Oxford University Press for the Royal Institute of International Affairs, 1976).

7. See, for example, the key works of: Charles Tilly, *Coercion, Capital and European States, AD 990–1990* (Oxford: Blackwell, 1976) and Gianfranco Poggi, *The State: Its Nature, Development and Prospects* (Oxford: Polity, 1990). Neither Tilly nor Poggi neglects the importance of war, or the international dimension as such (see, for example, Poggi, pp. 70–2, 83–5, 177–83), which makes it the more interesting that they barely touch on the question of the state's other external instruments, via foreign policy.

8. Richard Rosecrance, *The Rise of the Virtual State: Wealth and Power in the Coming Century* (New York: Basic Books, 1999) p. 211.

9. On Germany see Simon Bulmer, Andreas Maurer and William Paterson, 'The European policy-making machinery in the Berlin Republic: hindrance or handmaiden?' in Douglas Webber (ed.), *New Europe, New Germany, Old Foreign Policy? German Foreign Policy since Unification*, Special Issue of *German Politics*, vol. 10, no. 1, April 2001, pp. 182 and 198. The influence of the Länder is mainly felt indirectly, via consultations on EU IGCs and on the implementation of trade policy. Enlargement and migration are other obvious areas where the federal government has to work with the Länder. They also have a constitutional role in the Bundesrat, which has committees dealing with both foreign affairs and defence. Individual Länder like Bavaria only have occasional foreign visibility on matters like relations with the Czech Republic, or the politics of export promotion.

10. Views described by John Hall in his essay 'State', in Joel Krieger (ed.), *The Oxford Companion to Politics of the World*, (New York: Oxford University Press, 2nd rev. edn, 2001) pp. 802–6.

11. Rosecrance, *The Rise of the Virtual State*, p. 211.

12. This is not so distant from the view of diplomacy as 'a mediation between estranged individuals, groups or entities' provided by James Der Derian in his *On Diplomacy: a Genealogy of Western Estrangement* (Oxford: Basil Blackwell, 1987).

13. The Concert of Europe was supposed to deal only with diplomatic matters, unlike the Holy Alliance, but practice showed that the distinction could not be sustained. F.H. Hinsley, *Power and the Pursuit of Peace: Theory and Practice in the History of International Relations* (Cambridge: Cambridge University Press, 1967) pp. 213–37.

14. See Ángel Viñas, *Los pactos secretos de Franco con Estados Unidos: bases, ayuda económica, recortes de soberanía* (Barcelona: Grijalbo, 1981).

15. Samuel Williamson, *The Politics of Grand Strategy: Britain and France Prepare for War* (Cambridge: Harvard University Press, 1969).

16. Mitsumi Hirano, *The Implications of History Education for External Relations: A Case-study of the Japanese History textbook Disputes in the 1980s* (London School of Economics and Political Science, PhD thesis, 2001). History books often cause international conflict. The latest example is Moldovan outrage at pro-Russian accounts given to their own children. *The Independent*, 26 February 2002.

17. See James Tang, 'The external relations of China's provinces' (with Peter Cheung) in David M. Lampton, *The Making of Chinese Foreign and Security Policy in the Era of Reform* (Stanford: Stanford University Press, 2001).

18. Lord Marshall, 'Down to Business: the Pivotal Role of Commerce and Industry in International Affairs', lecture given at Royal Institute of International Affairs, London, 17 January 2001. The damage done to the airline industry by the terrorist attacks of September 2001 has painfully underlined companies' incapacity in this respect.

19. Samy Cohen notes that states and non-state actors increasingly need each other: 'Rivalry goes with a sort of complicity'. See Samy Cohen, 'Decision-making power and rationality in foreign policy analysis', in Marie-Claude Smouts (ed.), *The New International Relations: Theory and Practice* (London: Hurst, in association with Centre d'Etudes et de Recherches Internationales, Paris, 2001) p. 41.

20. This has not stopped various attempts to extend modern management measures to foreign policy. See William Egerton, 'Beyond the Balanced Scorecard. Performance Evaluation of Foreign Policy: how do the taxpayers know if they are getting a good deal?', MBA/DIC Dissertation, Imperial College of Science, Technology and Medicine, London, September 1998. Roy Ginsberg has assembled systematic data on the 'foreign policy actions of the European Community', where an action is defined as a 'specific, conscious, goal-oriented undertaking'. See Roy H. Ginsberg, *Foreign Policy Actions of the European Community: the Politics of Scale* (Boulder: Lynne Reinner, 1989) p. 2.

21. For the classical origins of rational choice theory see Anthony Downs, *An Economic Theory of Democracy*, and Mancur Olson, *The Logic of Collective Action: Public Goods and the Theory of Groups* (Cambridge, Mass: Harvard University Press, 1965). Important commentaries are to be found in Brian Barry, *Sociologists, Economists, and Democracy* (London: Collier-Macmillan, 1970); William C. Mitchell and Randy Simmons, *Beyond Politics: Politics, Welfare and the Failure of Bureaucracy* (Boulder: Westview, 1994), especially pp. xiii–xv, and 39–65; Donald C. Green and Ian Shapiro, *Pathologies of Rational Choice Theory: a Critique of Applications in Political Science* (New Haven, Conn.: Yale University Press, 1994), especially pp. 1–32.

22. Lawrence Freedman, 'Logic, politics and foreign policy processes', *International Affairs*, vol. 52, no. 3, July 1976. Also Martin Hollis and Steve Smith, *Explaining and Understanding International Relations* (Oxford: Clarendon Press, 1990), chapter 7; and Jonathan Bendor and Thomas Hammond, 'Rethinking Allison's models', *American Political Science Review*, vol. 86, no. 2, June 1992.

23. Raymond Cohen, 'Living and teaching across cultures', *International Studies Perspectives*, vol. 2, 2001, p. 153.

24. Most useful in this respect are Annette Baker Fox, *The Power of Small States: Diplomacy in World War II* (Chicago: Chicago University Press, 1959); David Vital, *The Survival of Small States* (Oxford: Oxford University Press, 1971); Ron Barston (ed.), *The Other Powers* (London: Allen and Unwin, 1973) and the Report of a Commonwealth Consultative Group, *Vulnerability: Small States in the Global Society* (London: Commonwealth Secretariat, 1995).

25. Even here, we should not assume that it was never possible for the GDR to pursue a subtly differentiated foreign policy, especially under Walter Ulbricht. See Peter Grieder,

The East German Leadership 1946–1973: Conflict and Crisis (Manchester: Manchester University Press, 1999), especially pp. 170–83.

26. Kalevi J. Holsti (ed.), *Why Nations Realign: Foreign Policy Restructuring in the Post-War World* (London: George Allen and Unwin, 1982).

27. Robert Gilpin, *War and Change in World Politics* (Cambridge: Cambridge University Press, 1981). Thucydides' comment is from the Melian Dialogue: 'the strong do what they have the power to do and the weak accept what they have to accept'. Thucydides, *History of the Peloponnesian War*, translated by Rex Warner (Harmondsworth: Penguin, 1972) p. 402.

28. Wolfram F. Hanrieder, 'Compatibility and consensus: a proposal for the conceptual linkage of external and internal dimensions of foreign policy', *American Political Science Review*, vol. 61, no. 4, December 1967, pp. 971–82.

29. Even a supposed realist like Wolfers stressed 'the many domestic goals which no government can ignore and which compete for resources with whatever external purposes the nation may be pursuing'. Arnold Wolfers, 'The goals of foreign policy' in his *Discord and Collaboration*, p. 72.

30. See Max Weber, 'Politics as a vocation' especially pp. 126–8, and 'Science as a vocation' in H.H. Gerth and C. Wright Mills trans., intro. and eds. *From Max Weber: Essays in Sociology* (London: Routledge and Kegan Paul, 1948). Also Francis Deng *et al.*, *Sovereignty as Responsibility: Conflict Management in Africa* (Washington, DC: the Brookings Institution, 1996) pp. 27–33.

31. Chris Alden's 'Solving South Africa's Chinese puzzle: foreign policy-making and the "two Chinas" question', in Jim Broderick, Gary Burford and Gordon Freer (eds), *South Africa's Foreign Policy* (London: Palgrave, 2001), traces the dilemmas of the Mandela government over the de-recognition of Taiwan.

32. Martha Finnemore, *National Interests in International Society* (Ithaca, NY: Cornell University Press, 1996) p. 145.

33. Rosecrance, *The Rise of the Virtual State*, pp. 18–19.

34. *Ibid.*, p. 211.

35. The novelist Julian Barnes gives an interesting example of the way we may evade responsibility by literally not providing a subject. He notes how couples get into the habit of saying 'love you', thus dropping the 'I': 'As if you weren't taking responsibility for the feeling any more. As if it had become somehow more general, less focused'. See *Love Etc* (London: Picador, 2001) p. 158.

36. By 1999 Cuba's forces had been overtaken in size also by those of Mexico, Colombia, Argentina and Peru – but were still larger than those of Canada. Since the US threat did not notably diminish before 1999 the conclusion must be that this was the result of fewer far-flung interventions. See *The Military Balance 2000–2001* (London: International Institute for Strategic Studies, October 2000).

37. David Campbell, *Writing Security: United States Foreign Policy and the Politics of Identity*, rev. edn (Manchester: Manchester University Press, 1998) p. 226.

38. *Ibid.*, pp. 68–72.

39. For detail on the particular British context, see Richard Little and Mark Wickham-Jones (eds), *New Labour's Foreign Policy: a New Moral Crusade?* (Manchester: Manchester University Press, 2000) and Christopher Hill, 'Foreign policy', in Anthony Seldon (ed.), *The Blair Effect: the Blair Government 1997–2001* (London: Little, Brown, 2001).

40. See Karen E. Smith and Margot Light (eds), *Ethics and Foreign Policy* (Cambridge: Cambridge University Press, 2001).

41. Christian Lequesne, 'The common fisheries policy', in Helen Wallace and William Wallace (eds), *Policy-Making in the European Union* (Oxford: Oxford University Press, 2000) analyses the interaction of communitarian, environmental and economic considerations.

42. Nicholas J. Wheeler and Tim Dunne, 'Good international citizenship: a third way for British foreign policy', *International Affairs*, vol. 74, no. 4, October 1998; also the same authors' 'Blair's Britain: a force for good in the world?' in Smith and Light, *Ethics and Foreign Policy*, pp. 169–70. This form of citizenship may be located in the classic liberal internationalist tradition, whereby interests and ideals are seen as converging, but it also has complex philosophical ramifications. See Andrew Linklater, 'What is a good international citizen?' in Paul Keal (ed.), *Ethics and Foreign Policy* (St Leonards, NSW: Allen and Unwin in association with the Australian National University, 1992).

43. The latest instance of this is the demand that European defence budgets rise so as to give real meaning to the new Common European Security and Defence Policy. François Heisbourg, *European Defence: Making It Work* (Paris: WEU Institute for Security Studies, Paris 2000), Chaillot Paper No. 42.

44. I have made this argument in relation to European foreign policy, but it has wider applicability, for example, to the United States and Russia. See Christopher Hill, 'The capability–expectations gap, or conceptualising Europe's international role', *Journal of Common Market Studies*, vol. 31, no. 3, September 1993, and 'Closing the capability–expectations gap?' in John Peterson and Helene Sjursen (eds), *A Foreign Policy for Europe?* (London: Routledge, 1998).

45. Paul Taylor, 'The institutions of the United Nations and the principle of consonance: an overview', in A.J.R. Groom and Paul Taylor (eds), *The United Nations at the Millennium: the Principal Organs* (London: Continuum, 2000) pp. 304–5.

46. Benjamin Barber, *Jihad vs. McWorld: How Globalism and Tribalism are Reshaping the World Order* (New York: Ballantine, 1996), cited in David Martin Jones and Mike Lawrence Smith, *Reinventing Realism*, p. 1.

47. In French it is *Label France*. See Michel Girard, 'States, diplomacy and image-making: what is new? Reflections on current British and French experiences', in Alan Chong and Jana Valencic (eds), *The Image, the State and International Relations: Conference Proceedings* (London: London School of Economics and Political Science, 2001), EFPU Working Papers 2001/2, p. 22. As Michel Girard points out, however, for French leaders 'France is far more complex than a label, or an image'. Moreover, the one developed country which does not feel the need to dabble in rebranding is the United States. A superpower knows that its foreign policy counts.

48. The two works entitled 'The Prisoners' (or for some 'The Slaves') are to be found in the Galleria dell'Accademia, Florence.

Index